Economic Liberalization and Political Violence

ECONOMIC LIBERALIZATION AND POLITICAL VIOLENCE
Utopia or Dystopia?

Edited by Francisco Gutiérrez and Gerd Schönwälder

Contributors: Einas Ahmed, Richard Banégas, Mauricio Barón, Jairo Baquero Melo, Frederick Golooba-Mutebi, Francisco Gutiérrez, Yao Kouman Adingra, Roland Marchal, Ramón Pajuelo Teves, Ricardo Peñaranda, and Alain Toh

and

International Development Research Centre
Ottawa • Cairo • Dakar • Montevideo • Nairobi • New Delhi • Singapore

First published 2010 by Pluto Press
345 Archway Road, London N6 5AA and
175 Fifth Avenue, New York, NY 10010

www.plutobooks.com

International Development Research Centre
PO Box 8500
Ottawa, ON, Canada K1G 3H9
www.idrc.ca / info@idrc.ca
ISBN 978-1-55250-482-6 (e-book)

Distributed in the United States of America exclusively by
Palgrave Macmillan, a division of St. Martin's Press LLC,
175 Fifth Avenue, New York, NY 10010

Copyright © International Development Research Centre 2010

The right of the individual contributors to be identified as the authors of this work has been asserted by them in accordance with the Copyright, Designs and Patents Act 1988.

British Library Cataloguing in Publication Data
A catalogue record for this book is available from the British Library

ISBN   978 0 7453 3064 8   Hardback
ISBN   978 0 7453 3063 1   Paperback

Library of Congress Cataloging in Publication Data applied for

This book is printed on paper suitable for recycling and made from fully managed and sustained forest sources. Logging, pulping and manufacturing processes are expected to conform to the environmental standards of the country of origin.

10   9   8   7   6   5   4   3   2   1

Designed and produced for Pluto Press by
Chase Publishing Services Ltd, 33 Livonia Road, Sidmouth, EX10 9JB, England
Typeset from disk by Stanford DTP Services, Northampton, England
Printed and bound in the European Union by
CPI Antony Rowe, Chippenham and Eastbourne

Contents

Foreword   vii
Frances Stewart

Introduction   1
Gerd Schönwälder and Francisco Gutiérrez Sanín

PART ONE

1. Mechanisms   13
   Francisco Gutiérrez Sanín

2. War, Peace, and Liberalism: A Quantitative Approach to the Relation between Economic Globalization and Armed Conflict   49
   Jairo Baquero Melo

PART TWO

3. Economic Liberalization and Politics in Uganda   93
   Frederick Golooba-Mutebi

4. Côte d'Ivoire: The Political Economy of a Citizenship Crisis   126
   Richard Banégas, Alain Toh, and Yao Kouman Adingra

5. Multiple Uses of Neoliberalism: War, New Boundaries, and Reorganization of the Government in Sudan   173
   Roland Marchal and Einas Ahmed

PART THREE

6. Colombia: The Restructuring of Violence   209
   Francisco Gutiérrez Sanín

7. War and Neoliberal Transformation: The Peruvian Experience   245
   Ramón Pajuelo Teves

8 Economic Liberalization and War:
   The Central American Scenario   285
   Ricardo Peñaranda and Mauricio Barón

Conclusions   327
Gerd Schönwälder

Index   343

Foreword

Frances Stewart

Since the Cold War, academics' and policy-makers' attention has been directed at two global phenomena—first, the combination of marketization, liberalization, and globalization, which has spread to almost every country in the world; and, second, the spate of civil wars that emerged after 1989, even as the wars-by-proxy fueled by the Cold War came to an end. While much has been written on the causes and consequences of both these developments, very little attention has been paid to the possible connections between them. Have the liberalizing pro-market reforms been responsible for provoking such opposition that violent civil war resulted? And what have been the consequences of the wars for reform?

It seems plausible that liberalization—with its acknowledged harsh consequences for income distribution and employment—might provoke violent opposition. Equally, globalization—which encompasses liberalization but goes beyond it, opening economies not just to the opportunities presented by global markets, but also to acute vulnerability associated with global cycles—might be thought to be likely to provoke rebellion as people lose their economic security. And in the reverse direction: One might expect that when such violent conflicts end, governments would cling to the security of planning and protection rather than opening their economies to the fierce internal and international competitive forces that result from liberalizing reforms.

This important book represents the first systematic attempt to explore these connections. It does so both theoretically and in practice, drawing on econometric cross-country evidence as well as case studies encompassing a range of situations.

The book shows that the connections between liberalization and conflict are far more complex and nuanced than suggested above. The causes of civil war are deeply rooted in group inequalities, poverty, and history, as well as in specific conjunctural events, on which reforms often have little bearing. Moreover, in some respects market reforms may reduce, rather than increase, the risk of conflict, as economic opportunities come to depend more on capabilities and less on connections. In terms of the reverse connection, war-ending seems to open the way for reforms, partly when it leaves a single victor powerful enough to overcome special interests, like in Peru, and partly when post-conflict donors insist on these reforms as a condition for the much needed reconstruction and recovery aid, as in Uganda. These complexities are powerfully illustrated by the evidence presented here. We see that in some cases, market reforms have accompanied conflict—such as Côte d'Ivoire and Sudan—although in both cases it is difficult to argue that they were the prime cause of it; and in other cases, liberalizing reforms have *followed* the end of fierce civil wars without reigniting conflict—such as Peru, Central America, and Uganda. More often than not, it seems that the end of wars has presented an opportunity for reform, and has not inhibited it.

While this book provides conclusive evidence that there are no simple relationships between globalization, liberalization, marketization and conflict, showing how complex the relationships are, further elapse of time may reveal still new connections. On the one hand, global recession may threaten political stability along with economic stability, and may also lead to an unraveling of some reforms. On the other, in many cases it seems that obsession with reforms has come at the expense of addressing some fundamental grievances that underlie the conflicts, including horizontal inequalities, land distribution, unemployment and poverty, and failure to address these grievances could lead to new outbreaks of violence in the future.

This book is essential reading for those concerned with the ever-present issues, any solution to which is of enormous importance to development and stability. The book offers enlightenment both to students of conflict and of the political economy of reforms, including policy-makers. The latter should be relieved to find that, in most cases, their reforms do not seem to have been responsible for conflict, although they have not stopped or prevented conflict either. But we cannot afford to be complacent: Grievances do need to be addressed if political stability is to be ensured, and the forces of globalization and market reforms cannot do so.

Introduction[1]

Gerd Schönwälder and Francisco Gutiérrez Sanín[2]

Globalization is as omnipresent as it is contentious. Lauded by some as a portent of peace and prosperity, it is accused by others as a harbinger of conflict and war. For some, the opening of societies, markets, and polities amounts to a "liberal utopia," where one good thing leads to another and violent conflict becomes a distant memory. Popularized by the likes of *New York Times* columnist Thomas Friedman (*The World is Flat*) or Johns Hopkins University professor Francis Fukuyama (*The End of History*), this view has been hugely influential, not least for international policymaking. Others, by contrast, see globalization as a threat to democratic governance and national sovereignty, fearing that it will further sharpen social cleavages and open new conflict fault lines. Partisans of this "liberal dystopia," such as Naomi Klein (*The Shock Doctrine*), point to Latin America, Southeast Asia, and other parts of the "Global South" where globalization has triggered waves of angry protests and unhinged whole political regimes.

Current theoretical and empirical studies of globalization offer support for the proponents of either position. Globalization advocates like to point to the growing evidence that more open economic policies and a liberal trade regime, often accompanied by a shift to representative democracy, indeed seem to decrease the likelihood that states will go to war with one another. This, at least, is the conclusion reached by some recent studies using aggregate data to track the relationship between economic openness and political violence.[3] Using various empirical measurements—among them the dataset on armed conflict jointly produced by the Conflict Data Project at Uppsala University and the International Peace Research Institute (PRIO) in Oslo—these studies challenge the idea that economic openness in general, and adherence to neoliberal policy prescriptions in particular, leads to more violence. In fact, they find a positive relationship between greater economic openness on the one hand and a *decrease* of politically motivated violence on the other, on the grounds that economic liberalization tends to produce more prosperity and improved governance, at least over the long term.[4] Based on these studies, the "liberal peace thesis," first coined by Immanuel Kant, still seems to hold.[5]

Globalization opponents are quick to challenge these results, pointing to numerous instances where economic liberalization has widened ethnic or social cleavages, facilitated the looting of natural resources fueling civil wars, produced riots over food shortages or deficient public service provision, or had other nefarious consequences. Again, there is some evidence to back up these claims. Amy Chua (2004), for example, describes how economic liberalization in Malaysia strengthened the hand of the already market-dominant Chinese minority, but also produced an anti-Chinese backlash by fueling simmering resentments. Paul Collier and his collaborators, certainly no anti-globalization crusaders, show how economic liberalization and bad governance help unscrupulous "war entrepreneurs" to take control of natural resources, sustaining and prolonging civil conflicts that would otherwise be short-lived (Collier, 2007, pp. 17ff.). Anti-globalization activists have documented the many forms of popular resistance against IMF-inspired austerity programs, culminating in the infamous "IMF riots" of the 1980s in response to reductions in food subsidies and public services (McMichael, 2004, pp. 137ff.). More recently, the "water riots" in Bolivia and elsewhere centered on privatization programs that threatened to exclude a large share of the population from public service provision.[6]

Dialogue between these two camps, when it happens, tends to be sterile and unproductive. In part, this is due to some fundamental differences in approach that have proved hard to bridge. Those who see globalization as broadly positive tend to argue that certain difficulties can be expected with change processes of this magnitude,[7] but that they do not invalidate the basic trend. Globalization opponents, by contrast, not only question the idea that globalization is a force for good, but also attack the empirical methodology used by their opponents for missing out on the day-to-day reality experienced by poor and marginalized people, particularly in the developing world.

This book presents a challenge to both perspectives, focusing squarely on the concrete impacts globalization has had on the ground. The individual contributions, each in their own way, make a forceful case that—quite apart from the fundamental, sometimes almost philosophical questions driving much of the globalization debate—far too little is known about these impacts and that new evidence is desperately needed. In order to keep the analysis manageable, the authors narrow globalization down to its *economic* aspects, but argue that the resulting changes can be observed both in the economic and political realms and are best captured by the notion of "neoliberalism." This results in a fine-grained, comparative analysis of the impacts of economic globalization the political incentive structure for violent conflict and war making. The analysis proceeds in two main steps: examining aggregate, global patterns using quantitative methods, then following particular trajectories in a set of qualitative case studies from Latin America (Colombia, Peru, El Salvador, and Guatemala) and sub-Saharan Africa (Côte d'Ivoire, Sudan, and Uganda). The findings demonstrate that, contrary to both the "utopian" and "dystopian" views, the shift to neoliberal policies has produced widely diverging outcomes in different contexts. Sometimes helping to end violent conflicts, these changes can also heighten the conflicts' intensity or otherwise transform them, and they can bring about new—especially criminal—forms of violence.[8] The case studies pursue this line of enquiry but drill deeper into specific country contexts, adding important insight and nuance.

The book's findings are remarkable in several respects. Most importantly, they show that neoliberalism hasn't created the world *ex novo* but instead, as a result of its interaction with previous regimes, produced ruptures and continuities. These effects can be deeply contradictory and are intimately linked with contextual factors, especially when neoliberal reforms are partial, incomplete, and end up coexisting with other, more established ways of doing things. As the case studies in this book demonstrate, this is far more common than one might expect, and it stands in stark contrast to the ideology-driven certainties of much of the globalization debate. In Côte d'Ivoire, for example, the demise of the state-centered economic model around the Caisse de Stabilisation des Produits Agricoles ("Caistab") did not lead to the hoped-for gains in efficiency and transparency, but instead to an unwieldy mix of formal, informal, and illicit arrangements that proved particularly hard to navigate for small agricultural producers, who were supposed to benefit the most from neoliberal reforms.

Another key insight is that neoliberalism is not a one-way street and that changes in the economic realm interact in often unforeseen ways with those in political, social, and other spheres. The chain of causality can go either way, often simultaneously: while it is true that economic changes can bring about political ones—opponents of neoliberalism rightly contend that it can weaken already feeble states and further undermine their capacity to shape and enact policy—

political developments can have a deep impact on the economic landscape. For example, in Peru, El Salvador, and Guatemala, the settlement of the armed civil conflicts *preceded* the enactment of neoliberal policies, in fact making these possible, not the other way around. Far from being a predictable, let alone inevitable, consequence of economic change, political events opened the door to subsequent shifts in economic policy that otherwise may not have been possible.

Closer to this collection's core theme, the studies' findings confirm that neoliberalism can result in more conflict and, perhaps more importantly, that it can produce new and different forms of violence. There can be little doubt that in Central America, for example, the introduction of neoliberal economic policies contributed to further weakening of already feeble states, which have been unable to put a stop to the growing public insecurity plaguing their societies. In Côte d'Ivoire, as mentioned, neoliberalism facilitated the siphoning off of agricultural resources to fuel the civil conflict, or just to line the pockets of powerful individuals. And in Colombia, neoliberal transformations allowed armed challengers to seek institutional basis within the state apparatus itself, perhaps heralding new forms of structural violence. At the same time, however, the studies in this book also suggest that neoliberalism can help bring ongoing conflicts to an end or prevent new ones from erupting; it allowed, for example, Uganda's Museveni to appease his political opponents and stave off popular dissent to his rule. Contradictory and counter-intuitive at first glance, these findings open new avenues for debate and investigation. They also highlight the need for innovative and targeted policies to confront challenges that so far have been ignored, dismissed, or not even recognized.

Shining a spotlight on the complex linkages between neoliberalism and political violence, and based squarely on evidence, the book's contributions are as rich as they are diverse. They pinpoint some of the concrete underlying mechanisms, at macro and micro levels, and they do so in a comparative fashion, drawing on cases from both sub-Saharan Africa and Latin America. By including both Southern and Northern authors, the book stands out in a debate where Northern voices and concerns still dominate. If nothing else, the book proves that highly complex issues such as neoliberalism and political violence are best approached from a truly global perspective.

The book is divided into three main parts, framed by this introduction and a conclusion. Part One sets out the comparative framework, arguing that neoliberalism is a worldwide, almost universal phenomenon that is associated with political violence in distinctive ways, and can be studied empirically. Francisco Gutiérrez Sanín, in his opening chapter, presents neoliberalism as a contested term. The chapter defines the concept, departing from Polanyi's famous dictum that the "great transformation" to a market economy can produce brutally violent outcomes. Showing that neoliberalism has in fact been global and all-encompassing, the chapter also stresses that its outcomes have diverged widely, both in terms of time and space. Contrary to liberal utopias and dystopias, neoliberalism has produced different equilibria, particularly with respect to violence and peace. The chapter goes on to discuss the underlying mechanisms, examining how neoliberal transformations, by altering and perturbing fundamental institutional arrangements, can modify the constraints and opportunities for potential challengers. These effects can be deeply contradictory, for example, by combining greater stability with deepening injustice and inequalities. At the same time, there are clearly observable impacts on conflict onset and continuation, as well as emerging conditions for, possibly, new confrontations.

The following chapter, by Jairo Baquero Melo, is built around a macro-analysis of economic globalization and conflict. It demonstrates that the aggregate landscape resulting from broad-based quantitative studies can defy what is often considered "common sense." Specifically, the data shows that neoliberalism has not given origin to a conflict-less paradise, but that it has not triggered havoc either. Neoliberalism, according to this study, is strongly associated with war termination but, on the other hand, it also sometimes increases the intensity of conflict, or the likelihood that other forms of violence will emerge. The chapter also probes problems such as regional and temporal variations.

Part Two begins with Frederick Golooba-Mutebi's piece on economic liberalization and politics in Uganda, the first of three chapters addressing sub-Saharan Africa. Golooba-Mutebi contends that having resisted neoliberal reforms for a long time, the government of Yoweri Kaguta Museveni discovered at the end of the 1980s that embracing these reforms could help stabilize and rebuild a country devastated by war and predatory governance. As external resources started to flow into Uganda, effective social policies (such as in education) became possible, and the regime now had sufficient resources to buy off its opponents. While supporters of neoliberalism expected economic liberalization to go hand in hand with greater political freedoms, and its opponents predicted that in the absence of such an opening political violence and repression would mount, the Ugandan model confounded all observers by combining relative pacification, open markets, and a non-democratic political regime. What made this possible? Essentially, Museveni's ingenious use of foreign resources to craft a clientelist, regionally-based answer to the internal tensions of his country, simultaneously increasing social investment. While successful in the short run, the long-term sustainability of this model remains in doubt.

Richard Banégas, Alain Toh, and Yao Kouman Adingra's chapter addresses the political economy of the crisis of citizenship in Côte d'Ivoire. Considered a showcase of successful state building in Africa until the late 1980s, the country fell into disarray when it embarked on a twin path of economic and political liberalization. The capacity of the state to adjudicate between competing interests broke down, and in the midst of political confrontation open violence flared up and divided the country politically, ethnically, and regionally. The conflict became about the very foundations of nationality and citizenship: it is justly termed an "identity war." But many of its drivers are rooted in the structural reforms that undermined the previously robust intra-regional pact, unraveling the very fabric of the country that gave life to its constitution and political regime. In particular, the demise of the Caisse de Stabilisation was a fatal blow to these regional arrangements. Going back further, the conflict in Côte d'Ivoire has its roots in the structural contradictions of its "plantation economy." Starting in the 1930s, these contradictions began to dominate political identities, demographic and territorial patterns, and ways of governing. Revealing a familiar tension between continuity and change—in particular, around the question of how to integrate rural economies with global markets and what role they should play in shaping developmental states—the problem became more acute with the later introduction of neoliberal policies.

Roland Marchal and Einas Ahmed's chapter on the "many uses" of neoliberalism in Sudan rounds out the second part of the book. It shows that the ruling elites' embrace of neoliberalism did little to quell the civil conflict in the country and even less to produce a political opening of the regime. Instead, the simultaneous adoption of neoliberalist policies and the Islamization of the public sphere helped these elites to sweep away the last vestiges of colonial rule and the societal order that had supported it, all the while strengthening their own control over the state apparatus. The relations between the state, the new economic elites, and the outside world were also profoundly changed, and were helped along but not caused by a growing reliance on oil revenues. This situation has proved to be immensely de-stabilizing, even spreading the conflict to peripheral regions of the country that had been previously relatively unaffected. Francisco Gutiérrez Sanín's piece on the restructuring of violence in Colombia is the opening chapter to Part Three, anchoring three case studies on Latin America. Gutiérrez Sanín argues that the Colombian case is unusual for Latin America. Neoliberalism in Colombia was introduced gradually, instead of by "shock therapy," and it was never the most pressing political issue. In fact, it failed to excite political tempers in Colombia as it did elsewhere, and the country's long internal war was triggered by problems that clearly predate the introduction of neoliberal reforms. Is there, then, a story to tell about the relation between neoliberalism and the armed conflict? The chapter shows that there is, and actually a very important one. Neoliberalism did not cause the conflict, but it did fundamentally transform it by upsetting established institutional arrangements. Three broad areas are examined: health policies, land distribution, and decentralization. In all three, the new institutional arrangements conceived by neoliberal reformers have changed the set of opportunities not only for political challengers but also for paramilitary groups. This has affected not only the way in which the war is waged, but also the nature and availability of peaceful settlements—which, contrary to liberal utopian thinking, can combine economic openings with political closures, and create more, not less, room for organized crime.

The following chapter by Ramón Pajuelo Teves on Peru provides a good example of neoliberal reforms leading to peace, at least at first glance. Bad governance and a closed economy, society, and polity permitted the development of a virulent internal conflict that cost the lives of nearly 70,000 Peruvians. With the ascent of a new political leadership in 1990—Alberto Fujimori and his entourage—subversion was quelled, and one of the most drastic neoliberal programs in the world produced years of strong economic growth. In the process, democracy was toppled, but due to a combination of internal and external pressures, Fujimori was replaced by genuinely democratic leaders, who maintained the liberal orientation of the economy. While this pre-empted the resurgence of the subversive challenge, the author points to a series of unresolved challenges, among them persistent poverty and deep regional disparities, that may well breed new sources of violence.

Contrary to Peru, Ricardo Peñaranda and Mauricio Barón's chapter on Central America describes how the civil wars in El Salvador and Guatemala came to an end through peace agreements, not outright victory by the state. In both cases, violence reached very high levels, and the insurgent movements successfully insisted on balancing economic liberalization with political liberties and social reforms. This was especially true in Guatemala, at least initially, even though the ambitious peace accords were never fully implemented. While both countries are examples of peace-making through economic and political liberalization, the outcome is more problematic upon closer scrutiny. Neoliberal policies fell short of the desired effect, and only a high level of external remittances—dependence on such external inflows being a problem in and of itself—prevented a certain economic crisis. Furthermore, foreign investment accelerated the privatization of security, which added to an already chronic and severe crime problem resulting from the end of the armed conflicts.

The conclusion by Gerd Schönwälder draws out some common threads—as well as some contradictory findings—from the individual chapters. It identifies avenues for future scholarship and again highlights the potential importance of the book's findings for practical policymaking.

NOTES

1. This book is the result of a research project supported by the International Development Research Centre (IDRC) in Ottawa, Canada.
2. Gerd Schönwälder is Director, Policy and Planning, at the IDRC. Francisco Gutiérrez Sanín is a researcher at the Instituto de Estudios Políticos y Relaciones Internacionales (IEPRI)—Universidad Nacional de Colombia.
3. See, for example, Hegre, Gleditsch, and Gissinger (2003), or more recently, Bussmann and Schneider (2007).
4. It is worth noting that the relationship is more complex and that trade in particular can also foster conflict. See, for example, Oli Brown, Mzukisi Qobo, and Alejandra Ruiz-Dana (in Khan, 2008).
5. Recent contributors to this debate have stressed that the underlying relationship is not automatic, highlighting the importance of intervening variables such as the quality of governance and political institutions. See, for example, Paris (2006), Hasenclever and Weiffen (2006), and Richmond (2006).
6. See also the research produced by the IDRC-sponsored Municipal Services Project (MSP) in South Africa: http://www.idrc.ca/en/ev-5490-201-1-DO_TOPIC.html.
7. Bussmann and Schneider (2007), for example, while not questioning the idea that economic liberalization is beneficial in the long run, show that greater economic openness does increase the risk of violence in the short and medium term. They argue that just like democratization, economic liberalization produces tensions

between winners and losers that make violence more likely, especially in the absence of effective governance arrangements that could cushion shocks and facilitate the necessary adaptation processes.
8. Including some that are reminiscent of the "new wars" described by Mary Kaldor (2007), where traditional warfare involving states intersects with organized crime and massive human rights violations.

REFERENCES

Brown, O., Qobo, M., and Ruiz-Dana, A. In Khan (2009).

Bussmann, M. and Schneider, G. (2007) "When globalization discontent turns violent: foreign economic liberalization and internal war." *International Studies Quarterly*, No. 51, pp. 79–97.

Chua, A. (2004) *World on Fire: How Exporting Free Market Democracy Breeds Ethnic Hatred and Global Instability*. New York City: Anchor Books.

Collier, P. (2007) *The Bottom Billion: Why the Poorest Countries are Failing and What Can Be Done About It*. New York: Oxford University Press.

Friedman, T. (2005) *The World is Flat: A Brief History of the Twenty-first Century*. New York: Farrar, Strauss, and Giroux.

Fukuyama, F. (1992) *The End of History and the Last Man*. Toronto: Maxwell Macmillan Canada.

Hasenclever, A. and Weiffen, B. (2006) "International institutions are the key: a new perspective on the democratic peace," *Review of International Studies*, No. 32, pp. 563–585.

Hegre, H., Gleditsch, N. P., and Gissinger, R. (2003) "Globalization and conflict: welfare, distribution, and political unrest." In *Globalization and Armed Conflict*, eds. G. Schneider, K. Barbieri, and N. P. Gleditsch. Lanham: Rowman & Littlefield.

Kaldor, M. (2007) *New and Old Wars*. Second Edition. Stanford: Stanford University Press.

Khan, S. R. (ed.) (2009) *Regional Trade Integration and Conflict Resolution*. Routledge and IDRC.

Klein, N. (2007) *The Shock Doctrine: The Rise of Disaster Capitalism*. Toronto: Macmillan.

McMichael, P. (2004) *Development and Social Change: A Global Perspective*. Thousand Oaks: Pine Forge Press.

Paris, R. (2006) "Bringing the leviathan back in: classical versus contemporary studies of the liberal peace." *International Studies Review*, No. 8, pp. 425–440.

Richmond, O. (2006) "The problem of peace: understanding the liberal peace." *Conflict, Security & Development*, Vol. 6, No. 3, pp. 291–314.

Shore, K. J. (2002) *Who Pays? Municipal Services in South Africa*. http://www.idrc.ca/en/ev-5490-201-1-DO_TOPIC.html, accessed August 28, 2008.

Part One

1
Mechanisms

Francisco Gutiérrez Sanín[1]

INTRODUCTION: NEOLIBERALISM AND CONFLICT REVISITED

A decade ago, in an already classic work, William Reno (1999) set up a careful consideration of the transformations of the African state, and their causes and consequences. One of his central theses was that by weakening and disorganizing an already precarious bureaucracy, neoliberalism was giving origin to a new way of governance characterized by the incorporation of private and public agents into networks of "militarized commerce" linked to global markets. "Less government has contributed not to better government but rather to warlord politics," he asserted (Reno, 1999, p. 1). Reno not only established a concrete method for evaluating neoliberal reforms, but he also proposed the mechanisms to help us understand why these reforms were likely to produce the predicted outcome. "A central premise of this study of the transformation of weak states to warlord politics lies in recognizing how rulers control markets to enhance their own power" (Reno, 1999, p. 15). The weakening of the state bureaucracy, and the empowerment of global markets, pushed already weak state organizations below the threshold of viability, and created a set of incentives that generated a "shadow state." Shadow states consist of an alliance of state officials and commercial networks that deeply criminalize the state (Bayart, 1989; Hibou, 2004), but that also change the way in which the state works and relates to society (Reno, 1999).

Many books and papers in the trendy "failed states" field have also flagged the potential relation between neoliberalism and violence. Why, then, is it necessary to revisit it? First of all, Reno's brilliant study had a regional focus, but are the phenomena that he identified for Africa also identifiable in other regions? Why or why not? What are the variations, in terms of a particular region or timeframe, in the impacts of neoliberalism? Second, there is a certain anomaly in the neoliberal dystopia. If shadow states and warlord politics were to become the predominant political form on a continent, or perhaps in the developing world, then we would expect a global increase in warlordism and violence (and perhaps a developmental slump). We would expect, after all, that the rule of unstable networks of militarized commerce would produce a more or less permanent state of confrontation.[2] We know, with a decent degree of confidence, that this has not occurred. We rather observe trends in the opposite direction.[3] How can this be explained?

One answer would be to affirm the liberal utopia, according to which the world is becoming a better place and phenomena like militarized commerce are simply transitional problems. Such a statement is in full harmony with what can be called the "liberal promise," according to which free economies and societies are able to manage adequately their conflicts, taking into account the interests of all the actors involved. The liberal promise has permeated international discourses and practices. In the United States, for example, independently of the party in power, foreign policy has consistently been tied to an effort of promoting free markets and free societies around the world. "The centerpiece of American foreign policy in the 1990s was the claim that promoting the spread of democracy would also promote peace. Clinton explained that promoting democratization would be a watchword of US foreign policy—because democracies never fight wars against each other, they trade freely with each other, and they respect the human rights of their citizens" (Snyder, 2000). The liberal promise is also so deeply embedded in several academic and policy circles that many a time it is simply taken for granted (see for example Diamond et al., 1997). Thus, the basic liberal idea of our times is based on the assumption that economies, societies, and polities are all isomorphic, which is to say not only that the more open they are, the better, but rather that openness in one domain has positive feedback effects in others.[4]

Despite its rather naïve and mechanical appearance, the case for the liberal promise is not hopeless. As seen above, after the demise of European "real socialism" there has been a decrease in civil wars since the end of the Cold War. Cases as prominent as El Salvador, Guatemala, and South Africa have seen accords between adversaries separated by many fundamental issues, but willing to find a common bargaining terrain in a set of liberal (in both the economic and political senses) transformations, related by concrete mechanisms that involved rational calculation by the elites (Wood, 2000; see below[5]). In other cases, like Peru, neoliberal administrations were able to impose a non-negotiated peace, and prevent the resurgence of any kind of nationally significant armed opposition, beyond declared ideological convictions.[6]

There is another reason for revisiting the relation between neoliberalism and conflict, which is both methodological and substantial. To understand it well, we should look at *both* neoliberal conflict and peace, and try to understand why in particular cases and contexts the implementation of neoliberal policies in the developing world produced particular outcomes (in terms of both state strength and conflict). Probably one of the main contributions of this collection is to show that neoliberalism generates *multiple equilibria*, and discussing in detail some of the main ones (the criminalization of the state, peace with stability, peace with instability, continuation of conflict).

The problem of understanding the different mechanisms through which neoliberalism can promote or quench political violence can be cast in the following way. First, as the quantitative analysis in this volume shows, it is not possible to deduce from general premises which consequences neoliberalism "should" have (see the conclusions for more detailed discussion). Neoliberalism is a transnational phenomenon,[7] but it is adopted, and adapted, by national actors in many different ways. The relation between neoliberalism and political violence depends on how neoliberalism is construed; what dimension of political violence we are speaking about;[8] and, on the complex set of direct and indirect implications that neoliberalism has on concrete polities given a specific context and trajectory. No satisfactory understanding of such a phenomenon can be fully covered by law-like or probabilistic models; mechanisms are indispensable tools if we are to understand historically shaped outcomes (see for example Elster, 2007). Second, the palette of problems and dangers triggered by the present "great transformation" does not boil down to actual violent conflict as measured, for example, by lethal events. In fact, Polanyi's basic insight was that liberal policies had been able to stabilize the world for decades, but at the same time had slowly created the conditions for its own destruction. Lest this sounds like "Hegelian" obscurantism it is worthwhile to recall that Polanyi was able to outline the concrete mechanisms that transformed liberal peace into a nationalistic–authoritarian backlash. In the present wave of liberalization, the sequence might be described in the following way: In the aftermath of World War II, a number of international institutions (like the World Bank) were created. Their role was to promote both development and peace. During the rise of neoliberalism, they became increasingly powerful transnational agents of neoliberal reform (this process has been described in detail by for example Stiglitz, 2002). Politically, early neoliberalism was not overly concerned with state reforms—it was not only liberal, but also libertarian. Then it started to merge with other trends, and eventually discovered a "state recipe" that was not only negative, i.e., that not only contained specifications about what the state should *not* do, but also prescriptions about desirable courses of action. For the contrast between the two, see Table 1.1. Actually, many of the core principles of neoliberalism were specifically conceived of as conflict prevention formulas (Sachs, 1989; Williamson, 1990; Harvey, 2005). Economic liberalization, a very active diplomacy by developed democracies, and a growing set of international institutions, in effect produced several positive results. However: (i) severe problems remain (*incompleteness*); (ii) other problems have been created (*counter-productiveness*); (iii) even some of the desirable outcomes may create the conditions for further turbulences (*potential blowback*).

What then is new? What is specific about the potentially conflict-breeding mechanisms of neoliberalism? Different waves of incorporation of late developers into international markets have *always* been both extremely traumatic and deeply transformative. This is yet another reason to revisit the theme of the relation between neoliberalism and violence: the building of the state in late-developing countries has more or less always been associated with long networks of militarized commerce (global markets protected by powerful actors) and has entailed a fair use of violence. Nkemdirim, for example, claims that African rebellions and revolutions throughout the twentieth century were always related to a transition from a more traditional to a more modern form of politics, driven by commercial activities that forced the joining of the continent to ever new international markets (Nkemdirim, 1977). Basically the same case has been made in great detail for Latin America (O'Donnell, Schmitter, Whitehead, 1986; Topik, Marichal, Zephyr, 2006). In this context, the Tocquevillian question—what is really new?—seems very much to the point. To capture the distinguishing flavor and characteristics of the neoliberal "great transformation" (using the terminology of Polanyi's classical work), it is necessary to examine the mechanisms that establish the link between global markets and late-developer state making—it is not the latter in general, but the particular forms that it takes in each situation that varies.[9]

Table 1.1 Evolving conceptions of neoliberalism

Dimensions	1980s	1990s
Assumptions	Principle of isomorphism, where free market and liberties reinforce each other. Any excessive state intervention ends up in the restriction of freedom. The idea of relating economic liberty to political liberty comes from the writings of neoliberal theorists. Their thoughts are addressed against forms of authoritarianism (Stalinist communism, German fascism, Keynesian thought).	Limitations of the market agents, which make state intervention necessary. The World Bank starts introducing concepts, such as social exclusion, which becomes a legitimacy issue, and proposes the implementation of redistributive policies. Poverty and inequality can be counterproductive for the market.
Economic impact	Inflation becomes a tremendously relevant issue that affects the political arena. Moderate advance in the process of privatization of services and public companies. Broadening the base of the VAT-type tax. The taxes on exports and imports start to get reduced. Public spending and operation of the state is being reduced.	There is a dynamic acceleration of the services and public companies. Juridical measures are enacted to promote foreign investment. There is an almost total abolition of the taxes on imports and exports. The base of the VAT-type tax continues being broadened. The land problem freezes, the concentration on land property gets worse, and the state abandons or makes little effort to overcome the situation. Health and education coverage become wider. Depending on the country, there is emphasis on one or another.
Political impact	Intervention of international organizations, such as the World Bank and IMF, into national economies, which weakens the role of the state. Forms of clientelism become altered, but they do not disappear.	More emphasis on the modernization of the state through decentralization and privatization. Gradually, security forces become unable to accommodate the needs of the countries. Simultaneously, the private security becomes a widespread phenomenon.
Role of the state	Neoliberalism does not promote simple laissez faire, but implements an ordered competition. The state plays a role in establishing that order. Economic order has to be supported by a legal structure. For example, technical committees regulate special markets. Another function of the state is to regulate the monetary policies.	The state emerges as a guarantor of the social rights fighting poverty and inequality. It leans on the resources provided by the World Bank and the IMF.

In sum, there are several reasons to come back to the neoliberalism–violence link. One of them is the importance of neoliberalism in the contemporary world. Another is the fact that real-world outcomes are so mixed and that, despite grim and well thought-out predictions, we seem to be heading towards a global scenario of multiple equilibria. This reinforces the need to understand mechanisms through which neoliberalism alters previous balances, producing more (like in Côte d'Ivoire) or less (like in Peru) violent political conflict. A final reason to reexamine the neoliberalism–violence link is the urge to answer the Tocquevillian questions and introduce into the analysis a historical perspective.

This chapter concentrates on the mechanisms that produce multiple equilibria and give neoliberal conflict and peace their distinctive characteristics. The first section shows that there is in fact a significant variability in the use and meaning of the term neoliberalism in the literature, and attempts to establish a new definition that is consistent and reasonably sound. The second section is dedicated to examining the failure of the predictions based on both the liberal dystopia and the liberal utopia. According to the former, the increase of inequality plus the weakening of the state—through more or less the mechanisms specified by Reno in his seminal work—would fundamentally destabilize society and produce unrest and violence. According to the latter, economic openness should foster social and political openness, and ultimately deflate violence, but what has really happened is much more complex and muddled. The third section focuses on the de-concentration of power, one of the core neoliberal transformations of the state. It shows that the context can determine the specific path that de-concentration can take. The fourth section returns to the criminalization of the state and the privatization of security, and the ways in which this is articulated in both neoliberal conflict and peace. It also discusses the phenomenon of multiple equilibria.

WHAT IS NEOLIBERALISM?

There are four main problems related to the term neoliberalism. First, despite a significant consensus regarding the vague intuition that today the socio-political and economic world seems different than it was two decades ago, there is no agreement on what the content of this difference is, or if the term neoliberalism is really able to denote something beyond the impressionistic statement that "something is going on out there." Second, reflecting a tendency in the social sciences in general, there is a definitional *crise d'abundance*, and part of this crisis has to do with the fact that authors tend to propose their own definitions, sometimes only marginally different from others, resulting in a kind of incommensurable dissonance (Evans, 2007). The third problem is the fact that the nomenclature has become so intricate that it is difficult to separate the territory covered by intimately related neologisms. Finally, neoliberalism has always been an evolving phenomenon, characterized by several incremental adjustments. Many of the definitions have difficulties capturing the whole of the neoliberal trajectory, and rather concentrate on its openly anti-state "Thatcherite" phase, which has long been left behind. Note that the real challenge is to show *simultaneously* the specificity of neoliberalism in relation to the old economic liberalism, and capture the complex evolution of neoliberalism itself.

In a very general way, several trends in the area of "definition-making" can be identified. The first one is characterized by a partisanship of denial.[10] The commentators in this group have several reasons to controvert the existence of neoliberalism:

- Lack of specificity. As shown in the introduction, it can be asserted that since the very beginning of capitalism we have witnessed phenomena that, like neoliberalism, are vague (e.g., the "marketization" of society).
- Confusion. Neoliberalism means different things to different people.
- Theoretical thinness. Authors that speak about neoliberalism generally eschew the fundamental contributions by Mieses, Hayek, and others, whose work was published a long time before the present wave of policies appeared, and who established the essential principles of contemporary liberal economic thought.

The second trend focuses on the relation between neoliberalism and the state. The main concern here is the weakening or retreat of the state from some key areas. According to Campbell and Pedersen, "Neoliberalism ... that is, a time of market regulation and market decentralization, and reduced state intervention into economic affairs in general ... Much debate has occurred over how extensive these changes have been and over their causes, but few doubt that neoliberalism has become an important part of our world" (2001, p. 1). The idea of neoliberalism weakening the state is for many authors related to the notion that neoliberal globalization represents the fading out of the nation–state (see for example Cadermatori, 2003). Evans (2007), among others, has argued forcefully against such intuition. It is obvious that neoliberal globalization has changed the state, but the question is in what sense? The purely quantitative perspective (more or less state) fails to establish a clear-cut separation between neoliberal and non-neoliberal periods. In Colombia, the administration of César Gaviria—the epitome of neoliberalism in the country—*increased* the size of the state during his administration by scaling up the investment in security and justice, but also in some social policies. Similar arguments have been made with regard to some periods of the Fujimori regime in Peru (Crabtree and Thomas, 1999).

Globally, it is true that the state has lost some of its monopolies, but to assume that the state is necessarily no more in vogue is not only far-fetched but also an immediate—and uncalled for—concession precisely to the main theories that feed liberal economic thought.[11] I would add that some of the loss of power of the state has been compensated by new, very powerful, regulatory capacities—think about reproductive policies—that have been made possible and necessary by technological change and demographic transformations. Not to mention the fact that stressing the promotion of a weak or inactive state is a definition too much associated with the first, Thatcherite, phase of neoliberalism.

The third trend defines neoliberalism as a set of economic policies. "The 1980s and early 1990s witnessed a wave of neoliberalism breaking across the developing world. Nationalized strategies of growth painted a broad consensus for targeting low inflation, balanced budgets, currency convertibility, export-oriented production, and privatization. In sub-Saharan Africa, at least twenty-nine countries have undergone almost a decade of structural adjustment, some longer" (Hanson and Hentz, 1999, p. 479).[12] As several authors have pointed out, these policies, to be implemented and work, require complex institutional transformations that reduce transaction costs, protect adequately property rights, guarantee the stability of (orthodox) policies, and offer a proper environment for the flourishing of private activity. This is the direct link between liberalization and the set of policies that try to make the state more transparent and "bring it over" to the citizen.

The fourth trend emphasizes market fundamentalism. According to Harvey, "Neoliberalism is in the first instance a theory of political economic practices that proposes that human well-being can best be advanced by liberating individual entrepreneurial freedoms and skills within an institutional framework characterized by strong private property rights, free markets, and free trade" (2005, p. 2). In Conaghan and Malloy's careful analysis of specific processes of implementation of neoliberal policies, the final conclusion is that neoliberalism is a term used "to denote economic policies that combine orthodox stabilization measures with a long-term commitment to restructuring the economy by reducing the role of the state and by subjecting economy activity to market forces" (Conaghan et al., 1990, p. 28).

As pointed out above, these lines of thought have quite a bit of variance. However, despite the idiosyncrasy of the definitions, almost all of them have something in common. "Most critics who use the term, however," says McCarthy,

> seem to work from a relative consensus that the term describes a near-global project over the past few decades to reconfigure economic and political governance in line with many of the founding precepts of liberal theory. According to researchers in this tradition, its three main pillars are what Polanyi (1944) called the "self-regulating market" as the institutional form most likely to produce optimal social outcomes; unremitting hostility toward the state (particularly the Keynesian and developmentalist states deposed by neoliberalization) as owner, provider, or regulator of goods or services; and faith in civil society, or its constituent communities, as the sphere best able to redress any market failures that do occur. (2006, p. 87)

The attacks on the Keynesian and developmentalist states have not stopped, but in the process the neoliberal managers and architects have discovered new types of states (especially what may be called the "social capitalist" state) that deserve to be buttressed. If in the first period, neoliberal policy and decision makers considered the state as part of the problem not of the solution, now they tend to see it as part of the solution—as long as the solution is a specific, transparent, and efficient, pro-civil society state (see, again, Table 1.1, which synthesizes the contrast between the two types of neoliberalism).

On the other hand, the isomorphism principle—which is an attempt to capture the most unique characteristics of today's socio-political and economic situation—should be added to any viable definition. In effect, though intellectually the theme precedes whatever policy implementation we may associate with neoliberalism, the practical political consequences of pro-free market orientations until the late 1970s was in the best of cases indifferent to public liberties, as Eduardo Galeano's renowned flippancy underscores.[13] Actually, there is a long and distinguished tradition—that includes some of the best early quantitative comparative studies about Latin America (Weyland, 1999 and Conaghan et al., 1990)—that wonders if very astringent free-market economic policies could possibly be implemented by a democracy. The political mechanism that justified such conclusion was at the same time credible and quite simple: at least in a first moment, free market policies do produce very negative impacts on the majority of the population, so the government is prone to be overthrown or, less dramatically, voted out.[14] The best way to guarantee the continuity of free market policies was to have stable dictatorships—this was called in the 1970s "monetarism." Democracies simply were not a good bet for neoliberal reforms. In this sense, the Tocquevillian question—always uncomfortable but always healthy—has an answer: some aspects of the neoliberal phenomenon—precisely those which are of biggest import for our discussion—are without doubt new.

The numerous definitions of neoliberalism available in the literature make it clear that the phenomenon they point to is a complex "syndrome," and one that manifests itself in several domains of political and economic life. In fact, neoliberalism trespasses at least three boundaries. First, and quite obviously, the economic–political one: neoliberalism refers to a set of decisions of both economic and political nature. Second, the global–national. Neoliberalism is related to the huge growth in power and even formal attributions of a set of trans-national agents (global regulators, as the WTO, the IMF, and the World Bank), but at the same time to a mode of decision making by national actors. The latter does not depend on the former; a margin of autonomy always remains. Finally, picking up the terminology of Peck and Tickel, neoliberalism covers two completely different domains from the point of view of intentionality (Table 1.2). "Both [globalism and neoliberalism] have been associated with a mode of exogenized thinking in which globalism/neoliberalism is presented as a naturalized, external 'force.' Both ascribe quasiclimatic, extraterrestrial qualities to apparently disembodied, 'out there' forces, which are themselves typically linked to alleged tendencies towards homogenization, leveling out, and convergence" (Peck and Tickell, 2002, p. 382).

Table 1.2 Homogenizing tendencies in neoliberalism

Global/National	Intentional/"Climatic"	Economic/Political
Transnational regulators	Structural adjustment	Economic opening
National decision makers	Technological change	State modernization

Neoliberalism, then, can be viewed as a syndrome with the following components:

- Large contexts and decision making chains (globalization: without the contemporary modalities of globalization neoliberalism would not be conceivable. Neoliberalism is a global project).
- Probabilistic, "restricted," contexts (structural adjustments). Structural adjustments preceded neoliberalism. Neoliberalism survived the structural adjustment phase. There is an association between them, but they are not equivalent. The relation is only probabilistic (the presence of neoliberalism increases the probability of structural adjustments taking place at certain moments in a country's trajectory).
- Core "climatic" characteristics, like economic opening. Campbell defines it as a "sharp increase since the mid-1970s in trade, production, and capital flows" (2004, p. 125). This has organizational implications: we are in a period in which new agents appear, and some old agents acquire radically enhanced new roles (for example, supra state regulators, as the IMF; global actors, as transnational companies; social actors, as NGOs and quangos).
- Core intentional, designed characteristics: the project of building a society around the market as the only or main regulator, independently of the level of development; the isomorphism principle (open economies, societies, and polities are equally desirable and reinforce each other); an adversarial stance towards the Keynesian and developmental modes of regulation; the building of an appropriate, "business friendly" interface to economic opening; a transformation in the structure of property rights.
- Consequences. Because of its core characteristics, neoliberalism logically and empirically entails some processes that derive from it but are conceptually distinct (the reform and modernization of the state).

Let us see if this specification resists the main challenges to which neoliberalism as a concept is open:

- Longitudinally, neoliberalism is clearly distinct from standard economic liberalism (for example, the isomorphism principle separates them neatly), but at the same time it is intimately related to it, as neoliberalism is a combination of the new and the old.
- Both neoliberalism phases—"Thatcherite" and "inclusive"— are captured by the type of definition proposed above.
- Neoliberalism has a clear area of intersection with its semantic kin, but remains a distinct concept.
- Both "climatic" and intentional dimensions are acknowledged. Economic and political patterns, and national and global ones, are included.

THE BASIC SYLLOGISMS OF ECONOMIC REFORM

In theory, it is easy to understand why neoliberalism is thought to increase political violence. First, it encourages a general retreat of the state, destroying a safety net for the most vulnerable sectors of the population. And by undermining bureaucracy, it weakens the capacity of the state to provide security and other public goods to the citizenship. Second, inequality—at least above a certain threshold—breeds violence. If we add the relative impermeability of new democracies to alternative economic policies, the picture is complete. In fact it can be comfortably put in liberal terms: the loyalty of individuals to the rules of the game is directly proportional to the results of the game and to their capacity to impact on them (Locke, 1997). The liberal argument against violence is that in a democracy people lack the reasons to engage in a rebellion because rational actors calculate that the probability of triggering change within the system is reasonable, and the differential costs of leaving it very high. Adding the two premises (neoliberalism is bad for the poor and it is difficult for them to change the situation), the immediate conclusion is that neoliberalism breeds violent reactions. In other words, if you systematically fare badly and you have small or no influence on establishing the rules that produce that negative outcome, you have no reasons for loyalty. The typical sequence would be the following: through certain policies, neoliberalism excludes from social participation huge sectors of the population, sometimes pushing them into dire poverty; *at the same time* it creates a situation in which those excluded actors have little hope of changing such policies democratically. For example, the political invariant of Peru in the last decade and a half has been the stability of neoliberal orientation, despite broad sectors of the population rejecting it, and sometimes even the majority voting against it (it is important to remember that the victory of Fujimori in 1990 was due in part to an anti-liberal vote[15]). Neoliberalism, in this view, brings forth radical politics and violent contestation.

The above explanation is neat but incomplete. Both quantitative and qualitative evidence, and aggregated data analysis and case studies, call it into question. Qualitatively, we find that a whole series of peace processes, termination of conflicts via a military victory, and/or democratic transitions were associated with neoliberal reforms. In this volume, we see this happening in El Salvador, Guatemala, Peru—even in Colombia the intensity of the conflict has certainly diminished. There are also prominent cases of peace and/or stabilization associated with neoliberalism in Africa (South Africa; also see the Ugandan case in this volume). Quantitatively, the landscape is complex and rather inconclusive. Inequality is probably—more or less strongly—a factor of violence. According to Baquero in this volume, neoliberalism catalyzes violent political conflict when it is raging, but at the same time helps to prevent it, and is very strongly associated with its termination. Even in Latin America, the continent where neoliberalism was introduced more abruptly— and where indeed it triggered more opposition—violent contestation *declined*. How can this be interpreted? What explanation can be offered to explain the failure of this popular economic syllogism, which stipulates that neoliberalism increases political violence?

The logic of the syllogism can be undermined by contesting its premises or the quality of its conclusion. Clearly, here the premises are open to contestation. That inequality and political violence are correlated has been put into question several times, and is still open to discussion. However, to my knowledge, the best—and last—words have been said by those who maintain that there is a positive association between inequality and political violence (the quantitative literature alone is enormous; Powell (1982) and Krain (1998) are some of the highlights). Our own statistical analysis also reveals an association, although not particularly strong (see Baquero). At least equally controversial is the impact of neoliberal reforms on inequality worldwide.

There are at least four prominent and distinct ways of measuring inequality. The first is the difference in inequality between countries.

The second is the difference in inequality within countries, calculated using continuous measures (Gini index). The third is the difference in inequality within countries measured using discrete measures. The last way of gauging inequality is to measure non-economic differences. Different measures, techniques, and forms of aggregation produce widely divergent results (see for example Stewart, 2000).[16] The relation between inequality and other socio-economic variables is far from simple.[17] But with all the necessary caveats, the case can be reasonably made that in a substantial part of the developing world inequality has worsened (see Figures 1.1–1.7, which depict the evolution of the Gini index in the cases covered in this volume). The retreat of the state from *some* social policies has been quite tangible.[18] In sum, though the premises of the economic syllogism are not foolproof, they are sufficiently strong so as to give them the benefit of the doubt.

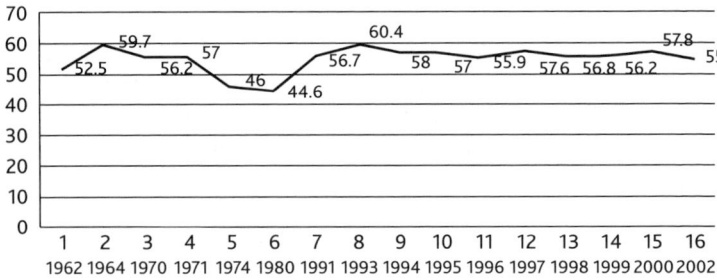

Figure 1.1 Evolution of Gini the index, Colombia, 1962–2002

Source: Calculations based on The Global Development Finance and World Development Indicators, available from www.worldbank.org/data.

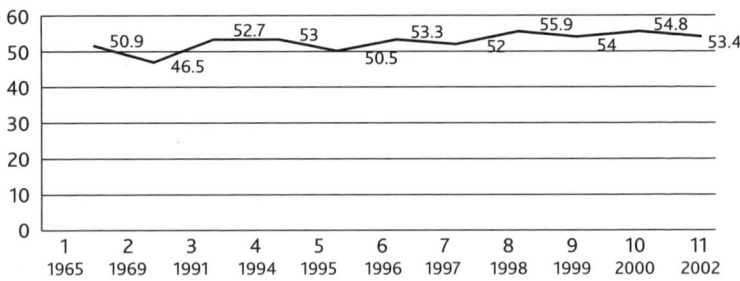

Figure 1.2 Evolution of the Gini index, El Salvador, 1965–2002

Source: Calculations based on The Global Development Finance and World Development Indicators, available from www.worldbank.org/data.

MECHANISMS 27

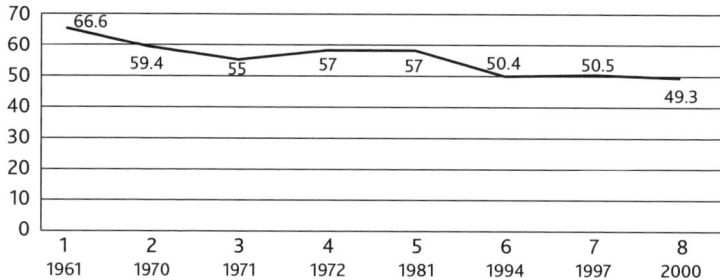

Figure 1.3 Evolution of the Gini index, Peru, 1961–2002

Source: Calculations based on The Global Development Finance and World Development Indicators, available from www.worldbank.org/data.

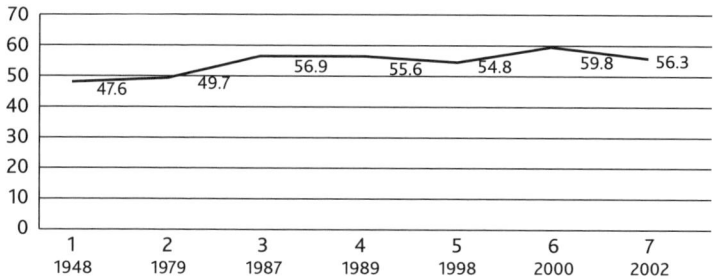

Figure 1.4 Evolution of the Gini index, Guatemala, 1948–2002

Source: Calculations based on The Global Development Finance and World Development Indicators, available from www.worldbank.org/data.

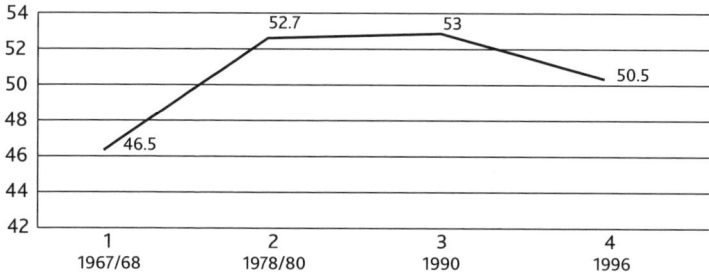

Figure 1.5 Evolution of the Gini index, Sudan, 1967/68–1996

Source: Calculations based on The Global Development Finance and World Development Indicators, available from www.worldbank.org/data.

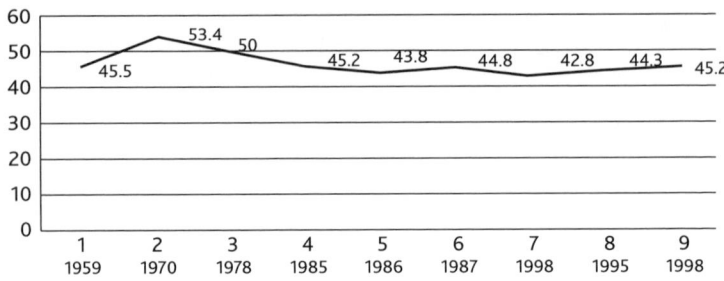

Figure 1.6 Evolution of the Gini index, Côte d'Ivoire, 1959–98

Source: Calculations based on The Global Development Finance and World Development Indicators, available from www.worldbank.org/data.

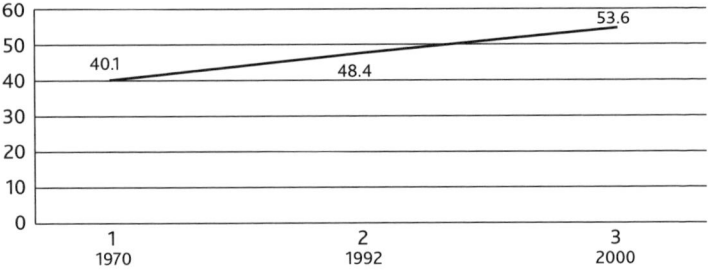

Figure 1.7 Evolution of the Gini index, Uganda, 1970–2000

Source: Calculations based on The Global Development Finance and World Development Indicators, available from www.worldbank.org/data.

Let us look at the conclusion then. The main problem with the conclusion is that it is based on an assumption that is not supported by facts. Neoliberalism can increase inequality, but it also changes everything else. Neoliberalism, thus, may curtail or solve social problems that have an explosive political potential, and that do not survive well in a neoliberal environment. The obvious example is hyperinflation. It can be conjectured that in good measure the Fujimori regime owed its early stability to its capacity to cut down inflation. Probably, in those countries where neoliberalism came hand in hand with solutions to burning preexisting macro problems—hyperinflation in Peru, security in Peru and Colombia—it was able to build a very strong social base *and* governing coalition that was willing to trade off the consequences of a severe economic environment for stability and predictability. Economic growth deserves a separate consideration. In countries where neoliberal reforms did not guarantee stable growth—like Bolivia[19]—mass opposition coalitions were likely to appear. When neoliberalism goes hand in hand with sustained growth, the upshot is different—even if growth is unequal (like in a coordination dilemma with asymmetrical Nash equilibria). For example in Peru, opinion polls have shown systematically that free-trade agreements enjoy broad support (Table 1.3). Growth, on the other hand, is not simply a product of policies but of the power relations that enable them. The characteristics of the neoliberal program implemented in each country, therefore, depend on the constellation of forces that support and oppose it.[20]

Table 1.3 Do you agree with the Free-trade Treaty? (Peru)

	2003 Nov	2004 Nov	2005 May	2006 Apr
Agree	73.4	64.4	63.7	81.0
Disagree	15.2	29.5	34.1	17.1
Does not know	11.4	6.1	2.3	1.4
Does not answer				0.5
Only respondents who declared that were informed about the treaty				
N	(178)	(123)	(206)	(237)

Source: Government of Peru.

All this fits well with the evidence coming from the experience of developmental states, the model that neoliberalism effectively shunned. According to neoliberal commentators, the developmental state is a type of state that is more vulnerable to contentious politics. This is because long-term development plans are likely to produce both political exclusion and high levels of state economic intervention. An active state can become a focal point for opponents. "States that form exclusive polities and states that intervene highly in capital accumulation tend to become very vulnerable to challenge and attack. Prolonged exclusion from the polity predisposes the excluded toward radical measures and insurgency. State intervention in capital accumulation also increases state vulnerability to challenge and attack. Highly interventionist states can readily become targets of attack during social conflicts" (Parsa, 2000, p. 10). By "effacing" the state from the public realm, and proposing the market as the only (multi-agent) viable social regulator, neoliberalism diffuses conflict—*after* the introductory period—and avoids the vulnerabilities of developmentalism.[21] Correspondingly, the retreat of the state can mean less, and not more, contention. For example, the privatization of state firms in Colombia weakened trade unions, already decimated by the activity of paramilitaries and other violent agents (see for example Duncan, 2005 or Ortiz, 1998). Colombia is only one extreme example; in Peru privatization had a similar effect.

Here, the role of neoliberalism in relation to social conflicts appears—at least in some contexts—to be a pretty clear tradeoff. On the one hand, it fosters inequality, which tends to produce if not violent then at least very polarized conflicts.[22] On the other hand, it eliminates, reduces, or diffuses polarized conflicts originating in other social problems. There are many more instances of this use of the market as a conflict resolution device. At the beginning of the 1960s, and throughout apartheid, a lively debate between South African Marxists and Liberals took place. The core of the discussion was the relation between capitalism and racism (Torchia, 1988; Callinicos, 1992; Williams, 1989). While the Marxists claimed that capitalism reinforced racism, and went into detailed explanations why, Liberals believed exactly the contrary. According to the latter, true market capitalism—without the developmentalist strictures that were associated with the racist regime—would free individuals from every single ethnic or communal adscription, and promote social mobility. Some of the propositions the Liberals advanced were clearly weak (for example, that the business community did not support apartheid; the reality was much more complex[23]). But the heart of their argument was that efficient markets would weaken racism in the long run by imposing the discipline of efficiency on entrepreneurs, and those who do not adapt to a color-blind logic of the market will become extinct.[24] Liberal ideas probably played a role in the negotiation process that ended in the devolution of power to the majority of the population (Wood, 2000). On the other hand, evaluating costs and benefits will depend on the moment and the context. In effect, introducing the neoliberal agenda entails state activism. At its beginning, neoliberalism can be extremely traumatic, precisely because it becomes the focal point that galvanizes social mobilization—and only if this first stage is successful, its diffusing effects may appear.[25]

In sum, the retreat of the state and the associated (hypothesized) increase in inequality trigger three types of mechanisms that act in different directions. First, the reduction of the loyalty to the law—the typically Lockean argument—by deepening disenfranchisement.

This should be more or less invariant where inequality jumps above a certain threshold. Second, the creation of a broad social base and of a stable governing coalition, where neoliberalism, simultaneously with the increase of inequality, is able to provide solutions to burning macro-social problems (inflation, security, eventually growth). Third, the effacement of the state from the public sphere, which (after the initial critical period) takes away from challengers a possible focal point for contestation, and multiplies the niches where the fight for power and decision making takes place. This, of course, is directly related to political reform.

In sum, the basic syllogism that feeds the liberal dystopia is based on a faulty (non-factual) evaluation of the tradeoffs that developmentalist states face. What about the liberal promise? Why hasn't it become true? After the first, Thatcherite phase, neoliberal hopes were, paradoxically, quite focused on the state. As several authors have underscored, to be implemented and work, neoliberal policies require complex institutional transformations, so as to be able to reduce transaction costs, protect adequately property rights, guarantee the stability of (orthodox) policies, and offer a proper environment for the flourishing of private activity. This is the direct link between liberalization and the set of policies that try to make the state more transparent and "bring it over" to the citizen. The most thoughtful liberal thinkers were well aware that this was only a "minimal program." For example, the bottom-line rationale that linked state reform and economic liberalization was, according to Centeno (1994), not that the latter offered in absolute terms an optimal growth strategy (see also Easterly, 2001), but that "state-led development" will produce developmental disasters where weak and predatory neopatrimonial states hold sway. It is better under these circumstances to have a leaner, "liberal" state with fewer economic tasks, combined with a long-term program of institutional reform to realize the "great transformation" of capitalist revolution. This, in essence, is what the neoliberal model now offers. Indeed, this has been a very central part of the neoliberal recipe for state building in the developing world in the last few years. Still "reinvigorating public institutions" was conceived of as the only way to trigger private initiative. This is an ever-deepening trend, due both to the fact that important financial institutions have espoused energetically the cause of state reform, and that the typical explanations offered by neoliberals when their program does not work is that we are in the presence of state and society failures (lack of social capital, wrong institutional designs, presence of informal institutions, etc.).

All this sounds very well but, like the assertion that neoliberalism necessarily increases political violence, it is an incomplete explanation. Several reasons explain the failure of the liberal promise. Above all, its minimal—and indeed defensive—program was keen on producing an environment that prevented the predatory drift of states. That this is not trivial is illustrated quite powerfully by the example of Uganda. Despite the fact that Uganda's present political regime is highly personalistic and very limited in terms of political competition, it is bound "from above" (by international actors, who provide a fair amount of the goods necessary for carrying out the everyday functions of the state) and "from below" (by a set of social and regional instances).[26] On the other hand, the identification of the state as the only potential predator is purely ideological, and misses completely the strong points that Reno made. Indeed, the very notion of self-regulatory markets is self-defeating, as Polanyi asserted in his brilliant analysis, and as is starkly revealed by our current world order. For example, despite all the double-speak about free trade, liberalization of certain goods coexists with global prohibitionist policies—of drugs, of the mobility of labor—which hit very hard both agents and states in the developing world.[27] For example, save Bolivia, there is no coca producer that has not undergone an internal conflict.[28] Entrepreneurs can be criminals, indeed, but those who are not can also be forced to act as criminals in certain contexts. As Reno predicted, in Colombia, Côte d'Ivoire, and Sudan, several agents (including multinational firms) have been able to create private–public arrangements and networks that have a high criminal component. What is new is that such arrangements are not necessarily attached to warlordism—in many cases criminal privatizations coordinated by the state produce peaceful political stabilizations (like in Colombia[29]) or diverse modalities of "armed peace" (like in Côte d'Ivoire and Colombia), which speaks very much to *one* type of peace that can be achieved through neoliberal reforms.

THE DE-CONCENTRATION OF POWER: IS SMALL BEAUTIFUL?

The Context

The particulars of the neoliberal "minimal program" described above—which include attempts to prevent the predatory drifts of developmental states, reduce transaction costs, limit actual or potential disasters—depend on the type of state with which it is associated. In the developing world, a substantial part of the political liberal reform was not oriented towards the organizational strengthening of the state, but towards the creation of a *cordon sanitaire* around it. While in the initial, Thatcherite period, neoliberalism meant radical individualism—according to which society did not exist—in the second period it meant de-concentration of power and promotion of social capital. The upshot is that the typical emphasis of the third wave of democratization has not been to buttress the checks and balances *within* the central state, but the creation of a cloud of surrounding non-state agencies that are directly linked with transnational actors and that almost always bypass national political institutions and bureaucracies. In other terms, both bureaucratization and the key Madisonian experience of institutionally endogenizing the friction between powers is absent from the third wave of democratization. For example, World Bank funding through NGOs grew in Africa from 6 percent of the total budget apportioned in 1989, to 40–50 percent between 1994 and 1997 (Manji and O'Coill, 2002). Several states—see the cases of Sudan and Uganda—simply will not make ends meet without international support. This is not so new. What is really new is that this support is not funneled through the state, but through civil society and private agencies, which will reduce transaction costs and escape the political economy of state agencies. Correspondingly, the developmental style of the World Bank has shifted towards a "micro" and "nano" project management, which emphasizes the role of local communities. The standard recipe for state reform in developing countries includes decentralization, a recipe that is not necessarily an imposition because it may result from endogenous traditions and democratic demands. These well-sounding ideas have been systematically evaluated and there is no evidence that microprojects are more successful than other ones, according to a paper commissioned by the Bank itself (Easterly, 2001; Tendler, 1997).

Decentralization

In all the cases considered in this investigation, multilateral agencies sponsored and supported vigorously the adoption of decentralization. In almost all of them—save perhaps in Guatemala—decentralization was an old, deeply rooted demand. It would be unreasonable to claim that decentralization is a neoliberal imposition or cabal. At the same time, transnational institutions and decision makers adopted it as one of the core items on the agenda of state reform in the developing countries.

Not being simply an exogenous recipe, real existing decentralization seems to have the following two main problems. First, frequently it lacked mechanisms for promoting national integration and inter-regional projects able to create common interests between the different regions. Thus, the territorial division of countries in conflict became a zero-sum competition for resources. Where certain key resources were concentrated in one part of the country, these competitions became ferocious. Such "resource driven fractures" became a very strong *casus belli*, but also a driver of a de facto decentralization in Côte d'Ivoire and Sudan.[30] Second, many regions—especially the poorest ones, which in theory should be favored by the reform—desperately lacked trained personnel, middle classes, media, and viable institutions. In these contexts, resource and power were rapidly captured by rural subnational elites and rent seekers (or by an alliance between them). The combination of zero-sum competition and devolution of power to the wrong people may have been particularly noxious in countries where other inflaming issues were already present. For example, in Colombia decentralization is a long-standing and completely endogenous institutional theme, but only got activated in the mid 1980s, and came to be accepted by politicians of all hues as a litmus test for the inclusive character of the regime. Decentralization endowed municipalities with fixed, earmarked income (growing transfers from the state, whose amount was established at the constitutional level). After a few years, this gave non-state armies a strong incentive to put pressures on the municipalities because: (i) municipalities, especially poor ones, were much more vulnerable and malleable than the central state; (ii) through municipalities the irregular armies could capture significant rents; (iii) the irregular armies could also influence local policies that were vital for the survival and subsistence of any given group. Decentralization was also intimately linked with the change in health policies. The Law 100 transformed the provision of health from a centralized, state-led (and very inefficient) service, into an open network, in which the state provides the resources and private operators (with a strong civil society component, represented by cooperatives) take care of the patients. In the typical neoliberal mood of "focalization on demand," the state allotted resources to each provider depending on the number of citizens–clients it had enlisted. The resources involved were enormous, and the system vulnerable, because the identity of poor citizens in need of subsidized health could easily be fabricated,[31] especially in some regions. This allowed the paramilitary to capture an important portion of these resources. More generally, the paramilitary involvement can be read as part of a subversion of the subnational elites against the state (Romero, 2002).

What about de-concentration of power qua democratization? It has the potential to prevent predatory rampages. Even when neoliberalism has co-existed with non-democratic regimes, these were sufficiently held back by international restrictions so as to exercise only bounded repression (Peru, Uganda). But an increased margin of maneuver for all actors can in effect produce suboptimal social results. In particular, in situations near a zero-sum competition, an external regulator can create cooperation through regulated distribution, backed by the threat of penalizing trouble makers (for example with marginalization), an outcome that is not accessible if the external regulator does not exist. For example, in Côte d'Ivoire and Colombia, several mechanisms (Caisse de Stabilisation, or "Caistab"; the Federación Colombiana de Cafeteros) permitted the national redistribution of rents created regionally, through a tightly monitored system of compensations above and below the table. As seen in the Côte d'Ivoire chapter in this volume, the system: (i) produced a sufficiently strong system of incentives so as to invite regional actors to cooperate with the central government; (ii) generated a monitoring system that allowed the central government to chide defectors. The Caistab seems to have been particularly successful in balancing citizen incorporation and economic themes (see the chapter by Banégas, Toh, and Kouman Adingra in this volume; also, for example, Tice (1974), or Toungara (1990)), and it is only after its destabilization that conflict ensued.

Table 1.4 shows the mechanism in a more schematic manner. Suppose the situation between the regions is a prisoner's dilemma, so the dominant strategy is mutual defection, which is socially bad. However, if an external regulator is able to create a new strategy, then defect-defect is not a Nash equilibrium any more, and the actors will use mixed strategies. Sometimes cooperation will ensue—under the condition that repression of trouble makers is not too costly for the regulator. The tradeoff (from the point of view of the regions) is a certain amount of "friction" (in terms of resources and power transferred to the center). Neoliberal reforms unhinged the Caistab mechanism, diminishing transaction costs and friction, but in the process destabilized the whole architecture of the Ivorian state—once one of the most successful African national experiences. In the spirit of Tocqueville, it has to be stressed that from the beginning the Ivorian state-building saga was market-oriented, which stresses neatly the differences between old and new liberalism.

Table 1.4 If B > 2, then Defect-Defect is not a Nash equilibrium

	Cooperate	Defect
Cooperate	5, 5	1, 7
Defect	7, 1	2, 2
Marginalize	A, 3	B, 0

This discussion seems to capture better the problem of the unraveling of old political agreements under neoliberalism than the standard claim that neoliberalism, by shrinking the state, diminishes the latitude of the ruler to distribute pork. It is nearly impossible to arrive at a credible generalization about this, but certainly some of our cases spectacularly disprove the proposition that neoliberal reforms always shrank the state. Fujimori probably distributed much more goods through clientelistic channels than his predecessors, only through new channels (see the "Vladi-videos" of Zapata and Montesinos[32]). In Colombia, the reform of the state also changed the nature of clientelism—shifting from emphasis on the payroll to emphasis on contracts—but did nothing to eliminate it; furthermore, the state grew, and quite substantially (Jimenez, 2005). Museveni has not been timid when bestowing goodies on his allies (see Golooba-Mutebi's chapter in this volume). He has also been able to create mechanisms of regional distribution, based on international aid. In Côte d'Ivoire, the "militia state" is based precisely on the reallocation of rents to different militias. Neoliberalism has not shrunk the pork barrel; sometimes it made it grow. What really seems to be new is the creation of social dilemmas in which increased liberty for all actors unsettled national arrangements of regional redistribution that regulated the main export economy.

In sum, democratization as de-concentration of power has had at least three conflict-generating effects. First, it has failed to promote processes of inter-regional integration, creating in some countries a politics of zero-sum competition. To the extent that this is true, assets and income being fought over are treated in practice as if they were non-divisible goods, with extremely negative consequences (Di John, 2006). Naturally, regional disputes can overlap with other ones (Sudan), creating diverse sources of "horizontal inequality" (Stewart, 2000). Second, democratization as de-concentration of power may open windows of opportunity for rent-seeking by state actors. This operates in both directions: decentralization can create rents, and rent-seeking can give origin to a de facto regionalization that mimics "small is beautiful" programs. Third, it can disorganize successful regulatory schemes that were able to link global markets, state building, and the political system, without offering some kind of surrogate.

Reasons for Contention

At the beginning of this text I stressed the importance of noting that neoliberalism was characterized by an isomorphism principle. For the first time in history, at the policy level we witness a worldwide effort to implement simultaneously—and as mutually reinforcing devices—political and economic liberties. This is the essence of the "third wave of democratization" (Diamond et al., 1997).

However, "third wave" democracies themselves can be quite imperfect regimes. In particular, economic and other key neoliberal policies can be insulated from political competition, which can promote the formation of a broad sector of disaffected voters, who may eventually choose an outsider (Weyland, 1999). Crucially, neoliberalism might also freeze the agrarian structures that are behind violent conflict. Since the rates of relapse into violence of countries that have suffered civil wars are high, maintaining a key facilitating factor of violence seems very dangerous. Indeed, this is less of a problem in countries in which the military and other forces carried out a genuine agrarian reform (especially Peru, but also El Salvador). But even there, peace arrived hand in hand with the preservation of very unequal structures.[33] However, the agrarian reform was instrumental to pass through the "mined period" of instability, because very soon the effects of capitalist modernization combined with the very effects of war produced a much more urbanized nation (Seligson, 1995), where an agrarian conflict was implausible (or marginal). The comparison between those countries that enacted their reforms on time (Peru, El Salvador) and those that did not (Colombia, Côte d'Ivoire, Guatemala) is quite telling. In Colombia, several authors have estimated that the rural Gini coefficient might go beyond 0.8 (see for example Rincón and Lucía, 1997), which is a degree of inequality that is probably incompatible with democratic governance (and perhaps with peace). Indeed, a very important part of the Colombian conflict is about agrarian property structures, and in the measure that the conflict has worsened steeply the situation—via the displacement of millions of peasants—such structures have become even more unequal and inefficient. This, also, is part of the explanation of the contrasting luck of Colombia and Peru—the latter had a much more virulent conflict, but was able to extricate itself from it much faster. In Côte d'Ivoire, the problem of land is associated with nationality and citizenship. In the initial phase of this "state planteur" (Banégas et al. in this volume), the patterns of distribution of land property rights were associated with regional mechanisms of coordination and, in the particular conditions of Côte d'Ivoire, with an incorporation of waves of migrants. That this incorporation was imperfect is shown clearly by an ex post facto analysis—though the imperfectness only materialized when the whole architecture of the state started to hover, giving incentives to politicians to enter political competition through the denunciation of aliens and the reformulation of the basis of Ivorian citizenship. In Guatemala, the proposals for a more equal distribution of land and other properties that stemmed from the peace accord were miserably defeated at the ballot box. Contrary to Peru, the agrarian elites are a very important component of the governing coalition. In other countries, as well, the way in which neoliberalism has transformed agrarian structures—freezing them or revolutionizing them, depending on the context—has proved to be highly contentious.[34]

Naturally, neoliberalism has also created new transnational realities, which limit the margin for maneuver of national decision makers and emasculate several national institutions. Today not only markets, but also democracy and peace have a strong global component of which economic policies are a key part. These can become focal points of opposition, as the logic of state politics (i.e., everyday, conventional politics) is still founded on the assumption that people self-determine and that, because of this, their decisions are relatively self-contained.[35] In other words, in some dimensions of globalization associated with neoliberalism, policy-making is insulated from national politics—which can give origin not to a policy characterized by reformist orientation, but to an antineoliberal politics. It may be the case, then, that neoliberalism is fostering and increasing a nationalistic tide, which expresses itself in several forms, and which may be potentially violent. This, of course, is a variant of Polanyi's vision. Obvious examples of this can be found in Africa (Sudan, but especially Côte d'Ivoire) and Latin America.

Because of all this, it can be safely conjectured that neoliberalism promotes contentious politics. Its inception is normally accompanied by a wave of protests. Once again, this phenomenon appears at different levels of development. It affected both Great Britain and

Argentina. There is a significant intersection area in the motives of anti-neoliberalism protesters around the globe. However, at low levels of development the wrong end of the ladder of development, the polarization triggered by neoliberalism can have more serious consequences. The reason for this is that national motives are added to social unrest. This assertion deserves two important caveats. First, the implementation of neoliberal measures is not necessarily the result of arm twisting. Hanson and Hentz (1999), comparing the development of neoliberalism in Zambia and South Africa, found that the preferences of the political elites played a key role. South African leaders had a much wider margin of maneuver, but both for strategic reasons and newly adopted beliefs decided to adopt a much clearer neoliberal course than their Zambian peers. Second, the population at large will not necessarily perceive neoliberalism or economic globalization as a threat. In Peru, opinion polls systematically have showed that the population has positive expectations towards the free-trade agreement with the United States. The same is the case in Colombia. But the positive opinion of the majority of citizens with regard to free-trade agreements, or more generally economic openness, should not blot out the fact that significant minorities can feel that they have been left entirely out of the socioeconomic pact. In Peru, the majority recognition of potential benefits of the free-trade agreement coexisted with a sense of social exclusion and despondency that—as practically all analysts believed—was the protagonist of the 2007 presidential election (see Pajuelo, 2004 and Ballón, 2006). The contrast between an enormous electoral volatility and the freezing of economic policies is an outstanding characteristic of the Peruvian polity.

AN ABSENT-MINDED WATCHMAN?

As seen in the cases we consider in this book—including the quantitative analyses—triggering a wave of contention is *not* synonymous with promoting armed conflict or violence. I believe it can more or less comfortably be asserted that neoliberalism destabilized societies throughout the developing world. In many parts of the world, this implied more violence (Côte d'Ivoire, Sudan). However, in many others it implied *less* violence (El Salvador, Peru, Uganda[36]). The aggregate landscape reveals one indisputable effect: Neoliberalism is associated (in the last decades) with conflict termination. This, of course, may change. The dynamics of society change rapidly. We do not know if the liberal conflict resolution devices will stand the test of time. We do not know if a backlash will take place or not. This is why—in terms of both analysis and policy—it is important to identify the mechanisms through which neoliberalism can generate peace or conflict, and then the type of peace and of conflict.

Why hasn't the creation of worldwide criminalized commerce networks, associated with "shadow states," produced a spike in violence and warlordism? First of all, private–public networks of militarized commerce need not be predatory or particularly aggressive. They can arrive in settlements in which they can conduct business and coordinate rent extraction with the private provision of security. As the case of Colombia suggests, the empowerment of such networks can result in a fall in the observable rates of violence, and a process of stabilization supported by the citizens at large (who would enter a Hobbesian pact: some order is better than no order at all). The critical issue is the solution of collective action problems within the state itself. States in developing countries are open to all types of pressure. Different agencies may obey different local and international dynamics. Stable arrangements in which criminals play a substantial role also depend on the level of tolerance of powerful international actors, and in particular on the legal or illegal character of the global market to which such arrangements are linked.[37] In other words, there can be a tradeoff between violence with contestation and peace without liberty, many a times mediated by criminal networks which reconfigure both state and society. Thus, the changes in the structure of the state prompted by neoliberal transformations can create propitious conditions either for peace or for violent conflict, but both of them can have a highly criminal component.

Contrary to the old liberalism—in which the role of the state was that of a night watchman—neoliberalism seems to be heading towards an "absent-minded watchman" model. While in theory the state keeps on trying to maintain a monopoly on legitimate violence—and provide security—in reality state security has undergone substantial privatization. This is clearly reflected in the cases discussed in this book and elsewhere. The two most extreme examples are Colombia and Côte d'Ivoire. In both, the deterioration of the provision of security by the state has taken place by both usurpation and delegation. On the one hand, rebels were able to launch and sustain successful challenges to the state, which materialized as specific forms of regional order.[38] On the other, the state found that for political or military reasons it had better allow the entrance of new security providers, which could attack challengers in a more agile form, short-circuit bureaucracies, and wage war in a more effective, or lucrative, manner. Indeed, in every case we studied in the research, the privatization of security is a phenomenon that precedes neoliberalism. In most of them (Colombia, Peru, Guatemala, El Salvador, Sudan, Uganda) privatization was a mechanism needed to face the insurgency challenge in a context of fiscal penury. The building of paramilitary organizations in these countries was determined by two main factors. On the one hand, rebels were able to launch and sustain successful challenges to the state, which materialized as specific forms of regional order. On the other, politically and fiscally outsourcing the use of force was more manageable. What neoliberalism did was to provide the conditions for scaling up the market for security services—also true in the developed world—legalizing many of the incipient and previously underground practices. In Central America, the number of private security personnel is larger than the number of police officers (Table 1.5). The same applies to Peru (also Table 1.5) and South Africa. The weaponry and functions of these forces have been escalated several times. Simultaneously, the direct relation of private agents with the security apparatus of the state has strengthened. Transnational firms pay for specific services, and fund the activities of some battalions (Pearce, 2005). For example, in 2004 in Guatemala, based on the figures of the Office of Private Security Control of the National Civil Police, there were 120 legal companies, which numbered 35,000 men. It must be pointed out that the Office of Private Security Control has only 48 agents to control the industry (Sieder et al., 2002).

Table 1.5 Private security services

Country	Total guards	Guards per 100,000
Colombia	190,000	4.56
Mexico	450,000	4.29
Brazil	570,000	3.13
Venezuela	75,000	3.04
Chile	45,000	2.87
Central America	105,000	2.67
Argentina	75,000	1.94
Peru	50,000	1.76
Other countries	70,000	
TOTAL	1,630,000	

Source: Adán Abelson, "Seguridad Privada en América Latina, 2003. Seguridad Privada en Chile," *Boletín de Seguridad Ciudadana* 6 (August 2006).

All these problems are not logically necessary—they are empirical instances of the implausibility of the liberal promise, not a proof of the dystopia. What they show is that the juxtaposition of economic and political liberalism can produce several equilibria. For example:

- Successful reform process, though different sectors paid differentially for the costs of the process (New Zealand).
- Suboptimal stagnation in the "fits and starts" cycle, in which the reforms are radical enough to produce strong opposition, but insufficient to produce a modernizing breakthrough.
- Hollowing out of democratic institutions (Giddens, 1991) and increasing inequality, entering the danger zone of political violence.
- Shadow state-like structures *characterized by peace*, in which armed private intermediaries pacify a territory and provide global market agents the minimum level of security and services.
- Shadow state-like structures *characterized by violence*, in which armed private intermediaries pacify a territory and provide global market agents the minimum level of security and services, but have to compete for the control of territory with other similar entities.

Instead of the standard single equilibrium version (economic, political, and social openness, according to the liberal promise; economic, political, and social disarray, according to the dystopia), the cases in this book show that there is a strong evidence in favor of the multiple equilibria argument. It should be noted that in none of the possible scenarios (save perhaps the first, above[39]) democracy is a necessity.

CONCLUSIONS

As many authors have noted, even in its most anti-statist mood, neoliberalism had to engage in state reform. From the very beginning, neoliberalism was conceived of as a form of reorganizing the whole of society in the image of the market. By prompting a distinct set of institutional macro changes, neoliberalism remodeled the set of incentives and constraints that all actors, economic and political, face, remodeling in the process the nature of violent contestation and state answers to challenges. In other words, neoliberalism sometimes has fueled the initiation of conflict, sometimes has perturbed it, and sometimes has played a fundamental role in pacification. I have discussed in this chapter several concrete examples that show how neoliberalism has:

- Transformed the state—stabilizing a specific type of political regime, promoting the de-concentration of power, creating a set of incentives that, as direct consequence or as a side effect, encouraged the privatization of security.
- Created a new form of checks and balances (not by "coordinating powers," but by "surrounding the state").
- Championed an economic program that increased several dimensions of inequality, many a time above a critical threshold.
- Continued several *longue durée* trends with respect to the articulation of the state vis-à-vis global markets, but changed the means to achieve this articulation. In particular, it reshuffled the articulation of regions to the national center. Some countries were able to improve their performance because of this; others fell into disarray.

Through all these paths, neoliberalism transformed the ways in which conflict is fought, and forced national re-adaptation practically everywhere (some successful, others not). Contrary to the expectations of the partisans of the liberal utopia (and dystopia), this change was multi-valued and multi-faceted. In some cases, it resulted in destabilizing dynamics; in others, it was associated with workable settlements. The combined effect can go in different directions depending on specific trajectories, which is precisely the type of evolution that is particularly difficult to capture through probabilistic cross-national models. The "myth" of the liberal promise is based on the illusion that "all good things come together" (Hirschman, 1970). The liberal dystopia is based on a flawed assumption that neoliberalism changes the levels of inequality, without altering the whole set of institutional arrangements.

The cases discussed in this book reveal that neoliberalism does affect conflict—both directly, by operating over crucial economic indicators, and indirectly, by changing the role and structure of the state.[40] But they also show that conflict perturbs the implementation of neoliberalism. Formulas crafted for societies without conflict ended up empowering criminal and violent actors. Ideas that were thought of as deeply democratic ended up weakening—sometimes critically—democracy. Certainly, this is also very context dependent:

Neoliberalism caused disasters in Côte d'Ivoire and Sudan, but is associated with different forms of sustainable stabilization in Uganda and Peru. Note that these stabilizations, with all their successes, have a rather dismal democratic record.

NOTES

1. Francisco Gutiérrez Sanín is a researcher at the Instituto de Estudios Políticos y Relaciones Internacionales (IEPRI)—Universidad Nacional de Colombia.
2. Actually, this is precisely the type of outcome described in Reno's study.
3. See Baquero's study in this volume. Also, PRIO http://www.prio.no/cscw/armedconflict/; Harbom and Wallensteen (2007).
4. I believe the novelty of the distinction between the two should not be overlooked. See below.
5. The feasible set for peace in these cases is easy to describe in an informal way: the rich wanted neoliberalism, the challengers wanted democracy. The rich would accept democracy if neoliberalism was more or less guaranteed, while the challengers would only accept the reverse: democracy then neoliberalism.
6. Peruvian rulers in the 1980s promoted, or at least coexisted with, certain forms of economic nationalism that presently are completely foreign to their thought.
7. See the first section of this chapter, and Baquero's work in this volume.
8. For example, if we limit our analysis to armed conflict, then neoliberalism may have different impacts on the conflict's onset, intensity, and termination (which is in fact the case—see the quantitative analyses by Jairo Baquero).
9. Or which, more accurately, is a reasonable candidate for variation.
10. Ghersi (2004) speaks about "the myth of neoliberalism."
11. Theories have created the image of a bad, rentist, and predatory state.
12. See also Hey and Klak (1999).
13. "People were in prison so that prices could be free," quoted in Cavanaugh (2003). Others stated that only "sufficiently stonyhearted" authorities could implement policies that made the markets work, and that this would be "slow and painful" for workers and peasants (Harberger, quoted in Brittain, 2005, n. 24).
14. Or, as has happened many times recently in Latin America, a combination of both.
15. See for example: Stokes (1996).
16. According to Stewart (2000), it is the overlap of several of these that more likely precipitates violent outcomes.
17. Naturally, it is possible that inequality increases and poverty shrinks at the same time, especially in the presence of vigorous growth. In Colombia, probably a more bizarre experience has taken place: the narco economy has produced more social mobility *and* more inequality. All this has impacts on the form in which the population evaluates its chances for success (and the policies that affect them).
18. Though certainly not all.
19. This is a particularly interesting case because it became a showcase of liberal—economic and political—reform for nearly two decades, and finally imploded.
20. See Polanyi's argumentation in his classic *The Great Transformation* (1944).
21. Is it far-fetched to assume that at least in some cases this came into the rational calculation of transnational policy makers? (Conaghan and Malloy, 1994).

22. Especially when the previous level of inequality was already very high. I will come back to this point in the conclusion.
23. Sampie Terreblanche, an economist linked to the National Party, was a strong representative of the intellectuals that linked closed economy (the racist developmentalist project) and closed society (apartheid itself). Entrepreneurs free from statism would shed the racist superstructure. This perspective does not seem to match the facts. Nattrass (1999).
24. Because they do not abide by the hard rules of the market that force agents to produce a system of incentives favorable *only* to the most efficient.
25. Some countries get stuck in the first stage, getting the worst of both worlds. Ecuador may be an example of this.
26. See Chapter 3 on Uganda, this volume.
27. Please note that the existence of those policies reaffirms Polanyi's point in two senses: (i) market self-regulation has an upper limit that cannot be surpassed; (ii) the intent of achieving the limit (what Polanyi called "the liberal utopia") destabilizes whole sets of human social arrangements.
28. Of the cases considered in this volume, Colombia and Peru fall into this category. El Salvador and Guatemala are not coca producers, but have become important points in the transportation chain, and exhibit very high levels of criminal violence. See CEG (2005).
29. Gutiérrez and Barón (2008).
30. Colombia might also be seen in this light, as initially the coca production was concentrated in the south. It probably makes more sense, though, to see issues as the relation between emeralds and oil production, on the one hand, and conflict, on the other (Gutiérrez and Barón, 2008; Pearce, 2005) as resource-driven fractures. In Latin America, Bolivia—a country which was presented as a showcase example of "proper" decentralization—has been deeply affected by resource-driven fractures.
31. These same citizens could simply sell their identity.
32. They were published on January 26, 2001. The video shows Montesinos bribing Congressman Zapata. See http://news.bbc.co.uk/1/hi/world/americas/1139544.stm.
33. There is a debate about the degree and type of agrarian inequality that characterized El Salvador. See for example Browning (1983) and Muller et al. (1989). But there is a consensus about the fact that the level was high.
34. For the South African case, see for example Schneider (2003).
35. For the evolution of this assumption, see Huber (1997).
36. Perhaps also Colombia.
37. For an in-depth study of these dynamics, see Snyder (2000), and Gutiérrez and Barón (2008).
38. Colombian insurgency claims that it dominates several regions of the country are exaggerated. At the same time, its influence in the regions in which it has a stable presence definitely transforms local social and political relations. In Côte d'Ivoire, different militias have been able to establish a relatively stable domination.
39. For reasons different from the isomorphism principle. See Przeworski et al. (1999).
40. I believe that probably the most interesting and biggest effect is the indirect one.

REFERENCES

Ballón, E. (2006) "Crecimiento económico, crisis de la democracia y conflictividad social. Notas para un balance del toledismo." *Perú Hoy: Democracia inconclusa y crecimiento*. Lima: DESCO.
Bayart, J. F. (1989) *L'Etat en Afrique*. Paris: Fayard.
Brittain, J. J. (2005) "A theory of accelerating rural violence: Lauchlin Currie's role in underdeveloping Colombia." *Journal of Peasant Studies*, Vol. 32, No. 2, pp. 335–360.
Browning, D. (1983) "Agrarian reform in El Salvador." *Journal of Latin American Studies*, Vol. 15, No. 2, pp. 399–426.
Cademartori, J. (2003) "The Chilean neoliberal model enters into crisis." *Latin American Perspectives*, Vol. 30, No 5. "Chile since 1990: the contradictions of neoliberal democratization," Part 1, pp. 79–88.
Callinicos, A. (1992) *Between Apartheid and Capitalism: Conversations with South African Socialists*. London: Bookmarks.
Campbell, J. (2004) *Institutional Change and Globalization*. Princeton University Press.
Campbell, J. and Pedersen, O. (2001) *The Rise of Neoliberalism and Institutional Analysis*. Cambridge University Press.
Cavanaugh, W. T. (2003) "The Unfreedom of the Free Market." See, http://www.jesusradicals.com/wp-content/uploads/unfreedom.pdf (accessed 14 September 2009). First published in *Wealth, Poverty, and Human Destiny*, eds. D. Bandow and D. L. Schindler. Wilmington, Del.: ISI Books, pp. 103–128.
Centeno, M. A. "Rocky Democracies and Hard Markets: Dilemmas of the Double Transition." *Annual Review of Sociology*, Vol. 20, pp. 125–147.
CEG (2005) *Inseguridad Pública: el negocio de la violencia*. Special Report, Center of Guatemalan Studies.
Conaghan, C. and Malloy, J. (1994) *Unsettling Statecraft. Democracy and Neoliberalism in the Central Andes*. Pittsburg and London: University of Pittsburg Press.
Conaghan, C., James, M., Malloy, M., and Abugattás, L. A. (1990) "Business and the 'boys': the politics of neoliberalism in the Central Andes." *Latin American Research Review*, Vol. 25, No. 2, pp. 3–30.
Crabtree, J. and Thomas, J. (1999) *El Perú de Fujimori: 1990–1998*. Universidad del Pacífico, IEP.
Diamond, L., Plattner, M., Yun-han Chu, Hung Mao Tien (eds.) (1997) *Consolidating the Third Wave Democracies. Themes and Perspectives*. Baltimore and London: Johns Hopkins University Press.
Di John, J. (2006) "The Political Economy of Taxation and Tax Reform in Developing Countries." Working Paper. Helsinki: Anthem Press and World Institute of Development Economic Research (WIDER).
Duncan, G. (2005) *Del campo a la ciudad en Colombia. La infiltración urbana de los señores de la guerra en Documento Cede 2005-2*. Electronic version, available at http://nuevagaceta.org/Del_campo_a_la_ciudad.pdf.
Easterly, W. (2001) *The Lost Decades: Developing Countries' Stagnation in Spite of Policy Reform 1980–1998*. Washington, DC: World Bank.
Elster, J. (2007) *Explaining the Social. More Nuts and Bolts for the Social Sciences*. Cambridge University Press.
Evans, P. (2007) *Instituciones y desarrollo en la era de la globalización neoliberal*. Bogotá: ILSA.

Ghersi, E. (2004) "The myth of neoliberalism—El Mito del Neoliberalismo." September 29. www.cepchile.cl.
Giddens, A. (1991) *Modernity and Self-Identity: Self and Society in the Late Modern Age*. Stanford, CA: Stanford University Press.
Gutiérrez, F. and Barón, M. (2008) "Órdenes subsidiarios. Coca, esmeraldas: la guerra y la paz." *Revista Colombia Internacional*, No. 67, Universidad de Los Andes, Facultad de Ciencias Sociales, pp.102–129.
Hanson, M. and Hentz, J. J. (1999) "Neocolonialism and neoliberalism in South Africa and Zambia." *Political Science Quarterly*, Vol. 114, No. 3, pp. 479–502.
Harbom, L. and Wallensteen, P. (2007) "Armed Conflict, 1989–2006." *Journal of Peace Research*, Vol. 44, No.5, pp. 623–634.
Harvey, D. (2005) *A Brief History of Neoliberalism*. Oxford and London: Oxford University Press.
Hey, J. and Klak, T. (1999) "From protectionism towards neoliberalism: Ecuador across four administrations (1981–1996)." *Studies in International Comparative Development*, Vol. 34, No. 3, pp. 66–98.
Hibou, B. (ed.) (2004) *Privatizing the state*. New York: Columbia University Press.
Hirschman, A. O. (1970) *Exit, Voice and Loyalty*. Harvard University Press.
Huber, E. (1997) "The paradoxes of contemporary democracy: formal, participatory, and social dimensions." *Comparative Politics*, Vol. 29, No. 3, "Transitions to democracy: a special issue in memory of Dankwart A. Rustow," pp. 323–342.
Jimenez, W. (2005) "Reforma administrativa y carrera administrativa en Colombia: frustraciones, razones y oportunidades." In *X Congreso Internacional del CLAD sobre la Reforma del Estado y la Administración Pública*, Santiago de Chile.
Krain, M. (1998) "Contemporary democracies revisited: democracy, political violence, and event count models." *Comparative Political Studies*, Vol. 31, No. 2, pp.139–164.
Locke, J. (1997) *Political Essays*. Cambridge University Press.
Manji, F. and O'Coill, C. (2002) "The missionary position: NGOs and development in Africa." *International Affairs*, Vol. 78, No. 3, pp. 567–583.
McCarthy, J. (2006) "Neoliberalism and the politics of alternatives: community forestry in British Columbia and the United States." *Annals of the Association of American Geographers*, Vol. 96, No. 1, pp. 84–104.
Muller, E. N., Seligson, M. A., Hung-der Fu, and Midlarsky, M. I. (1989) "Land inequality and political violence." *The American Political Science Review*, Vol. 83, No. 2, pp. 577–596.
Nattrass, N. (1999) "The Truth and Reconciliation Commission on Business and Apartheid: a critical evaluation." *African Affairs*, Vol. 98, No. 392, pp. 373–391.
Nkemdirim, B. A. (1977) "Reflections on political conflict, rebellion, and revolution in Africa." *The Journal of Modern African Studies*, Vol. 15, No. 1, pp. 75–90.
O'Donnell, G., Schmitter, L., and Whitehead, L. (1986) *Transitions from Authoritarian Rule: Latin America*. Johns Hopkins University Press.
Ortiz, R. (1998) "Guerra Civil y descentralización de la violencia: el caso de Colombia." *Papeles de Cuestiones Internacionales*, No. 65.
Pajuelo Teves, R. (2004) "Perú: crisis política permanente y nuevas protestas sociales." *Observatorio Social de América Latina*, OSAL, No. 14. Buenos Aires: CLACSO.
Parsa, M. (2000) *State, Ideologies & Social Revolutions*. Cambridge University Press.
Pearce, J. (2005) "Policy failure and petroleum predation: the economics of civil war debate viewed from the war zone." *Government and Opposition*, Blackwell Publishing.

Peck, J. and Tickell, A. (2002) "Neoliberalizing space." *Antipode*, Vol. 34, Issue 3, pp. 380–404.
Polanyi, K. (1944) *La gran transformación*. [Ed. 1992], México: Juan Pablos (ed.).
Powell, B. (1982) *Contemporary Democracies: Participation, Stability and Violence*. Cambridge and London: Harvard University Press.
Przeworski, A., Stokes, S., and Manin, B. (eds.) (1999) *Democracy, Accountability and Representation*. Cambridge University Press.
Reno, W. (1999) *Warlord Politics and African States*. London: Lynne Rienner.
Rincón, D. and Lucia, C. (1997) *Estructura de la propiedad rural y mercado de tierras*. Universidad Nacional de Colombia, Facultad de Ciencias Económicas. Departamento de Economía. Masters Degree in Economy. Director Absalón Machado.
Romero, M. (2002) *Paramilitares y autodefensas, 1982–2003*. Bogotá: Iepri-Planeta.
Sachs, J. D. (1989) "Social Conflict and Populist Policies in Latin America." NBER Working Papers No. 2897.
Schneider, G. (2003) "Neoliberalism and economic justice in South Africa: revisiting the debate on economic apartheid." *Review of Social Economy*, Vol. 61, No 1. pp. 23–50.
Seligson, M. A. (1995) "Thirty years of transformation in the agrarian structure of El Salvador, 1961–1991." *Latin America Research Review*, Vol. 30, No. 3, pp. 43–74.
Sieder, R., Thomas, M., Vickers, G, and Spence, J. (2002) *Guatemala Five Years After the Peace Accords. Who Governs?* Cambridge, MA: Hemisphere Initiatives.
Snyder, J. (2000) *From Voting to Violence: Democratization and Nationalist Conflict*. New York: W.W. Norton.
Stewart, F. (2000) "Crisis Prevention: Tackling Horizontal Inequalities." QEH Working Paper Series—QEHWPS33. Available at http://www3.qeh.ox.ac.uk/pdf/qehwp/qehwps33.pdf.
Stiglitz, J. (2002) *El malestar en la globalización*. Bogotá: Taurus.
Stokes, S. (1996) "Economic reform and public opinion in Perú, 1990 and 1995." *Comparative Political Studies*, Vol. 29, No. 5, pp. 544–565.
Tice, R. D. (1974) "Administrative structure, ethnicity, and nation-building in the Ivory Coast." *The Journal of Modern African Studies*, Vol. 12, No. 2, pp. 211–229.
Tendler, J. (1997) *Good Government in the Tropics*. Johns Hopkins University Press.
Topik, S., Marichal, C., and Zephyr, F. (2006) *From Silver to Cocaine: Latin American Commodity Chains and the Building of the World Economy, 1500–2000*. Durham: Duke University Press.
Torchia, A. (1988) "The business of business: an analysis of the political behaviour of the South African manufacturing sector under the nationalists." *Journal of Southern African Studies*, Vol. 14, No. 3, pp. 421–445.
Toungara, J. M. (1990) "The apotheosis of Côte d'Ivoire's Nana Houphouet-Boigny." *The Journal of Modern African Studies*, Vol. 28, No. 1, pp. 23–54.
Weyland, K. (1999) "Neoliberal populism in Latin America and Eastern Europe." *Comparative Politics*, Vol. 31, No. 4, pp. 379–401.
Williams, R. (1989) *The Politics of Modernism: Against the New Conformists*. Ed. Tony Pinkney. London and New York: Verso.
Williamson, O. E. (1990) *The Firm as a Nexus of Treaties*. London: Sage.
Wood, E. J. (2000) *Forging Democracy from Below. Insurgent Transitions in South Africa and El Salvador*. Cambridge University Press.

2
War, Peace, and Liberalism
A Quantitative Approach to the Relation between Economic Globalization and Armed Conflict[1]

Jairo Baquero Melo[2]

INTRODUCTION

Significant political, economic, social, and environmental changes have taken place around the world over the last decades. Among them, the deepening of the globalization processes since the 1970s, the adoption of democracy by a number of countries after the collapse of the Soviet Union, and, as Gutiérrez (Chapter 1) stresses, the expansion and strengthening of neoliberalism. A global opening towards a "great transformation" in Polanyi's sense is apparent, with economic systems in an increasing number of countries undergoing liberal reforms, and a wider opening by countries already showing high degrees of liberalization.

After the fall of the Berlin Wall, world economies started showing increasing liberalization trends, democratic political systems became strengthened, and a loss of confidence in the state as a developmental tool became apparent. Armed conflicts, on the other hand, did not vanish. While some conflicts had ended before the end of the Cold War, others have emerged after the fall of the Berlin Wall, while others still have become protracted and have undergone changes over time.

This study looks at the ways in which armed conflicts have been transformed or affected by globalization. The possibility of "new wars" (in the sense of Kaldor, 1999) is not being considered here. This research suggests that both the introduction of neoliberal reforms and globalization have, in some ways, had an impact on armed conflicts—those still continuing, those coming to an end, and those that have emerged in the midst of these processes. Linguistic, religious, or tribal differences alone do not explain the complexity surrounding armed conflicts.

Using a quantitative approach, this chapter looks at the ways in which *economic globalization* processes have had an influence on armed conflict. It looks at both *direct ways* in which globalization may have influenced the intensity of conflicts and their characteristics, and at *indirect ways*—indirect variables that can be used to account for the occurrence and intensity of these conflicts.

The chapter then addresses the question: What are the possible links between economic globalization and armed conflict? To this end, an analysis of the direct and spillover effects of economic globalization on armed conflict is performed, drawing on a distinction among conflict intensity, occurrence, and termination. Other dependent variables—such as the number of homicides, robberies, and mobilizations, all considered globalization-related factors—will be reviewed as well. Statistical methodologies (SEM, OLS, and Logit models) are applied to a sample of 90 countries for the period of 1970–2005.

The main findings of this study show that: (i) armed conflict (intensity and occurrence) can be accounted for by increasing inequality, ethnic fragmentation, illegal trafficking and, to a lesser extent, by the presence of natural resources; (ii) economic globalization has a direct impact on the occurrence and intensity of higher-level conflicts (recording a larger number of casualties) by opening new windows of opportunity to conflict actors; (iii) economic globalization has a positive relation with the *termination* of armed conflicts, especially those ending in a military victory; (iv) economic globalization is linked with a lower *occurrence* of armed conflict (without taking into account the *scale*), suggesting the likelihood of a "liberal peace"—liberal in the sense explained in the theory section below (although this kind of peace may not be entirely peaceful and take a long time to achieve); (v) economic globalization has spillover effects on armed conflict as well, especially through its impact on the state (on military expenditure in particular); (vi) new ways of conflict have become apparent, such as a crime, robberies, and popular mobilizations; (vii) a suggestion is made that the quest for peace should involve reducing inequality, combating the illegal trafficking of resources, increasing democracy, strengthening—rather than weakening—the state, and increasing wealth and enhancing its distribution patterns.

THEORY AND RESEARCH HISTORY

The following section talks about three issues relevant to this study: (i) the theoretical correlation between liberalism and war; (ii) the (empirically assessed) impacts economic globalization has on other variables; and, (iii) studies in the root causes of conflicts.

Liberalization and Armed Conflict from a Theoretical Stance

To simplify the analysis, liberalism in this study is defined as a set of principles and institutions characterized by features such as individual freedom, political participation, private property, and equal opportunities. These characteristics are, to a larger or lesser extent, shared by most liberal states and societies.[3]

A claim has been advanced that market forces and democracy could have a direct effect on de-escalating war. In *The Great Transformation*, Polanyi (1997) talked about a change in which land and labor would become goods, thus reinforcing the capitalist economy in industrialized countries first and then in all societies. Market institutions capable of defusing or diminishing violence would be established. And the motivation of individual profits supersedes the rationale for subsistence. Of course, many of these changes do not come about peacefully, since the market is "the result of a conscious, and often violent, intervention of the State, which has enforced the market organization on society for non-economic purposes" (Polanyi, 1997, p. 391). Schumpeter, too, examines the interaction between democracy and capitalism as the foundations of the so-called "liberal pacifism." Schumpeter argues that capitalism, in the production process, drains its citizens' energies (which could otherwise be utilized in a process of social unrest), and that it "individualizes" them and creates "subjective opportunities," which replace traditional hierarchical societies' "static" modes of operation.[4] Despite this, capitalism has not always been as peaceful as it has been portrayed to be.[5]

On closer examination of economic globalization and war, state-related issues also become an important matter. On the one hand, neoliberal changes tend to reform (and shrink and weaken) the state and its institutions.[6] Tilly (1978) suggests that states are strengthened by wars, because wars reinforce taxation systems, bureaucracy, and national identity.[7] "Classical" definitions of the state talk about it as an institution that has a legitimate monopoly on the use of force in a territory, a monopoly which often runs contrary to other stakeholders' (e.g., rebel groups') interests. To achieve a military victory over rebel groups, for example, states build up their own army. But, because of budgetary constraints, international pressure, and the reduced availability of Cold War era aid,[8] many state armies (e.g., in Africa), have seen their military activities curtailed. This has led rebel groups to fund war through the exploitation of natural resources and trade in other commodities.[9] It should be highlighted that in countries where neoliberalism is just beginning to take hold, it has an impact on the state, failed states,[10] and "quasi-states."[11] While some states are simply unable to control the territory they are officially said to control, other states have become what has been referred to as "shadow states,"[12] in which the bureaucracy apparatus becomes informal. Reno (1995, 1998) claims that warlords use international trade networks to trade natural resources to create domestic legitimacy. Also, "institutionalized primitive accumulation" processes occurred when armed groups displace people from their lands.[13]

Although most research work has been focused on strategic factors,[14] the end of armed conflicts may also be linked to elements of neoliberalism. Wood (2000, ch. 5) examines the threats that South African economic elites were faced with because of labor unrest and financial sanctions imposed on them due to allegations of discrimination against the black population. El Salvador economic elites, aware of the high cost that rejecting peace would have for them, persuaded government elites to negotiate peace.[15] Humphreys (2005) argues that war termination is linked with natural resources because when the supply of resources is being threatened stakeholders have an incentive to end war.

Finally, mention should be made of Berdal's work (2003). According to this author, economic globalization has a two-way relation with war: an *indirect* one, through which economic globalization brings about poverty and, therefore, violence; and a *direct* one, related to the economic agenda of conflicts. Economic globalization increases the incentive for trade in legal and illegal goods, opening windows of opportunity to armed actors. But this does not mean that economic concerns[16] were not involved in wars of the past.[17] Wars may undergo change and continuity processes, and material and non-material conditions are a part of how these processes influence war.[18] War and the market may coexist, which does not mean that war is due to material conditions alone. For example, Duffield shows the impact of coffee trade dynamics on the war in Sudan (2004, p. 198).

The Impact of Globalization on the Contemporary World

Some research work on the impact of economic globalization is expanded upon here.[19] Dreher (2003) argues that, although global economic growth is spurred on by globalization, this has not reduced poverty. By impairing their ability to become union members, globalization has affected less-skilled workers (Dreyer and Gaston, 2005). The debate on inequality is open, and some authors claim that inequality is growing.[20] Due to the soaring growth of Asian countries and other OECD countries vis-à-vis countries in Africa and Latin America, inequality between countries and regions is on the increase. However, as suggested by other studies, the impact of globalization is unclear. Bourguignon and Morrison (2002) argue that the Gini index increased during the nineteenth century, keeping its upward trend during the twentieth century, getting "stalled" at 0.65. Dreher and Gaston (2008) have found that, while wage inequality in industrialized countries has increased because of economic globalization starting in the 1970s, this has not been the case in developing countries.

On the other hand, when countries where an ethnic minority holds economic control over the majority of other ethnic groups,[21] economic globalization and democratization can generate conflicts, although democracy reduces the likelihood of conflict if no economically prevailing minorities exist.[22]

Furthermore, legal and illegal features are also embodied in globalization. Illegal components include drug trafficking, trafficking in persons, arms trafficking, and other types of organized crime based on networks designed and supported by channels this process generates.[23] And common crime is also related to globalization, in particular when social mobility is non-existent.[24]

Armed Conflict Origin and Rationale

The current debate revolves around a greed-and-grievances-based rationale. Although Collier et al. argue that conflict emerges from a greed-induced decision of the combatants (Collier and Hoeffler, 2004), this claim could be rebutted through an analysis of insurgent movements' cohesion and commitment vis-à-vis the few incentives available to them and the high risk levels they are faced with.[25] The argument has been advanced that violence incentives may be generated by wealth when armed groups seek to control both resources and the state.[26] A claim has been also made that it is more likely for civil wars to occur in poor countries,[27] and that it is not wealth itself that is the problem, but rather how it is shared.[28]

Inequality is another factor contributing to armed conflict. The relative deprivation,[29] political process, resource mobilization,[30] and rational choice[31] theories have been propounded to elucidate why, even within the institutional structure, grievances explain political violence.[32] While studies show that this link is negligible,[33] authors, such as Muller (1985), argue that extreme inequality generates class conflicts. Krain (1998) contends that the relation between inequality and armed conflict does exist. He points out that the way to measure inequality and violence influence the results. Schock (1996) argues that inequality-triggered grievances interact with political opportunities to generate conflict.[34] The World Bank has questioned this correlation,[35] suggesting that measuring inequality on the basis of the Gini index is problematic.[36] According to some claims, another type of inequality between ethnic groups or regions exists: horizontal inequality.[37] Inequality of land distribution has been reviewed by Midlarsky (1982, 1988), who claims that highly inequitable societies breed greater grievances. Although his findings are not too significant, Midlarsky suggests that violence can be explained by the difference between those who have more and those who have less land. Muller, Seligson, and Fu's (1989) findings are, however, more conclusive.

In our analysis, we deem natural resources, oil, and diamonds in particular, as armed conflict breeders and withstanders.[38] This is because, among other reasons, armed conflict harms economic performance, makes governments frail and less accountable, and provides incentives to set up independent states. But, as some have suggested, not all agricultural products are related to wars.[39] The probability for the outbreak of civil war in oil, gas and diamond-producing countries has shown a steady rise from the 1970s. Conflict duration is linked with the "illegal trafficking" of precious stones, timber, and drug trafficking.[40] And per Humphreys (2005), conflicts start because of the former production of natural resources.

As far as ethnic fragmentation is concerned, Fearon and Laitin (2003) claim that countries showing high ethnic and religious fragmentation rates have not experienced significant violence in this period. Instead, conflict is accounted for by poverty, a weak state, political instability, mountainous terrain, and population size. In addition, developmental policies can be responsible for unequal distribution of wealth among ethnic groups, thus giving rise to discrimination.[41]

THE RELATION BETWEEN ECONOMIC GLOBALIZATION AND ARMED CONFLICT

We will now examine the results of our study, which looks at the link between economic globalization and armed conflict, and other impacts globalization has on variables such as crime and political demonstrations.

Correlations Analyzed

Hypothesis 1: Armed conflict determinants exist

Variables studied as armed conflict determinants include inequality, natural resources, ethnic fragmentation, GDP per capita, conflict background, and the occurrence of conflict in neighboring countries.

Hypothesis 2: The link between economic globalization and armed conflict

As discussed in the theoretical framework, some linking modes between economic globalization and armed conflict may exist. Three possible correlations are evaluated in this study:

- *The link between economic globalization and armed conflict intensity.* The violence *level* in armed conflict (as measured by the number of casualties) will be analyzed, as well as how this variable correlates with the economic globalization level. Countries with and without armed conflict are included in the sample.
- *The link between economic globalization and the occurrence of armed conflict.* Whether or not armed conflict is present and number of years it lasts will be taken into account.
- *The link between economic globalization and termination of armed conflict.* The link between economic globalization level and conflict will be explored. To evaluate this hypothesis according to a set of variables, an armed conflict termination probability exercise will be conducted (Probit model).

Economic globalization may have direct and spillover effects on armed conflict.

- *Direct effects*: conflict intensity may be heightened by economic globalization because all conflict stakeholders want to take advantage of the opportunities offered by the globalization process.

- *Spillover effects*: armed conflict is triggered by globalization because of the latter's impact on other variables, such as inequality, already analyzed in the first hypothesis.

Hypothesis 3: Economic globalization goes along with state reforms, which also have a bearing on armed conflicts

The state can be (militarily and bureaucratically) strengthened to fend off rebel groups. War can also strengthen the state through an increase and consolidation of bureaucracy, tax systems, etc. But the state tends to shrink as a result of neoliberal policies and the effects of the state reduction on conflicts can become apparent. These effects will be examined here through the link between war and selected variables, such as military expenditure as a GDP percentage, public expenditure as a GDP percentage, and the taxation level as a GDP percentage.

Hypothesis 4: A global trend towards enhanced democratization in countries is apparent—a fact that may have an impact on armed conflict

Democracy can be analyzed as a variable mediating among the causes, occurrence, and intensity of conflicts. Bearing conflict determinants in mind, increased political opportunities and enhanced democracy may address past grievances and help prevent armed conflict.

Hypothesis 5: Economic globalization is linked with other forms of conflict

Although conflicts may not occur in a large number of countries, social problems, such as crime, have been on the increase in recent decades. Likewise, a trend towards the occurrence of social mobilizations reflecting social unrest is being noticed, a fact that can lead to the destabilization of political regimes. Therefore, in a world that is more globalized at the economic, political, social, cultural, and environmental levels, other forms of conflict may emerge, reflecting problems that have so far been unsolved (or have been exacerbated) due to the economic globalization model.

Hypothesis 6: Globalization involves an armed, conflict-linked illegal component

Globalization involves an illegal component, linked with trafficking in persons, drugs, weapons, and (smuggling) of goods. This illegal trafficking had and still has an impact on the occurrence and escalation of armed conflict[42] in African and Latin American countries.

Hypothesis 7: Existing control variables should be taken into account

Significant social changes and processes taking place in many countries should be borne in mind, such as a push towards urbanization and socio-demographic changes leading to the aging of the population. Variables, such as the specifics of the region, should also be taken into account.

The Data and Variables

To conduct statistical exercises, a database of 90 countries (see Annex), for the 1970–2005 period,[43] was compiled. Variables included in the database, together with their definitions and sources, are examined below.

Dependent variables

As shown below, the Structural Equation models (SEM) are the basic methodology applied, making it possible to evaluate more than one dependent variable at a time and in simultaneous regressions. Therefore, five dependent variables are included, as follows:

- Political violence: number of casualties in armed conflicts; combatants and non-combatants for each year and country[44] (source: Fearon and Laitin, and PRI-Uppsala).
- Occurrence of political violence: dichotomic variable with a one (1) value if there is conflict, and a zero (0) value if there is no conflict, for each year and country (source: Fearon and Laitin, PRI-Uppsala and Armed Conflict Database).
- Homicides: number of criminal homicides for each country and year (source: United Nations Survey on Crime and Justice, several years).
- Robberies: number of robberies for each country and year (source: United Nations Survey on crime and justice, several years).
- Mobilizations: number of marches, protests, and demonstrations threatening the stability of the political regime, including the executive branch, and changes in the legislative branch.[45]

To look into the termination of armed conflicts, an additional dependent variable is included:

- Termination of armed conflict: The years in which countries were involved in armed conflict are drawn from the database. The variable was constructed to show whether conflict continued (0) or terminated (1) for each year.[46]

Explanatory variables

Economic globalization. For each country and year, an economic liberalization indicator is introduced, according to the economic globalization index produced by the KOF Project (globalization index[47]). This indicator goes from 0 to 10, where 0 accounts for less globalization and 1 for more globalization and so on.[48]

Inequality. The Gini income index[49] is included on the basis of UNU-WIDER World Income Inequality Database (WIID) data. Although no data are available for a large number of countries, other inequality indicators are available, such as the percentage of people with a given income.[50]

Natural resources. Two indicators are included: (i) export of raw materials in each country as a GDP percentage (WDI, 2006); and (ii) a dichotomic variable indicating whether the country is (1) or is not (0) an oil exporter (WDI, 2006).

Ethnic fragmentation. A variable the World Bank uses to estimate ethnic fragmentation in each country. The lower the indicator, the less fragmented the country will be.

Political globalization. This indicator is also drawn from the KOF Index of Globalization, taking into account variables such as number of embassies, membership in international institutions, and participation in UN activities.

Social globalization. This indicator is also drawn from the KOF Index of Globalization, taking into account variables such as telephone traffic, money transfers, tourism, telephone lines, the internet, and the media.

Political regime trends. For operational reasons, and acknowledging the constraints many democracy indicators show, the Vanhanen (2000) democracy index is included. This index classifies the political regime of countries according to two variables: (i) electorate participation level, and (ii) competitiveness and electoral freedoms.

Military expenditure. Military expenditure as a GDP percentage (WDI, 2006) is used as an indicator of the state strength.

Taxation. To take a rough measure of the strength of the state, we have taken into account the percentage of taxes collected by the government as a percentage of the GDP (WDI, 2006).

Public expenditure. Another state-dependent variable is the public expenditure level, which is now being measured as a percentage of GDP (WDI, 2006).[51]

Trafficking in illegal resources. A dichotomous variable is included in the dependent variable to indicate whether or not countries are involved in illegal trafficking of resources, diamonds and cocaine in particular (Ross, 2004).

GDP per capita. This variable is being used as a proxy for wealth. It is also used as a result control variable (WDI, 2006).

"Time" variables. An urban population percentage indicator is included for each country and year (WDI, 2006). To assess how population is aging, a percentage indicator for those 64-years-and-older is included (WDI, 2006).

Africa and America regions. Two dichotomous variables are included to indicate whether countries are located in Africa, or in Latin America and the Caribbean.

Contiguousness of conflict. A variable indicating the number of neighboring countries with internal conflicts was constructed for each year and country.

Termination of the Cold War. A dummy variable indicating the years elapsed after the fall of the Berlin Wall is included, taking note of a worldwide structural change.

Residual violence. This variable shows the occurrence of armed conflict in previous years (two lag periods are included, one lasting one year, and another one lasting five years).

METHODOLOGIES USED

Structural Equation models (SEM) are the main methodology used in this study. To the extent that different relationships between variables are taken into account by the theoretical approach, and some are explained in turn by others, an appropriate methodology is the Structural Equation Model (SEM) or the LISREL model, which is a multidimensional causal structural equations model.[52] Using more than one dependent variable, it allows us to examine the relations between many variables. The use of latent variables (which are constructed on the basis of perceived or actual variables) allows the complexity of links between many variables to be captured. While other methodologies, such as multiple regression, factor analysis, and multivariate analysis of variance (ANOVA) provide powerful tools, they can only estimate one relationship at a time. SEM models are an extension of some multivariate techniques, such as simple regression, multiple regression, and factor analysis. These models also help to comprehensively assess relations, and constitute a transition from the exploratory analysis to the confirmatory analysis. SEM models are characterized by two features: (i) the ability to estimate multiple and crossed dependency relations; and, (ii) the ability to represent concepts not perceived in these relations, and include the estimation process in the measurement error.[53]

Structural Equation Model Specifications

On the basis of the hypothesis examined, the likely theoretical correlations between variables are established. Figure 2.1 shows these relations (the SEM model), in which five dependent variables are included: (i) armed conflict intensity (number of casualties); (ii) the occurrence of internal armed conflict in the country; (iii) the number of (criminal) homicides; (iv) the number of robberies; and, (v) the number of social mobilizations threatening the stability of the political regime. Explanatory variables included are economic globalization, inequality, export of natural resources, ethnic fragmentation, political globalization, social globalization, political regime tendency, military expenditure as a GDP percentage, public expenditure as a GDP percentage, taxes as a GDP percentage, illegal trafficking (supply side), GDP per capita, control variables (urbanization and population aging), region (Africa or Latin America), number of conflicts in neighboring countries, the post-Cold War period, and armed conflict history.

Figure 2.1 shows correlations being evaluated in the model. As explained above, the model includes some latent variables, which are shown in rectangles. These variables are estimated on the basis of variables perceived and included in the database.[54]

As shown in Figure 2.1, the five dependent variables included are explained by the remaining independent variables. The type of indicators estimated is shown in the figure: ζ are the ratios between perceived and latent variables (measurement model); β are the ratios between latent explanatory variables and dependent variables; γ are ratios estimated between the explanatory variables. The other explanatory variables linked with economic globalization are shown in the figure, thus dotted lines go to an arrow pointing to this variable. The spillover effects of economic globalization will be estimated in the next section.

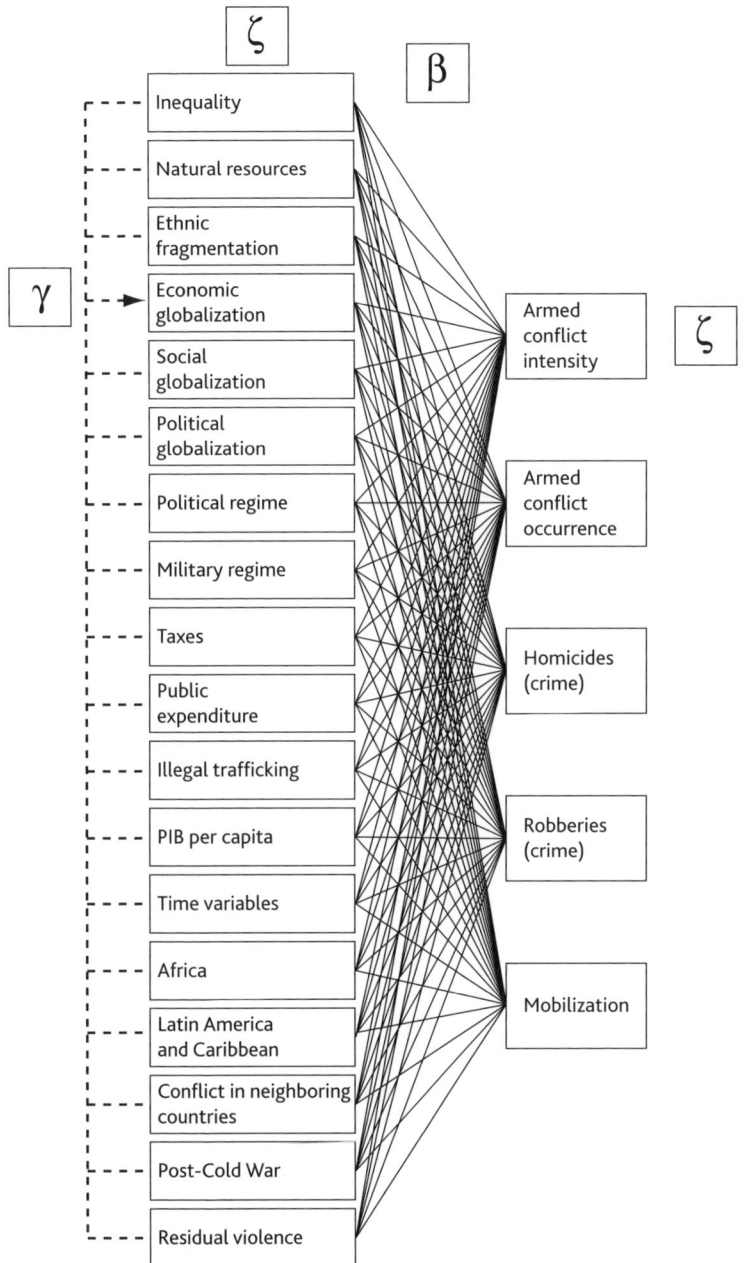

Figure 2.1 SEM model including all (latent) variables

STATISTICAL RESULTS

The statistical results shown in this section do not show precise causal relationships between variables. Rather, they provide empirical evidence or a "global" picture of links between variables, and explore the likely existence of trends and event–occurrence probabilities, which depend on the occurrence or behavior on other variables or events. It is clear that each conflict has its own specific characteristics, history, and evolution, which is why this book includes case studies that shed light on the links between economic globalization and armed conflict in particular countries.

Structural Equation Model (SEM) and Ordinary Least Squares (MCO) Results

It is worth mentioning that as suggested statistical methodologies such as SEM, the specification of the model was revised and changed depending on the demands of theoretical approaches and the availability of sufficient data for the cases included. This process involved adding and removing variables, until the final version of the model shown was obtained. Likewise, most results remained unchanged in relation to estimates made.

Some elements should be taken into account in order for the results of the SEM and MCO models to be interpreted. The SEM model links estimations with error term and, therefore, gets closer to an analysis of the relationship between some variables' "peaks" or highest values. On the other hand, the MCO model is used to examine what usually happens in the relationship between different variables. Thus, the SEM model results are closer to explaining the variations in the highest variable values, in the context of high variations in other variables, and the MCO model explains what happens on average and with a variable, depending on the behavior of one or more variables.

The determinants of armed conflict (Hypothesis 1)

The statistical results of the model shown in Table 2.1 summarize the determinants of both armed conflict and the occurrence of armed conflict. Table 2.1(a) shows the SEM model results, and Table 2.1(b) shows the MCO model results. Variables with a high significance level over variables explained are highlighted in bold. Hypothesis 1 suggests that some variables have been deemed as armed conflict determinants. These variables include inequality, natural resources, ethnic fragmentation, GDP per capita, armed conflict, or violence lags, and the occurrence of conflicts in neighboring countries.

Determinants of armed conflict intensity. Among variables mentioned in Table 2.1, the largest number of conflict casualties (SEM result) is explained by high inequality (0.057), natural resources (0.003), ethnic fragmentation (0.064), residual violence (0.816), and the occurrence of conflicts in neighboring countries (0.080). In terms of the average relationship of variables (MCO result), armed conflict intensity is positively explained by ethnic fragmentation (0.155) and the occurrence of conflicts in neighboring countries (0.119).

Determinants of armed conflict occurrence. SEM results show that this variable is linked with high inequality values (0.071), ethnic fragmentation (0.060), residual violence (0.494), and the occurrence of conflicts in neighboring countries (0.191). The trend to export natural resources fails to explain the occurrence of armed conflict (insignificant 0.004); this could mean that in cases in which countries record a very high level of exports of this kind (the largest exporters of natural resources, among natural-resource exporting countries) high armed conflict levels are likely, but we can't say that being a natural resource export country can be linked with the occurrence of armed conflict. As for MCO results, the occurrence of conflict is linked with ethnic fragmentation (0.196) and the occurrence of conflicts in neighboring countries (0.488). Natural resources-related values back the previously reached conclusion: on average, the trend to export natural resources—oil or other resources—is inversely related to the occurrence of conflict (with −0.511 and −0.116 ratios respectively). For its part, a higher GDP per capita is linked with both: a less intense armed conflict (−4.686) and lower trends for armed conflicts to occur (−0.479).

As for inequality, Table 2.1 results show that inequality is positively and significantly related in SEM models to the intensity (0.057) and occurrence (0.071) of conflict. It would therefore be wrong to claim that inequality is not linked with armed conflict. These results show that countries recording the highest inequity are those most prone to armed conflicts, and to more intense conflicts (with a high number of casualties). This would confirm the grievance hypothesis as an explanation to the occurrence of conflicts in very inequitable societies.

The relation between armed conflict and economic globalization (Hypothesis 2)

The link between economic globalization and the intensity and occurrence of armed conflict will be analyzed in this section. The direct impact of economic globalization on conflict will be examined first, and the spillover effects second.

Table 2.1 Ratios estimated on (a) SEM model (maximum likelihood) and (b) ordinary least square basis

Dependent variables: armed conflict intensity (number of casualties log), and occurrence (1.0). Significant results are highlighted in bold.

Variable	Dependent variable		Variable	Dependent variable	
	Armed conflict Intensity SEM direct effect (standardized)	Armed conflict occurrence SEM direct effect (standardized)		Armed conflict Intensity MCO ratio	Armed conflict occurrence MCO ratio
Inequality	0.057	0.071	Inequality	0.281	0.154
Natural resources (grouped)	0.003	0.004	Non-oil exports	-0.366	-0.511
			Oil exports	0.192	-0.116
Ethnic fragmentation	0.064	0.060	Ethnic fragmentation	0.155	0.196
Economic globalization	0.549	0.428	Economic globalization	0.843	-0.305
Political globalization	0.016	0.056	Political globalization	0.202	0.455
Social globalization	-0.012	-0.005	Social globalization	-0.752	-0.276
Political regime	-0.229	-0.469	Political regime	-0.455	-0.136
Military expenditure	-0.582	-0.869	Military expenditure	-0.895	-0.645
Taxes	-0.504	-0.583	Taxes	-3.210	-0.741
1-Public expenditure	1.181	1.460	1-Public expenditure	1.351	-0.173
Illegal trafficking	0.142	0.126	Illegal trafficking	2.367	0.579
Time variables	0.135	0.113	Urbanization	0.251	-0.126
			Population aging	-6.299	-1.010
PIB per capita	-0.586	-0.453	PIB per capita	-4.686	-0.479
Conflict in neighboring countries	0.080	0.191	Conflict in neighboring countries	0.119	0.488
Post-Cold War	-0.291	-0.213	Post-Cold War	0.207	0.447
Residual violence	0.816	0.494	Violence (-1)	0.003	
			Violence (-5)	0.002	
Africa	-0.267	-0.405	Africa	-0.413	-0.158
Latin America and the Caribbean	0.041	0.004	Latin America and the Caribbean	-0.357	-0.518

WAR, PEACE AND LIBERALISM   65

(i) Direct effects of economic globalization on armed conflict. Results shown in Table 2.1 are useful to inquire into the direct effects of economic globalization on armed conflict. According to the SEM results, economic globalization has a direct link with or effect on the *intensity* of armed conflict, an effect which is statistically significant. Hypothesis 2 is thus substantiated, suggesting that the existence of windows of opportunity created by globalization tends to increase the intensity of armed conflict. Regarding globalization-derived networks and resources (funding, weapons, trade, etc.) that armed actors have access to, conflicts tend to account for a larger number of casualties, and the scale of conflict is also higher. MCO results show that increased economic globalization is, on average, inversely related to the occurrence of armed conflict. Thus, it is important to differentiate between the occurrence of armed conflict and its intensity. Although on average globalization has no relation with the occurrence of conflicts, market opening-related processes, capital movements, and increased investment, etc., are indeed related to *increased-intensity* armed conflicts. And economic globalization is, on average, linked with a lower tendency for armed conflict to occur, bearing in mind that both industrialized and developing countries are included in the database, many of the former being more involved in the globalization process and most of them not having a record of internal armed conflicts.

(ii) Spillover effects of economic globalization on armed conflict. It has been shown that economic globalization has a direct and positive impact on the intensity of armed conflict. We now look at the spillover effects that economic globalization has on armed conflict (i.e., the impact this process may have on other variables, thus having an impact on armed conflict). On the basis of statistical information recorded in the database, an estimate has been made of these spillover effects. What follows is a brief explanation of how spillover effects have been estimated, and Table 2.2 shows a summary of values observed.

An example of how to find the spillover effects is shown in Figure 2.2.[55] In this case, an effort is made to estimate the spillover effect of economic globalization on the intensity of armed conflict, through its relation with or effect on inequality. To do so, we estimate the resulting outcome between the direct effect of economic globalization on inequality (Y_{21}), and the direct effect of inequality on the intensity of armed conflict (β_{32}), thus obtaining the spillover effect ($Y_{21}\,\beta_{32}$). The spillover effects of economic globalization were

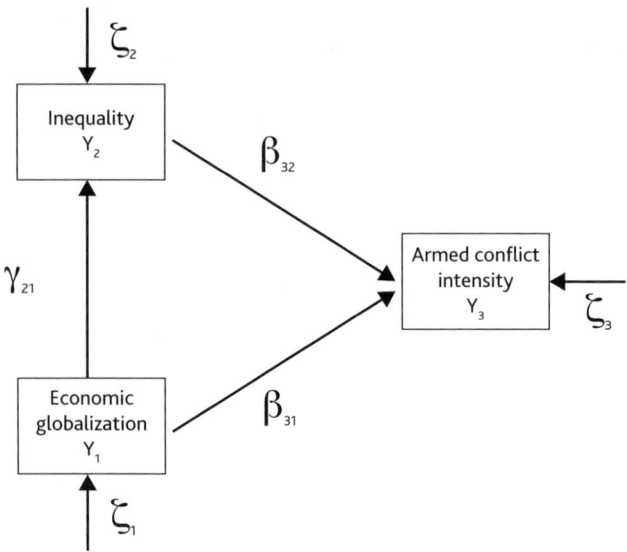

Figure 2.2 Spillover effects calculated among variables

thus estimated on the basis of the remaining variables. Results are shown in Table 2.2.

Please note: These results have been estimated on the basis of the SEM model. We should not forget that, within the variables analyzed, these effects of the SEM model take into account the higher value cases in particular.

Data in the first column of Table 2.2 show that wherever higher economic globalization levels occur, they are linked with: increased inequality (0.004, although the ratio is not very significant), a lower endowment of natural resources (–0.013), and ethnic fragmentation (–0.237). Economic globalization is also linked with enhanced democracy (0.354); lower military expenditure (–0.375); increased tax burden (0.030); increased urbanization and population aging (0.561 grouped) and higher GDP per capita (0.621). An increased trend towards economic globalization is, for its part, related to a lower occurrence of conflict in neighboring countries (–0.101), and it has a negative ratio with both regions, Africa (–0.241) and Latin America (0.011, insignificant), showing that, despite reforms being implemented aiming at a wider opening in these regions, they have a tendency to record a lower economic globalization level than countries in other regions in the world.[56] On the other hand, it is worth mentioning that higher economic globalization levels are linked with the highest public expenditure (the variable [1 – public expenditure] has a negative result equal to –0.251, Table 2.2).

Table 2.2 Economic globalization spillover effects

Variable	Relation with economic globalization	Dependent variable	
		Armed conflict intensity	Armed conflict occurrence
Inequality	0.004	0.0002	0.0004
Natural resources	–0.013	0.0000	–0.0001
Ethnic fragmentation	–0.237	–0.0147	–0.0213
Political globalization	0.558	0.0089	0.0469
Social globalization	0.288	–0.0032	–0.0020
Political regime	0.354	–0.0789	–0.2474
Military expenditure	–0.375	**0.2123**	**0.4860**
Taxes	0.03	–0.0147	–0.0261
1-Public expenditure	–0.251	–0.2884	–0.5467
Illegal trafficking	0.035	0.0048	0.0066
Time variables	0.561	0.0735	0.0948
PIB per capita	0.621	–0.3546	–0.4198
Conflict in neighboring countries	–0.101	–0.0079	–0.0287
Cold War termination	0.53	–0.1500	–0.1685
Residual violence	–0.136	0.1078	–0.1002
Africa	–0.241	0.0624	0.1458
Latin America and the Caribbean	0.011	0.0320	0.0056

Dependent variables: armed conflict intensity (number of casualties), and armed conflict occurrence (1.0).

Bearing these correlations in mind, Table 2.2 (second column, where statistically significant values are shown in bold) shows that, through military expenditure (0.212), economic globalization has a spillover effect on the intensity of armed conflict, meaning that the entry of economic globalization, implying large military expenditure reductions, may lead to an exacerbation of highly intense armed conflicts.[57] In the taxation field, economic globalization is also linked to increased tax collection rates and with a lower conflict intensity (–0.0147).[58] Economic globalization coincides with the post-Cold War period, and according to the indicator linking both variables, their combination is linked with a lower intensity of armed conflict (–0.150).[59] In protracted conflicts, economic globalization has also been linked with a lower intensity of armed conflicts (–0.1078). For its part, economic globalization is linked with higher intensity conflict, especially in Latin America (0.032), whereas in Africa the relationship is also positive but less significant.

The relation of economic globalization's spillover effects with inequality should be mentioned. While the results show that economic globalization has a positive spillover effect on higher intensity conflicts through increased inequality (0.0002), the result is not significant. This could be due to the type of variable used (Gini); however, even if Gini is not the best information source available, it should be highlighted that we cannot rule out that in many countries inequality has increased with economic globalization, and that this has led to increased conflict intensity. Case studies should be conducted and include new definitions of inequality, such as horizontal inequality,[60] which, as mentioned in the theoretical framework, may have increased with economic globalization (in cases in which neoliberal reforms have benefited some social, ethnic groups, etc., at the expense of others)—a factor which could further elucidate the relationship between economic globalization and armed conflict.

As for the occurrence of armed conflict (column three), it is less likely to happen through the spillover effect of economic globalization with increased democracy (−0.247), and reductions in public expenditure in countries (from −0.546 in the 1-public expenditure variable).[61] And economic globalization has a positive spillover effect on the occurrence of armed conflict, through a high military expenditure (0.486). Thus, countries with a higher military expenditure as a GDP percentage, and increased economic globalization, are linked with the less likely occurrence of armed conflict.[62] But in Latin American countries, increasing economic globalization in the continent has been associated both with the occurrence of armed conflict (0.0056) and a higher intensity of armed conflict (0.0320).[63]

In short, what the previous sections have shown is that economic globalization has both direct and spillover effects on armed conflict. There are direct and positive effects on armed conflict intensity (more casualties, or greater scale of conflict); the MCO model shows an inverse long-term relationship with the occurrence of armed conflict. Spillover effects occur through military expenditure (military expenditure and globalization combine to generate increased conflict intensity, and may lead to its occurrence). However, economic globalization can lead to a lower scale of conflict, if higher taxes are collected by the state. Economic globalization combined with enhanced democracy could result in fewer occurrences of armed conflict, while economic globalization and reduced public expenditure are related with a lower intensity of armed conflict.

Some of these results lend credence to the "liberal" peace thesis. But as we shall see below, the "pacification" process that long-term liberalization may entail is not entirely peaceful—it is linked with military victories.

Likewise, what we are witnessing is that the market may well coexist with war, adapting to it, and high levels of economic liberalization may be found together with high levels of violence. To illustrate this point, we offer the examples of the thriving coffee market during the war in Sudan, markets dealing in illicit products and resources during the war in Colombia, or the diamond markets in Africa. In most of these cases, both reforms aiming at strengthening the market and structural adjustment programs were implemented.

(iii) Termination of armed conflict and economic globalization. In this section we look at the role of economic globalization in ending conflicts. A statistical conflict termination probability analysis is conducted for a sample of countries engaged in armed conflicts from 1970 to 2005. For an analysis of the determinants of armed conflict termination, we refer to data gathered by Humphreys (2005), who in turn draws on Walter's (1997), and Fearon and Laitin's (2003) data. In his study, Humphreys examines conflict termination-related factors, with an emphasis on conflict correlation with and termination in the presence of natural resources. His most significant findings show that natural resources wealth is associated with peace achieved through military victories. At the same time, according to this author, we cannot say that the abundance of natural resources is always an obstacle to negotiated solutions (i.e. there could be a "negotiated peace" in the midst of wealth, but the probability is lower). His explanations show that if armed groups derive income from the exploitation of resources, such as diamonds, a peace negotiation is unlikely. In the case of oil, conflict termination is linked with swift military victories by one side, due to the fact that external actors get involved or exert influence in conflicts— because of the gains they expect to obtain from oil revenues—to bring them to an end. These outside influences strengthen one side helping it to defeat the other. On the basis of a methodology similar to Humphreys', logistic model (Logit) analyses have been conducted using explanatory variables, such as conflict termination through military means and by negotiation, as well as with an indicator accounting for both variables simultaneously. The value-added of this work is an analysis of the influence of economic globalization-related variables as a process involving the participation of

international economic stakeholders, capital, and investment, all of which are present in countries with conflict and may play some role in its termination.

Table 2.3 Probability (Logit) models for armed conflict termination through military victory, negotiation, and grouped together

Variable	Conflict termination grouped	Conflict termination military victory	Conflict termination through negotiation
Economic globalization	30.97	81.15	25.53
	(2.79)	(6.86)	(0.10)
Public expenditure	−12.26	−23.60	106.5
	(3.16)	(5.45)	(1.82)*
Military expenditure	−0.48	−0.88	−6.80
	(1.04)	(1.94)*	(2.68)
Taxes	−31.5	−33.0	−67.0
	(6.92)	(4.28)	(0.39)
Political globalization	1.17	3.94	−3.80
	(0.64)	(3.05)	(0.37)
Inequality	0.03	0.03	0.09
	(0.53)	(0.24)	(0.14)
Democracy	0.009	0.04)	0.20
	(0.10)	(1.18	(2.61)
Commodity export	7.25	16.45	−194.3
PIB percentage	(3.26)	(9.57)	(2.34)
Non-oil exporting country	−0.18	0.10	−6.72
	(0.04)	(0.007)	(1.47)**
Oil exporting country	6.06	6.47	15.15
	(8.96)	(7.60)	(0.00)
Illegal trafficking	0.48	0.28	−3.21
	(0.12)	(0.029)	(0.00)
PIB per capita	12.37	11.12	179.0
	(0.99)	(0.60)	(3.98)
Urbanization	−4.22	1.90	−72.1
	(0.68)	(0.10)	(4.37)
Population aging	18.42	46.2	−184.2
	(0.45)	(1.47)**	(1.72)*
Intercept	−3.24	4.19	−189.2
	(0.16)	(0.16)	(3.34)
No. of observations goodness of fit (Square Chi) likelihood ratio	310	305	296
Score	38.38	50.36	29.6
Wald	49.33	69.64	29.6
	20.96	21.93	7.75

*   95 percent significance level
** 90 percent significance level

Table 2.3 shows that economic globalization has a positive and meaningful correlation with conflict termination. The data also shows, however, that this correlation is especially strong in conflicts terminated by a military victory of one side (81.15), and not particularly significant in a conflicts that ended through negotiation (here the ratio is 25.53, but the statistical figure is 0.10). Therefore, increased economic flows, trade and financial opening, the inflow of direct foreign investment and, in general, the opening of opportunities for all armed groups, may coincide with (or press for) the deactivation of armed conflicts.

The data suggest that domestic and international economic stakeholders play a key role in economic liberalization processes. First, by helping one actor to achieve success, which, following Humphreys' line of reasoning, could take place because of the interest economic stakeholders have in future earnings promised by economic liberalization. And second, through the victory of one side, especially the side that supports market institutions. According to the results shown in Table 2.3, which support Humphreys' (2005) findings, the first mechanism seems to be more important, since the presence of natural resources is positively correlated with the military victory of one of the sides (16.45).[64] In instances of negotiated settlements, democracy seems to play a critical role (the 0.20 ratio is positive and significant).

Building on Humphreys, the correlation between armed conflict termination and greater economic globalization could be seen in two ways: (i) as simply coincidental or circumstantial: the overlapping between termination of some armed conflicts in the midst of an avalanche of neoliberal reforms taking place globally should be borne in mind, including structural adjustment programs, trade liberalization, a higher inflow of direct foreign investment, and increased capital flows, among others; and (ii) as *causal* and *political*: a claim could be made that, within a trend towards enhanced liberalization, multilateral financial institutions support structural adjustment policies as a strategy to solve economic and social problems, as well as foreign trade and increased foreign investment as strategies for economic growth and development. This would involve institutional changes within countries where those policies are implemented.[65]

The results considered thus far show that the entry of international economic stakeholders, increased direct foreign investment, and other factors, can be linked with violence. This contradicts the views of multilateral institutions which argue that, by increasing the availability of resources in societies,[66] direct foreign investment has an impact on reducing political violence. This is not to say that in the midst of economic globalization, conflicts that are in their final stages cannot also give rise to new market-deepening economic (and also social and political) structures. There are cases in which peace negotiations (or victory of one side) have led to a market expansion, seeking to include the entire population (at least in the labor market), as in South Africa. But in most cases, external actors militarily support and strengthen one side helping to defeat their opponent. The latter seems to have taken precedence, especially in regions where natural resources are plentiful (oil in particular). In Table 2.3, the coefficient of the variable "oil exporting country" is 6.47 when armed conflict termination occurred with military victory of one armed actor.

Other interesting results suggest the following: increased military expenditure is linked with fewer options to end an armed conflict, either through negotiated peace (–6.80), or with a military victory of one side (–0.88). Taxes are linked with a lower probability to terminate conflict (–31.5),[67] and political globalization (a country's commitment to bilateral and multilateral treaties) is linked with an enhanced possibility to end the conflict—though not through negotiation (–3.80), but through the victory of one side (3.94).[68] Another significant outcome is that higher wealth rates measured by the GDP per capita are mostly linked with the negotiated termination of conflict (179.0). This suggests that a fairer distribution of wealth makes it easier to negotiate termination of conflict.

State, economic globalization, and armed conflict (Hypothesis 3)

Table 2.1 shows that higher military expenditure (–0.582) and taxes (–0.504) tend to be linked with lower levels of armed conflict. These links could mean that in countries where the levels of armed conflict are very high, the state "is not as strong," if strength is to be linked with increased military expenditure and higher taxes, measured as a GDP percentage. It should be borne in mind that economic globalization is linked with a lower military expenditure, and that this spillover effect has a relation with both an escalated armed conflict and with the occurrence of armed conflict. The reduction of military expenditures is not linked with the reduction in conflict intensity because of a trend to use private security and mercenaries. Tax increases, on the one hand, are linked with less intensity (–0.504) and occurrence (–0.583) of armed conflict. On the other hand, economic globalization, coupled with a reduction in total public expenditure (as a GDP percentage), is linked with lower occurrence of armed conflict (−0.546 in Table 2.2). This does not mean that the reduction in public expenditure will lead to peace. This chapter does not claim that the solution is to reduce public spending to achieve peace. In many developed countries with higher levels of liberalization and with consolidated democracies the probability of armed conflict is low.[69]

The role democracy plays (Hypothesis 4)

The SEM model (Table 2.1) shows that higher levels of democracy are linked with a lower intensity (−0.229) and occurrence (−0.469) of armed conflict. The relationship is similar in the MCO model (albeit insignificant). Table 2.2 shows there is a positive correlation between economic globalization and democracy (0.354), generating a negative spillover effect on both the occurrence and the intensity of armed conflict. Table 2.3 shows how democracy is related to a higher likelihood of terminating conflicts through negotiated peace (0.20), but as we have seen before, it is more likely that conflicts will terminate through a military victory by one side. These results could be due to the fact that democracy makes it less likely for high-intensity conflicts to occur and, while generally making conflict less likely. But when talking about conflict termination, the role of democracy tends to be less important than that of coercive instruments.

Lastly, a higher level of democracy is linked with the occurrence of more homicides (0.97) and robberies (0.932, MCO model), and with the occurrence of popular mobilizations affecting the stability of political regimes (3.236, SEM model).

Other modalities of conflict and economic globalization (Hypothesis 5)

This study examines the additional impacts economic globalization may have on other modes of conflict or violence. These include criminality represented in the number of murders and robberies, and the number of popular mobilizations likely to destabilize political regimes. Table 2.4 shows statistical results for these variables using SEM and MCO models.

According to these results, the forms of criminality examined here do not have a close relation with higher levels of economic globalization (homicides −0.472; robberies −3.511). In the MCO model, economic globalization seems to have a positive effect on social mobilizations (0.128), although the result is not significant. In a different way, a high number of homicides (SEM model) is explained by time variables (0.051) (urbanization and population aging), and relates to the post-Cold War period (0.187), thus this form of conflict has arguably increased. And (MCO model) homicides have, on average, a positive correlation with inequality (0.282), democracy (0.977) and GDP per capita (57.4), while having a negative correlation with variables such as military expenditure (−15.783), the post-Cold War period (−12.676), and regional variables for Africa (−35.5) and Latin America (−29.8). Likewise, homicides have a positive correlation with the occurrence of illegal resource trafficking (25.26).

As for robberies, their highest levels (SEM model) are linked with the trend to natural resources exports (0.025), higher taxes (0.449), illegal resource trafficking (0.595), and the post-Cold War period (1.507). The MCO model points out that, on average, robberies have a positive (and significant) relation with variables such as inequality (0.277), democracy (0.932), illegal trafficking (25.305), and GDP per capita (57.89). They are inversely linked with ethnic fragmentation (−11.21), military expenditure (−16.12), the post-Cold War period (−13.45), and regional variables for Africa (−36.8) and Latin America (−29.3).

Popular mobilizations aiming to destabilize political regimes have a positive link with higher military expenditure (7.24) and taxes (6.47), as well as with the occurrence of democratic regimes (3.23) (SEM model). They are also negatively linked with natural resources exports (−0.053), ethnic fragmentation (−0.814), reduced public expenditure (−15.28), and illegal trafficking (−0.56). The MCO model shows that when the GDP per capita is higher (−0.302), it is less likely for popular mobilizations of this kind to occur.

According to these results, the role that economic globalization plays in these processes is not so clear, and, as previously mentioned, economic globalization is mainly linked with the likelihood for popular mobilizations aiming to destabilize the political regime. However, as already noted, problems of crime and mobilizations are highly associated with the illegal flows (of merchandize, persons, etc.) taking place in the processes of globalization. This point will be discussed below.

The role illegal markets play in armed conflict (Hypothesis 6)

As illustrated in Table 2.1, the illegal trafficking of natural resources, diamonds, and cocaine in our case study is positively and significantly linked with armed conflict intensity and occurrence. Table 2.2 also showed a positive (although not significant) relation with economic globalization, which has a spillover effect on armed conflict intensity

Table 2.4 Ratios estimated on the basis of (a) SEM model (maximum likelihood) and (b) ordinary least square basis

Dependent variables: number of homicides, robberies and mobilizations. Significant results are highlighted in bold.

Variable	Dependent variable SEM direct effect (standardized)			Variable	Dependent variable		
	Homicides	Robberies	Mobilizations		Homicides	Robberies MCO ratio	Mobilizations
Inequality	0.071	0.275	−0.783	Inequality	**0.282**	**0.277**	0.119
Natural resources (grouped)	0.005	**0.025**	−0.053	Non-oil commodity exports	61.378	62.320	**0.610**
Ethnic fragmentation	0.006	0.394	**−0.814**	Oil commodity exports	8.269	11.319	0.303
Economic globalization	−0.472	−3.511	−7.000	Ethnic fragmentation	−10.965	**−11.213**	−0.178
Political globalization	1.062	**2.395**	**−0.641**	Economic globalization	−9.156	−9.453	0.128
Social globalization	0.002	0.065	0.608	Political globalization	**−84.855**	**−85.283**	**0.222**
Political regime	−0.423	−1.547	**3.236**	Social globalization	0.556	0.569	−0.609
Military expenditure	−0.163	−1.478	**7.245**	Political regime	**0.977**	**0.932**	−0.242
Taxes	−0.102	**0.449**	**6.470**	Military expenditure	**−15.783**	**−16.122**	−0.344
1-Public expenditure	0.139	−0.601	**−15.281**	Taxes	96.307	10.597	0.214
Illegal trafficking	0.149	**0.595**	**−0.565**	1-Public expenditure	−85.866	−90.471	−0.183
Time and control variables	**0.051**	−0.596	−1.192	Illegal trafficking	25.264	25.305	**0.385**
				Urbanization	50.176	45.984	0.752
PIB capita	−0.509	3.469	7.582	Population ageing	−67.884	−71.084	−0.289
Conflicts in neighboring countries	−0.416	0.000	0.000	PIB capita	**57.465**	**57.897**	**−0.302**
Cold War termination	0.187	**1.507**	2.995	Conflicts in neighboring countries	−26.503	−26.564	0.150
Residual violence	0.118	0.000	0.000	Post-Cold War	−12.676	−13.458	−0.125
Africa	−0.104	0.067	**3.775**	Africa	−35.556	−36.821	0.206
Latin America and the Caribbean	0.176	0.677	−0.788	Latin America and the Caribbean	29.893	−29.351	0.752

and occurrence. And Table 2.4 showed that illegal trafficking is linked with other crime modalities, such as homicide and robbery, and also (albeit to a lesser extent) with mobilizations. In all models, this is the only variable keeping a significant and positive relation with armed conflict and crime. Thus, illegal resource trafficking is a problem linked with most recent social and political conflicts, and deserves to be examined in more detail; also, policies that address the root causes of armed conflict should be drafted and enforced by national and international authorities. In particular, demand-side policies should be strengthened because supply-side control policies have been rather ineffective, and have been linked with increased violence. This situation should be reassessed in depth, and market laws amended to include these illegal goods. This is because their illegal nature not only increases their price, harming many countries experiencing internal conflicts, but also generates high crime rates in developing and in industrialized countries alike.

Control variables and other relevant results (Hypothesis 7)

As stated in the theoretical framework, liberal reforms go hand in hand with a number of social and institutional changes in societies where liberalization is implemented. Among them, urbanization plays a meaningful role in deactivating armed conflict. Table 2.1 numbers confirm this hypothesis (MCO model). Higher urbanization (–0.126) and aging population (–1.010) are, on average, linked with a lower occurrence of armed conflict. When armed conflicts are more intense (SEM model), their increased intensity, accounted for by the number of casualties, has a positive relation with the latent variable joining urbanization and aging (0.135) together. Such more intense conflicts could imply both rural and urban violence, and involve larger population sectors.

The post-Cold War years variable is linked with fewer armed conflicts (–0.291) and with a lower likelihood of armed conflict (–0.213) (SEM model). On the other hand, and according to the MCO model, this variable is, on average, positively linked with armed conflict intensity (0.207) and occurrence (0.447). This would imply a greater likelihood of more intense armed conflicts in the post-Cold War period. However, more intense conflicts occurred before the end of the Cold War, measured by the number of casualties recorded. Table 2.2 results show that economic globalization is linked with increased urbanization and aging rates (time variables in this table). And with regard to new conflict modalities, these variables are particularly linked with high homicide rates (Table 2.4).

The regional impacts in Latin America, Africa, and the Caribbean are also examined in this analysis. Results show that the "African dummy" is inversely linked with high-intensity armed conflicts (–0.267) and their occurrence (–0.405), while the "Latin American dummy" is positively linked with higher intensity conflicts (0.041). Using the MCO models, both regions show a negative relation with the occurrence of armed conflict (–0.158 and –0.518, respectively). This means that just because countries are located in these regions, they do not have a particular predisposition to get involved in armed conflict. Likewise, both regions are inversely linked with the occurrence of homicides (–35.55 and –29.89) and robberies (–36.82 and –29.35, MCO models, Table 2.4), and the Latin American dummy is linked with the possible occurrence of mobilizations aiming to destabilize the political regime (0.752). And Africa is also linked with a lower economic globalization (–0.241, Table 2.2), while Latin America and the Caribbean show a positive (but insignificant) relation with economic globalization (0.011).

CONCLUSIONS

First, a methodological conclusion. We should differentiate between root causes of conflict, its occurrence, and its termination. Also, we should differentiate the explanations for higher-intensity conflicts (SEM model) from those for lesser or average intensity conflicts (MCO model). Regarding armed conflict *intensity*, its higher level according to the SEM model is linked with inequality, ethnic fragmentation, occurrence of natural resources (to a lesser extent), occurrence of conflicts in neighboring countries, and residual violence. The *occurrence* of more intense conflicts, meanwhile, is linked with higher inequality, ethnic fragmentation, conflicts in neighboring countries, and residual violence. As for the MCO model, conflict intensity is, on average, linked with ethnic fragmentation, but not with the occurrence of primary resources. Inequality, therefore, seems to be mainly linked with higher-intensity conflicts.

With regard to the correlation between economic globalization and armed conflict, this study examined three conflict-related variables: intensity, occurrence, and termination. The data shows three important conclusions:

- On the one hand, higher rates of economic globalization are linked with a higher intensity of armed conflict. The market opens up opportunities to armed groups, but also to international economic stakeholders in countries besieged by armed conflict.
- Second, higher rates of economic globalization are linked with a relative *absence* of armed conflict. In other words, it is less likely for armed conflict to occur in countries showing higher levels of economic globalization. This could mean that a market-driven "liberal peace" is indeed possible. But, as noted above, the process of getting there is not necessarily peaceful,[70] and often lengthy.
- Third, higher rates of economic globalization are linked with the *termination* of armed conflict. This typically occurs through a military victory of one side (and less by negotiation), often supported by international economic stakeholders, especially if natural resources are involved. At the same time, countries with higher levels of democracy may be more likely to terminate conflicts through negotiated solutions.

Globalization also has some spillover effects on armed conflict. The data examined show that economic globalization has a spillover effect in terms of military expenditure, since reductions in military expenditures may lead to further escalation and intensification of armed conflicts (probably through greater involvement of private security agents). In this sense, the shrinking of the state (by reducing military expenditure as a percentage of GDP) does not reduce violence. On the other hand, economic globalization is linked with higher tax collection rates which would lead to reduced conflict intensity.[71]

The data thus show that, on the one hand, higher economic globalization rates are linked with higher-intensity armed conflict, both in a *direct* way, through opportunities that conflict actors take advantage of, and in an *indirect* way, through the impact on economic globalization of variables such as reduced military expenditure (due to a trend of hiring private security agents, mercenaries, and the like). Results also show that economic globalization can be present at the end of armed conflicts for several reasons: by coincidence; by voluntary and conscious planning of policy designers or by governments as a peace building strategy; or by the introduction of opening and adjustment policies, just after the termination of war.

The data thus suggest that the "peacemaker" role of the market is not as clear (in the short-term at least) as the "liberal peace" thesis claims.[72] War may adapt to the economy and vice versa. Local economies in war zones can be very dynamic and the market, working in a better or a worse way, can exist in regions[73] besieged by conflict. Armed groups may benefit from opportunities opened by the market economy (legal and illegal international markets, trafficking networks, smuggling networks, tax havens, incoming foreign exchange flows, international trade, etc.), as well as neoliberal-type reforms and restructuring programs that act against the state.[74] Mention should also be made of the fact that international economic stakeholders are likewise able to find opportunities in countries besieged by armed conflict (for example, multinational corporations and international banking, in sectors such as the exploitation of natural resources).[75]

Furthermore, a combination of variables exert pressure to terminate armed conflicts. The market is not the only peacemaker—also required are political factors that are conducive to both domestic and external peace, and to the adoption of policies involving national and international stakeholders. The data show that a military victory by one side best explains the termination of many conflicts, but the market and its stakeholders often seem to play a supportive role. Increased efforts are therefore required to monitor the activities of national and international economic actors in countries involved in armed conflict, to ensure that human rights are not violated, and to prevent an exacerbation of violence. Likewise, economic liberalization policies should be revised to monitor or "close" the windows of opportunity that these policies have opened to some actors involved in armed conflicts. Instances in which market stakeholders are making a contribution to peace should be distinguished from instances in which they exacerbate the violence, and from instances where the stakeholders' role is more complex than it appears to be. Moreover, the weakening of the state and the handover of state functions to the private sector in countries in conflict seems to have a bigger impact on increasing violence.

Could economic globalization become both a discourse and a set of policies to advance the cause of peace? If so, additional efforts are needed, including: a reduction of inequality, a reduction of illegal resource trafficking, higher levels of democracy and a stronger state. Therefore, a more stringent surveillance of the windows of opportunity that economic globalization opens up should be ensured, relating to both local and external conflict actors, including

international economic stakeholders. Similarly, improvements in socia
economic sectors must be made—with the support of the state—and espe
in countries involved in armed conflicts. Last but not least, enhanced effor
needed in the fight against illegal resource trafficking, although, as we have
armed conflict is driven by more than the presence of natural resources al

ANNEX: COUNTRIES INCLUDED IN DATABASE

East Asia and the Pacific	Western Europe	Latin America and the Cari
Australia	Austria	Argentina
China	Belgium	Bolivia
Fiji	Cyprus	Chile
Hong Kong, China	Denmark	Colombia
Indonesia	Finland	Costa Rica
Japan	France	Ecuador
Korea, Rep.	Germany	El Salvador
Malaysia	Ireland	Guatemala
New Zealand	Italy	Honduras
Philippines	Netherlands	Jamaica
Singapore	Norway	Mexico
Thailand	Spain	Nicaragua
Eastern Central Europe and Central Asia	Sweden	Panama
	Switzerland	Paraguay
Albania	United Kingdom	Peru
Bulgaria	**North America**	Trinidad and Tobago
Croatia	Canada	Uruguay
Czech Republic	United States	Venezuela, RB
Estonia	**Sub-Saharan Africa**	**Middle East and North Afr**
Hungary	Botswana	Algeria
Latvia	Burundi	Bahrain
Lithuania	Côte d'Ivoire	Egypt, Arab Rep.
Poland	Madagascar	Greece
Romania	Mauritius	Israel
Russian Federation	Nigeria	Jordan
Slovak Republic	Rwanda	Kuwait
Slovenia	Senegal	Morocco
Turkey	South Africa	Portugal
Ukraine	Uganda	Syrian Arab Republic
Southern Asia	Zambia	Tunisia
Bangladesh	Zimbabwe	
India		
Nepal		
Pakistan		
Sri Lanka		

NOTES

1. From a paper drafted within the framework of the project *Economic Liberalization, Politics and War: A Comparative Study of Africa and Latin America*, financed by the IDRC-Canada. The author acknowledges the contributions made by Francisco Gutiérrez Sanín, including his comments and suggestions, and by the project's working team members, including Diana Mendoza, Mauricio Barón, and William Mancera. Also, the author is grateful for the suggestions made by the project participants, in particular Richard Banégas, Roland Marshall, Frederick Golooba-Mutebi, James Putzel, Gerd Schönwälder, and Ricardo Peñaranda. The contributions of those attending the presentation of this paper at IEPRI—especially Jaime Andrés Niño, Arlene Tickner, Andrés López, Jorge Pulecio, and Gabriel Misas—are also acknowledged, as are the comments made by the members of the Observatory of Human Rights of the Vice-Presidency, and the International Crisis Group (Bogotá). More details on the statistical analysis underlying this chapter can be obtained from the author (bajeromix@yahoo.com).
2. Jairo Baquero Melo is an economist with a Master's degree in Political Studies (IEPRI, Universidad Nacional de Colombia) and a Master's degree in International Relations and African Studies (Universidad Autónoma de Madrid). He has worked as researcher at IEPRI, Universidad Nacional de Colombia, and as fellowship scholar at African Studies Group, Universidad Autónoma de Madrid.
3. For an in-depth analysis of liberalization, economic globalization, and neoliberalism, see Chapter 1 (Gutiérrez) in this volume, which attempts to conceptualize these processes. In economic terms, liberalism has been recently linked with the market economy and economic globalization, and neoliberalism has been associated with the expansion processes of this economic model.
4. These approaches could be critically discussed from different points of view. From one perspective, history shows that societies with different degrees of hierarchy, or hierarchism, in their social structure do exist.
5. Small and Singer (1976), and Schumpeter (1950), quoted in Michael Doyle (1986). Polanyi also argues that liberalization and the introduction of a market economy are not necessarily peaceful processes and, sometimes, through their impact on other variables, may escalate conflicts.
6. Nozick (1988). The goal of neoliberal reforms, through structural adjustment programs, is greater state efficiency through privatization, reduction of public expenditures, eradication of corruption, and a larger role for the private sector. A claim has been advanced, though, that adjustment policies have had negative social impacts.
7. War played an important role in Europe: it forced the state both to implement more efficient tax collection systems, and to improve its administrative and economic managerial skills. It also brought about unifying symbols linking the population with the state, making authority legitimate. But, as Herbst (1996) claims, many African states have failed to solve these problems: a situation that impairs their ability to consolidate power and evolve their political economy.
8. Herbst (1996).
9. For example, the MPLA and UNITA funding sources in Angola, which went from the Soviet Union and the United States' financial support, respectively, to oil-based (MPLA) and diamond-based (UNITA) funding. See Ferreira (2005).

10. Milliken and Krause (2002).
11. Jackson (1990).
12. See for example: Reno (1995, 1998), Ballart, Ellis, and Hibou (1999), and Newbury (2002).
13. See Richards (1996) and Skinner (1999).
14. See, for example, Coser (1961), Mack (1975), Massoud (1996), Kecskemeti (1970), and Wittman (1979).
15. Both in South Africa and in El Salvador, the negotiated transition to political democracy amounted to a liberal revolution, where insurgents have won political inclusion and abandoned their defiance by armed means.
16. In other words, economic interests are often present where it is alleged "new war" is taking place (Berdal, 2003, pp. 489, 493).
17. In the Clausewitzian sense, for whom war was the continuation of politics through other means.
18. Berdal (2003), p. 486.
19. Reference should be made to economic globalization, which is related to increased flows of some types of economic capital (investment and goods, mainly), and reduced barriers to these capital flows. In the variables included in this study, migration is considered inside the "social globalization" index (KOF Globalization index. See in the next section of this chapter, the data and variables definitions).
20. Birdsall et al. (2001) argue that globalization is good for the rich and bad for the poor, because it is able to reduce global poverty while inequality increases. Wade (2002) claims that global inequality is increasing through technological changes and financial liberalization. Between 1988 and 1993, the world income share among 10 percent of the world's poorest people fell by a quarter, while the 10 percent of the richest share rose by 8 percent. And for Cornia (2003), country-level inequality has increased by two-thirds in the 73 countries in the sample under review, due to deregulatory policies in force in those economies.
21. Bezemer and Jong-A-Pin (2007).
22. The arrival of democracy and free markets can engender hatred among ethnic groups. But the existence of a minority that dominates the market is not a necessary or sufficient condition to generate conflict.
23. UNODC (2006), p. 10. US Department of State (2003), p. 1.
24. Fajnzylber et al. (2000).
25. Gutiérrez (2004). The rationale comes closer to Hobsbawm's social banditry thesis. See Sánchez and Meertens (1983).
26. Keen (2001), Bates (1973).
27. According to the GDP per capita indicator. See Collier and Hoeffler (2000) and Fearon and Laitin (2003).
28. Humphreys (2005), p. 3.
29. Davies (1969), Gurr (1970).
30. Oberschall (1973), Tilly (1978).
31. Lichbach (1989).
32. Tilly (1978), Tarrow (1994).
33. Powell (1982).
34. Schock and other authors examine mediating variables between conflict and its causes, such as democracy, democratic culture and political opportunities. See Homer-Dixon (1994).
35. Auvinen and Nafziger (1999).

36. Krain (1998).
37. Analyzing horizontal inequity for a large sample of countries is complicated because there are no global databases on a panel to give account about the evolution of this indicator.
38. Ross (2002).
39. Ross (2004).
40. Ross (2006).
41. Rothschild (1981), p. 2.
42. Providing armed actors with funding and access to weapons, among other things. Drug trafficking from developing to industrialized countries remains very profitable, due to the high prices these goods fetch in international markets; therefore production also remains high. Likewise, rebel groups in drug-producing countries make the picture more complex because these groups are involved in production and trafficking. Trading in products such as cocaine, diamonds, and timber, provides resources to governments and insurgent groups alike in countries in Africa, Asia, and Latin America. And illegal trade networks take advantage of the technological innovations and transport facilities globalization has to offer.
43. Originally, the database was made up of 125 countries. As further variables were included, some countries for which no information was available were eventually deleted. The final version examined includes 90 countries from all over the world (see Annex).
44. The Fearon and Laitin database uses a lower eight-casualty threshold. For the statistical exercises, an estimation was made of the natural logarithm of this variable.
45. We appreciate the assistance of historian William Mancera at the National University of Colombia. The number is based on a review of books, newspapers and the Internet. The main sources are *The New York Times*, *Le Monde Diplomatique*, and the BBC.
46. A probabilistic model is being applied, following Humphreys' (2005) methodology.
47. See data and its explanation at the KOF Index of Globalization: http://globalization.kof.ethz.ch/.
48. For the construction of this indicator, the following data, divided into two subsets, is included: one for current flows and another for data on restrictions:
    (a) Current flows:
    - Exchanges, trade (% of GDP), WDI (2005)
    - Direct foreign investment, DFI (% of GDP), WDI (2005)
    - Investment Portfolio (% of GDP), IFS, 2005
    - Revenue Payments to nationals abroad (% of GDP), WDI (2005)

    (b) Data on restrictions:
    - Hidden barriers to imports, Gwartney et al. (2005)
    - Average rate, Gwartney et al. (2005)
    - Tariffs (% of current revenue), WDI (2005)
    - Restrictions on capital account, Gwartney et al. (2005)

    For more details about the construction of this indicator, see the KOF Index of Globalization (http://globalization.kof.ethz.ch/).
49. The Gini index ranges between 0 and 1, and the smaller the value, the lesser the inequality in income distribution.

50. Likewise, the importance of other forms of inequality is acknowledged, such as "horizontal" inequality, which could be a better indicator for examining its relation with armed conflict. However, enough information on this variable for an overall analysis is unavailable. For this reason, the Gini ratio is being included.
51. An inverse indicator of this variable, constructed by subtracting the initial percentage from the unit, was used in the statistical exercises (i.e., 1 − public expenditure as a GDP percentage). The higher the value, the smaller government spending.
52. For the theoretical and conceptual details on this type of model, see for example Kline (2005).
53. The SEM model (Structural Equation Model) is composed of two parts: a consistency measure model of the variables observed with latent variables and a structural equation model, or confirmatory model. The consistency measuring model specifies the consistency level in which empirically observed variables define latent variables as theoretical determinants hypothesis, and are used to describe measuring validity and reliability properties of the variables observed. The structural equation model specifies causal relations of latent variables or theoretical determinants hypothesis, and it is used to describe causal effects and the importance of the unexplained variance. When measure and structural models are estimated, weights provide estimations of indicators and determinants as a whole.

   The ordinary least squares method (OLS) models are based on the estimation of linear equations of the equation:
   $$X_i = a_i + bY_{ij} + e_i$$
   Where X_i is the vector of i observations of the independent variable; a_i is the constants vector; b is the vector of j β ratios estimated for the relation between the j independent variables and the dependent variable X; Y_{ij} is the matrix of i observations of the j independent variables; and e_i is the vector of error terms of estimations.

   And the logistic model (Logit) estimates a logistical binary choice model, where conflict continues (y=0) or ends (y=1), according to a set of variables. These factors are reflected in a vector X, so that
   $$Prob\ (Y=1) = F(X, B)$$
   $$Prob\ (Y=0) = 1 - F\ (X, B)$$
   The parameters B vector reflects the impact X has on the probability.
54. Due to the large number of explanatory variables included, only the links examined between latent variables are shown in Figure 2.1. Most latent variables are calculated on the basis of an observed variable. Latent variables, which include more than one observed variable, are: natural resources (including an observed variable indicating whether the country is a primary exporter of oil resources, and other variable for non-oil natural resources); time variables (the urbanization and population aging levels were included for each country); and violence laggardness (which includes a one-year lag, and another five-year lag, to examine the conflict history impact on the subsequent violence).
55. Bollen and Stine's (1990) methodology is applied. The methodology for estimating standard errors, applied in this chapter, is also explained in their work.
56. This does not mean that economic globalization is not present in Africa and Latin America. What we are showing here, is that despite the economic

opening, in comparison with countries in regions such as Asia, Europe, and North America, economic globalization remains lower than in these areas in the world (see list of countries included in the Annex). See Chapter 1 (Gutiérrez) in this volume, to learn how the process of economic globalization has made progress.
57. This could be linked to a reduction in military expenditure though, on the other hand, it could also lead to higher private security expenditures, and to the use of mercenaries and private armies, which tend to generate increased violence and a larger number of casualties.
58. As the theory claims, the hypothesis that higher taxes are a proxy for a stronger state, a fact that could be linked with lower armed conflict intensity, should not be ruled out.
59. Comparing conflicts ranging from the 1970s—the first year in the sample included in the database—to the end of the Cold War.
60. Stuart (2005).
61. A more in-depth analysis should be conducted to see under what conditions an argument could be advanced that a public expenditure reduction, linked with enhanced economic globalization, may be associated with a lower probability for the occurrence of armed conflict. This could be true in the cases where the state has become "criminalized."
62. This could occur in states showing less democracy, and an increased trend to autocratic regimes and military dictatorships.
63. We should not rule out that, in this region, persistent inequality may be a part of this relationship. We should remember, as some authors have stressed, that inequality has continued in Latin America since the early 1980s, with very few indications that the trend is decreasing; this has been the background, against which structural adjustment reforms have been implemented. See Korzeniewicz and Smith (2000). The highest worldwide land distribution inequality levels are also present in this region, surpassing regions like the Middle East and North Africa, North America and sub-Saharan Africa. See Kliksberg (2007).
64. The mechanism elucidated by Humphreys is that expected future resource-originating earnings encourage these actors to support one side.
65. For example, an enhanced definition of property rights, increased efficiency and less corruption in public institutions, and an improvement in legal institutions, among others.
66. Likewise, some studies argue that high direct foreign investment levels may be linked with less conflict in resource-poor societies, and with increasingly more conflict in resource-rich societies. See Rothgeb (1990).
67. If the state controls an important quantity of resources, explained because it collects a high level of taxes, at some points during the confrontation, there could be incentives to continue the war (but this subject deserves more research).
68. This includes membership in international security agencies, regional blocs, and multilateral organizations, as well as commitments to agreements entered into with other countries. Many of these instruments may be used to negotiate peace, but also, apparently, to increase military actions in countries besieged by armed conflicts.
69. This does not preclude other conflictivity modalities, as we shall discuss below.
70. Violence may increase as a result of the opportunities open to some actors involved in armed conflicts.

71. Economic globalization seems to increase tax collection revenues, thus strengthening the state and reducing armed conflict intensity and occurrence. Therefore, strengthening the state may be linked with reduced armed conflict intensity.
72. Maybe the market will, in the long-term, become linked with the presence of peace, considering that countries showing higher economic globalization rates show a stronger trend towards *domestic* peace than to the occurrence of *domestic* armed conflicts. This is not to say that there are not other conflict modalities, such as crime and social mobilizations, also examined in this chapter. Or the occurrence of international conflicts, involving more liberalized countries (Doyle, 1986).
73. See the previously quoted example regarding the coffee trade in the war zone in Sudan (Duffield, 2004).
74. See the example of the social security sector in Chapter 6 on Colombia (Gutiérrez), in this volume.
75. It would be worthwhile to more thoroughly look into the moral hazard many states, companies, etc., incur by economically and politically intervening in countries besieged by armed conflict.

REFERENCES

Auvinen, J. and Nafziger, E. W. (1999) "The Sources of Humanitarian Emergencies." *Journal of Conflict Resolution*, Vol. 43, No. 3, pp. 267–90.
Ballart, J. F., Ellis, S., and Hibou, B. (1999) *The Criminalization of the State in Africa*. Oxford: James Currey.
Bates, R. H. (1973) "Ethnicity in contemporary Africa." *Eastern African Studies*, No. 14. Syracuse, NY: Syracuse University.
Berdal, M. (2003) "How 'new' are 'new wars'? Global economic change and the study of civil war." *Global Governance*, Vol. 9, pp. 477–502.
Bezemer, D. and Jong-A-Pin, R. (2007) "World on Fire? Democracy, Globalization and Ethnic Violence," University of Groningen, Draft Paper, 4.
Birdsall, N., Behrman, J. R., and Szekely, M. (2001) "Economic Policy and Wage Differentials in Latin America." CGD Working Paper 29. Washington, DC: Center for Global Development (http://www.cgdev.org/content/publications/detail/2761, accessed July 2007).
Bollen, K.A. and Stine, R. (1990) "Direct and spillover effects: classical and bootstrap estimates of variability." *Sociological Methodology*, Vol. 20, pp. 115–140.
Bourguignon, F. and Morrison, C. (2002) "Inequality among world citizens: 1820–1992." *American Economic Review*, Vol. 92, No. 4, pp. 727–744.
Collier, P. and Hoeffler, A. (2000) "Greed and Grievance in Civil Wars." World Bank Working Paper WPS 2000-18. Washington, DC: World Bank.
Collier, P. and Hoeffler, A. (2004) "Greed and grievance in civil war." *Oxford Economic Papers*, Vol. 56, No. 4, pp. 563–595.
Cornia, G. (2003) "The Impact of Liberalization and Globalization on Income Inequality in Developing and Transitional Economies." CESIFO Working Paper 843. (http://www.cesifo.de/pls/guestci/download/CESifo%20Working%20 Papers%202003/CESifo%20Working%20Papers%20January%202003%20/ cesifo_wp843.pdf, accessed July 2007).

Coser, L. (1961) "The termination of conflict." *The Journal of Conflict Resolution*, Vol. 5, No. 4, pp. 347–353.

Davies, J. (1969) "The J-curve of rising and declining satisfactions as a cause of some great revolutions and a contained rebellion." In *The History of Violence in America: Historical and Comparative*, eds. H. Graham and T. R. Gurr, pp. 690–730. New York: Praeger.

Doyle, M. (1986) "Liberalism and world politics." *American Political Science Review*, Vol. 80, No. 4.

Dreher, A. (2003) *Does Globalization Affect Growth?* Mannheim: University of Mannheim.

Dreher, A. and Gaston, N. (2005) "Has Globalization Really Had No Effect on Unions?" Arbeitspapiere / Working Papers, No. 110. Zurich: KOF Swiss Economic Institute, ETH Zurich.

Dreher, A. and Gaston, N. (2008) "Has globalization increased inequality?" *Review of International Economics*, Vol. 16, No. 3, pp. 516–536.

Duffield, M. (2004) *Las nuevas guerras en el mundo global, la convergencia entre desarrollo y seguridad*. Madrid: La Catarata Ed.

Fajnzylber, P., Lederman, D., and Loayza, N. (2000) "Crime and victimization: an economic perspective." *Economia* (Fall), pp. 219–302.

Fearon, J. and Laitin, D. (2003) "Ethnicity, insurgency and civil wars." *American Political Science Review*, Vol. 97, No. 1, pp. 75–90.

Ferreira, M. E. (2005) "Development and the peace dividend insecurity paradox in Angola." *The European Journal of Development Research*, Vol. 17, No. 3, pp. 509–524.

Gurr, T. R. (1970) *Why Men Rebel*. Princeton, NJ: Princeton University Press.

Gutiérrez, F. (2004) "Criminal rebels? A discussion of war and criminality from the Colombian experience." *Politics and Society*, Vol. 32, No. 2, pp. 257–285.

Gwartney, J. and Lawson, R., with Gartzke, E. (2005) *Economic Freedom of the World: 2005 Annual Report*. Vancouver, BC: The Fraser Institute.

Herbst, J. W. (1996) "Responding to State Failure in Africa." *International Security*, Vol. 21, No.3, pp.120–144.

Homer-Dixon, T. (1994) "Environmental scarcities and violent conflict: evidence from cases." *International Security*, Vol. 16, No. 1, pp. 4–40.

Humphreys, M. (2005) "Natural resources, conflict, and conflict resolution: uncovering the mechanisms." *Journal of Conflict Resolution*, Vol. 49, No. 4, p. 3.

Jackson, R. (1990) *Quasi States: Sovereignty, International Relations and the Third World*. Cambridge: Cambridge University Press.

Kaldor, M. (1999) *New and Old Wars: Organised Violence in a Global Era*. Cambridge: Polity Press.

Kecskemeti, P. (1970) "Political rationality in ending war." *Annals of the American Academy of Political and Social Science*, Vol. 392, "How Wars End," pp. 105–115.

Keen, D. (2001) "The political economy of war." In *War and Underdevelopment: Volume 1: The Economic and Social Consequences of Conflict*, eds. Frances Stewart, Valpy Fitzgerald, et al. Oxford: Oxford University Press.

Kliksberg, B. (2007) *Equidad en América Latina*. CIDI / CIDES/ OAS. (www.sedi.oas.org/ddse/documentos/.../14.%20Equidad.ppt, accessed October 7, 2009).

Kline, R. (2005) *Structural Equation Modelling*. New York: The Gilford Press.

KOF Index of Globalization. http://globalization.kof.ethz.ch/ (accessed October 7, 2009).

Korzeniewicz, R. and Smith, W. C. (2000) "Poverty, inequality, and growth in Latin America: searching for the high road to globalization." *Latin American Research Review*, Vol. 35, No. 3, pp. 7–54.

Krain, M. (1998) "Contemporary democracies revisited: democracy, political violence and event count models." *Comparative Political Studies*, Vol. 31, No. 2, pp. 139–164.

Lichbach, M. (1989) "An evaluation of 'Does economic inequality breed political conflict?' studies." *World Politics*, No. 41, pp. 431–470.

Mack, A. (1975) "Why big nations lose small wars." *World Politics*, Vol. 27, No. 2, pp. 175–200.

Massoud, T. G. (1996) "War termination." *Journal of Peace Research*, Vol. 33, No. 4, pp. 491–496.

Midlarsky, M. (1982) "Scarcity and inequality: prologue to the onset of mass revolution." *Journal of Conflict Resolution*, Vol. 26, pp. 3–38.

Midlarsky, M. (1988) "Rulers and ruled: patterned inequality and the onset of mass political violence." *American Political Science Review*, Vol. 82, No. 2, pp. 491–509.

Milliken, J. and Krause, K. (2002) "State failure, state collapse and state reconstruction: concepts, lessons and strategies." *Development and Change*, Vol. 33, No. 5, pp. 755–756.

Muller, E. (1985) "Income inequality, regime repressiveness, and political violence." *American Sociological Review*, Vol. 50, No. 1, pp. 47–61.

Muller, E., Seligson, M., and Fu, Hung-der (1989) "Land inequality and political violence." *The American Political Science Review*, Vol. 83, No. 2, pp. 577–596.

Newbury, C. (2002) "States at war: confronting conflict in Africa." *African Studies Review*, Vol. 45, No. 1, pp. 1–20.

Nozick, R. (1988) *Anarquía, Estado y Utopía*. Mexico City: Fondo de cultura económica.

Oberschall, A. (1973) *Social Conflict and Social Movements*. Englewood Cliffs, NJ: Prentice Hall.

Polanyi, K. (1997) *La gran transformación. Critica del liberalismo económico*. Madrid: Ediciones de La Piqueta.

Powell, B. (1982) *Contemporary Democracies: Participation, Stability and Violence*. Cambridge, Mass. and London: Harvard University Press.

Reno, W. (1995) *Corruption and State Politics in Sierra Leone*. Cambridge: Cambridge University Press.

Reno, W. (1998) *Warlord Politics and African States*. Boulder, CO and London: Lynne Rienner.

Richards, P. (1996) *Fighting for the Rain Forest: War, Youth and Resources in Sierra Leone*. Portsmouth, NH: Heinemann.

Ross, M. (2002) *Natural Resources and Civil War: An Overview*. Washington, DC: World Bank.

Ross, M. (2004) "How do natural resources influence civil war? Evidence from 13 cases." *International Organization*, Vol. 58, No. 1, pp. 35–67.

Ross, M. (2006) "A closer look at oil, diamonds, and civil war." *Annual Review of Political Science*, Vol. 9, pp. 265–300.

Rothgeb, J. M. Jr. (1990) "Investment dependence and political conflict in Third World countries." *Journal of Peace Research*, Vol. 27, No. 3, pp. 255–272.

Rothschild, J. (1981) *Ethnopolitics: A Conceptual Framework*. New York: Columbia University Press.

Sánchez, G. and Meertens, D. (1983) *Bandoleros, gamonales y campesinos: el caso de la Violencia en Colombia*. Bogotá: El Ancora Editores.
Schock, K. (1996) "A conjunctural model of political conflict." *Journal of Conflict Resolution*, Vol. 40, No. 1, pp. 98–133.
Skinner, E. (1999) "Child soldiers in Africa: a disaster for future families." *International Journal on World Peace*, Vol. 16, pp. 7–22.
Stuart, F. (2005) "Horizontal inequalities: a neglected dimension of development." *UNU-Wider, Wider Perspectives on Global Development*. London: Palgrave.
Tarrow, S. (1994) *Power in Movement: Social Movements, Collective Action and Politics*. Cambridge and New York: Cambridge University Press.
Tilly, C. (1978) *From Mobilization to Revolution*. Reading, MA: Addison-Wesley.
United Nations Office on Drugs and Crime (UNODC) (2006) *Informe Mundial sobre las Drogas 2006*. UNODC: Vienna.
US Department of State (2003) *Trafficking in Persons Report 2003*. Washington, DC: US Department of State.
Vanhanen, T. (2000) "A new dataset for measuring democracy, 1810–1998." *Journal of Peace Research*, Vol. 37, No. 2, pp. 251–265.
Wade, R. H. (2002) "Globalization, Poverty and Income Distribution: Does the Liberal Argument Hold?" LSE Development Studies Institute Working Paper No. 02-33. Draft July, 2002. (http://www.lse.ac.uk/Depts/destin/w_papers.html, accessed July 2007).
Walter, B. F. (1997) "The critical barrier to civil war settlement." *International Organization*, Vol. 51, No. 3, pp. 335–364.
Wittman, D. (1979) "How a war ends: a rational model approach." *The Journal of Conflict Resolution*, Vol. 23, No. 4, pp. 743–763.
Wood, E. (2000) *Forging Democracy From Below: Insurgent Transitions in South Africa and Salvador*. Cambridge and New York: Cambridge University Press.
World Development Indicators (WDI) (2005, 2006) Washington, DC: The World Bank. (http://data.worldbank.org/data-catalog/world-development-indicators).

Part Two

3
Economic Liberalization and Politics in Uganda[1]

Frederick Golooba-Mutebi[2]

INTRODUCTION

At independence in 1962, Uganda had a healthy economy and brighter prospects than most former colonies (Lateef, 1991; Ochieng, 1991), and made positive strides in the economic and social spheres during its first decade as an independent country. Things, however, started to change with the violent seizure of power by General Idi Amin in 1971. From a multi-party democracy at independence, it took the country less than a decade to descend into political violence and, subsequently, economic decline. At the root of the change in fortunes were political exclusion, disregard for constitutionalism, violent change of government, insurgencies, and civil wars.

It all started with the Prime Minister, Milton Obote, supported by a politically partisan military, overthrowing President Edward Mutesa in 1966, abrogating the independence constitution and declaring himself President in 1967. He went on to stifle political competition by banning all political parties save for his Uganda People's Congress (UPC). Obote's disregard for constitutionalism set a precedent that was later followed by his successor, Idi Amin. Obote's narrowing of space for participation in national politics effectively locked out his and UPC's competitors for power, and placed the country firmly on the road to violent changes of government, political instability and, consequently, economic decline.

From the 1971 coup d'état until 1980, the economy declined considerably. During this period, for example, GNP per capita fell at an annual rate of 6.2 percent. While inflation between 1965 and 1973 averaged 5.6 percent, between 1973 and 1980 it rose to 45 percent per annum. Export volumes fell, averaging 9.5 percent per annum. In the social sector, primary school enrolment between 1965 and 1980 declined, and the ratio of population per physician doubled. After he seized power, Idi Amin maintained the ban on political parties, abolished parliament, ruled by decree, and expelled from the country the Asian minority who had hitherto made up the bulk of the country's industrial and business class. The departure of the Asians in 1972 had a negative effect on the country's economy. Agricultural and industrial production declined precipitously as did the whole formal sector and the employment opportunities it had provided (Jamal, 1998; Maxwell, 1998; Collier and Pradhan, 1998).

Idi Amin's intolerance for opposition and his decision to maintain the ban on political competition and close the already narrow space for political competition, led his opponents to resort to insurgency as the only viable means of changing government.[3] A combination of political instability brought about by political repression and insurgency diverted the government's attention and national resources away from development-related activities to those related to security and regime maintenance. The expulsion of the Asian business class—whose skills, industriousness, and business acumen had hitherto contributed greatly to the country's prosperity and advancement—and the subsequent economic mismanagement, contributed to the decline in Uganda's economic fortunes.

After several unsuccessful attempts by Ugandans in political exile to topple Amin's government through insurgency, they eventually succeeded in 1979 with the assistance of the Tanzanian military (Avirgan and Honey, 1982). However, Amin's overthrow brought about only temporary respite, as disagreements among the former exiles about how to move the country forward perpetuated the elite polarization that had hitherto played an important role in fomenting political instability (ibid.). Disagreements about whether or not to hold elections in 1980, right after Amin's deposition, and whether or not to re-introduce multi-party politics only compounded the elite fragmentation and undermined chances for quick stabilization of the country's politics. Amidst sharp disagreements, multi-party elections were held in 1980 and won by the Uganda People's Congress against the background of accusations of fraud by other parties and sections of the public. The UPC's contested victory returned Milton Obote to power nine years after Idi Amin had toppled his first government.

The second Obote administration (Obote II) inherited a virtually collapsed economy, a political environment that was already poisoned by accusations of electoral rigging, and a realistic threat of renewed civil war by losers unwilling to accept the election results. Rather than devote its energies and resources to repairing the country's torn political fabric and rebuilding the economy, the new regime found itself caught up in an insurgency that further poisoned the political environment and polarized the country's political elites. The new administration made an effort to implement, with the support of the World Bank and the IMF, economic reforms and even scored some successes. However, their sustainability was undermined by the civil war and the damage it inflicted on the productive sectors and, consequently, the country's revenue-earning capacity.

ECONOMIC LIBERALIZATION AND POLITICS UNDER OBOTE II

The accession to power by the Obote II government coincided with the beginning of pressure by the Bretton Woods institutions on African governments for economic reform. In Uganda it was therefore the Obote II government which was the first to implement the IMF's earliest economic restructuring programs in Africa. Before we look at the reforms it attempted to carry out in the economic sphere, however, it is important to point out that the 1980 elections which were held after nearly a decade of dictatorship, were not the outcome of the pressure donors were exerting on African governments to adopt multi-party politics alongside economic liberalization. Instead, they were the outcome of acrimonious debate among local political elites about the form of government best suited to the country's circumstances following years of despotism and political turmoil. Rather than usher in a period of peace and stability as would have been expected by war-wary Ugandans and foreign observers, the elections sparked a five-year civil war responsible for the limited success of the IMF-backed economic reform program and which eventually led to the collapse of Obote's second administration.

By 1980, the economic devastation wrought by the Amin regime rendered efforts at economic reconstruction an absolute necessity. As with other countries undergoing economic reform, in Uganda the central objective was to reduce the need for external financial support. In 1981, under the guidance of the IMF, the government embarked on programs of economic stabilization. In what has been characterized as "the first experiments in structural adjustment programs for Third World countries," the donor community insisted "on liberalizing (or floating) the Uganda shilling and a considerable reduction in state expenditure as the price of financial assistance" (Hansen and Twaddle, 1998, p. 2). They sought to "halt the deterioration of the economy, revive production,[4] restore confidence in the Uganda shilling, eliminate price distortions, improve fiscal and monetary discipline, and lay a firm foundation for sustained recovery" (Ochieng, 1991, p. 44).

The economy responded positively, leading to the transformation of GDP growth rates from negatives to positives during 1981–83. In 1982 and 1983, all the sectors experienced positive growth. Only electricity (1982) and agricultural primary processing (1983) did not. However, the economy had negative growth rates during 1983 and 1984. Although in agriculture the area planted and production of all food crops increased between 1980 and 1983, both declined between 1983 and 1985. While for cash crops there was no change in the area planted, production increased between 1980 and 1983, only to decline and register negative growth rates from 1984. The industrial sector also showed signs of revival in capacity utilization, but only temporarily. Only soft drink and cigarette production maintained the revival momentum and were operating at 40 percent and 75 percent capacity respectively by 1985, while other industries operated at less than 20 percent capacity utilization (Ochieng, 1991, p. 46).

Under Obote, the adjustment program had therefore managed to attain only short-term success in reviving the economy. The major cause of the government's failure to sustain its reform success was the damage inflicted by the civil war on the productive sectors and its drain on the government's meager resources. There were, however, other factors not related to the war. According to Hansen and Twaddle (1998, p. 2), the reforms begot a great deal of corruption among ministers and officials seeking to benefit from the black market sale of foreign currency, which discredited Obote's government and increased support for the insurgents. In July 1985, the embattled Obote government fell to a military coup led by the army commander, General Tito Olara Okello. Behind the coup were ethnic divisions that had severely factionalized the military, and its inability to contain the insurgents. The putsch ushered in a short-lived government which, following failure to negotiate peace with the insurgents, was toppled in 1986 by the Museveni-led National Resistance Movement (NRM), the largest and best-organized of the several armed groups that had declared war on the Obote II regime following the 1980 elections.

The failure by the Obote government to sustain the initial successes of its economic reform efforts and to carry out a successful economic reconstruction program was the outcome of the civil war into which it was plunged after the elections. The civil war itself was the consequence of two related phenomena. First was the failure by the country's political elites to reach a consensus about how to move the country forward following the collapse of the Amin regime. Second was the systematic and arrogant manipulation of the pre-election political process and the elections themselves by Obote's allies in the transitional Military Commission government. Also, after the war broke out, the government steadfastly refused to engage the insurgents in talks to try and resolve their differences peacefully, and instead sought to defeat them militarily. Further, as the civil war grew in intensity, the Obote government and its allies took to harassing and eliminating members and supporters of opposition parties—activities that served only to isolate it from major sections of the general public.

Furthermore, the government failed to impose discipline on and create cohesion within the military and the security agencies. Widespread indiscipline culminated in the military and security agencies committing atrocities against civilian populations, especially in areas where the insurgents were active, thereby forcing many civilians to join the armed rebellion.[5] Conflicts within the military, especially between the dominant Acholi and Langi factions, undermined its effectiveness as a fighting force, leading to a failure to defeat the insurgents and eventually to the Acholi-led coup d'état of 1985.[6] Such were the demands on the government's energies, resources, and organizational capacities that made failure in the twin arenas of economic reform and post-war reconstruction inevitable. Indeed, it was in the midst of trying to respond to the exigencies of the civil war and its effects, against the advice of the IMF, that the latter withdrew its support.

It is clear, therefore, that the main factor behind the failure of reform under the Obote II regime was political instability and its underlying sources: elite polarization and the consequent zero-sum politics underlain by the desire on the part of competing political factions, once they acquired power, to monopolize it and hold on to it for as long as possible. As the next section shows, upon seizing power from the Acholi-led military junta that had toppled Milton Obote, the National Resistance Movement embarked on an ambitious agenda to create an elite consensus around the rules of the political game and to end, once and for all, the zero-sum politics of its predecessors. The prevailing international environment also demanded that it embrace the agenda for economic reform championed by the IMF and the World Bank.

ADJUSTMENT PART II: ECONOMIC LIBERALIZATION AND POLITICAL REFORM UNDER THE NRM ADMINISTRATION

Like the Obote II government, the NRM government inherited an economy in shambles and in free fall. By 1986, most of the positive gains of the 1982–83 period had been eroded by the acceleration of the negative trends that had started in 1984. The new government was faced with "low and declining production; shortages of goods, services and foreign exchange; uncontrolled government deficits and excessive monetary expansion; galloping inflation; widespread parallel markets and smuggling; balance of payments problems and high levels of insecurity" (Ochieng, 1991, p. 49). In addition, the NRM administration was as yet to bring the entire country under its complete control, with its authority still contested by remnants of its predecessors' armies in some regions. Amidst all these challenges, the government adopted a skeptical, if not hostile, attitude towards the IMF and its reform programs (Kiyaga-Nsubuga, 1995).

Faced with intractable problems in the economic sphere that had the potential to assume dangerous political dimensions, however, the government was forced to reconsider its attitude. After intense debate within its inner circles, an economic recovery program was eventually agreed upon with the IMF in May 1987, reflecting, for the most part, the IMF's diagnosis and approach.[7] Producers were to be given incentives through increased prices; government deficits and monetary expansion had to be reduced; price controls would be dismantled; flexible exchange rates adopted in place of fixed ones; the shilling devalued; and public enterprises divested (Ochieng, 1991, pp. 50–51).

Whilst the economy continued to experience instability, the program registered some gains: GNP rose by 4.5 percent in 1987; the industrial sector grew by 15 percent; good weather and higher producer prices for cash crops led to an increase in agricultural production of 8.5 percent. The economy as a whole, however, failed to adjust. Inflation shot up at the end of 1987 and remained high at an annual average rate of about 24 percent. Exports fell by 18 percent because of a lower volume of coffee sales due to a fall in prices on the international market and delays in donor assistance. The economy had failed to respond promptly to the domestic consequences of external shocks. Other reasons for poor performance included "an expansionist fiscal and monetary stance, internal and external security threats,[8] poor budgeting, and a weak institutional administrative capacity" (Ochieng, 1991, pp. 56–57).

In March 1988, another stabilization attempt was launched amidst political resistance and skepticism because of the failure of the previous stabilization program. The IMF and World Bank, however, continued to insist on draconian policy measures as a condition for releasing funds. The new reform package consisted of privatization of the state enterprises; downsizing of the civil service; reduction in public expenditure; decentralization; military demobilization; and abolition of commodity marketing boards, which had been conceived by the colonial administration to protect the incomes of small and poor farmers. The economy remained destabilized, but once again progress was made. For example, real GDP per annum grew by 7.2 percent in 1987/88, the highest in sub-Saharan Africa. Other sectors also registered high positive growth rates: industry 25.1 percent; monetary agriculture 8.5 percent; agricultural processing 40 percent, forestry, fishing, and hunting 39.2 percent; manufacture of goods 31.3 percent; miscellaneous manufacture 22.4 percent, construction 19.6 percent, and non-monetary economy 5.2 percent. But serious problems remained. For example, the cost of living index for low- and middle-income groups grew by an annual average rate of 197.6 percent and 189.0 percent respectively in 1988. Total exports continued to decline from US$333.7 million in 1987 to US$272.9 million in 1988, a fall of 18.2 percent. The government reduced spending on all development projects and social services (Mugyenyi, 1991, p. 72; Ochieng, 1991, pp. 58–59). Nonetheless, by this time it was showing commitment to the program, not least because, following its agreement with the IMF and the consequent disbursement of resources by donors, it had realized, as Mugyenyi (p. 71) points out, that the IMF's leverage was not simply related to the money it loaned out, but that it also acted as gatekeeper for all other bilateral and multi-lateral funds (de Torrenté, 2002).

The government's new-found commitment and willingness to embrace liberalization under the stewardship of a one-time self-professed socialist president[9] earned it praise within donor circles and, in due course, a reputation as a showcase of economic success on the African continent. As a result, Uganda received increasingly large amounts of foreign assistance to enable it to implement the reform policies, and with each success registered by the reforms, it acquired more political capital (de Torrenté, 2002).

IMPLEMENTING THE REFORMS

In terms of specificity, accounts of the reforms' implementation process are as scanty for the NRM period as they are for the Obote II regime, and are often at best inconsistent and at worst contradictory. The most consistent and focused analysis, at least for the NRM period, is the examination of the privatization of state enterprises. For the most part, that is the focus of this section.

After it abandoned its initial reluctance to accept the IMF's prescriptions and embraced the economic reform agenda, the NRM government remained grudging in its implementation of aspects of the reform program, such as the divestiture of state enterprises, of which there were 150 when the reform process began in May 1987 (Tangri and Mwenda, 2001). With time, however, divestiture showed itself to possess high potential as a political tool. Just as they had been a source of considerable patronage under its predecessors, state enterprises or their divestiture became a source of patronage for the NRM regime. Mostly as a consequence of weaknesses in its implementation, the divestiture process was suspended twice (in March 1993 and August 1998) by parliament amidst allegations of political favoritism, influence-peddling, lack of transparency, and outright graft. Although broadly successful, the divestiture process became synonymous with lack of transparency and was sullied by impropriety amidst persistently high levels of poverty. Commenting during the late 1990s, for example, the World Bank denounced the process for its lack of transparency, insider dealing, conflict of interest, and corruption (see Mwenda and Tangri, 2005, p. 454).

Nonetheless, donors generally perceived the entire range of reforms as particularly difficult, and consequently gave the government a great deal of latitude in implementing them (de Torrenté, 2002). Demonstrating sophisticated political skills, the government took advantage of this to implement the reforms in a way that allowed it to respect the donors' requests, while taking care of its own interests. Mwenda and Tangri (2005, p. 452) show that state officials exploited their considerable discretionary powers of implementation, access to state resources, weak accountability, and governance mechanisms "to serve their personal interests as well as to enhance the political dominance of the regime." They argue that the cozy relationship that developed between donors and the government ended up reproducing a corruption- and patronage-based government and become a pivotal factor in enabling it to tighten and maintain its grip on power. Despite its shortcomings, however, the divestiture process was completed, albeit unsatisfactorily, leaving the state free of the burden of subsidizing unprofitable enterprises. In addition, nonetheless, the state had lost an important source of political patronage.

It is important at this point to note one significantly stabilizing development following the NRM's seizure of power: with the partial exception of northern Uganda, conflicts—including those surrounding privatization—were now handled politically by parliament, albeit within a semi-autocracy. In addition, they were widely reported by fairly free mass media through which ordinary citizens had an avenue, hitherto unavailable, for participating in national debate and venting their anger and disquiet (Mwesige, 2004). Instead of fighting or rioting against the economic reforms, as was the case in a number of African countries, members of the public in Uganda could vent their anger in newspapers and on radio, and feel that they had been heard, especially since the government was relatively open to criticism. This was important, as divestiture and reform more generally impacted negatively on large sections of the public. Also, the government and president Museveni were still new in power and, in most parts of the country, basking in the enormous popularity and legitimacy bestowed upon them by their status as freedom fighters who had liberated the country from dictatorship.

GROWTH AND DISTRIBUTION OUTCOMES OF THE REFORM

By the time liberalization under the Obote government ended abruptly in 1984, it had produced some positive outcomes, including for small farmers who, thanks to improvement in cash crop prices and after years of retreat into subsistence agriculture, had rejoined the market. As already seen, however, the gains were short-lived and by the time the Museveni-led NRM seized power, the economy had once again virtually collapsed as had been the case following the overthrow of Idi Amin in 1979. Of immediate significance to the ordinary person was the fact that basic consumer goods (e.g., sugar, salt, soap, paraffin) were seriously in short supply and had to be imported from neighboring Kenya. Shortages of consumer goods had led to smuggling and expansion of the informal economy. Inflation was very high and foreign exchange reserves very low (Kiyaga-Nsubuga, 1995).

After realizing the inevitability of embracing and committing to the reforms if it was to secure much-needed external assistance (Mugyenyi, 1991), the NRM regime went on to preside over a high-growth economy with growth rates higher than those of the Tanzanian and Kenyan economies. Economic growth averaged 7.3 percent between 1988 and 1995, dropped to 6.3 percent from 1996 through to 2000, and has hovered at about 5.8 percent since.

Foreign investment also slowed down with time as rising political uncertainty, especially during the period leading up to the February 2006 general elections, unsettled investors (Barkan et al., 2004). Poverty levels have also been on the rise. The proportion of the population living below the poverty line, which had been on the decline through the 1990s, rose from 35 percent in 2000 to 38 percent in 2003 (Government of Uganda, 2004). Progress on the economic front has also been hindered by factors such as rising levels of corruption and the government's apparent lack of political will and commitment to tackling it effectively.[10]

It is also possible that gains in growth and redistribution have been affected by other—intended and unintended—changes brought about by the reforms. Some of the changes in question are those ensuing from policy decisions intended to reduce government expenditure, but which ironically led to higher expenditures. For example, the reduction in civil service employees, which began in 1992, was one such reform. Despite the trimming down of numbers, public service expenditure went up (de Torrenté, 2002; Kiyaga-Nsubuga, 1995). Also, the size of the army was reduced by more than 50 percent under the donor-funded demobilization program, yet military spending shot up from "$44 million in 1991 to $88 million in 1996, over $155 million in 2003, and $196–203 million in 2004" (Mwenda and Tangri, 2005, p. 456).[11]

In the absence of evidence to the contrary, it can be conjectured that the increase in military spending has boosted the government's capacity to deal decisively with violent contestations of its authority. Overall expenditure on public administration, on the other hand, could be explained by the creation, at the urging of the same donors who sought to cut down on public service costs, of specialized executive agencies and commissions, a measure which sought to speed up reform. In addition, costs rose as a consequence of the government hiring a wide array of political functionaries into the civil service from outside the framework of formal recruitment, which had been put on hold by civil service reform. Many of the appointees, such as Resident District Commissioners and presidential advisors and assistants,[12] have been selected on the basis of religious affiliation or ethnic or regional origin and, more recently, loyalty to the National Resistance Movement. They have been instrumental in the dispersal of the spoils of power to different interest groups and, consequently, in securing and maintaining political support for the regime in areas and regions that have traditionally supported rival political groupings and interest groups, such as Pentecostal churches, which in the past had no known political leanings.

Another consequence of liberalization was increase in revenue collection through introduction of new taxes, such as VAT, and improvement in the collection of taxes and duties. A combination of increased revenue generation and donor largesse has, since the 1995 Social Summit in Copenhagen,[13] helped the government channel large amounts of resources into the social sectors. This includes the launching, in 1997 and 2006 respectively, of universal primary and secondary education, both entailing the provision of free education to young people who would otherwise have not had a chance to go to school or advance after primary school. While the details of these programs raise questions about their long-term sustainability, they do not detract from the importance of efforts made in the interest of channeling benefits to the poor who would otherwise have missed out. The increase in social sector spending has taken place within the framework of the Poverty Eradication Action Plan (PEAP), Uganda's version of the PRSP and one of the earliest on the continent. The PEAP itself has benefited from resources accruing to the country from the HIPC initiative of which it was an early beneficiary. Resources saved by the country through debt relief have gone into a Poverty Action Fund (PAP) directed only at activities and programs—health, education, and infrastructure—that have a direct impact on poverty (Hickey, 2003; Brock, 2004).

This, however, is the more recent story. The early phases of structural adjustment and the economic recovery it engendered took place, thanks to its macroeconomic character, amidst low expenditure on social services and inattention to the poorest sections of society. Due to scarcity of empirical data and time constraints, it has not been possible to establish the extent to which low expenditure on social services affected the ordinary person who in the past depended more on personal ingenuity than on public provision.[14] There is, however, a view that adjustment policies heightened the effects of the crisis by increasing food prices, cutting subsidies to the poor, reducing wages, causing retrenchment in civil service employment, and reduction in private-sector employment opportunities (Maxwell, 1998, p. 98). It is to the credit of the NRM government, as we shall see shortly, that, unlike in countries such as Zambia (where, for example, food riots broke out), in Uganda the reforms did not cause public disturbances.

Liberalization and the restrictions it imposed on the state with regard to financing social services did, however, have an unexpected positive, if limited, outcome. It led to an explosion in the voluntary sector as foreign and local NGOs stepped in to fill the gaps left by public service provision (Brock et al., 2004). Over the years, NGOs have played a critical role in service provision (Dicklitch, 1998; Brock et al., 2004). In a sense, also, the explosion in the voluntary sector has widened the community of civil society organizations which have, to different degrees, contributed, albeit only marginally owing to a number of factors, to further democratization of the country's politics (as human rights advocates, etc.). One of the effects of the crisis (or crises) on people's livelihood strategies engendered by economic restructuring was the increase in ruralization of urban centers as people took to diversifying their livelihood strategies, including practicing urban agriculture (Jamal, 1998; Maxwell, 1998).

ECONOMIC LIBERALIZATION AND POLITICS: WHY THE NRM GOVERNMENT SUCCEEDED

Donor pressure on African governments to liberalize their economies came hand in hand with pressure for political liberalization. Donors blamed previous failures in the economic sphere on excessive state intervention, while in the political sphere they were blamed on excessive centralization of decision-making processes and political monopoly that narrowed space for participation in public affairs by rival actors to the elites in power or eliminated it altogether. Consequently, political liberalization envisaged the dispersal of powers, resources, and responsibilities from the center to local governments (decentralization), and the opening up of political space to allow for multi-actor participation in politics and public affairs. This invariably meant the introduction of multi-party politics. Liberalization of the economy and politics were therefore meant to occur in tandem.

POLITICAL LIBERALIZATION IN UGANDA: INTRODUCING NEW RULES OF THE GAME

The National Resistance Movement came to power armed with an ambitious agenda whose twin objectives were the creation of a consensus about the rules of the political game, and the ending of the spoils politics of its predecessors, both of which had produced the political turmoil of the first two decades of independence. The successes it scored in the political sphere led to a prolonged period of peace and stability in most of the country, again with the partial exception of northern Uganda. In addition, they were pivotal in ensuring the successes in economic reform and post-war reconstruction, which earned the regime a large reservoir of approval and political capital within and outside Uganda.

Just as it had started off with a healthy and promising economy at the time of independence, Uganda also began life in 1962 as a multi-party democracy. But democracy was short-lived and lasted only four years. In 1966, the military carried out its first intervention in the country's politics by helping Prime Minister Milton Obote carry out a number of illegal and illegitimate acts. Five years later, he too was deposed in a military coup by the same military that had helped him assume power unconstitutionally. The rise to power by General Idi Amin marked the beginning of a long period of political upheaval, economic decline, and mass political exodus.[15]

After Amin was toppled by the Tanzanian armed forces and Ugandan exiles, there was a brief respite from violence, the outcome of the returnees' efforts to forge a government of national unity.[16] The respite was ended by civil war that broke out immediately after the 1980 elections. The war, launched by several insurgent groups led by veterans of the anti-Amin struggle,[17] eventually became a two-way contest between his government and the best-organized of the insurgent groups, the Museveni-led National Resistance Movement/Army (NRM/A). Within a context of a determined insurgency and generalized political turmoil, Obote's economic stabilization program was from the beginning destined at best to achieve very little and at worst to fail.

Upon seizing power, the National Resistance Movement, whose leadership had been opposed to the re-introduction of multi-party politics in 1980[18] saying it would be too soon after years of autocracy and war, suspended political party activity and opted for no-party politics within a broad-based government bringing together people of different political persuasions and outlooks, including members of political parties whose activities had been suspended. Political parties were not banned, but prohibited from sponsoring candidates for election. Henceforth, candidates vying for political office would contest the elections in their individual capacity, on their individual merit. The intellectual justification for the suspension of political party activity was the claim that pre-industrial societies, such as Uganda's at the time, which have a tendency to fracture along ethnic and religious lines, were unsuited to multi-party politics. Having officially placed multi-party-ism on hold, the government embarked on consolidating the alliances it had sewn together while still a guerrilla movement (Mugyenyi, 1991, p. 61) and on building a wide coalition with other political groups with which it was otherwise destined to compete for power.

There is mileage in the claim that multi-party-ism was put on hold in order to safeguard the country against ethnically-inspired political violence or politically-inspired ethnic conflict. Underneath this seemingly charitable gesture, however, was, it would seem, a clever scheme. Aware of their own inexperience in the affairs of government, the NRM leadership sought to use the absence of political party activity to exploit the talents of more experienced politicians and allow the NRM to build up a support base of its own in preparation for future contests with more established and better-known political groups. Whatever the intention behind it, however, the move, by bringing potential rivals for power together and preventing the early outbreak of destabilizing political arguments and contestations, allowed the government ample time and space to focus its attention on issues of economic reconstruction.

Also contributing to the stabilization of the polity was the decision to write a new constitution for the country. The whole process, which started with the appointment of a constitutional review commission, country-wide public consultations, and finally the election of a constituent assembly to debate the commission's findings and promulgate a new constitution, lasted about six years. In the light of the previous (1967) constitution, which had been approved by members of parliament who had not even read it,[19] this was unprecedented and revolutionary. In 1995, a new constitution based broadly on views contributed by members of the general public, and debated and approved by their elected representatives, came into being.[20] Despite causing sharp disagreement among the political elites who by then were polarizing around the question of whether or not to re-introduce multi-party politics by maintaining the ban on political party activities, the constitution was welcomed by many as reflecting broad consensus about the rules of the game.

Another significant factor in the processes of stabilization was that during the first few years of the NRM government the donor community accepted the argument that political parties were guilty of destabilizing the country and that they should therefore be held in abeyance while the country recovered from its political wounds. Consequently, they allowed the government breathing space to practice its brand of individual merit, broad-based, no-party or movement politics, while pressuring other autocracies, such as Kenya, to open up to multi-party politics.

In addition, in line with the thinking of the donor community, which at the time the NRM came to power was exercised by questions about the best way to promote good governance and improve the effectiveness and efficiency of the state (de Torrenté, 2002), the new government embarked on decentralization. Decentralization had started during the guerrilla war, with the introduction by the NRM of elected councils (resistance councils) through which people in areas occupied by the insurgents exercised responsibility for matters of common interest and collectively played roles and performed functions of direct benefit to the insurgency, such as recruitment of fighters, intelligence gathering, and resource mobilization.[21] After the NRM seized power, these councils were introduced country-wide and came to form the foundation of a new and local administration system. Behind its introduction was the conviction by the NRM's leadership about the necessity to widen participation in decision making. Funded generously by donors, the formal decentralization program for which the government subsequently won accolades started with the passing of the Decentralization Statute in 1993.[22]

Decentralization led to two outcomes with far-reaching implications for political stability. First, it dispersed power from the center, redistributed it to local-level actors, and in the process opened the way for wider participation in decision-making and administration. Secondly, it gradually channeled vast amounts of resources from the center to the local level, and in the process diminished its importance as the arena of competition for resources. In addition, as a result of decision making according to local priorities, service delivery improved considerably with the public better able to monitor policy implementation than when it was the preserve of the central government and its local-level representatives.

Today more than ever, the public generally think of services as a right, not as gifts from the central government. Weaknesses notwithstanding, the degree of positive change is palpable. The assertion by one analyst that Uganda's decentralization program amounts to "a radical re-engineering of the mechanisms of governance in Uganda towards real political, administrative and fiscal devolution of power" (Steffensen et al., 2004, p. 45) is therefore broadly accurate. Among the achievements of decentralization is that it is now legally and institutionally well anchored, supported by a strong legal framework, the basis of a local government system in which different levels of local government possess actual decision-making powers and are generally accountable with a well-defined service delivery mandate. The cumulative effect of the reforms, recent signs of a tendency to re-polarization notwithstanding, has been to contribute to the strengthening and stabilization of the Ugandan state and politics.

To forestall the chances of future polarization and endangering of the gains already made in both the political and economic spheres towards the first presidential elections in 1996, donors started calling for the opening up of political space and leveling of the political field to enable all eligible political and interest groupings to participate equally in politics. By then, the grand coalition crafted by the NRM in the bush in its early days in power, was falling apart with the exit of advocates of multi-party politics who had joined the government in the hope that no-party politics was a temporary arrangement.

THE NRM'S RESPONSE TO PRESSURE TO OPEN UP

In direct contrast to their temporary opposition to IMF prescriptions and eventual capitulation and embrace of economic liberalization after a brief period of flirting with socialism and barter trade, the NRM leadership stood steadfast in their refusal to yield to pressure to re-introduce multi-party politics. As Hansen and Twaddle (1998, p. 8) point out, the politics of the NRM, unlike its economics, were non-negotiable. The NRM's intellectual elites claimed that in the past the country had been plunged into turmoil by attempts to practice multi-party-ism in a society that was not ready for it. These assertions formed the basis of their resistance to pressure to open up to multi-party politics so soon after they had introduced broad-based politics under which people vying for elected office did so on the basis of individual merit, not party affiliation or sponsorship.

Nonetheless, in order to demonstrate that the door had not been closed completely on multi-party politics, a provision was made in the 1995 constitution for referenda to be held every five years to allow people to choose between no-party and party politics.[23] This opening served to re-assure donors that the NRM presided over a gradually, if slowly, evolving political system that might open up to pluralism in due course. In addition, it left the door sufficiently open for its opponents not to conclude, as the NRM itself had done after Obote won the 1980 elections, that violence was the only option they had. This, combined with the NRM government's embrace of economic reform and the lingering fear among donors that the country was still susceptible to instability, explains why they treaded carefully, just in case too much pressure proved disruptive and counter-productive (de Torrenté, 2002). Meanwhile, despite failure to enlist strong donor support for their agitation for pluralism, political parties persisted in their demands for opening up and were occasionally harassed by the police, the military, and security agencies.

Altogether it took 20 years for the government to re-introduce multi-party politics, and it did so only after it became clear that donors were willing to play for high stakes and withhold international assistance if the government continued to resist and ignore their wishes. Indeed, in a speech to the Movement's National Executive Committee in a 2003 meeting to discuss the possible lifting of restrictions on parties, President Museveni cited "intolerable donor pressure" as the main reason he supported it. It was also the reason he was recommending it and the conversion of the "movement" into a political organization, the National Resistance Movement Organisation (NRM-O). It is also true, nonetheless, that domestic pressure for liberalization was mounting and threatening to become a source of destabilization, and in the process ruin the NRM's achievements. The fear of the impact of political destabilization and donor withholding of aid on the country's ability to safeguard the gains of the previous two decades of economic liberalization played a significant role in persuading the NRM to end its political two-decade institutionalized political monopoly.

THE IMPACT OF THE NRM'S REFORMS ON THE LOGIC OF WAR

Political reform in Uganda and the consequent stabilization of the polity for the last two decades has provided a firm foundation for economic liberalization and a peaceful environment in which significant gains could be made. Also, economic and political reform, although for many years the latter did not fit the template of conventional political liberalization based on political parties, have had a significant impact not necessarily on the logic of war, but on the way politics is practiced in Uganda. While they have not prevented war from breaking out, they have brought about changes in the practice of politics in the country.

Mayall (2003, p. 47) points out that the structural adjustment programs (SAPs) had difficulty factoring political stability into their effects and that where the state had failed to take deep roots, rolling it back might threaten to roll it out of existence and open the way to war of all against all—the Hobbesian "state" of being. Food riots that occurred in some countries implementing SAPs, such as Zambia, in reaction to the removal of food subsidies and subsequent rise in food prices, are one indicator of the SAPs' disregard of politics. The divestiture of state enterprises is another. African governments especially have been criticized for maintaining unprofitable and failing state enterprises as sources of political patronage. This is largely true, but focusing merely on the patronage side of things always missed the large picture.

In many cases, the patronage served the important purpose of spreading the spoils of power widely enough to safeguard the political system from destabilization by those who might feel left out. Divestiture therefore deprived governments of instruments for maintenance of stability without replacing them with anything else. In Uganda, however, divestiture was used as a source of patronage to benefit government supporters and bribe potential opponents. While it rendered the old form of political allocation unfeasible in the new liberal environment, it provided the basis for the creation of a new form of political allocation that turned out to be just as useful as the old one. Following its completion, and thanks to the financial support from the donor community, the government was able to create more public service jobs outside of the mainstream civil service. They replaced the traditional sources of patronage, such as the divested state enterprises, in their role as sources of stability maintenance.

Political reform in the form of decentralization, and the introduction of elections and liberalization in the form of the reintroduction of multi-party-ism, have also been influential. Besides being of great administrative value, decentralization produced a number of political dividends for the NRM regime. First, it instantly created a large number of political jobs which have served to oil the patronage machine. From 33 districts in 1986, when the NRM seized power, the number of districts has grown to 88 in 21 years. Also, the expanded local government system has created openings for many people to take up positions of leadership at the local level, right down to the village level. This has brought many people into the decision-making processes, and created a sense of participation and inclusiveness that, after securing legitimacy for the NRM, removed incentives for people to wage war in a bid to seize power, as was the case during the Milton Obote and Idi Amin regimes.

The devolution of financial resources has also been important. Actual financial transfers from the center to the districts have been growing year after year since formal decentralization started in 1993. On the one hand, the availability of large volumes of resources at the local level has simply extended patronage networks from the center to the local levels. On the other hand, however, it has led to an increase in the volume (if not always quality as well) of services delivered to the people. Education and health facilities have been built, infrastructure repaired, and in some cases livelihoods improved. Election to a numerically expanded parliament, even before the return to multi-party-ism, has over the last 20 years guaranteed people jobs and incomes. They, too, are unlikely to want to engage in forms of contestation of state power that might put their careers in jeopardy. This emergence of new political elites with vested interest in the status quo has narrowed the scope for violent conflict and widened space for deliberative forms of contestation.

Commitment to reform by the Uganda government led to the development of a particularly close relationship with members of the donor community who then not only provided more resources to facilitate the implementation of reforms, but also took it upon themselves to try and shield the regime from criticism or even turn a blind eye to some of its excesses (de Torrenté, 2002). Success in Uganda had to be ensured and protected at all cost, and this in a way eventually engendered a situation in which talk of a possible return to all-out war became common especially in the period running up to the amendment of the 1995 constitution to allow for unlimited presidential terms, and to the 2006 elections. However, it is one thing for those in opposition to threaten war and quite another for them to acquire the capacity to wage it successfully.

There are several reasons why war in Uganda has become more difficult to organize and prosecute. After several years of armed conflict, there is general war fatigue in the country, especially in regions in the north, east, west, and Buganda, which have borne the brunt of war in the past. War fatigue is best illustrated by the decision by local youths in Teso in eastern Uganda and in Acholi in the north to take up arms and fight the Lord's Resistance Army when it invaded the region and fought running battles with the Uganda People's Defence Forces (Behrend, 1998). The relative peace and prosperity of the last two decades have also made war unattractive, especially to those who have prospered as a result of the prevailing peace and stability, and don't want to see war jeopardize their achievements. While in recent times Museveni's regime has come to be seen as a dictatorship, there is a general acceptance that it is a benign autocracy, in many ways preferable to its predecessor regimes. This acceptance is captured by the widely used justification for voting for Museveni during elections: "at least we are able to sleep these days." The phrase is used to contrast life under the NRM with life under previous regimes, especially under Obote II, when, as a result of the fear of being attacked and possibly killed in one's house at night by unruly soldiers, people opted to spend sleepless nights hiding in the bushes. The fear of returning to the bad old days makes war unattractive to many who still support Museveni as "the devil we know." Increased reach and capacity of the state to police its territory has also complicated the logistics of planning, training for, and executing a war.

The extent of the state's reach is suggested by the sheer number of security arrangements the government has instituted. The NRM government has made possibly the largest number of defense and security-related appointments in Uganda's history. In addition to a Minister of Defense, there is a Minister of Security, as well as a Presidential Advisor on Security. The military has a chieftaincy of military intelligence in addition to the internal security organization (ISO) and the external security organization (ESO), and a number of shadow (some argue also unconstitutional) paramilitary organizations, all working to ensure peace, stability, and regime maintenance (see Mwenda and Tangri, 2005, pp. 459–460; Rubongoya, 2007). The importance of security to the Museveni regime can be seen in its historically large defense budgets, about which even its allies in the donor community have often expressed unease (de Torrenté, 2002).

The general return to peace in the neighboring countries of Rwanda, Sudan, and the Democratic Republic of Congo has also made war a more difficult prospect today than it was in the past. Rebellions in all these countries have historically had a link to, or a spillover effect on Uganda. Historical links and spillover effects can be simultaneously demonstrated by the successive Uganda governments' support for the Sudan People's Liberation Army (SPLA), and the support by successive Sudanese governments for Ugandan insurgents (Rwehururu, 2002; Behrend, 1998). In the DRC, the weakening of the state by the various wars in that country has made it possible for Ugandan insurgents, sometimes in collaboration with insurgents fighting the Congo government, to train and organize attacks from within its borders.[24]

By virtue of the large volumes in which it has flowed into the country over the last 20 years (thanks to the government's commitment to economic reform and post-war reconstruction), foreign aid has enabled the NRM, through service delivery and various forms of co-optation of numerous political actors, to consolidate its hold on power and strengthen its dominance over potential competitors (Mwenda and Tangri, 2005, p. 453; Rubongoya, 2007). In addition, large amounts of aid have enabled the government, through decentralization and reforms, such as the revamping and strengthening of its law and order function, to establish control over more of the country's territory than its predecessors. Through service delivery and co-optation, the regime has succeeded at legitimizing its hold on power and diminishing threats to its existence. Through enhanced control over the country's territory, it is much more difficult for insurgents to organize and launch successful armed struggle.

Alongside measures aimed at strengthening national security, such as the creation of numerous security agencies, some outside the ambit of the constitution and extending their reach into the countryside, the government has also used resources at its disposal, some accruing from activities linked to economic liberalization, for patronage aimed at preserving peace and stability (Mwenda and Tangri, 2005). A specific form of this kind of patronage has included appointments to ministerial and other positions in government and government-related bodies. Uganda has one of the largest cabinets in the world, adding up to more than 70 ministers and their deputies (some with as many as five). Many appointments are made in the name and interest of regional—in reality ethnic—balancing. Regional and ethnic balancing, and other sectional considerations, also apply to the identification and appointment of the more than 70 presidential advisors, special assistants, and their deputies.[25] Many of these earn ministerial salaries and enjoy related perks. However, only some of them advise, let alone get to meet, the president.[26]

In Uganda, ethnicity counts for a great deal and ethnic groups complain about not being "represented" in government or having too few "representatives" in important positions. Consequently, appointment of their supposed representatives carries great significance and determines which way they apportion their political support. The size of the Uganda parliament has also been increasing over the last 21 years. From the 38-member National Resistance Council, which served as the legislature soon after Museveni seized power in 1986, it grew to 80 by 1989, and before the end of that year, had expanded again to 130 members. The 1996 elections brought in 284 MPs. In 2001, the number grew to 304. The 2006 elections brought in a total of 333 MPs.

As in other spheres, donor largesse has allowed the government to divert its own resources into funding a disproportionately large legislature in which the NRM (through ballot rigging, bribery, intimidation, and other tactics) ensures majority representation for itself. Members of parliament draw large salaries and allowances and, save for the most diehard of the NRM opponents, are happy to support a government (and party) that secures their positions and livelihoods. The sense of gratitude some MPs feel towards the government as a result is evident in the many sycophantic praise statements they make in parliament and in forums attended by Museveni. For example, "Permit me to extend my sincere gratitude to the NRM government and its leaders for having come out of the bush with clear cut policies which favor women."[27]

At face value, extra-territorial military adventures by the Uganda military, such as the incursions deep into the Congo in 1998, bear no relationship to economic liberalization. Deeper scrutiny by analysts (Tangri and Mwenda, 2003), though, points to an important connection: liberalization, as we have seen above, led to a rapid and large increase in foreign assistance to Uganda by donors pleased with its commitment to reform. The large inflows of resources allowed the government to channel increasing amounts of money into the defense budget, which over the last 21 years has been classified and beyond the purview of even the government's own Auditor-General. It is these same resources that have enabled the government to fund counter-insurgency wars in Uganda and in Congo.

With specific reference to Congo, Tangri and Mwenda (2003, pp. 539–540) point out: "By most accounts, the Uganda People's Defence Force (UPDF) advanced into areas of Eastern Congo to profit financially from the plunder of natural resources." Here then lies the crux of the matter: "Corrupt military procurement and economic plunder have benefited key UPDF officers as well as promoted their loyalty to the regime," and turned the army into "a partisan instrument of the NRM government." The NRM's determination to retain support in the military can be best understood by looking back at the relations between the military and Obote's two previous governments (1962–71 and 1980–85). In both instances, Obote was deposed by disgruntled key military officers.

It seems reasonable to argue, therefore, that a regime with a contented officer corps, whatever their source of contentment, stands little risk of contestation of its power by the military. Another important element of all this is that military procurement, even if riddled with corruption, resulted overall in substantial (re) equipment of the UPDF and the boosting of its counter-insurgency capacities. This must have contributed to the defeat of the insurgent groups that have emerged and disappeared, although in some cases, as in that of the Lord's Resistance Army, the UPDF's weaknesses, including corruption, have rendered it unable to measure up to the task of guaranteeing the security of the people of northern Uganda.

This view is amply supported by a committee of inquiry (the Tinyefuza Committee) set up by the Military High Command in June 2003, and chaired by Major-General David Tinyefuza, currently coordinator of security agencies, which inquire into incidences of corruption and indiscipline in the army. During the late 1990s, Major-General Tinyefuza resigned from the army after he accused fellow officers of corruption, for which act the military tried to "discipline" him. To avoid punishment, he requested to retire from the army, but the request was rejected by the Military High Command—a decision widely believed to have been directly influenced by President Museveni. Major-General Tinyefuza then sued the government, arguing that he had a constitutional right to withhold his labor. He won the case and left the army, only to return later and become a member of the regime's current inner circle.

The inability by insurgent groups to sustain war should not, however, be attributed simply to the effects or impact of liberalization, be it of politics or the economy. President Museveni's considerable role in talking and bribing insurgents out of the bush (when it has suited his interests) must be acknowledged. Unlike its predecessors, the NRM government has applied multiple tools to its counter-insurgency strategies, ranging from co-optation, bribery, to outright war. The recognition of the shortcomings of using war as the sole response must account for the number of times insurgencies, active and incipient, have been successfully ended or averted.

An important outcome of liberalization has been the sheer explosion in the numbers of NGOs and other civil society organizations, of which the vast majority are indigenous. From a modest 160 registered in 1986, they had grown in number to 600 in 1990, to 3,500 in 2000, and 4,000 in 2003. In addition, at any one time there have been large numbers of unregistered NGOs and community-based organizations (CBO), some of a transient nature, having been formed to respond to specific situations, including availability of funding for certain activities.[28] The principal reasons behind the rapid growth in their numbers have been the challenges of post-war reconstruction and, more specifically, gaps in service delivery left by the state's inability, due to human and financial resource constraints, to fully fulfill its service delivery functions (Dicklitch, 1998). There are questions about the extent to which NGOs can legitimately claim to reach the poor or influence government policies and actions, and policy outcomes.[29] The questions are inspired by not only the proliferation of "briefcase NGOs" targeting donor funding by pandering to the changing fashions in their policy preferences and funding priorities, but also by restrictive legislation, such as the 2003 NGO bill, which the government uses as an instrument of control.

Nonetheless, despite the restrictions and the tendency by civil society groups to seek to assume an apolitical stance, some, about 6 percent of the total,[30] have been involved in advocacy in various domains: human and minority rights, good governance, and anti-corruption in addition to service delivery. Through advocacy, groups such as the Uganda Debt Network (UDN), Foundation for Human Rights Initiative (FHRI), and the Uganda Debt Coalition (UDC) among others, have contributed to improvement in the quality of governance and policy-making.[31] Earlier on, during the mid 1980s, civil society played an explicit role in the economic recovery program (ERP), which unveiled the government's pro-poor agenda for the first time. Courtesy of the donor community, which has catalyzed their inclusion in policy discussions by encouraging the government to involve them in sector working groups, task forces, and budget conferences, some civil society organizations participate actively in various policy processes.[32] On the whole, however, despite strong donor support, civil society is far from being an effective vehicle for pressuring the state and holding it to account (Dicklitch, 1998). Consequently, during the 20 years when political parties were forced to remain inactive, there were no organized interests to scrutinize or contest the government's policies and actions, making Uganda virtually a one-party state.

INTERNAL CONFLICT: VIOLENT CONTESTATIONS OF STATE AUTHORITY

All post-colonial governments in Uganda have had to deal with violent contestation of their authority. A careful examination of the conflicts and their causes suggests a strong correlation between the type of regime (tyrannical, uncompromising, or accommodative) in power at any one time and the nature of politics (exclusionary, violent, or peaceful) it practiced.

The earliest of these contestations dates back to two years after independence when the kingdom of Buganda[33] asked the central government to vacate its territory and relocate the capital city as a result of anger at what it perceived as the central government's encroachment on its federal rights conferred on it by the independence constitution. The resolution, passed in the Buganda regional parliament (Lukiiko), led to armed reaction by the central government and to scattered acts of armed confrontation between ordinary Baganda[34] and state agents in various parts of the kingdom. Disorganized and uncoordinated, these acts of violence were quickly put down, followed by the abolition of monarchies. At the center of this particular "uprising" and its violent quenching were, on the one hand, questions about the incorporation of a traditionalist, mildly separatist and highly assertive Buganda kingdom into a modernizing, would-be socialist, and centralizing state. On the other hand was the government's preference for using confrontation rather than negotiation to solve political conflicts.

Idi Amin's regime (1971–79) witnessed the most sustained and intense violent contestation of its authority. The brutality of its rise to power and the uncompromising stance it adopted towards its critics and opponents led to the exodus of large numbers of political refugees into the neighboring countries of Kenya and Tanzania, and to Europe and the Americas. Over the eight years of Amin's rule, 23 insurgent and pressure groups were formed by exiles to fight or de-campaign the regime at home and abroad. Although before they were organized and armed by the Tanzanian government, the insurgent groups did not pose much of a threat to the regime, their sustained campaign had galvanized international opinion against it.[35]

After Idi Amin's departure, attempts were made by the newly returned former exiles to put into place institutional arrangements that would, for the first time since independence, introduce a politics of consensus. For a short while it seemed as though the country had been firmly placed on a stable footing, and insurgency as well as violent contestation for power generally effectively ended. However, the fledgling stability lasted only a short while before the country plunged once again into violence after the disputed 1980 general elections. The elections had been planned in an atmosphere of protracted arguments about whether or not it was the right time to re-introduce multi-party politics so soon after the country had been freed from years of dictatorship. Advocates of multi-party politics had won as a result both of their dominance within the Military Commission government, which subsequently prepared the elections, and support from a partisan military. The losing side, which was in favor of broad-based politics bringing together people of different shades of opinion under one political umbrella, therefore went into the polls dissatisfied and disgruntled. The preparation for the elections added to the growing tensions as the Military Commission government was accused by its opponents of planning to rig them in favor of the Uganda People's Congress, whose supporters dominated both the government and the army. Yoweri Museveni, at the time the leader and presidential candidate for the Uganda Patriotic Movement (UPM), which had been hastily formed by people who had opposed the early return to multi-party politics, warned of war if the elections were rigged.

The elections were marred by irregularities and the winning party, the Uganda People's Congress, was accused of fraud. True to his word, Museveni led his supporters into war against the newly-elected government, under the umbrella of the Popular Resistance Army (PRA), later christened the National Resistance Movement (NRM). Other rebel groups also emerged, leading to what, until the emergence of the Lord's Resistance Army in the 1990s, had been the most violent and protracted insurgency in the country's history. Again, the violence can be explained by the insurgents' determination to seize power by force, the government's inability to prevent them from planning and waging war, and its commitment to ending the insurgency by military means. Unlike the anti-Amin insurgencies, which were organized and staged from outside the country, the anti-Obote insurgencies were organized and executed from within its borders, which was the first time such a thing had happened. The state had been rendered so weak by eight years of dictatorship and mismanagement under Idi Amin and by the effects of the war that had toppled him, that the new government lacked the capacity to prevent determined contestation. Indeed, its determination to seize power and its superior organizational skills in comparison to other insurgent groups eventually enabled the NRM to seize power and embark on the reforms we examined earlier on.

As with its predecessors, the NRM government had to contend with violent contestation of its authority right from the beginning. A number of insurgent groups, consisting of supporters and members of its predecessor regimes, particularly that of Milton Obote, sprang up as soon as it installed itself in power. Other groups had emerged as a reaction to the new government troops' misconduct towards civilians while on mop-up operations against elements of the defeated army. Also, still seeking to re-take power were groups of former soldiers and supporters of the defunct Amin regime, who since his departure had waged war on all subsequent governments.[36] While some of the insurgents were based across Uganda's borders in Sudan, Kenya, and the then Zaïre, others attempted to organize, recruit, and wage war from inside the country. Invariably, like all insurgencies before them, they claimed to be fighting for democracy and freedom, although in reality each had its own agenda and not entirely democratic ideologies that it sought to impose. At least three of the groups (the Holy Spirit Movement, the Lord's Resistance Army, and Allied Democratic Forces) sought to set up theocratic regimes.

Unlike its predecessors, in dealing with insurgency, the NRM government adopted a two-pronged strategy: negotiation involving co-optation and bribery, and violent confrontation. Only one of them, the Holy Spirit Movement, was defeated militarily, while another, the Allied Democratic Forces, have reportedly been severely weakened. The Lord's Resistance Army, currently engaged in talks with the government thanks to pressure from a war-weary Government of South Sudan eager to devote its energies to post-war reconstruction, has survived repeated military assaults. Other insurgencies have ended through negotiations as a result of which their leaders have been rewarded financially and with government or military appointments, and their rank-and-file fighters were either absorbed into the Uganda People's Defence Forces or assisted to resettle in their areas of origin with retirement benefits.

Economic liberalization has played an important role in all this by making available to the government large amounts of financial resources, including from foreign aid, that have enabled it to buy off insurgents and to maintain large defense budgets. This in turn allowed it to build up a numerically strong army and also provide it with equipment for use against insurgent groups. At the same time, for over two decades political liberalization, notwithstanding the government's reluctance to open up to multi-party politics, has kept the political terrain sufficiently open, which has allowed a broad range of interest groups and actors to participate in the affairs of the state. In the past, zero-sum politics and political monopoly by small groups of elites have been the major causes of political violence, when those seeking power have had to fight for it. In contrast, after they seized power, the leaders of the National Resistance Movement decided to share it with their rivals and potential competitors within the framework of an inclusive, broad-based government set up on the basis of widely-agreed rules of the game. This, more than any other factor, has prevented the growth of potentially destabilizing discontent, and accounts for the 20 years of relative peace and stability, and failure by insurgents to win popular support not only across the country, but also in their areas of operation.

CONCLUSIONS

At 1962 independence Uganda had great potential. That potential, though, remained largely unexploited for nearly a quarter of a century thereafter, as the country swung from one violent political upheaval to the next, with different groups of elites struggling for power, and, once they got it, seeking to retain it while excluding and sometimes physically eliminating or seeking to eliminate their rivals and competitors. It all started with the first independence government led by the prime minister (later President) Milton Obote who, after unilaterally abolishing monarchies, abrogating the independence constitution, and banning political parties, sought to use military force and exclusion to remain in power. Obote's actions led to growing instability that eventually culminated in his deposition by General Idi Amin.

Whilst in the beginning the Amin government rallied significant and politically disparate elites around it in what seemed like a departure from Obote's politics of exclusion and persecution of perceived enemies, it soon deepened the elite disunity that had facilitated and precipitated Obote's downfall. Within a short time, those wishing to play a role in the country's politics outside of the parameters set by his government had to flee the country to save their lives. Having fled to safety, the exiles set about planning the next violent change of government. Amin's intolerance of dissent and opposition had convinced them that war provided them with the highest chances of taking over power. The exiles, encouraged and emboldened by the support they received from anti-Amin governments and porous borders, set about conducting insurgent activities inside Uganda. Although until 1979, when the Tanzanian government intervened directly and contributed soldiers and other resources to support the war that toppled Amin, these activities had had no significant immediate effect on his government, they diverted its attention and resources from other spheres of governance to the military and security. In addition they led to intensified misrule as the regime sought to neutralize its enemies, real and perceived.

Unfortunately, and in keeping with what had by then become something of a pattern, the formerly exiled elites who assumed power after Amin seemed not to have learnt any lessons from either Obote's or Amin's regimes. Within a short time of assuming power, the new governing elite took to fighting over control of the state. The unity that the Tanzanian government had helped them forge under the auspices of the umbrella Uganda National Liberation Front (UNLF) soon gave way to factional fighting and short-lived governments. It had been hoped that the 1980 elections, the first ones in nearly two decades, would open a new chapter of political stability and democratic rule. Instead, they led to a civil war which, fought mostly in some of the country's most agriculturally productive areas, wreaked havoc on the very foundations of the economy. While before this the economy had suffered more from mismanagement and neglect due to acute political instability, the 1980s civil war targeted the economy as one way of accelerating the collapse of the government.

The war also eventually brought to power a government determined to re-orient the country's politics from its zero-sum and cut-throat nature towards more inclusiveness and consensus building around the basic rules of the political game and political discourse. It is this new approach which, more than anything else, has helped stabilize Uganda's otherwise volatile politics. Economic liberalization has obviously helped, not least by availing resources—including vastly increased aid flows—that have enabled the state to discharge its security and service delivery functions, build a reasonably robust military and security apparatus, and buy peace by paying off its rivals and opponents. However, without a measure of political stability right from the start, founded on an elite consensus, albeit a fragile one, that the NRM government helped to build, this would not have been possible.

NOTES

1. I thank Francisco Gutiérrez Sanin and the entire team on the Economic Liberalization and War project for their useful comments, critiques, and suggestions, and the Crisis States Programme at the London School of Economics and Political Science, University of London, for funding and facilitating some of the research that has informed the preparation of this chapter.
2. Frederick Golooba-Mutebi is a Senior Research Fellow at the Makerere Institute of Social Research, Makerere University, and an Honorary Senior Researcher, MRC/University Rural Public Health and Health Transitions Research

Unit (Agincourt), School of Public Health, University of the Witwatersrand Johannesburg.
3. See, for example, A. Ruzindana, "When freedom fighters become fascists." Interview by Michael Mubangizi, *The Weekly Observer*, January 3–9, 2008.
4. In agriculture this envisaged the recapture of the peasantry who had retreated into pure subsistence production, but who would be attracted back to the market by the process of being able to earn a profit for their produce.
5. It was, for example, the harassment and murder of members of the Rwandese Tutsi refugee community on the grounds that they were supporters of the NRM that drove thousands of them into the ranks of the guerrilla movement's armed wing, the National Resistance Army (Omara-Otunnu, 2000; Prunier, 1997).
6. For a full story of the Obote II years, see Kiyaga-Nsubuga (1995).
7. For a detailed account of the government's initially negative attitude and evolution of the situation towards accommodation with the IMF and the World Bank, and a change in approach by the rest of the donor community, see Mugyenyi (1991).
8. These consisted of insurgencies based within the country itself and cross-border attacks by those operating and receiving support from neighboring Kenya and Sudan.
9. See Museveni (1992).
10. The government's failure to effectively deal with corruption is often attributed to its senior officials' and leaders' (as well as supporters in the army and other government departments) involvement in corrupt activities.
11. In 2003/04, defense expenditure amounted to 23 percent of public administration expenditure and 20–23 percent of total government expenditure.
12. Altogether there are more than a hundred of these, some with undefined or ill-defined duties and responsibilities.
13. The summit saw the introduction of the 20:20 principle, whereby donors would allocate 20 percent of all their aid to health and education in return for the recipient government also allocating 20 percent of its budget to the same social sectors. The donors had recognized the needs of the poorest people who benefited least from structural adjustment (Hansen and Twaddle, 1998, p. 9).
14. See, for example, Whyte (1991).
15. For a detailed examination of this period see, for example, Kyemba (1977), Mutibwa (1992), and Karugire (1988).
16. See Avirgan and Honey (1982).
17. During his eight-year rule, 23 exile groups were formed (in Kenya, Tanzania, Zambia, Europe and the Americas) to fight Amin's government (Avirgan and Honey, 1982).
18. Avirgan and Honey (1982).
19. After they had approved the 1967 republican constitution, the MPs were told to pick up their copies from their pigeon holes, which explains why it came to be known as "the pigeon-hole constitution."
20. For a detailed account of the constitution-making process see, for example, Odoki (2005).
21. For an early study of the role and functioning of resistance councils, see Tidemand (1995).
22. The legislation has been revised twice (in 1997 and 2006) to correct weaknesses and further strengthen the system.

23. Two referenda were held, in 2000 and 2005. Controversially, the former led to the retention of no-party politics while the latter endorsed its re-introduction (Bratton and Lambright, 2001; Golooba-Mutebi, 2007).
24. See, for example, "Uganda, DR Congo to force Kony out of Garamba Park." *The New Vision*, Monday January 7, 2008.
25. See, for example, F. Golooba-Mutebi, "Redundant Ministers and Political Patronage." *Sunday Monitor*, October 21–27, 2007.
26. Personal communication from a former government functionary (Resident District Commissioner) and member of NRM (December 2006).
27. Tamale (1999, p. 80).
28. See De Coninck (2004); Wallace et al. (2007).
29. See, for example, Golooba-Mutebi (2007).
30. Wallace et al. (2007, p. 79).
31. De Coninck (2004, p. 60).
32. Brock (2004).
33. The most influential of four ethnically distinct kingdoms within Uganda, containing the country's seat of government.
34. The people of Buganda.
35. See Avirgan and Honey (1982).
36. For a full account of insurgencies the NRM government has had to confront, see Amaza (1998).

REFERENCES

Amaza, O. O. (1998) *Museveni's Long March from Guerrilla to Statesman*. Kampala: Fountain Publishers.

Avirgan, T. and Honey, H. (1982) *War in Uganda: The Legacy of Idi Amin*. London: Zed Press.

Barkan, J. et al. (2004) "The Political Economy of Uganda: The Art of Managing a Donor-Financed Neo-patrimonial State." Background paper commissioned by the World Bank in fulfillment of purchase order 7614742.

Behrend, H. (1998) "The Holy Spirit Movement's new world: discourse and development in the north of Uganda." In *Developing Uganda*, eds. H. B. Hansen and M. Twaddle. Kampala: Fountain Publishers.

Bratton, M. and Lambright, G. (2001) "Uganda's referendum 2000: the silent boycott." *African Affairs*, Vol. 100, pp. 429–452.

Brock, K. (2004) "Ugandan civil society in the policy process: challenging orthodox narratives." In *Knowledge, Actors and Spaces in Poverty Reduction in Uganda and Nigeria*, eds. K. Brock, R. McGee, and J. Gaventa. Kampala: Fountain Publishers.

Collier, P. and Pradhan, S. (1998) "Economic aspects of the transition from civil war." In *Developing Uganda*, eds. H. B. Hansen and M. Twaddle. Kampala: Fountain Publishers.

De Coninck, J. (2004) "The state, civil society and development policy in Uganda: where are we coming from?" In *Knowledge, Actors and Spaces in Poverty Reduction in Uganda and Nigeria*, eds. K. Brock, R. McGee, and J. Gaventa. Kampala: Fountain Publishers.

De Torrenté, N. (2002) "Pragmatism as principle? The donors and 'no party democracy' in Uganda." In *Transformations in Uganda*, eds. N. K. B. Musisi and C. P. Dodge. Kampala: Makerere Institute of Social Research, and New York: Cuny Center.

Dicklitch, S. (1998) *The Elusive Promise of NGOs in Africa: Lessons from Uganda*. Basingstoke: Macmillan Press.

Golooba-Mutebi, F. (2007) "Uganda in 2005: Political, Economic and Social Trends." In *L'Afrique Orientale: Annuaire 2005*, eds. H. Charton and C. Médard. Paris: L'Harmattan.

Government of Uganda (2004) "Poverty Eradication Action Plan." Ministry of Finance, Planning and Economic Development.

Hansen, H. B. and Twaddle, M. (eds.) (1998) *Developing Uganda*. Kampala: Fountain Publishers.

Hickey, S. (2003) "The Politics of Staying Poor in Uganda." CPRC Working Paper 37. Manchester: Chronic Poverty Research Centre.

Jamal, V. (1998) "Changing poverty patterns in Uganda". In *Developing Uganda*, eds. H. B. Hansen and M. Twaddle. Kampala: Fountain Publishers.

Karugire, S. R. (1988) *Roots of Instability in Uganda*. Kampala: Fountain Publishers.

Kiyaga-Nsubuga, J. (1995) "Political Instability and the Struggle for Control in Uganda, 1970–1990." PhD dissertation, University of Toronto, Canada.

Kyemba, H. (1977) *A State of Blood: For Five Years a Top Cabinet Minister in Amin's Uganda*. London: Paddington Press.

Lateef, K. S. (1991) "Structural adjustment in Uganda: the initial experience." In *Developing Uganda*, eds. H. B. Hansen and M. Twaddle. Kampala: Fountain Publishers.

Maxwell, D.G. (1998) "Urban agriculture: unplanned responses to the economic crisis." In *Developing Uganda*, eds. H. B. Hansen and M. Twaddle. Kampala: Fountain Publishers.

Mayall, J. (2005) "The colonial legacy." In *Making States Work: State Failure and the Crisis of Governance*, eds. S. Chesterman, M. Ignatieff, and R. Thakur. Tokyo: United Nations Univerty Press.

Mugyenyi, J. B. (1991) "IMF conditionality and structural adjustment under the National Resistance Movement." In *Developing Uganda*, eds. H. B. Hansen and M. Twaddle. Kampala: Fountain Publishers.

Museveni, Y. K. (1992) *What is Africa's Problem?* Kampala: NRM Publications.

Mwenda A. and Tangri, R. (2005) "Patronage politics, donor reforms, and regime consolidation in Uganda," *African Affairs*, Vol. 104, No. 416, pp. 449–467.

Mutibwa, P. (1992) *Uganda Since Independence: A Story of Unfulfilled Hopes*. London: Hurst and Co. Publishers.

Mwesige, P. (2004) "'Can You Hear Me Now?' Political Talk Shows and Participation in Uganda." Unpublished PhD dissertation, Indiana University, June.

Ochieng, E. O. (1991) "Economic adjustment programmes in Uganda, 1985–8." In *Developing Uganda*, eds. H. B. Hansen and M. Twaddle. Kampala: Fountain Publishers.

Odoki, B. J. (2005) *The Search for a National Consensus: The Making of the Uganda Constitution*. Kampala: Fountain Publishers.

Omara-Otunnu, O. (2000) "An historical analysis of the invasion by the Rwanda Patriotic Army (RPA)." In *The Rwanda Crisis from Uganda to Zaire: The Path of a Genocide*, eds. H. Adelman and A. Suhrke. New Brunswick, NJ: Transaction Publishers.

Prunier, G. (1997) *The Rwanda Crisis: History of a Genocide*. London: Hurst & Co.

Rwehururu, B. (2002) *Cross to the Gun: Idi Amin and the Fall of the Uganda Army.* Kampala: Monitor Publications.

Rubongoya, J. B. (2007) *Regime Hegemony in Museveni's Uganda: Pax Musevenica.* New York & Basingstoke: Palgrave Macmillan.

Steffenson, J., P. Tidemand, and E. Ssewankambo (2004) "A Comparative Analysis of Decentralisation in Kenya, Tanzania and Uganda: Country Study." Nordic Consulting Group.

Tamale, S. (1999) *When Hens Begin to Crow: Gender and Parliamentary Politics in Uganda.* Kampala: Fountain Publishers.

Tangri, R. and Mwenda, A. (2001) "Corruption and cronyism in Uganda's privatization in the 1990s." *African Affairs*, Vol. 100, No. 398, pp. 117–133.

Tangri, R. and Mwenda, A. (2003) "Military corruption and Ugandan politics since the late 1990s." *Review of African Political Economy*, No. 98, pp. 539–552.

Tidemand, P. (1995) "The Resistance Councils in Uganda: A Study of Rural Politics and Popular Democracy in Africa." PhD dissertation: Roskilde University, Denmark.

Wallace, T. et al. (2007) *The Aid Chain: Coercion and Commitment in Development NGOs.* Kampala: Fountain Publishers.

Whyte, S. R. (1991) "Medicines and Self-Help: The Privatisation of Health Care in Eastern Uganda." In *Developing Uganda*, eds. H. B. Hansen and M. Twaddle. Kampala: Fountain Publishers.

4
Côte d'Ivoire: The Political Economy of a Citizenship Crisis

Richard Banégas, Alain Toh, and Yao Kouman Adingra[1]

INTRODUCTION

With a population of nearly 20 million people, one-third of whom are immigrants, and plentiful agricultural (coffee, cocoa) and natural (oil[2]) resources, Côte d'Ivoire has always been considered the "economic lung" of West Africa—its economy accounts for nearly 40 percent of the GDP of the countries that are members of the Economic and Monetary Union of West Africa (UEMOA). It has also been the "showcase" of the French–African relations that had been forged well before the country's independence on the basis of a close collaboration between the French elites and Felix Houphouët-Boigny, the then Minister of the Fourth Republic. Long regarded as an island of peace and stability in West Africa, Côte d'Ivoire entered in the late 1990s into a cycle of violence marked by the proliferation of coups d'état, rebellion movements, and the radicalization of political debates around the Ivorian identity and citizenship issues. On September 19, 2002, the country tumbled into a conflict that split the territory between north and south, separated by a front line under the surveillance of UN, international, and French forces. For five and a half years, until the signing of the Political Agreement of Ouagadougou in March 2007, the Ivorian society lived in an unstable "neither war nor peace" situation, which has been the source of much turmoil.

In the southern region of the country controlled by government forces, this situation has given rise to both a powerful nationalist movement of Young Patriots and a myriad militias in the service of the regime of Laurent Gbagbo, who, to make up for his lack of legitimacy, engaged in anti-colonialist rhetoric, blaming France for the country's hardships and presenting the conflict as a war for national liberation. Taking advantage of the business sector liberalization reforms promised before its arrival in power, the regime has managed to consolidate its position by formally and fully implementing a cash economy (including the coffee–cocoa sector) and by diversifying its resources as the state and society quickly became increasingly criminalized. In the northern regions, the uprising of the New Forces (FN),[3] led by Guillaume Soro (appointed as Prime Minister after the signing of the Ouagadougou Peace Agreement), has gradually become organized and institutionalized, with the establishment of a state army, a territorial administration, and a two-tier military and political headquarters based in Bouaké. A war economy has also been organized under the leadership of the rebel chiefs, around the exploitation of mineral (diamonds) and agricultural resources (cocoa and, primarily, cotton grown mainly in the north), and the predatory collection of taxes on all commercial activities.

How is it then that Houphouët-Boigny's country, known for its stability and tolerance, descended into a spiral of war and regional conflicts that were thought to be confined to the Mano River country? How can we explain the way violence, in just a few years, became the main resource for political fights and what links can we find between this violence and the forced liberalization process that the country went through in the 1990s? How should we interpret the emergence of rebel movements and, at the same time, the trajectory of the Laurent Gbagbo regime? As a spillover effect from the neighboring conflicts in Liberia and Sierra Leone, as some argue?[4] Some of the things that have happened in western regions could suggest that the regionalization of war has been achieved at the expense of the state, which, facing "ethnic leagues" and transnational rebellion movements recruiting mercenaries throughout the subregion,[5] was unable to control its borders. Following the now classic claim of association between "war economies" and "failed states," other observers believe that the protagonists' quest for profit and greed are at the heart of the Ivorian conflict: "the stakes in Ivorian politics are largely economic, although the debate is predominantly phrased in ethno-nationalist terms"; "much of the rhetoric of division and ethno-nationalist hatred on both sides of the conflict is highly theatrical and a cover for illicit economic gain" (ICG, 2004). Others still, many of whom are in the government or the ultranationalist Patriotic Youth, feel that Côte d'Ivoire is facing a neocolonial economic war covertly waged by France and the French multinational firms involved in the Ivorian cash economy. In this view, the conflict was intended to restore or maintain the economic hegemony of French firms in the face of increasing international interest in African resources (new scramble for Africa).[6]

Although these various interpretations, both etic and emic, do not stand up to a factual observation, they do make us question the relationships that may exist between, on the one hand, the forced liberalization of the Ivorian economy (and in particular the agro-export sectors) and the transformations of a cash economy-based developmental model; and, on the other hand, the crisis of the political regulatory system and the spread of violence in the context of the criminalization and militarization of the economy. We will see as well that the reasons for the conflict lie in the historical formation of a plantation-based economy that has deeply shaped political identities, demographic relationships, territorial inequalities, and political regulatory systems.

Our first argument is that the violence that spread throughout the country since the late 1990s (coup d'état in December 1999), more specifically since the emergence of the armed rebellion in September 2002, may be seen as the result of the political exhaustion of a regulatory system based on a political economy driven by extraversion and institutionalized clientelism and hinged on the famous "Caistab," the Agricultural Commodities Stabilization Fund. What happened is that the foundations of this "postcolonial compromise"[7] collapsed under the impact of the economic crisis, the liberalization of sectors undergoing structural adjustment, and the rise of the new generations (in the civil and military sectors) which, after the death of Houphouët-Boigny in December 1993, competed to succeed him.

Contrary to the views mentioned above, which tend to see rebellions and nationalist mobilizations as an epiphenomenon of the competition for the country's resources, we argue that this is a highly political conflict. It is a crisis of citizenship that deals primarily with the principles of nationalism and sovereignty, and aims to settle the seemingly simple questions, "Who is Ivorian and who is not?" "What is the nation?" and "Who is a part of it?" Thus, this conflict is plainly over the rights—political, economic, land-related, educational, cultural, and marital—that come with having documents establishing one's identity. Two different conceptions of citizenship clash with each other: the first refers to open citizenship and the second to citizenship based on a political ideology of autochthony, implying exclusion. In other words, the

CÔTE D'IVOIRE: POLITICAL ECONOMY OF A CITIZENSHIP CRISIS   129

conflict is about a "war of identification," which has a long-standing colonial and postcolonial history. Our hypothesis (the first section of this chapter) is that this conflict, which revolves around issues of sovereignty and access to citizenship, also indicates difficulties renewing the social and political contract in the context of a swiftly moving economic and political liberalization.[8] In our opinion, the conflict over rights reflects a dual process: (i) the erosion of the political pacts that permitted the assimilation of certain categories of the population into the political economy of the "planter state," and (ii) the leveling of the representations of otherness that developed as part of the colonial and postcolonial extraversion of a cash economy.

But, beyond this etiological analysis of the crisis, this chapter aims to put to the test a second type of correlation focused on the situation of conflict itself, namely, the possible link between: (1) economic neoliberalism (particularly the privatization of agro-export sectors); (2) the rise of violence and war economies (both in the north and the south of the country); and, lastly, (3) the changing governance patterns. Based on a close look at the situation prevailing in the rebel-held areas as well as in the government-held areas,[9] we put forward several complementary hypotheses, which are expanded upon in the second and third sections of this chapter:

1. The forced and accelerated liberalization of various sectors, and the privatization of entire economic and social sectors, have contributed to the implementation of a power-based economy in the south and the development of a war economy in the north, reproducing, paradoxically, the predatory instruments of the old "planter state."
2. Patronage and clientelist regulation have not disappeared with liberalization, but, rather, have become more diverse, complex, and privatized, contributing to fragmentation as well as to an increased spreading of supervisory power fostering opacity and predation. In other words, our hypothesis here is that the spread of violence goes hand in hand with the spread and/or privatization of patronage functions.
3. These neoliberal reforms and the war have contributed to the criminalization and militarization of a large part of the state and the economy, leading to the exacerbation of conflicts over land, but also to the privatization of violence and the "militarization" of the social and political space. In the south, this phenomenon translates into the "para-militarization" of the regime, which

resembles a "militia state"; in the north, it results into the spread of the predatory violence of the New Forces.

THE SOURCE OF POLITICAL VIOLENCE: THE CRISIS OF THE CASH ECONOMY AND THE EROSION OF THE PLANTER STATE'S REGULATORY TOOLS

As indicated above, what is at stake today in the Ivorian crisis is the very foundations of the state, as it developed during colonialization and under the long reign of Felix Houphouët-Boigny. The situation nowadays could be largely explained by the erosion or regulatory mechanisms that are under increasingly violent attacks and by the socio-political compromises made by the father of independence. These reached a crisis point in the 1980s and 1990s, and the pivotal issue of how citizenship can be exercised came back to the forefront, more acute than ever.

Houphouëtism: the Political Economy of a "Planter State"

The trajectory of Houphouët-Boigny's country has been the subject matter of a large number of analyses that have, sometimes, turned into academic and political controversies between, for example, dependentist neo-Marxist[10] interpretations, liberal approaches[11] and the "Ivorian developmental model." We won't go over these debates here. For our purposes, it is enough to say that the Houphouëtist system was a form of state capitalism, the regulation of which was based on the structure of the plantation-based economy.[12]

But what was the Houphouëtist political economy? Choosing to stay in the French fold, thus going against the anti-colonial and pro-pan African schism encouraged by his neighbors N'Krumah and Sekou Touré, Houphouët-Boigny built the prosperity of his country on its natural resources, in particular on coffee and on cocoa, of which Côte d'Ivoire quickly became the world's leading producer. We should point out that these extraversion resources were not limited to the global bean market: they also included the massive exploitation of foreign labor and strong international alliances with the Western world in general, and France in particular (through French businesses, army, as well as technical assistants posted in all key positions within the administration). Let us also point out that the Ivorian developmental model, inherited from the colonial value-added model of development, has always had as its background a fully recognized and declared economic liberalism. The state, nevertheless, did play a central role in this agro-export model that could be described as state-centered liberalism, or state capitalism. Houphouët-Boigny was emphatically anticommunist, despite having been at the outset of his career at the head of a party (the RDA) affiliated to the French Communist Party, clearly supported the market economy (and the Western camp), even though many countries on the continent hesitated between several options and tested the socialist developmental model. The liberal model would never be challenged in Côte d'Ivoire, despite the economic setbacks that gripped the country starting in the late 1970s. When Laurent Gbagbo, who had socialist sympathies and a Marxist background, became head of state, in October 2000, this ideology did not change—quite the opposite, as we shall see later on. In fact, in the long history of Ivorian state-centered liberalism, the most important fiasco has been the imposition, from 1981 onwards, of structural adjustment plans (SAPs), which have deeply shaken the social pacts and political regulatory systems of the extraversion-based economy.

In this cash economy, the Houphouët-Boigny administration played a prominent role at all levels of production and marketing, including the organization of production systems; the control of cooperative groups; the provision of inputs; the structuring of marketing channels; as well as in price setting and stabilization. The institutional control (as described by Bruno Losch) of the agro-export sectors by the state apparatus was total. At the core of this economic and political plan was a full range of stabilization mechanisms dating back to the colonial period—1954 to be precise, a time when the first ancestor of the famous stabilization fund was first established. From the mid 1950s onwards, according to Losch, "we witnessed […] a constant strengthening of state control that has led to an instrumentalization of the stabilization plan. This plan would become the central tool for levies and redistribution within a centralized, discretionary, and clientelist management system" (1997, p. 213).

The stabilization system originating from colonial times was changing very quickly from a financial tool meant to regulate prices to a tool geared towards regulating all aspects of the market. The Caistab (fund to support and stabilize agricultural products' prices, the CSSPPA, which became known as Caistab in 1966) became the central instrument in this Plan. The competences of the Caistab, a state corporation, would gradually expand beyond stabilizing prices to deal with the organization of domestic (hiring of professionals, definition of domestic prices, charging of transport costs) and international (export control, shipping licenses, sales policy, etc.) marketing. In 1968, a coffee–cocoa export quota system was implemented, further strengthening both administrative control over the sector, and the Caistab's influence. The fund became the very heart of the Houphouëtist clientelist regulatory system:

- Through the schedules and the organization of the centralized distribution of the market value between economic agents and social categories, with the guarantee of a remuneration fixed *ex ante* per kilo [...];
- Through export controls and the organization of a levy by Caistab, corresponding to the difference between the scale [price] and the price of futures contracts. This levy would yield plentiful resources [...] that went primarily into the special state investment budget (BSIE), although substantial amounts were left behind, with no clear allocation (total lack of transparency of Caistab's accounts);
- Through agreements and quotas, with the possibility of distributing benefits on a clientelist basis by assigning rights to non-professionals,

giving birth to the highly sensitive category of "political quotataires," trusted accomplices of the authorities, who could sell their "rights" to other exporters (Losch, 1994, p. 214).

In short, the purpose of implementing the plan to control the production and marketing of farming products was first and foremost the political stabilization of the regime. Beyond the personal euergetism of the head of state who routinely handed potential opponents suitcases full of banknotes, it is this rather subtle clientelist system of capture and redistribution of rent that has allowed the party in power to establish sound social foundations as well as alliances in many layers of society.

The state established alliances with planters who, for a long time, were shielded from market fluctuations and supported by the state through favors giving access to land (to protected forests, in particular). This contributed to the emergence and consolidation of a new "planter bourgeoisie," often members of the state cabinet (and also, it should also be stressed, members of the Baoulé ethnic group—the group the President belonged to), to the point where one could talk of "senior civil servants capitalism" (Losch, 2003, p. 60).

Alliances, and compromises, were also arranged with foreign firms involved in this corrupt system—if these firms were willing to hire Ivorians, they were granted a number of advantages, often of a fiscal nature. Losch (2003, p. 48) noted that power could play with export quotas to support a given player in the field. The liberalization that took place in the 1990s significantly altered the situation in this area by upsetting the cocoa oligopolies system.

This double commitment on which the planter state was based was finally balanced by alliances and related arrangements with three other important groups: immigrant labor; the intermediary elites in the rural regions in the south (who had been promised upward social mobility through education and paid employment in the civil service or in the private sector); and the urban petty bourgeoisie, often from the civil service, who enjoyed the benefits of the cash economy in the form of various advantages (housing, grants, subsidies, for example).

These subtle rent capture-redistribution mechanisms worked therefore as an institutionalized and centralized clientelism system, and permeated a large part of Ivorian society. In short, if the stability of Côte d'Ivoire had been preserved for such a long time under Houphouët-Boigny's dictatorship, it is, first and foremost, because of the regulatory mechanisms and political–economic commitments arising out of what Bayart (1989) called the "passive post-colonial revolution."

Nevertheless, we must emphasize two facts that would come to play an important part. First, this mechanism was not only clientelist. Because of the resources generated by this system, it worked in conjunction with large-scale public redistributive policies, in such fields as education, health, or land-use planning. It was mainly due to this clientelist game that a semblance of territorial balance was maintained. But even if this system was redistributive, it was also highly unequal and largely based on the exploitation of the wealth produced by farmers and on their exclusion from the political rent management arena.

Such is, in a sense, the paradox of the Houphouëtist "planter state": The central role of the coffee–cocoa sector and the various related alliances went hand in hand with the increasing exclusion of planters from the management system of the plantation-based economy. While independence had been achieved through the mass action of their union,[13] the planters were then prevented from organizing themselves into co-operatives or trade union structures that could influence decision-making mechanisms. Losch points out that this exclusion resulted—over a 30-year period—in the hoarding of 50 to 70 percent of the world price of coffee and cocoa through the support of the coffee and cocoa sectors and of the state. Concretely, he writes, such an "expropriation" could only, in fact, happen under the cover of a political discourse designed to maintain the myth of the planters' preeminence—as epitomized by the President, Côte d'Ivoire's top planter—and to justify the way the nation and its leader annually conferred distinctions to the best farmers. The cohesion of the system was reinforced by subservient media and by the direct dialogue that was encouraged between the president and the vast planters' community, which had an opportunity to show its "affection" to the "father of the nation" when hearings were granted to them, reinforcing the idea of a sacred pact between the state, embodied by the "old man," and his peasantry (Losch, 1997, p. 222). As we shall see below, the economic crisis, the falling prices, and the structural adjustment wrecked this "sacred pact," gradually eroding the foundations of this state clientelism. It will then have to be determined if the liberalization reforms implemented in these sectors at the turn of the year 2000, and the promise made by Laurent Gbagbo to "return power to the farmers," did change this situation of exclusion. We will see that, unfortunately, they did not.

Houphouëtism was more, however, than an extraversion-driven political economy. It was also a fine concoction of social relationships based on what Francis Akindès (2004) has called the "peanut roaster philosophy." For the hegemony of the clan in power to continue and be—more or less—accepted by the groups that were excluded from it, it had to be accompanied by subtle co-optation, redistribution, and enrichment mechanisms that, at the national level, ensured geopolitical balance and, at the individual level, let everyone hope they could succeed at the game. This "philosophy" encompassed a set of culturally constructed and accepted practices and representations (an ethos, a moral economy, or a governmentality, one could also say, in reference to the "belly politics" Bayart (1989) talked about), that legitimized the predatory redistribution mechanisms mentioned above. Under Houphouët-Boigny, the state's political patronage, clientelism, and patrimonialism were not shameful and hidden practices. Quite to the contrary, they were legitimized and encouraged, as illustrated by the famous proverb: "we do not look into the mouth of him who roasts the peanuts." In other words, the diversion of a part of the production is not only accepted, but also legitimate from a moral point of view. "To be clear," Akindès explains, "it is the legitimization of prevarication, of primitive accumulation, with one specificity in Côte d'Ivoire: the purpose, for President F. Houphouët-Boigny, was to create, through this mean, a state bourgeoisie" (2004, p. 13). The declared objective, as pointed out in this quotation, was to create, by illegal enrichment if necessary, a national bourgeoisie capable of transforming itself into classes of investors and local entrepreneurs interested in offsetting the foreign interests, French in particular, who controlled the Ivorian economy.

In hindsight, one could say that this silent watchword, echoing Guizot's ("Enrich yourselves!"), has in part succeeded because the state bourgeoisie did truly emerge in the wake of the planter state.[14] It first emerged in the 1970s, assumed more and more important positions in both the administration and the economy, with a constant connection to the ruling party. Postcolonial Côte d'Ivoire thus saw the constitution, in the midst of the patrimonial state and cash economy, of a real business bourgeoisie, and a social class of elected officials personally indebted to the prince for his favors and recognizable for their conspicuous consumption and a great contempt for those excluded from the system. After the death of Houphouët-Boigny, his successor, Henri Konan Bédié, took this logic of enrichment and ostentation to the end, publicly celebrating with champagne each new billion of CFA francs accumulated. Today, in the context of what has been called the Refoundation, in which the new elites have seized power, the economic–political "tontine" practiced by the peanut roaster, far from ending, amplified and sped up, as though the new leaders, aware of the fragility of their position, were trying to hoard as much as possible and as quickly as possible.

The Political–Economic Pacts on the Immigration Issue

Finally, we must mention one last structuring principle of Houphouëtism, still at the heart of the Ivorian crisis today: the admittance of immigrants. Again, a great continuity between the colonial and postcolonial situations is apparent. The history of migrations to Côte d'Ivoire has, indeed, been inextricably linked to that of imperial "development" and the construction of a plantation economy, renewed and strengthened by the Houphouët-Boigny government. As shown above, this "developmental" policy and its postcolonial substitutes, which had led to the famous "Ivorian miracle," were made possible by the massive use of a foreign workforce, mostly originating from the neighboring Sahel countries. From the 1920s, colonization has encouraged large population movements into Côte d'Ivoire. To provide major infrastructure projects with a strong workforce and to meet the labor needs of European farms, the government implemented a special recruitment policy to access the "reservoirs of labor" in the neighboring Sahel colonies. By the early 1930s, in the forest areas in the west, villages of agricultural workers from Upper Volta, the future Burkina Faso, started to sprout up. This immigration would happen under duress until 1946, when immigration flows seemed to ease up as a result of the abolition of forced labor. The difference in development between the Côte d'Ivoire colony and neighboring areas continued to attract large numbers of seasonal and permanent workers. From the 1950s onwards, with the creation in 1951 of SIAMO (Syndicat interprofessionnel d'acheminement de la main d'oeuvre, an inter-professional union to channel the workforce), designed to streamline recruitment, voluntary immigration intensified and became institutionalized. Migrants were not only from Upper Volta and French Sudan. Côte d'Ivoire attracted people from all over French West Africa, many from Senegal, Togo, and Dahomey, primarily in urban areas, in commercial activities, and in government jobs. Their stays in Côte d'Ivoire gradually grew longer and they eventually started settling land. The phenomenon had already started during colonization but was encouraged by the Ivorian authorities perpetuating the French West African exploitative practices.

The famous Houphouët-Boigny motto, "Land belongs to who tills it," would in fact exacerbate the above phenomenon and result in major changes in the economic, demographic, and political balance of the country. In the 1970s, the years of the famous Ivorian miracle, immigrants already accounted for nearly a quarter of the country's total population (the last census of 1998 established the rate of immigrants at 26 percent, but according to estimates, it is closer to 30 percent). Their presence is mostly visible in the urban fabric, with the creation of many exclusive neighborhoods or encampments hardly permeable to other groups (here, too, the colonial legacy is undeniable). In fact, contrary to the common and rather ironical idea that Côte d'Ivoire is a good host country, it should be pointed out that the reality of inter-community relations has been tense. Rather than being a melting pot, in Côte d'Ivoire's cities communities lived side by side and shared work, each group occupying an "ecological niche," to quote Dembelé. "In this human system, there is no real social fusion, no assimilation, but, instead, a subtle cosmopolitism of ethnic groups which, if integrated to the maximum, would look like a strong social and spatial emulsion. [...] In this new social and spatial arrangement, men cross paths but do not mingle" (Dembelé, 2002, pp. 140–141). In addition to this spatial division, the communities were also divided along economic lines, a fact we should keep in mind in trying to understand the stakes in this conflict. Because of Houphouët-Boigny's commitment to a strongly extraversion-driven state capitalism, the issues of the economic integration of "foreigners" and of citizenship (in the socio-political, not legal, definition of the term) had become confused. It is probably in the area of land ownership that this problematic is at its strongest. The story is fairly well known. The pace of migration picked up and stays lengthened, and migrants who had come as farm hands became planters themselves. More and more of them started to own land, instead of the "traditional" native land holders. They entered legal–political agreements and social arrangements (especially the famous "mentoring" institution) finding them more or less to their advantage. The "Peasant State" (as Chauveau, 2000 has called it) played a major arbitration role. Conflicts between native people and foreigners were certainly not absent, but they were regulated by a whole set of social institutions and intermediation structures which, eventually, entered into a crisis.

Similarly, in urban areas, the economic and social integration of foreigners was fairly easily achieved through a social division of work, which could be roughly summarized by the following formula: Ivorians of Ivorian descent (a common way of describing southern populations) took over salaried jobs in the civil service and major public enterprises or para-state enterprises; foreigners and people from the northern regions (including Dioulas), took over petty trade, transportation, and all small informal jobs. This social division of labor flowed from the colonial development policy that rested, as we have said, on a division of roles between native people and foreigners. This division also went hand in hand with a moral economy and a vision of success where salaried work and school diplomas were highly valued. This conception of upward social mobility, organized around the central figure of the civil servant, was particularly vivid among people from the country's southern and central regions who—we should remember—had been the first to become integrated into the colonial state. We should also point out that, today, the willingness to settle the colonial legacy is accompanied by a questioning of these models of upward social mobility and these old representations of success and achievement.[15] Many of the Young Patriots we interviewed questioned the civil servant social model associated with the colonial legacy and the Houphouëtist state, and its counterpoint, the appreciation of private enterprise and individual initiative as the key to empowerment and self-realization.

This economic integration—urban and rural—of immigrant populations also went with a political pact that was at the heart of the Houphouëtist governance. This is to say, an informal understanding was reached between, on the one hand, a regime practicing liberalism with regards to immigration and land issues and, on the other, the immigrants who, in return for the freedom they were granted in their activities on the territory, had to support the government in power. This tacit compromise, agreed upon with the foreigners, was an example of the "principle of triumphant alien-ness," identified by Dozon (1997). To simplify, we can say that in Côte d'Ivoire foreigners enjoyed a form of "economic citizenship": anyone working in Côte d'Ivoire and participating in the development of the country was regarded as Ivorian. Interestingly, Houphouët-Boigny, in 1966, had wanted to legally extend this arrangement by granting dual citizenship to nationals of countries of the Entente Council (Dahomey, Togo, Upper Volta, and Niger), but Parliament refused. Lacking the authority to include this arrangement in the country's legislation, the president, who wanted "pan-Africanism in one country," decided to grant "rights" to his foreign allies under the authority of small informal clientelist agreements. These political arrangements were reinforced with Côte d'Ivoire's opening to a multi-party system in 1990 and, above all, the approaching presidential election of 1995. To ensure support against an increased partisan competition and growing social protest, the PDCI (Côte d'Ivoire Democratic Party) distributed with great largesse identity cards to foreign nationals. This aroused strong reactions from the opposition, which denounced the scandalous use of "electoral livestock." Since then, the FPI (Côte d'Ivoire People's Front), Laurent Gbagbo's party, has repeatedly called for a clarification of the civil status and the identification process (i.e., the issuance of identification documents) to break out of the informality of the Houphouëtist governance (including his successor) and to rebuild the state and help Côte d'Ivoire become a modern nation. Much of the current conflict therefore finds its origin in these practices, which flowed, not only from a political need but also from a historical trajectory based on extraversion rents.

The End of the Colonial Pact and the Ethno-Nationalist Affirmation of Ivority

This model of integration of foreigners hobbled along until the late 1970s when, under the influence of various factors, it would enter into a crisis. With arable land becoming scarce and increasing pressure on the land, with declining agricultural prices and a pioneer exploitation system in crisis, with a fiscal crisis and diminishing public resources to lubricate the system, with the bankruptcy of an upward social mobility model based on education and rural exodus, and, finally and most importantly, with the structural adjustment measures and the implementation of sector privatization policies, the foundations of this model of integration were undermined and the workings of the political–client regulatory system, that had been implemented since before independence, seized up. In the late 1980s, the foundations of this system collapsed because of the impact of economic liberalization, the affirmation of the new generations (civil and military), and the political ambitions of the Houphouëtism heirs. In 1990, under popular pressure, particularly the FPI and the Fesci (Student and School Federation of Ivory Coast, the main student union) calling for democracy, Houphouët-Boigny had to accept a multi-party system. But the crisis was not resolved. Quite to the contrary: the process of democratization, granted "from above," did not ease the tensions that had been building throughout the 1990s. The economic and political liberalization of the Houphouëtist system had paved the way for increasingly violent protests against the ruling order based on a plantation economy and its concessions to the immigrant workforce.

Indeed, the political crisis was accompanied by a progressive questioning of one of the structuring principles of the "Ivorian miracle"—the admittance of foreigners—and a radicalization of debates around immigration and autochthony. This process was already at work in the years 1970–80, in fact, pushing the government to initiate an "Ivorization" policy with regards to the recruitment of civil service cadres. But it was mostly under the regime of President Henri Konan Bédié (December 1993–December 1999) that tensions worsened as, with the elections in mind, he opened up the Pandora's Box of Ivority. After Houphouët-Boigny's death in December 1993, as president of the National Assembly and, therefore, constitutional successor of the head of state, Bédié came to power. Having been Finance Minister, well versed in the arcane workings of the party and of the administration, a Baoulé like Houphouët-Boigny, and a native of the Dimbokro region, Bédié, however, did not have the same charisma as his illustrious predecessor. He came to power after a brief but intense war of succession between heirs, moderated by France. Alassane Ouattara, whom Houphouët-Boigny had appointed Prime Minister in 1990 to save the country from economic decline, was also in the running. Pushed aside by the ruling party in 1993–94, he founded his own party, the Assembly of Republicans (Rassemblement des républicains), and sided with Laurent Gbagbo's FPI party to form an opposition front to boycott the 1995 presidential elections. After these were thwarted, H. Konan Bédié, head of the PDCI, retained power, but with minimal legitimacy.

It is in this tense transition context that "Ivority" claimed its central position in the political discourse. The notion of Ivority, of which there were already signs in the early 1970s, was conceptualized by a few PDCI intellectuals who designed a restrictive and ethno-nationalistic definition of citizenship. According to a founding text published in 1996, "the Ivorian people must first assert their sovereignty, their authority vis-à-vis the messages of dispossession and subjugation, be it immigration or the economic and political power" (CURDIPHE, 1996, p. 21). "Ivority appeared as a system [...] whose coherence supposes closure. Closure and control of our borders [...]. The identification of the self naturally supposes the differentiation of the other and demarcation propounds, whether we like it or not, discrimination" (ibid., p. 40). "To build a 'We,' we must to make a distinction with a 'Them'" (ibid., p. 26). Under the "white mantle of Ivority" (to quote Bédié), a xenophobic approach to social relationships was taking hold. On a more subtle level, behind the concept of "Ivority," the PDCI ideologues were outlining a "Baoulity" or an "Akanity," marginalizing not only foreigners but also all other groups—and northerners in particular—who did not belong in the "ethno-cultural" space in the center and the southeast, regions which, since the late 1950s, had built its hegemony country-wide. In hindsight, we can say that the twin processes of economic and political liberalization have resulted in a strong polarization of the population over the issue of rights in Côte d'Ivoire.

This ethno-nationalistic radicalization by the Bédié regime caused great tension in the country, as a large portion of the population (from the neighboring countries or simply from the northern and western regions of Côte d'Ivoire) felt increasingly marginalized and even threatened. The adoption in 1998 of the nationalist Rural Land

Code (which excluded non-Ivorians from land ownership) further fed suspicions and conflicts multiplied in the countryside, as those who considered themselves "natives" used these provisions to chase "foreigners" out of their land. This constituted a major fracture in the founding principles of Houphouëtian liberalism ("Land belongs to who tills it"), and it led to outbreaks of inter-community violence. This was the case in late 1998 in Tabou, near San Pedro, where pogroms were launched against Burkina Fasans who had settled in the region decades earlier. Indeed, the "popular success" of the Ivority issue must be understood not just in terms of the political race for the presidency (A. Ouattara). The main reason why this issue took such a dimension is that it fed on the employment crisis in urban areas as well as on a "crisis of rurality,"[16] which, for a long time already, had been giving rise to many land conflicts between "natives" and "foreigners." The Ivority issue became a social language for advocacy and for expressing the frustration of those who had been left behind by the "Ivorian miracle" based on the liberalism of the plantation economy. When they returned to their village, after failing to find jobs in the cities, as promised by the model of upward social mobility, and found out that there was no more land available because their parents had sold it for almost nothing to the Mossi, young school dropouts took the autochthony registry by storm to claim their rights. Today, organized in rural militias, they are the first to invoke "tradition" (sometimes against their own elders) to contest foreigners' land ownership rights. Similarly, in urban areas, structural adjustment has left on the street hundreds of thousands of Ivorians from the south who had in the past put their faith in salaried work, congruent with the upward social mobility system mentioned above. When they turned to small jobs in the informal sector to earn a living, they ran into the monopoly of Dioula and foreign small shop owners who long occupied these economic niches.[17] It will be easily understood, here again, how easy it was for the Ivority ideology to spread through these social groups. A classic response, in such situations, is the identification of a scapegoat—the immigrant—against the backdrop of economic impoverishment and a multifaceted social crisis.

But there is obviously more to the situation than that. This issue should also be considered in the continuum of the formation of the state and agrarian capitalism. The issue of Ivority, and its ethno-nationalist versions, is rooted in the history of Côte d'Ivoire's political economy. Indeed, the issue of the relationships between natives and foreigners has been a constant topic in the Ivorian political debate since the 1930s and has led, on many occasions, to xenophobic violence against immigrants (in particular, in 1958, against Dahomeyans). But this issue had never been as politicized before, targeting not only foreigners in the strict sense of the term, but also many Ivorian citizens whose geographic origin, ancestry, religion, or name (notably those with a "northern" consonance) made them "second class citizens" of "dubious nationality." Against this background of hardening positions regarding otherness, northern nationals, mostly Muslims, would be more and more systematically seen as "foreigners" and stigmatized by southern citizens who, persuaded by a skillful politicization of the notion of Ivority, saw themselves as the "true Ivorians." These are the tensions and stigmatizations of Ivority that led to the coup d'état by General Gueï in December 1999 and, in September 2002, to the rebellion of the New Forces who took control of the whole northern region of the country, while the regime of Laurent Gbagbo retained its control over the southern regions.

REBELLION OF THE NEW FORCES IN THE NORTH: DISSEMINATION OF VIOLENCE, LOOTING ECONOMY, AND STATE MIMETISM

In the second and third sections of this chapter, we will try to see how, on both sides of the front line, the relationship between three interlocking dynamics took shape: (i) the war economy; (ii) political violence; and (iii) governance systems that were deeply affected by the first two variables. Our hypothesis is that the liberalization–privatization processes in various sectors combined with the war context have contributed to the taxing of the economy both in the north and in the south, and to the paradoxical replication of former predatory mechanisms of the "planter state." We shall show that rather than disappearing, rent capture functions and clientelist regulations became more complex and privatized within the framework of a more comprehensive process of fragmentation and dispersal of power (both in rebel-held and in government-held areas). In the north, a proto-rebel state was established with mechanisms to control the war economy, in an effort to centralize resources. We will quickly review "war economy" hypotheses, showing that the involvement of fighters in the rebellion cannot be explained solely by utilitarian arguments. In the south, we will see that the state started a multifaceted policy to mobilize resources which, paradoxically, was facilitated by the neoliberal privatization reforms. We will argue that these reforms and the context of conflict have contributed to a three-fold process of criminalization of the economy, privatization of violence, and informalization of the state, a process which is akin to the consolidation of a "militia state."

Centrifugal and Centripetal Dynamics of a War Economy

Let's first look at the transformations at work in the northern regions under FN control. Who were the rebels that tried to seize power during the night of September 19, 2002 and, having failed, withdrew into Bouaké, the second city in the country? The first group to speak up in the aftermath of the attack was the MPCI (Patriotic Movement of Côte d'Ivoire), which demanded guaranties regarding citizenship and the departure of Laurent Gbagbo. First led by junior military spokespersons, the MPCI then saw the rise in its midst of a political wing led by Guillaume Soro (a former student leader of the Fesci), as well as of senior officers who had defected from the loyalist army. Many of these rebel leaders shared a common military and political past; some had played a particularly active role in the 1999 coup d'état. During the 2000 military transition, they had headed various armed factions—for example, the Red Brigades, Cosa Nostra—and had experienced repression and exile. When General Gueï picked up the Ivority torch, some of these northerners, Ouattara sympathizers, felt betrayed, then threatened. Later on, hunted down by the government of Laurent Gbagbo, who had been the victim of a new coup attempt, they fled to neighboring countries: Ghana, Liberia, Mali, and mainly Burkina Faso, where they were rather well received. It was there, in the suburbs of Ouagadougou, that the rebellion was organized under the leadership of Cosa Nostra headed by Staff Sergeant Ibrahim Coulibaly, known as "IB." This movement clearly had the support of Burkina Faso authorities—already involved in conflicts in Liberia and Sierra Leone—who provided rebels with meaningful political and logistical support. In late November 2002, two other rebel movements emerged in the west: the MPIGO (Popular Movement of the Great West, or Mouvement Populaire du Grand Ouest) and the MJP (Movement for Justice and Peace, or Mouvement pour la Justice et la Paix)—two distinct rebellion movements made up of Yacoubas who were former Gueï supporters and of militiamen recruited in surrounding countries, particularly Liberia and Sierra Leone. In reality, these two rebellion movements originated in the MPCI, that was trying to circumvent the October 17 ceasefire signed in Bouaké. The three movements came together elsewhere under a new name—the New Forces (FN)—at the time of the negotiations held under the aegis of France, at Marcoussis and Paris (Kleber summit), in January–February 2003.

In the field, the FN became organized and institutionalized, and a real army was organized as well as a territorial administration, and a military and political headquarters based in Bouaké. Gradually, after the start of the rebellion in 2002, the apparatus of military conquest transformed into a proto-rebel state,[18] replacing the structures of the central state whose staff had fled or had been driven out of the region. Dealing first with military and security issues, to cope with the anarchic multitude of fiefdoms run by uncontrollable warlords, the general secretariat of the FN split up its territory into ten military command areas, placed under the authority of an area commander, the "Area Com," directly appointed by headquarters. This command and administration system was based on subdivisions of urban and rural space into "operational commands" and "outposts." The "rebel state" is thus first and foremost a military administration of the land. It is seconded by a political administration, headed by the general secretariat (SG) and in particular by the SG's "civilian cabinet," largely made up of former Rassemblement des Républicains (RDR) and Fesci militants. Gendarmerie, police, and custom schools were also created along the lines of what existed previously. Media (radio, TV, Internet sites) were set up by the rebels, and new banking structures emerged (People's Savings and Credit Fund in Côte d'Ivoire, or Caisse d'épargne populaire et de crédit en Côte d'Ivoire). But despite these structuring efforts, the FN remained a fragile coalition of local cliques led by warlords who did not always obey the movement's formal leaders and controlled their men through looting prebends. The organization of the rebel state remained more theoretical than real in many parts of the northern regions, where its actual operational capabilities rely on personal influence and the logic of fiefdoms controlled by strong men—local warlords turned "Area Com," who have almost all the power and are not very accountable to Bouaké.

The proto-FN state also armed itself with important instruments for controlling economic activities, within what can be regarded as its Ministry of Economy and Finance, the famous "Economic Head Office," set up in Bouaké under the direct authority of the SG. Having quickly understood that it would take them time to win the war, rebels in the north had to secure resources to meet the movement's funding needs. The MPCI therefore encouraged the establishment of a parallel economy by opening the borders with hinterland countries and setting up a taxation system that amounted to institutionalized racketeering. The splitting of the country in two resulted in the development of informal trade flows with neighboring countries (Mali, Burkina Faso, Guinea, and Ghana). This strategy was a reaction to the policies of the authorities in Abidjan, aimed at isolating occupied zones by preventing them from getting supplies, starting with commodities.

The institutionalization of the war economy happened in several stages. During the first months of conflict, nothing was really structured: rebels had their own resources (still of unknown origin, as we write) and let their fighters manage their areas to their own advantage. The general secretariat in Bouaké made an effort to centralize its operations with the creation of a Directorate for Resource Mobilization (Direction de la mobilisation des ressources, DIRMOB) and a Center for Unification of Mining and Agricultural Resources (Centre d'unification des ressources minières et agricoles, CURMA). The purpose of these structures was to centralize and manage mobilized resources to meet the movement's needs and those of the populations left onsite after the outbreak of the conflict. In September 2003, these bodies were replaced by La Centrale, which would become truly functional a few months later, in March 2004.

Under the direct control of the Secretary General of the New Forces, Guillaume Soro, assisted by the National Secretary for Economic Affairs, La Centrale became the main "regulatory" body of the war economy in rebel areas. It was initially made up of three structures: the Department of Agriculture and Forestry; the Department of Trans-border Resources, responsible for monitoring trade with neighboring countries; and, the Department of Oil and Mineral resources (in charge, among other things, of the exploitation of diamonds, an important resource of the rebels' war economy). In November 2006, La Centrale was split into five major departments, reflecting the rebel state's economic ambitions and the way it mimicked the central government: DGPB (General Directorate for Budget Planning, or Direction générale de la planification budgétaire); the DFFPM (Direction of Paramilitary Forces, or Direction des forces paramilitaires); DGI (General Tax Office, or Direction générale des impôts); DCCA (Central Directorate for Army Commissions of Rehabilitation, or Direction centrale des commissions de la réhabilitation des armées); and, IGA (Inspectorate General of the Armed Forces, or Inspection générale des armées). Alongside these, bodies and sub-branches in charge of specific areas were also established, such as the monitoring committee of the cotton sector resolutions (Comité de suivi des résolutions de la filière coton). Finally, in response to the closure of banking branches after September 2002, the New Forces established a substitute financial structure, the Credit du Nord, which was only in place for two years due to mismanagement.

La Centrale has branches in the ten areas under the control of the New Forces, and its agents are deployed at checkpoints on the outskirts of cities and country borders. Each area is administered by a commissioner and his deputy, assisted by "tax agents" stationed at the entrances and exits of each urban area under control of the New Forces. These "tax agents" are the equivalent of town hall collection agents. The administrators are trusted men in the inner circles of Guillaume Soro, Secretary General of the FN, and often have been politically active with him within the Fesci. Their tax collection activities are governed by a taxation scale codified by La Centrale. All activities are taxed by the rebel state,[19] which collects large amounts of money especially in the so-called "safe corridors." The resources mobilized by tax agents are expected to be repaid to the commissioner responsible for authorizing expenditures in the area to pay for, for example, the military allocations (5,000 CFA francs per month per soldier), the food needs of the population, and wages earned by the local New Forces administration staff. In addition to mobilizing resources to finance the rebellion, La Centrale was also intended to maintain the flow of economic activity in the occupied areas, operating under the same principles as the former Caistab. For example, it became involved in food quotas to prevent artificial shortages in areas under FN control. The tax system implemented was, to a large extent, a replication of the fiscal and para-fiscal devices used to structure sectors in the days of the Caistab.

All of this shows the rebel forces' political willingness to institutionalize and centralize economic resources in the areas under its control. Sector liberalization and privatization—particularly in the cotton sector—encouraged the takeover of economic sectors by enhancing management ambiguity, increasing cooperative and umbrella structures, and rebuilding the capital and oligopolies structures. But, behind this parallel institutional device and its objectives, a real underground economy evolved, based on the exploitation of forest resources in the west, and of gold and diamond resources in the south. A plundering economy, combined with a "checkpoint economy," has grown to a considerable size over time. The signing of the Ouagadougou Agreement in March 2007 should have been accompanied by a restoration of the free movement of persons and property, as state authority was restored throughout the territory. But the Agreement has not substantially changed the rebel war economy. On the contrary, as we found in our research, racketeering is still highly pervasive or has even increased in some areas. The decline in the number of checkpoints did not have a significant impact on the road duties incurred by carriers and their passengers. For example, a Bouaké visitor taking the Yamoussoukro–Bouaké highway may welcome the disappearance of the Djébonoua checkpoint, as it saves him the 300 CFA francs fee required at the "identity papers control post." But this decrease in fees is only an illusion. That's because the traveler who used to pay between 600 and 900 CFA francs at the southern corridor,[20] will now be ordered to pay between 900 and 1,200 CFA francs. This 300 CFA francs increase is designed to make up for lost earnings due to the dismantling of the Djébonoua checkpoint. The same thing happens on most routes and it amounts to the implementation of a strategy to consolidate the red tape inflicted on travelers in the north, after the Ouagadougou Agreement. As one Bouaké carrier stated:

> When we say that people have removed the checkpoints, we are wrong. It is a policy. In any case, on those roads on which politicians travel a lot, some checkpoints have been removed. And when politicians come to the area, they automatically think that there are no more checkpoints. They just pretend, because they want to show that there is peace since the Ouagadougou Agreement, even though the checkpoints are still there in other places.[21]

"Greed vs. Grievance": a Socio-political Rereading of the Engagement of Rebel Fighters

The conflict which began in September 2002 undeniably contributed to the structuring of a rebel war economy with conflicting characteristics: it is at the same time centralized and decentralized; territorialized (as it is ruled in each territory, by the local "Area Com") and de-territorialized (because it is pegged to the economy of globalized trade and financial investments in the international real property markets); and it is subject to centrifugal and centripetal dynamics that we feel are symptomatic of a war economy at the core of the new neoliberal order.

Should we therefore conclude, in accordance with the now classic theories of the "war economy,"[22] that these are the variables ("greed, not claims") that control the conflict and the eventual way out of the crisis? Research work recently conducted by Moussa Fofana (2008),[23] on what drives the engagement of individual FN combatants, lead us to put in perspective this line of reasoning and to avoid this overly economistic view of the war mobilization process (and, ultimately, the demobilization process). Fofana shows, first, that the recruitment of New Forces troops was not very difficult. There was, at the onset of the conflict, a rather massive and spontaneous movement of young northerners seeking to be enlisted. Most fighters interviewed joined voluntarily, often following in the footsteps of people they knew, in a contagion effect, or through a "big brother." Informal "teapot" gatherings ("grins"[24]), seem to have played a significant role in the recruitment of young Malinké fighters—the grin being a social institution characteristic of the cultural Mandingo space. We can also notice that the grin solidarity was reconstituted in the ranks of the rebellion and in military camps. The contagion effect, Fofana believes, was important: "Friends belonging to the same grin enlisted almost all in the same period and most often wanted to be stationed in the same camp or under the command of the same leader" (2008, p. 42). He also notes that family and community structures have played a significant role in individual decisions:

> In several stories, recruitment candidates were preceded within the rebellion by his brothers, his "big brothers," his friends. Those often seem to play the role of a scout, or facilitator of their integration into the armed forces. They were often close relatives—father or uncle, for example. So it is almost natural for the decision to join the rebellion to become a subject of interest at the family level. Also, the decision to recruit potential combatants was often made following a family discussion. At the same time, there was throughout the village or the neighborhood an exalted speech extolling enrolment. It was as if enlisting was necessary to assert individual commitment to the efforts of the community under attack. It is no exaggeration to say that families whose member chose not to enlist (for whatever reasons), risked a sort of social quarantine. [...] In most cases [...] those interviewed who chose to enlist would ask for the approval of family members. The father, uncles, and other male figures of the extended family take part in the decision-making. Opposition on the part of the family group sometimes led to a decision not to enroll. When a fighter enrolls without telling his parents, he often finds a mediation

mechanism, once mobilized, to get his family's approval. (Fofana, 2008, p. 42)

It even seems that the structure of polygamous families, the most common family type among the Malinké and Senufo in the south, had an influence on youth engagement, as each one of the wives pushes her son to enlist to prove to everybody that her son is, indeed, the legitimate son of the father (according to an old legend dating back to Samori wars, any woman who has never deceived her husband has a 90 percent chance to see her child back safe and sound from combat).

To break out of the economistic approach, we need, in the second place, to look at what motivates the stakeholders to join the movement, and at the rhetoric they use to justify the armed struggle—in short, at the subjective factors driving individual enrollment. His surveys of ranked military helped Fofana verify "that their ways of seeing and understanding the 'war' are not necessarily or unavoidably the same as those of the political and military leaders [...]. These youngsters have developed their own discourse on the nature of the crisis" (2008, p. 26). At the core of their discourse are, among others, the ideas of freedom and liberation. Like their counterparts in the patriotic movement, most FN fighters had a very deep sense that they were participating in a "noble cause" (the term turns up constantly), namely in the "liberation of the country," the "liberation of the Motherland," or "Fasso Kêlê" in the Malinké dialect. Enlisting can be driven by the values of freedom, but it is also seen as a sacrifice for the Motherland and for the parents. In this perspective, the use of weapons is justified and legitimate. This is the only way in the eyes of these young people to change the country, to induce political and social transformations nationwide. This idea of a struggle for a more equitable world, for a recognition of the rights of everyone in the city and, ultimately, for individual and collective freedom, must not be neglected or seen as empty rhetoric. Everything indicates that this has been a decisive factor in the commitment of MPCI troops at the beginning of the rebellion. We could hypothesize that enlistment in the armed struggle is a means of testing freedom, a paradoxical form of "subduing-freeing"[25] that can be found on the other side of the frontline, among young militiamen of the patriotic galaxy. The similarity in rhetoric is striking:

We had to come down carrying weapons to say that we are here today. You must free the country so that youngsters may take advantage of their possessions. (T., 26 years old)

> I think it sometimes happens in the history of a nation that [...] this nation needs patriot volunteers [...] to sacrifice themselves, to sacrifice themselves to help their country move forwards, evolve. Because when everything is stuck, instead of remaining in a system that degrades us, that denies us our rights, it is good when you have tried everything—and I stress that point—when you have tried everything, [...] it is good to accept your responsibilities and to do it [that is to say, to take up arms]. (Fadiga Khalil, JFN officer)

Fofana concludes: "In summary, people analyze, interpret, and understand 'war' in Côte d'Ivoire at different levels where it is implied that the violence engendered can no longer be considered as gratuitous or absurd. The underlying logics of the various players often reflect a certain social and political vision of 'life together'" (2008, p. 31). This conception of citizenship and advocacy of rights is at the heart of the FN fighters' rhetoric of engagement. Although they don't have the same background, all of them have experienced traumatic episodes of discrimination, marginalization, racketeering, and even violence linked to the issue of Ivority. Their struggle, as we pointed out earlier, is first and foremost a war for "papers," a struggle to obtain an identity card or, more accurately, to have their contested identity papers recognized, for people to admit, once and for all, that they are Côte d'Ivoire citizens like anybody else, and not second or third rate citizens. Young FN fighters also want "to protect the community"—a recurring theme in their discourse. The feeling of insecurity, due to discrimination, and the violence perpetrated by controlling forces have often been at the root of young FN fighters' thirst for revenge which, in turn, legitimates armed violence.

It is, therefore, clear that for most young people who enrolled, political and ideological motivations have largely prevailed over material and financial considerations. For those who have abandoned their paid activities, the war has even meant the loss of their income. One could then speculate that demobilization for these young FN fighters will be a relief and an opportunity to rebuild their lives. But it's important to keep in mind that changes in the material

CÔTE D'IVOIRE: POLITICAL ECONOMY OF A CITIZENSHIP CRISIS   151

realities have taken place during the five years of conflict and war economy. For some fighters, conflict—providing opportunities for systematic racketeering and looting—has been a chance to get rich quickly. As Fofana has found out in his research, the figure of "the looting warrior" has acquired, early in the conflict, a sort of prestige in CNO (Center, North, and West) zones.

> When someone returned to the neighborhood for the first time after enrolling, in his fatigues, [...] people shouted *"guerrier ... guerrier ... guerrier!"*[26] So, in the neighborhood, there were the children, the women and especially the mothers who acclaimed them and even more ... they had the father's blessing. (Mr. Konaté, chairman of the committee of students remaining in FN areas)

Fofana stresses that:

> FN military leaders have not officially encouraged looting by fighters, but the "legitimate" targets of looting were more or less known (police officers, gendarmes, customs officers, and anything that could represent the state—Author's Note). Fighters were in a way given *carte blanche* to help themselves, as remuneration for their job. A black market for disposing of the loot even appeared in Bouaké. At the same time, some families whose sons had enlisted began to ostentatiously exhibit signs of their new prosperity, while household heads, as a result, found ways to invest in sectors of the new war economy (housing, mass transit, import of goods, establishment of plantations, etc.). Young people who pledged to *fasso-kèlè* were then seen as noble and proud warriors who could "legitimately" get rich by looting. [...] New wealth was thus formed through looting and investing in new smuggling sectors of the war economy. Many fighters have benefited from the reconstruction of economic circuits to set up small businesses. They mostly are to be found in second-hand clothing shops, real estate or in the sale of household appliances, electro-mechanics, and electronics and so on. The glamorized image of the "looting warrior," who succeeds both in business and in the chain of command of the rebellion, has become one of the social success models that should be emulated. (2008, p. 46)

The issue of retribution for armed engagement or disengagement goes beyond these more tangible aspects. In the context of armed struggle as in that of trade union militancy, symbolic reward is crucial to maintaining and reinforcing allegiances. Reward often amounts to the moral recognition by the community of the personal sacrifice one has made. Moreover, research on the remuneration of militancy[27] shows that deferred compensation is also a condition for maintaining investment in collective action. Regarding the New Forces, Fofana underscores the role of "rewards" or, more accurately, *promises* of rewards in engagement and disengagement:

> All the young people interviewed admitted that they willingly enlisted and that no promise whatsoever was made to them. They said that their rallying was never motivated by either opportunism, or by the desire to loot or acquire property. However, to the question to find out, whether they had something—by way of reward—they unanimously accepted the idea. There is no lack of arguments to justify the fact that "something" must be done for them; "something" must be given to them for their action. It is difficult to establish a desire to get richer as a determining factor in their enrolment. On the other hand, if it is not a key criterion for enrolling, the idea of reward seems to be a condition for a young fighter to leave the forces. [...] We have shown above how the ideas of sacrifice and courage impregnated the perceptions of young people and motivated their involvement in the conflict. Similarly, the idea of reward logically colors their perceptions of the post-war period. All the time they were mobilized, they received assurances that they would receive a reward. [...] Without taking the form of a firm promise, the idea of a reward seems to transform itself into something that they demand, that is owed to them. The expectation of a reward to come, though not admitted at the beginning, is, therefore, a common feeling throughout mobilization. We have found that the expectation of this "something" becomes more and more precise and firm, particularly in the face to the enrichment of warlords and collaborators of the rebellion.[28] (2008, p. 46)

In some ways, this hope of reward fueled the fighters' "convictions" throughout their mobilization. But, again, could their commitment

CÔTE D'IVOIRE: POLITICAL ECONOMY OF A CITIZENSHIP CRISIS 153

be limited to an economistic reading? The elements shown above indicate this is not the case.

ECONOMIC PREDATION, PRIVATIZATION OF VIOLENCE, AND RECONFIGURATION OF THE STATE AT WAR: THE HYPOTHESIS OF A MILITIA STATE IN THE SOUTH

How has the state of Côte d'Ivoire reacted to the armed insurrection that has led to the emergence of a proto-rebel state and of a full-fledged war economy in the northern regions? Threatened by the armed political opposition, the government in power in Abidjan deployed a three-pronged ultranationalist strategy: an "ultranationalist" mobilization, a "militianization" of society, and a capture of resources, which could be read as the establishment of a militia state. Paradoxically, the privatization of violence and the liberalization of some key sectors of the economy fostered the consolidation of the state.

The Paramilitarization of Rural Areas (West and Central West)

Very soon, at the very beginning of rebel offensives in western regions, in the fall of 2002, President Gbagbo and his advisers realized that they could hardly count on the national army, which was weakened and divided, to resist and to eventually re-conquer the territory. To overcome this structural weakness, the Gbagbo government used a dual strategy of privatization and "paramilitarization" of the conflict: on one hand, they recruited foreign mercenaries (Angolans, South Africans, Ukrainians, Israelis, French) who were primarily given supervision, intelligence and training roles; and, secondly, they promoted the creation of various paramilitary movements to confront rebels and ensure the regime's stability.

These movements fell in three categories: paramilitary forces in the west; rural militias; and the Young Patriots urban movements and militias. It's important to keep in mind that this typology is purely analytical. That's because, on the one hand, the on-the-ground boundaries between these various movements are very porous; and, on the other hand, these movements belong to the same nebula of parallel forces that are organized and financed by those close to presidential power. Although not homogeneous and not always coordinated, these parallel forces can be considered as belonging to a continuum of privatization of violence and paramilitarization of power.

It is, above all, in the western conflict region that this "counterinsurgency" strategy was applied, with the creation of genuine paramilitary organizations, similar in their structure and operations to those deployed by Latin American governments to fight narcoguerrillas.[29] Parallel armies were set up with the support of the national army, but also with the help of Liberian trainers, in a context of increasing transnationalization of the conflict. These paramilitary groups, made up of volunteer recruits who had no real fighting experience when they joined, quickly learned how to fight with the help of their Liberian "advisors." The direct experience of war and of atrocities in regions where those were massive, have transformed these men into killing machines. Fighters received accelerated military training, but they are said to have also participated in mystical protection (*kanké*) sessions that gave them, and still does today, a higher sense of power and invincibility.

The movement was not confined to the regions bordering Liberia: it spread elsewhere, in particular in the "cocoa belt" in the central western region. In these areas, war and ultranationalist propaganda radicalized natives and sharpened the appetite of young people for foreigners' land and crops. Numerous conflicts have occurred. These violent episodes are clearly rooted in local history and land conflicts, but they are also directly linked to the paramilitary strategy of the government in Abidjan and to the regionalization of war. Indeed, research on this topic[30] shows that paramilitary groups were organized and funded by close presidential advisors (in this case Kadet Bertin, former Defense Minister, advisor to the head of state, and related to Laurent Gbagbo, as well as Eloi Oulaï, director of Côte d'Ivoire radio) and trained by Ivorian army commandos, in conjunction with the Liberian rebels mentioned above. Today, these paramilitary groups are still closely related to the defense and security forces and to local administrative authorities.[31]

In this Ivorian "Far West," the most important paramilitary group is the Forces for the Liberation of the Great West (Forces de libération du grand ouest, FLGO), founded by "General" Denis Maho Glofiéhi, assistant to the mayor of Guiglo and a member of the FPI Central Committee. The other main militias are:[32] the Ivorian Movement for the Liberation of the West of Côte d'Ivoire (Mouvement Ivoirien pour la libération de l'ouest de la Côte d'Ivoire, MILOCI), led by "pastor" Gammi who claims to be a man of God, and who was trained in Liberia; the Patriotic Wê Alliance (Alliance patriotique Wê, AP-Wê), led by Julien Gnan Monpého, known as "Colombo"; the Union of Patriots for the Resistance of the Great West (UPRGO), led by Gabriel Banao, former customs officer and "Senegalese tirailleur"; and the FS Lima:[33] fairly loose groups of Liberian mercenaries based in Duékoué, who were led at the start by Maho Glofiéhi and were part of the Lurd troops that toppled Taylor.[34]

But that is not all. Within the framework of this overall FPI "resistance" strategy, a strategy designed to encourage the creation of supplementary forces, the authorities also encouraged the formation in villages of a large number of "self-defense groups," in particular in the western and central western regions. In a context of growing insecurity, these rural self-defense groups proliferated since the beginning of the war, to the point that they can now be found in almost all rural communities. Initially based on the village militias model, and comparable to the urban "vigilante" system, these informal patrols were rather quickly structured, with the support of local authorities, into hierarchical organizations of "Young Rural Patriots," echoing their Abidjan counterparts.

In many communities, militias of Young Patriots were organized under the guise of village associations. These are fairly structured and are headed by a president, a treasurer, a supervisor, and officials assigned to various types of security and mobilization activities. They sometimes coordinate with nearby villages' associations and try to establish themselves as regional federations. This political–administrative structure goes with a genuine process of enlisting and identifying volunteers. Bobo and Chauveau reported that, "Everyone carries an identification card proving that he is a patriot serving his country, with on it his name, age, and village of origin. The card works as a laissez-passer, following instructions from the prefect" (2003, p. 20). Concurring data show that, as DDR/DDM (Demobilization, Disarmament and Reintegration / Disarmament and Dismantling of Militias) approached, the number of enlisted members also multiplied.

We should stress the fact that relationships between these rural militias and local authorities are very strong (elected officials, deputies and administrative officers such as prefects and subprefects), and the latter play a crucial leadership and coordination role in the militianization of rural areas. This trend towards the weaving together of administrative and military logics illustrates the process of informalization of the FPI regime which, since the war began, has relied more and more on parallel structures and shadow "organization charts," where networks of political, economic, military, and paramilitary influence are inextricably connected.

These rural structures made up of young patriots generally perform several types of tasks. These tasks obviously vary depending on the particular situation, but they are characterized by a double logic of protection and extortion—the same logic as that of all militia self-defense structures. As stated above, these structures are often born out of a "spontaneous" movement to fight against insecurity. As they were entrusted by the elders of the village with the protection of the city, the youths first screened visitors and controlled village access by erecting checkpoints, often quite informal. Gradually, in many cases, this "police" role of checking identities was recognized by local public authorities and security forces who found it a useful complement to their own screening system. These checkpoints appeared on all main roads, causing serious problems in terms of freedom of movement. This is because the checkpoint activity quickly proved lucrative. In other words, if the first roadblocks erected in 2001–02 were primarily intended to prevent rebel infiltrations, they have since turned into opportunities for racketeering, with increasingly structured procedures.

That is still not all. In addition to the "taxation" function, rural militias were also given "power over land," which they exerted increasingly frequently, by expropriating land. Backed by local authorities and some citizens in the region who are influential in Abidjan, groups of Young Rural Patriots have set up a reign of terror in some western regions, where they expel "foreigners" (including southerners, Burkina Fasans, but also people of Baoulé origin) from their land, before having local big-men "legally" take this land over. They can also intervene, if the occasion arises, to put pressure on an agro-industrial group in the region, so that it will pay a "fee" to the new "landlords." The rubber boom seems to have indeed reinforced these trends. In this land extortion process, the young militiamen obviously resort to violence and do not shy away from invoking "traditions" and "customs" that were abandoned by their parents, according to them, to reassert the rights of the natives over the land.

In some cases, these local rural self-defense groups also fulfilled functions tied to the war, acting as proxy forces for the national army in the western counter-offensive. It is important to note, here, the extreme porosity of the borders separating these groups that often mix on the ground. Finally, against the backdrop of an upcoming electoral campaign, these local militias were increasingly entrusted with political tasks: "Instead of being asked to attack former rebel fighters, the mission of militiamen has been changed to better fit the struggle being fought at the time," as an observer remarked in

2005. Thus, in the south-western forested areas, the instruction given to the militias was clear: on the one hand, they were to protect areas under the political influence of the ruling party against any incursions by the opposition. In regions like Gagnoa, Guibéroua, and Divo, elected posts (deputies, mayors, and presidents of county councils) could remain the exclusive property of the FPI. On the other hand, the government militiamen must work on "pushing" the opposition parties out of the areas where they hold political posts. "In the next elections, there will be no PDCI or RDR mayor, deputy, or president of the general council in our region. These parties are rebel parties and we will oppose the vote of their militants," confided a Diégonéfla militiaman.[35]

The Abidjan Young Patriots: the Emergence of a New Political Generation

The militianization and militarization of the youth is therefore an important phenomenon in rural areas. It also became commonplace in the streets of Abidjan where, under the leadership of great media leaders, the Young Patriots have taken over power on the streets. This movement, in all its organizational, ideological, and sociological complexity is, without doubt, the most obvious expression of the evolution of the Gbagbo regime in the war—a regime which, unable to rely on a powerful army and strong international alliances, relies on the militianization and ultranationalist radicalization of society to impose political order and to resist all forms of external interference.

The Alliance of Young Patriots for National Survival (Alliance des jeunes patriotes pour le sursaut national), led by Charles Blé Goudé, was born in the wake of the September 19, 2002 enemy incursion, as a movement to support the government in power and provide resistance against assailants from the south. In June 2001, Blé Goudé had already set up the core of the future "patriotic galaxy," namely the COJEP (Congress of Young Patriots, or Congrès des jeunes patriotes), which remains today the most powerful and most structured organization of the patriotic movement. Very quickly this movement spread into areas under government control and mobilized impressive crowds at major events in the economic capital of the country. Stigmatizing the enemies of Côte d'Ivoire (the rebels, neighboring countries, and their foreign supporters, especially France), the Young Patriots quickly became forefront political actors in the Ivorian crisis. They also became the militia serving those in power, responsible for monitoring opponents, controlling neighborhoods, and enforcing a reign of terror in the city, sometimes acting in concert with the notorious death squads responsible for kidnappings and summary executions.

At the outset, however, the Alliance was born as an alternative political movement, bringing together a heterogeneous coalition made up of half a dozen associated organizations or trade unions that had become known under the regime of General Gueï for having participated in the Constitutional and Electoral Consultative Commission where, in line with the arguments of Ivority, they had pushed for a restriction of political rights to "natives"[36] only. Later on, the Young Patriots movement would become structured around three major federations, each comprising numerous associations: the Alliance of Young Patriots for National Revival (AJPSN, mentioned above) led by "General" Blé Goudé; the Union for the Total Liberation of Côte d'Ivoire (UPLTCI, or Union pour la libération totale de la Côte d'Ivoire), chaired by "Marshal" Eugene Djué; the National Coalition of Resistance of Ivory Coast (CONARECI, or Coalition nationale des résistants de Côte d'Ivoire), led by Damana Adja, nicknamed "Pickass," also an influential member of the FESCI and the J-FPI, who later became political advisor to the FPI president.

Since the crisis began, the Young Patriots in Abidjan have become a shock weapon of the Laurent Gbagbo regime. Used as an instrument by the government in power, who generously pays their leaders, the Young Patriots have played a particularly pivotal role in the very ambivalent relationship with France, as shown by the violent demonstrations that took place after the Marcoussis Agreement in January 2003, or those of November 2004. Recruited in large numbers, armed and daily trained in the streets of Abidjan, they are a formidable apparatus of social and political control, at the service of the regime. The multiplication of "parliaments," "agoras," and "senates," which have been established in most neighborhoods and modeled on the Plateau "Sorbonne,"[37] illustrates this desire to control the urban areas which, insidiously, have been subject to the law of patriotic militias. This movement has quickly spread into major southern cities, but also to rural areas, where the leaders of the Young Patriots, encouraged and supported financially by the government in power, have helped structure similar organizations. The patriotic movement has thus experienced an amazing rise and an impressive growth in the government-held area in the early years of the conflict. In hindsight, one can even say that Young Patriots have saved the regime from defeat, especially by allowing it to withstand the various pressures and demands of the international community. In Abidjan, as in the west, a myriad militias and paramilitary forces can be found, that are more or less established and operational. But it is the Group of Patriots for Peace (GPP, or Groupement des patriotes pour la paix), chaired by Bouazo Yoko Yoko, that is the closest to a paramilitary movement in the city. The GPP, and its associated militias within the Union of Self-defense Movements of the South (UMAS, or Union des mouvements d'autodéfense du sud) and the tank that is the Fesci (the student union militia), are in a way the armed wing of the "patriotic galaxy." Our surveys of members of the GPP showed, however, that they insist on the difference that exists between their movement, committed to armed struggle and armed resistance, and other patriotic organizations that "are fighting with words." GPP members see themselves as "dressed bodies," which they are since, until recently, they wore uniforms identical to those of loyalist forces. Enlisted combatants also have identification cards similar to those of members of the national army. But despite all these efforts to stress the differences, the rhetoric of the movement leaders, as well as that of low-rank militia, is very close to that of Young Patriots. Their battle is fought using the resistance's heroic talk about saving the republic, as a national liberation struggle.

> Our politicians are the hostages of the French colonial pact system. They are hostages; the proof: we had Thomas Sankaras, where were they? And we had Lumumbas, where were they? What I am saying is that those who really want to defend the homeland, to claim some ... the real independence of their country, they are made a minority [...], reduced to a minority, and then they are dismissed one way or another. So the first battle of youth is to serve as a rear base for all our powers. [...] There is power in truth. So if we continue to make our brothers, our friends, more aware, this awareness will eventually ... prevail. And we will free our country, all of us. And our economy, our wealth, currently held at the French Treasury, we will return it. Because it is not right.[38]

The Group of Patriots for Peace was founded at the beginning of the conflict as an army of "reservists" by Charles Groguhé, a former leader of the Fesci, who was followed by Touré Zéguen, who was himself replaced by Bouazo Yoko Yoko, following a series of internal divisions. The GPP recruited in Abidjan hundreds of fighters who had been armed and trained by the government. Among them are many former soldiers, policemen, and gendarmes who are not new to arms. They are the ones who, jointly with loyalist army instructors, train new recruits in the camps of the economic capital. The GPP have several regrouping and training camps in the city (Vridi, Yopougon-Sable, Yopougon-Gesco, Abobo PK-18, Bingerville, and even Cocody or the Riviera), often spaces that they took over by force, as was the case with the Institut Marie Thérèse d'Adjamé. In Abidjan, the movement organized itself into a dozen companies, each one of them in charge of a well-defined sector. It is difficult to accurately assess the number of fighters available to the GPP in the country. The craziest numbers are quoted here and there. When they were grouped at the Institut Marie Thérèse, they were about a thousand. The GPP militiamen do not receive wages; they are only fed, housed and dressed, and often resort to racketeering activities. Their looting and extortion practices have led to many conflicts with the population, as in Yopougon-Azito in November 2006. Clashes have also occurred quite frequently between militia and the police who, in one case, tried to restore order and were attacked by the militiamen. The militiamen were later pardoned by P. Mangou, the Chief of Staff of the Ivorian Defense and Security Forces (SDS) itself. The Diarra government, at the time, had even tried, unsuccessfully, to dissolve the GPP (for forgery and use of forgeries!). However, the GPP was forced to leave the Institut Marie Thérèse, and became dispersed throughout the city. We found some of them who returned to their homes but still think of themselves as mobilized fighters. Others gathered in less conspicuous camps in the suburbs. They continue training and are ready to reclaim the streets if necessary. But the motivation of many of them has significantly diminished by now.

Indeed, over time, the patriotic movement has become fragmented and divided. Fairly quickly, the "patriotic galaxy" underwent a scission, which has seen the birth of a multitude of groups led by minor chiefs who had become rich and disputed among themselves their monopoly on being patriotic and, above all, on the presidential favors that go with it. Without going into detail,[39] we will say that this decline has been accompanied by growing rivalries between the leaders of the various organizations and a comprehensive slowing down of the movement. Could one still claim that this mobilization of the Young Patriots is limited to simple material conditions? We obviously cannot deny that some individuals used the structures of the patriotic galaxy as a means to build up wealth and gain social status. But this functional explanation of an "alimentary patriotism," which sees the Young Patriots as merely "tummy patriots,"[40] is not sufficient. Our research shows that this line of reasoning ignores the patriotic militants, the ones who stand up or come every day to listen to the debates at the Plateau "Sorbonne," or the common "statutory member" militants of neighborhood "agoras." Some of those people find in this political activity a part of their daily bread, but the lavish lifestyle of the "patriotic galaxy" leaders should not conceal the relative poverty of their troops, as we have seen on the ground.

Like any nationalist mobilization, that of the Young Patriots finds its strength in the social imagination, which has been deeply affected by widespread violence. Our hypothesis is that this mobilization based on a violent anti-colonialist rhetoric is made even more effective by the fact that it is articulated around these three dimensions (among others): a religious and quasi-prophetic eschatology of deliverance; an occultation of national history; and, most importantly, an individual and collective struggle for the emancipation of the young against a background of intergenerational relationships in turmoil.[41]

Regardless of the motivation of their leaders and of their relationship with power, these patriotic militias, which have proliferated since September 2001, reflect a major development. The mobilization of Abidjan patriots, such as that of rural militiamen, illustrates an important sociological phenomenon that already has long-term consequences for the operation of the state: the reconfiguration of intergenerational relationships and the rise of a new political generation. Because of the war, youths stand up like men and show their power. At both local and national levels, young people increasingly strongly affirm their commitment to war and shake off the yoke of birthright relationships, trying to assert themselves on the public stage. This quest for autonomy is of course not new, but it has been accelerated by war, which made youth a political stakeholder in its own right.

Similarly, militias are not the only place of this "generational revolution" but, both in the cities and in the countryside, they are one of the most significant catalysts for it. As indicated above, this movement is noticeable in the rural areas, where young people are given the weapons and the responsibility to defend the community. Their work at the checkpoints gives them, through racketeering, some financial autonomy, but it also grants them a sovereign authority in the management of the city borders. It is their responsibility now to ensure the security of the community, control the flow of people and goods, and settle some of the disputes (often through violence). They are in some way the "new sovereigns" of the local public space. This movement is also very significant in urban areas where the crisis has seen the emergence of powerful groups of Young Patriots who have taken over control of the streets. This might be the most spectacular phenomenon in the Ivorian crisis. One could reasonably object by saying that these militia movements are peons to the authorities, and are used by the presidency as a popular nationalist mobilization strategy. But the role that their leaders—Blé Goudé, Djué, Pickass—now play in the national political game, shows that they have also gained considerable influence over the management of public affairs, up to the highest state level. The prospects for ending the crisis after the signing of the Ouagadougou Agreement and the appointment of Soro as the prime minister further reinforce this trend, as they show the increasing strength of a new political generation—Young Patriots and rebels alike—that is taking over the reins of power. What is striking is the fact that most of the key players in this upcoming generation come from the same matrix: that of trade union militancy within the Fesci, where political rivalries were already settled through violence. It is in this trade union melting pot, very close to the FPI but also to the RDR of Alassane Ouattara, that the political careers unfolding today took shape, particularly those of "General" Blé Goudé, leader of the "patriots" in Abidjan, and Guillaume Soro, political leader of the MPCI, who became Prime Minister in 2007, both of whom ruled the Fesci. At all levels in the administration, former militant trade unionists coming from the patriotic galaxy or from the rebellion are gaining influence, to the point where we could talk about a fascist model of upward mobility.

Conclusions: Informalization of the State and Criminalization of the Economy in a Context of War and Neoliberal Reforms

The growing influence of these paramilitary structures and of the new generation of militants within society and the Ivorian administration has led us to develop the idea of a "militia state."[42] This concept is likely inadequate to describe a regime that, despite the obvious state belligerence, seems to operate almost normally. But it is a way to show that, since the outbreak of the conflict, sovereignty and legitimacy are no longer the domain of official institutions; they are also found in the neighborhoods and on the boulevards controlled by militiamen through checkpoints and racketeering. That the leader of the Alliance of Young Patriots, "General" Charles Blé Goudé, proclaims himself "President of the Public Roads" is not a trivial matter. Behind the bragging, there is indeed a significant evolution of the ways the government is operated, mobilization is approached and the public space is controlled by parallel forces and paramilitary groups more or less loyal to the state.

In conclusion, we would like to emphasize that, in the context of war and swift liberalization of the economy, the structures of governance in Côte d'Ivoire became increasingly fragmented, opaque, and disseminated. From the onset of the conflict, trends towards informalization of the exercise of state power are evident. By informalization of state power, we mean a threefold process of fragmentation of the administrative apparatus, erosion of the official hierarchical authority structures in the organization, the corresponding development of other chains of command and of decision making following partisan, activist, clan, ethno-regional, and other sorts of reasoning.

The deregulation of the operation of the public service had already started under previous regimes. But it increased with the outbreak of the war, with the neoliberal reforms of sector privatization and, more recently, with the introduction of a series of instruments to help break out of the crisis. The transition and national reconciliation governments have clearly had a perverse effect on governance: as each party that signed the agreements obtained one or more cabinet posts, "government solidarity" soon transformed into rivalry between government offices and departments that variously supported FPI, RDR, PDCI, UDPCI, or FN. The trend seems to further exacerbate after Ouagadougou and its prospects of recovery as well as its promises of assistance from the international community. In this context of "a new scramble for Côte d'Ivoire," each ministry was seen as a rent by the party holding it. The conditions imposed by the international community for ending the crisis paradoxically contributed to greater ministerial confusion. The implementation of policies to end the crisis was accompanied by the exponential multiplication of *ad hoc* structures and bodies dedicated to the management of this or that aspect of post-conflict reconstruction. Each administration created its own structure, sometimes encouraged by donors, while the Prime Minister's office, allegedly in charge of coordination, had neither the capacity nor the will to steer the whole thing. This trend towards administrative "agencying" and "scissioning" is a well-known phenomenon in the context of governance reforms, particularly in war-end situations. It was particularly sharp in Côte d'Ivoire.

More generally, one can easily notice a growing informalization and criminalization of the economy and the state since armed violence erupted in 1999 and, mostly, since the conflict broke out in 2002. Corruption reached unprecedented heights, greatest than at the worst moments of the Houphouët-Boigny and Bédié regimes. Most economic sectors are under the thumb of special political interests. Under the guise of privatization and liberalization reforms, the plundering of the country's resources and of various sectors has increased. What happened in the coffee–cocoa sector is a good illustration of these developments. As we saw in the first section of this chapter, this sector has historically played a central role in the country's governance, providing not only the resources for political regulation, but also the sociological and ideological foundations of the state. These foundations, as we said, were deeply affected by the implementation of structural adjustment reforms aimed precisely at breaking up the logic of this institutionalized clientelism. Bretton Woods institutions—and the opposition parties who criticized corruption—pushed very hard for the privatization of the sector and the dismantling of the Caistab. Houphouët-Boigny, with France's support, resisted these pressures and his successor, Bédié, did the same by making the reforms hollow. But in the late 1990s, the process picked up some speed. In January 1999, Caistab was indeed closed and replaced by a new private regulatory body: the "new Caistab," in which the state was a minority partner. After failing, the new Caistab was dismantled in May 2000 by the General Gueï junta. The liberalization of the sector had been achieved. But instead of the old regulatory system, we saw the implementation of a whole series of structures designed to manage the industrial sector on behalf of the state and growers: the ARCC, the BCC, the FRC, the FDPCC, and the FGCCC,[43] and a myriad umbrella organizations of co-operatives also claiming a regulatory role. All these bodies, while supposedly private, would in fact be taken over by individuals close to power or groups connected to the state. Without going into detail, we can see that the liberalization of the sector has not led to a withdrawal of the state or to less government intervention in this sector, quite the contrary. Privatization did not result either in lower levies on cocoa production, but in higher levies, each "regulatory" body now imposing taxes, where the Caistab used to exert its fiscal and para-fiscal monopoly. Indeed, the predation on the coffee–cocoa sector, far from falling, was rather exacerbated with the neoliberal reforms. "The minimum state" found other tricks.[44] The war has further exacerbated this predation on cocoa resources by the clan in power, which found new ways to consolidate its position and to finance war. Huge sums of money were diverted since the beginning of the conflict as shown by various research reports.[45] Indeed, we can see that the neoliberal reforms did not fundamentally affect the former patronage mechanisms and regulatory clientelism instruments, which have now simply become diversified, privatized, and disseminated in a multitude of structures, each offering new opportunities for corruption in the context of great ambiguity reinforced by war.

The diversion of public money and the display of the wealth thus obtained have reached such proportions today in Côte d'Ivoire that we can actually speak of a personal privatization of the state. These practices, far from being hidden, are performed in an ostentatious way, legitimized by the highest authorities of the Republic, in line with the "philosophy of the peanut roaster" referred to above. The war has undoubtedly sharpened these old trends which, since 2002, have made a qualitative leap. This is plainly visible every day in the streets of Abidjan, where the number of large 4x4 vehicles is on the increase and large villas are sprouting up like mushrooms. Cynics might say that conflict plays a part in the primitive accumulation of capital, that peace in Côte d'Ivoire is at the end of the check book because today everything and everyone can be bought. It has been clear, lately, that political allegiances, divisions, and oppositions resume and come apart extremely quickly with the help of suitcases full of cash. The opposition parties have all been weakened by internal divisions and senior-member defections which, for the most part, were caused by stipendiary strategies being implemented by the Presidency. The fact that Laurent Gbagbo has managed to co-opt much of the armed opposition by appointing the rebel leader, Soro, as the prime minister, and offered him new sources of accumulation in compensation for his political powerlessness is yet another significant example of this money- and corruption-based governance.[46]

These institutional informalization processes have their counterparts in the Ivorian society, where a collapse of social norms and reference points is also visible. The increase of criminality and the total impunity for crimes of all kinds committed since the outbreak of the crisis are evidence of the dissolution of legitimate social practices, and are broadly seen by the public as such. Since the war, in the words of the people from low-income neighborhoods of

Abidjan, "Côte d'Ivoire is under a sheet," which is to say anyone can do anything without being held accountable for it. The spectacular boom of the "coupe-décalé"[47] musical movement is in itself indicative of this new state of mind, where whoever makes a bad shot and deceitfully accumulates money—like Nigeria's "419" or Cameroon's feymen—is regarded as a social hero; where the DJs' "wisdom" is a function of this scam-based moral economy; and where "work" is no longer a way to earn money, but, on the contrary, synonymous with ostentatious squandering. In short, neoliberalism, which has spread like wildfire across the planet and has been presented as a real philosophy of life by its designers, resulted in a crisis and in the upturning of social norms in Côte d'Ivoire.

How to interpret these new configurations of power and social relations based on the informality of structures, the fragmentation of areas of sovereignty, the significance of hierarchical interpersonal relationships, the top-to-bottom redistribution of favors (and therefore debts), the articulation of chains of dependence based on generational clan logics, and so on? Should we, as Dembélé suggested,[48] speak of a tendentious feudalization of society and the state in Côte d'Ivoire? Or, more simply, a fragmentation of institutions of power, coupled with state populism, that seeks to demystify the excesses of the pyramidal state power of the Houphouëtian age? It is difficult to unequivocally answer this question.

Whatever it may be, this global trend towards the informalization of power, economy, and society is a major constraint to be taken into account if we are to understand the recent—and perhaps future—developments of Côte d'Ivoire in the context of liberal globalization. On the one hand, it should encourage us to look at the issue of the nature of post-conflict reconstruction programs: Most donors involved in Côte d'Ivoire are there because of a rehabilitation and restoration logic—they want to return Côte d'Ivoire to "normal." But what is this "social normalcy" and "economic or political order" that should be restored? And what does it mean for some of the players who have been operating for years according to an entirely different logic and in another state of normalcy? Our research shows that, for part of the unemployed youth, normalcy is the culture of the ghetto, of the street, of violence and of grabbing. They don't see further than their daily scrambling, where they squirm and try to find themselves. As the highest state level is setting the example with predation, since the rebels who fought the government with weapons became ministers and since theft and violence have become almost normal ways to rise in society, these youths basically come to the conclusion that this is what is normal and there is no reason for them to be more virtuous than the others.

Moreover, because of the dynamics of informalization mentioned above, one must raise again the now classic question of the governance of states coming out of war and, perhaps, see in a different light the argument of "fragile states" that has become the new magic word of international cooperation. Why? Because, on the one hand, one can recognize in Côte d'Ivoire a form of institutionalization of power that seems to fit with the bankrupt states or "failing states" theory. There are definitely signs of fragility in this country, which, despite its huge resources, is not implementing any mechanism whatsoever to regulate its society. We also saw in the first section of this chapter that structural adjustments contributed to the massive erosion of the regulatory mechanisms that had previously assured the country's stability. But on the other hand, it is also plain that this Ivorian state, in spite of its adjustment reforms and in spite of the war, is indeed present and remains, all in all, quite operational. Unlike other conflict situations, it must be remembered that, in Côte d'Ivoire, the state never ceased to operate, despite the scission of the territory. Most administrations and economic and social sectors continued to function almost normally. State resources remained at a high level, and, thanks to large oil discoveries, have even increased during the conflict. Tax collections—a good indicator of the effectiveness of the state—far from falling, dramatically increased in recent years.[49] Similarly, social and political control grew significantly under the rule of a state supported by what we described earlier as a militia state. The war also helped strengthen nationalist fervor and devotion to the nation-state. Finally, this state, in spite of very strong international constraints, as it was placed under a quasi-trusteeship system by the United Nations, still found ways to produce its own peace agreement, forcing the international community and donors to endorse its options!

What weight do the requirements, admonitions, and conditions of the international community have in this context? Far from offsetting the excesses of the regime, the mass return of international aid strengthened the foundations of this increasingly corrupt state. The trick played by history is that the consolidation of Côte d'Ivoire was achieved, amidst violence, through a clever implementation of neoliberal reforms that made it possible to replicate the "peanuts roaster philosophy" in new, now privatized, finery.

NOTES

1. Richard Banégas teaches at University Paris 1. This chapter was written with the collaboration of Alain Toh, University of Abidjan and Yao Kouman Adingra, University of Paris 1.
2. With the starting up of the Baobab oil fields on the Ghana border, oil production increased by 71 percent in 2006, to become the country's number one export. Starting in 2004, the oil sector-based tax collection has shown a steep rise, amounting to 193.6 million FCFA in 2007 (source: General Tax Office).
3. The term "New Forces" was coined in January 2003, during the Marcoussis negotiations, to bring together the three rebel movements that had emerged in September and October 2002: the Patriotic Movement of Côte d'Ivoire (MPCI), established in Bouaké; the Movement for Justice and Peace (MJP); and the Popular Ivorian Movement of the Great West (MPIGO), created in the western region.
4. See Galy (2004).
5. See Marshall and Ero (2003).
6. See pamphlet written by Mamadou Koulibaly, President of the National Assembly (with A. Ahua Jr. and G. K. Bush) (2003), pp. 8–9.
7. According to Achille Mbembe (1992).
8. We will show the concomitance between the various liberalization reforms of the agro-export sectors and the emergence of armed violence in 1999 and in 2002.
9. It should be noted that this research was conducted in three different areas: in Abidjan, in the western region under the control of government militias, and in the northern region under the control of the rebel forces.
10. See, for example, Amin (1967, 1970); Campbell and Lubeck (1987); and, for an updated version of the dependentist discussion, Campbell (1997).
11. See, in particular, Fauré and Médard (1982).
12. See Amondji (1984).
13. The SAA (African Farming Union) created in the 1930s by Houphouët-Boigny, before he set up the PDCI-RDA (Democratic Party of Ivory Coast–African Democratic Coalition), which would become the Single Independence Party and would remain in power until December 1999.
14. See Fauré and Médard (1982).
15. See the *Politique africaine* dossiers "Figures de la réussite et imaginaires politique." No. 82, June 2001 (coordinators R. Banégas and J.-P. Warnier).
16. According to Chauveau's (2000) formula.
17. See Le Pape (1997).
18. The expression is from Galy (2007).
19. For example, the Bouaké market is directly managed by the FN Central, instead and in place of City Hall, absent since the onset of the crisis. Market traders hand over to tax collector agents the daily taxes fixed as follows: seamstress 100 to 200 FCFA; extension workers 100 FCFA; butcher shops 2,300 FCFA per head of cattle slaughtered, and 100 FCFA as market tax; market stalls: 6,000 FCFA; taxi drivers 300 FCFA; phone booth administrators 1,800 FCFA.
20. Checkpoint located south of Bouaké on the Bouaké–Yamossoukro highway.
21. Personal communication.
22. See Berdal and Malone (2000), Collier (2001). For a critical view of these approaches, see Marchal and Messiant (2002), Gutiérrez Sanín (2004).

23. The paragraph that follows draws on his data.
24. *Grins* are informal places where friends meet to have their evening tea. These places can also be found in Burkina Faso, as well as in Mali and in Côte d'Ivoire.
25. We borrow this notion from Xavier Audrain who, drawing on Foucault, illustrates the case of young Mouride disciples of Cheikh Modou Kara in Sénégal. By making body and soul subordinated to the marabout, they become free from family tutelage and assert themselves as moral and political subjects. See Audrain (2004).
26. This French term has not been translated into the local dialect.
27. See, among others, Gaxie (2005).
28. Our research shows that young southern fighters denounce, more and more frequently, the wealth accumulated by their leaders. Indeed, because of the war, the use of cross-border trade channels and the development of a new market fueled by smuggling led to the disappearance of former players and to the emergence of new entrepreneurs. The new commercial activity has given rise to the *nouveau riche* phenomenon. They have very frequently received financial support from members of the rebellion—but are not themselves part of the rebellion—and reinvested the money in the business sector.
29. See Lair and Sanchez (2004).
30. See Marshall and Ero (2003).
31. Besides, this close coordination has been publicly acknowledged by policymakers. On May 8, 2007, at Bloléquin, during a meeting between senior and local officials, Eloi Oulaï directly claimed responsibility: "Tchéidé Gervais [vice-chairman of the General Council of Guiglo], Daouho Benoit [Mayor of Bloléquin], it is we who have given weapons to these young fighters and have equipped them to repel the rebellion [...] If people were to go before the CFI, it is us. It was at my office that the distribution of weapons and the organization of different groups were settled. Also, the organization of the visit of the head of state and the awareness campaign for the dismantling of self-defense groups must be our business." *Le Nouveau Réveil*, May 9, 2007.
32. To this non-exhaustive list, another structure, which is somewhat different in nature, should be added: the Groups of Patriots for Peace (Groupes de patriotes pour la paix, GPP), which are urban militias in the south (Abidjan and San Pedro regions), now headed by Bouazo Yoko Yoko, who lives in Abidjan. The GPP claims an extraordinarily large number of fighters in the south-west, but their claims could not be confirmed.
33. According to a direct witness-actor, in this case Sian Rachel, camp commander of the APWE in Duékoué: "When LIMA came to Côte d'Ivoire to [...] by signing an agreement with Côte d'Ivoire, an agreement with the President of the Republic, they said: we have come to help you, after this war you had, you will give us weapons to go liberate our country as well. That's how they came to Côte d'Ivoire." Testimonial obtained by a member of the research team, Alain Toh, Duékoué, May 26, 2007.
34. Since July 2005, Maho leads and officially represents these five militia groups, now known collectively as the Resistance Forces of the Great West (Forces de résistance du grand ouest, FRGO). Also invested with the responsibilities of a traditional chief, he is regarded as the leader of militia leaders in the west. He has full access to the offices of the President of the Republic in Abidjan, where he is a regular visitor.
35. Konaté (2005).

36. See Konaté (2003).
37. See Bahi (2003), Banégas and Toh (2006), Konaté (2003).
38. President of the GPP, a conversation collected by R. Banégas in September 2006 at his home in Adjamé (220 rooms).
39. See Koné (2007).
40. In reference, of course, to what has commonly been called "belly politics." See Bayart (1989).
41. For further empirical details, see Banégas (2007).
42. See Banégas (2006).
43. Respectively: Coffee and Cocoa Regulatory Authority; Coffee and Cocoa Exchange; Coffee and Cocoa Regulatory and Control Fund; Fund for Development and Promotion of Coffee and Cocoa Grower Activities; Coffee and Cocoa Co-operatives Guarantee Fund.
44. Coussy (1994).
45. See, in particular, the Global Witness report, June 2007.
46. A device this corruption-based governance has resorted to, is to turn a blind eye to the practices of this or that minister (in particular from the opposition) to later have a hold on him through compromising files. If not loyalty, at least some form of allegiance is thus ensured.
47. See Kolaghen (2006).
48. Personal communication.
49. Between 2002 and 2003, tax revenues fell by 12 percent, but thereafter they have risen steadily to impressive proportions: +4.1 percent in 2004; +16.6 percent in 2005; +15.3 percent in 2006; +16.8 percent in 2007 (source: General Tax Office). This increase is partly, but not only, due to oil discoveries. It is also indicative of the broadening of the tax base and greater collection efficiency by the state. See Bossuroy and Meseil (2008).

REFERENCES

Akindès, F. (2004) *Les racines de la crise militaro-politique en Côte d'Ivoire.* Dakar: CODESRIA.
Amin, S. (1967) *Le développement du capitalisme en Côte d'Ivoire.* Paris: Editions de Minuit.
Amin, S. (1970) "Capitalism and development in the Ivory Coast." In *African Politics and Society*, ed. I. L. Markovitz. New York: Free Press, pp. 277–288.
Amondji, M. (1984) *Felix Houphouët-Boigny et la Côte d'Ivoire.* Paris: Karthala.
Audrain, X. (2004) "Devenir 'baay-fall' pour être soi. Le religieux comme vecteur d'émancipation individuelle au Sénégal." *Politique africaine*, No. 94, pp. 149–165.
Bahi, A. (2003) "La Sorbonne d'Abidjan: rêve de démocratie ou naissance d'un espace public?" *Revue africaine de sociologie*, Vol. 7, No. 1.
Banégas, R. (2006) "Costa d'Avorio, lo Stato delle milizie." *Limes*, No. 3.
Banégas, R. (2007) "Côte d'Ivoire, les jeunes se lèvent en hommes." *Les Etudes du CERI*, No. 137.
Banégas, R. and Toh, A. (2006) "La France et l'ONU devant le 'parlement' de Yopougon. Paroles de 'jeunes patriotes' et régimes de vérité à Abidjan." *Politique africaine*, No. 104, pp. 141–158.
Banégas, R. and Warnier, J.-P. (2001) "Figures de la réussite et imaginaires politiques." *Politique africaine*, No. 82 (dossiers).
Bayart, J.-F. (1989) *L'État en Afrique. La politique du ventre.* Paris: Fayard.

CÔTE D'IVOIRE: POLITICAL ECONOMY OF A CITIZENSHIP CRISIS

Berdal, M. and Malone, D. (eds.) (2000) *Greed and Grievance: Economic Agendas in Civil Wars*. Boulder and London/Ottawa: Lynne Rienner and IDRC.

Bobo, S. and Chauveau, J.-P. (2003) "La situation de guerre dans l'arène villageoise. Un exemple dans le centre-ouest ivoirien." *Politique africaine*, No. 83, p. 20.

Bossuroy, T. and Meseil, N. (2008) "Note sur la situation macroéconomique de la Côte d'Ivoire," French Development Agency, AFD / RCH / REC.

Campbell, B. (1997) "Le modèle ivoirien de développement à l'épreuve de la crise." In *Le modèle ivoirien en questions*, eds. B. Contamin and H. Memel-Fotê. Paris: Karthala, pp. 37–60.

Campbell, B. and Lubeck, P. (1987) *The African Capitalist Bourgeoisie in Nigeria, Kenya and the Ivory Coast*. Boulder and London: Lynne Rienner.

Chauveau, J.-P. (2000) "Question foncière et construction nationale en Côte d'Ivoire. Les enjeux silencieux d'un coup d'État." *Politique africaine*, No. 78, pp. 94–125.

Collier, P. (2001) *Economic Causes of Civic Conflicts and Their Implications for Policy*. Washington, DC: World Bank.

Coussy, J. (1994) "Les ruses de l'Etat minimum." In *La réinvention du capitalisme*, ed. J.-F. Bayart. Paris: Karthala, pp. 227–248.

CURDIPHE (1996) *L'Ivoirité ou l'esprit du nouveau contrat social du président Henri Konan Bédié*. Abidjan: Presses universitaires de Côte d'Ivoire—PUCI.

Dembelé, O. (2002) "La construction économique et politique de la catégorie 'étranger' en Côte d'Ivoire." In *Côte d'Ivoire, l'année terrible. 1999–2000*, eds. M. Le Pape and C. Vidal. Paris: Karthala, pp. 140–141.

Dozon, J.-P. (1997) "L'allochtone et l'étranger en Côte d'Ivoire." In *Le modèle ivoirien en question*, eds. B. Contamin and H. Memel-Fotê. Paris: Karthala, pp. 786–787.

Fauré, Y.-A. and Médard, J.-F. (eds.) (1982) *État et bourgeoisie en Côte d'Ivoire*. Paris: Karthala.

Fofana, M. (2008) "Les déterminants de l'enrôlement des jeunes combattants de la rébellion du Nord de la Côte d'Ivoire." Oxford: Crise Working Paper.

Galy, M. (2004) "De la guerre nomade: sept approches du conflit autour de la Côte d'Ivoire." *Cultures & Conflits*, No. 55, pp. 163–178.

Galy, M. (2007) "Politologie d'une rébellion. Une gouvernance par la violence au Nord de la Côte d'Ivoire?" *Cultures & Conflits*, No. 65, pp. 137–155.

Gaxie, D. (2005) "Rétributions du militantisme et paradoxes de l'action collective." *Swiss Political Science Review*, Vol. 11, No. 1, pp. 157–188.

Global Witness (2007) *Chocolat chaud. Comment le cacao a alimenté le conflit en Côte d'Ivoire*. Washington, DC: Global Witness.

Gutiérrez Sanín, F. (2004) "Criminal rebels? A discussion of civil war and criminality from the Colombian experience." *Politics & Society*, Vol. 32, No. 2, pp. 257–285.

International Crisis Group (ICG) (2004) "Côte d'Ivoire: following the money." *ICG Africa Report*, No. 74, pp. 2–3.

Kolaghen, D. (2006) "Frime, escroquerie et cosmopolitisme. Le succès du coupé-décalé en Afrique et ailleurs." *Politique africaine*, No. 100, pp. 92–105.

Konaté, F. (2005) "Bouaflé, Oumé, Diégonéfla, Hiré ... Les milices préparent un coup," *24 Heures*, February 16, 2005.

Konaté, Y. (2003) "Les enfants de la balle. De la Fesci aux mouvements de patriotes." *Politique africaine*, No. 89.

Koné, G. (2007) "Comprendre l'émergence du mouvement des Jeunes patriotes à travers l'engagement de ses leaders." Oxford: Crise Working Paper.

Koulibaly, M., Ahua A. Jr., and Bush, G. K. (2003) *La Guerre de la France contre la Côte d'Ivoire*. Abidjan: La Refondation.

Lair, E. and Sanchez, G. (eds.) (2004) *Violencias y estrategias colectivas en la región andina*. Bogotá: Grupo Editorial Norma, IFEA, IEPRI.

Le Nouveau Réveil, May 9, 2007.

Le Pape, M. (1997) *L'énergie sociale à Abidjan: économie politique de la ville en Afrique noire, 1930-1995*. Paris: Karthala.

Losch, B. (1997) "A la recherche du chaînon manquant. Pour une lecture renouvelée de l'économie de plantation ivoirienne." In *Le modèle ivoirien en questions. Crises, ajustements, recompositions*, eds. B. Contamin and H. Memel-Fotê. Paris: Karthala, pp. 205–230.

Losch, B. (2003) "Libéralisation économique et crise politique en Côte d'Ivoire." *Critique internationale*, No. 19, p. 60.

Marchal, R. and Messiant, C. (2002) "De l'avidité des rebelles. L'analyse économique de la guerre selon Paul Collier." *Critique Internationale*, No. 16, pp. 58–68.

Marshall, A. and Ero, C. (2003) "L'ouest de la Côte d'Ivoire: un conflit libérien?" *Politique africaine*, No. 89.

Mbembe, A. (1992) "Tradition de l'autoritarisme et problèmes de gouvernement en Afrique sub-saharienne." *Africa Development*, Vol. 17, No. 1, pp. 37–64.

5
Multiple Uses of Neoliberalism
War, New Boundaries, and Reorganization of the Government in Sudan

Roland Marchal and Einas Ahmed[1]

INTRODUCTION

The military junta's takeover by coup d'état in June 1989 in Sudan was not simply a historical blip. While the army had already led extra-constitutional takeovers in 1958 and 1969, this time it played an ambiguous, and perhaps secondary, role to the extent that the government after June 30, 1989 cannot be considered a praetorian regime. Right away, the Islamists, members of the National Islamic Front (NIF)[2] led by Hassan al-Turabi, appeared as the actual commanders, a state within the state—even though this characterization is up for debate. As a result the government's authoritarianism was less characterized by the coercion unique to the military ethos than by the setting up of real disciplinary constraints tinged with religious overtones, which affected both the public and private spheres.

The new government undertook an ambitious program to change the social and economic field that went beyond simple political repression. International public opinion remained focused on the unilateral imposition of the Arabic language and Islamic practices in a country where linguistic and religious plurality—including within groups calling themselves Arab and Muslim—had never been fundamentally threatened, despite several periods of intolerance since the end of the colonial period. The media concentrated, and rightly so, on the human costs of a bloody war being waged in the south of the country[3] against the Sudan People's Liberation Movement (SPLM)—which, according to the agreed formula, was supposed to represent the Christians and animists in that part of the country—but portrayed the brutalization of society to the north in a much more superficial way.

Nevertheless, the new government had no intention of establishing an immutable order and, unlike its predecessors, became resolutely involved in the state's radical reforms. After almost a decade of economic status quo, it implemented neoliberal economic policies, the terms of which confirmed an Olivier Roy statement: "Islamism is about the Sharia (Islamic law) and the IMF, like the Soviets were about the kolkhozes and electrification."[4] Therefore, it is less the content of these policies that would line up with IMF frameworks than the ways in which they were implemented that interests us, because they were not a product of expert logic but rather a very political agenda for the stability of the government in the north and the continuation of war in the south.

This challenge to the regulations of the post-colonial Sudanese state under the aegis of neoliberalism was led in a very specific context. On the one hand, the country was already off-limits to most multilateral and especially the Bretton Woods organizations, because of its calamitous management of the country's debt since the beginning of the 1980s. This international ostracism was intensified when the United States placed Sudan on its list of State Sponsors of Terrorism in 1993, and was toughened by the vote for UN sanctions after the Khartoum government was implicated in the assassination attempt on the Egyptian president in June 1995. Moreover, the accelerated liberalization policy was implemented while war was tearing apart a large part of the country's south in such a way that certain policies that were applied seemed to cause the convergence of both a neoliberal economic rationality and a devastating yet effective counterinsurgency strategy.

The result is even more interesting to assess since the exploitation of Sudanese oil, which was located for the most part in zones of war or split allegiance, led to an intensification of neoliberal policies starting in December 1999, while giving the government a key economic dimension because of its role in the allocation of oil rent.

The intention of the following analysis is to underline some of the facets of this political and economic reality that took shape in both a very authoritarian[5] (northern Sudan) and war-torn (the country's "great" south[6]) context. It shows that the neoliberalism applied in the Sudanese context only provided the conditions for dismantling part of the traditional elite (and incidentally the political parties that they supported) and for setting up a security apparatus that overlaps both the government apparatus and the private sector. Rather than resulting in a radical transformation of the social and economic fabric, the major effect was a reconfiguration of the elite, the elimination or forced marginalization of a large percentage of this elite, and the emergence of a new group. This new group was more plebeian in its social origins, more educated than the previous generation, more internationally minded, and above all it coexisted symbiotically not only with the government but with its security apparatus, whose ramifications in the economic and social sphere indicate that it was an increasingly important autonomous economic and political player.

Theoretical conclusions cannot be drawn based on a single case study, but it would seem that the neoliberalism that was implemented in Sudan allowed for the reconstruction of a political sphere polarized by the National Congress Party (NCP), successor of the NIF and dominant today, despite the promise of free and transparent elections in 2009. But perhaps just as much as reviewing the radical challenges to the regulations brought on by the colonial government, neoliberalism made it possible to grasp other important aspects of the Sudanese government machine, notably the devolution of violence to private groups, the militia-ization of forces in rural settings, creating the conditions for a true civil war between Southern Sudanese starting in 1991, thus intensifying the war against the Khartoum government as well as in Darfur starting in 2003 (without even going into previous episodes). The application of neoliberal formulas to the Sudanese case revealed the methods for devolving power between public and private entities, a political geography of the government that could not be simply reduced to urban vs. rural relations, and especially the capacity for identity destabilization that undoubtedly traumatized the rural settings more than urban centers.

Our first section provides a historical framework of the construction of the government and the Sudanese economic sphere before the June 1989 coup d'état. As Polanyi stated, no market exists alone and the declaration of neoliberal public policies is always unique and takes into account the history of national economic structures. In particular, this historical reminder underlines just how the creation of political parties was possible through the support of parts of the economic elite who were themselves configured by the colonial administration. The relationships of dependence between the government, parties and the bourgeoisie therefore were structural. The Islamists—the new kids on the political and economic scene, even though their leaders were the children of the most traditional elite—took this history into account and, without caving in to theories of historicism or conspiracy, fervently implemented their political program because it was part of the process to dismantle the historical regulations that kept them in the margins of political power.[7]

The second section strives to analyze the macroeconomic policies followed since June 1989 and their rationality in the briefly aforementioned international context. As much as the rather dogmatic adherence to neoliberalism, this will involve showing how the rhythm of reforms followed a very political course, the major stakes of which seem retrospectively to have been to make it impossible to form any political opposition and to finance a gigantic security apparatus by companies whose importance today in the import–export industry, service sector, and oil borders on a quasi-monopoly.

The third section examines land colonization and border changes in the case of Kordofan. Subsequently, we discuss several questions regarding the relationship between neoliberalism and war activities, as well as regarding the ambiguities of African liberalization that have already been voiced for over a decade (lessons that were little or poorly considered in the measures implemented in the former Soviet Union).[8] The question of international economic sanctions and the survival of a government apparently outlawed by the Western community prompts a closer examination of land settlement policies used determinedly and often with violence in the 1990s; the imposition of the new border was not a collateral effect of privatization, because it also served as a veritable counterinsurgency strategy and, based on official statistics used by the World Bank, it is the increase in these agricultural exports during this period of isolation that allowed the government to escape, albeit at an enormous social cost.

This liberalization had other effects that appeared increasingly significant as time went on and military crises recurred despite the signing of a peace agreement with the rebels in Southern Sudan in January 2005. Therefore, two important aspects will be quickly examined: first, the privatization of the security sector, and second, the dynamics of individuation under the guise of Islamism that cannot be reduced only to the success of the consumerism which is today so visible in Khartoum but not elsewhere in Sudan.

GOVERNMENT, BOURGEOISIES, AND WARS IN SUDAN BEFORE 1989

Colonized by the Ottoman Empire between 1821 and 1885, the territory that would later make up modern-day Sudan did not have a proper governmental organization. Therefore, the Ottoman period included the building of administrative machinery, the introduction of taxes, and an institutionalization of Islam and the legal practices associated with it. The conquest of Sudan also corresponded to a key moment in the construction of the Egyptian state, its expansion being financed by the quest for slaves to serve in the imperial army, and for gold and additional revenue derived from the exploitation of Sudan.

A Mahdist uprising put to rout the Ottoman troops led by General Gordon in 1885. But the Mahdist government never found peace because the ever-present British in Egypt quickly moved in to give rise to internal opposition before undertaking their re-conquest in 1898. This long decade for Sudan may be interpreted in various ways because of the traumatic events (notably multiple wars, droughts, and the extensive forced displacement of the population) that took place. It was also the founding moment of contemporary Sudanese nationalism, the indigenization and appropriation of government structures that were imposed under the Ottomans (resources needed to be centralized in order to defend themselves against the return of the Egyptians who were supported by the British), the ambiguous and delicate end to the slave trade, and the imposition of a simpler Islam.

The collapse of the Mahdists and the imposition of an Anglo-Egyptian condominium over the country marked the beginning of two main modern political forces in Sudan: a pro-Ottoman and pro-Egyptian trend that long connected Sudan's fate with that of its neighbor to the north and was often under the denomination of unionists whose leaders had always been members or close relations of the al-Mirghani family, which leads the Khatmiyya Sufi brotherhood; a trend that proclaimed the Mahdist movement and reinserted the holy war scheme and eschatological expectations into a nationalism that was circumspect with regard to the first Ottoman colonization led by the descendants of Mahdi.[9] Several decades later, these political forces led the country to independence and, through a variety of skillful factional alliances, ruled the country until 1989, with the exception of course of two long and ambiguous military parentheses (1958–64 and 1969–85).[10]

Until the beginning of World War I, the new authorities did in fact promote the religious elites who had been faithful to them during the Mahdist War. These elites were mainly grouped together in Sufi brotherhoods, such as Khatmiyya led by the al-Mirghani family, and therefore very Egyptian in philosophy. Although they had a rural foundation, they formed the core of urban bourgeoisie battalions and were granted by the administration significant economic privileges, notably import licenses and jobs in the colonial administration.

At the same time, the British made every possible effort to curb the hostility of those defeated and appease their relations with Mahdi's descendants, especially Abdel Rahman, and their partisans (known as the Ansar, or the companions). Starting in 1908, they granted large landholdings to Sayyed Abdel Rahman al-Mahdi on Aba Island in the White Nile region and later also granted him other incomes, so much so that in 1936, al-Mahdi controlled a 4,500-employee company on his land. Similarly, this support allowed for the growth of a commercial middle class largely tied to the agricultural sector and export crops.

Without delving into the historical details here, the British quest for equilibrium between rival Sudanese political forces was motivated by the perceptible increase in the strength of Arab nationalism at the start of the Turkish war in 1915. This context and the more peaceful relations between the British administration and the partisans of the Mahdist movement also made it possible for these groups to formulate a new political doctrine called neo-Mahdism, in which civil political competition was recommended and eschatological upheaval not required: this doctrinal evolution made it possible to form a pacifist political sphere for both of the two main political forces, despite their reverence for the nineteenth-century civil war as their founding moment.

These reminders aim to highlight the rooting of a certain number of socio-political workings that clarify the policies put in place after the June 1989 coup d'état. First, the colonial government gave structure to the emergence of relatively separate economic groups and did so with a specific goal: to support the political forces that were specifically connected to them. The political organizations that were taking shape at the end of World War II conveyed this reality through a religious as well as financial dependence vis-à-vis these two economic and/or religious groups, which were represented by the two Sayyeds: Sayyed Ali al-Mirghani and Sayyed Abdel Rahman al-Mahdi. Therefore, it is on a dual organic state/bourgeoisie/political sphere relationship that Sudanese politics have been built since 1945, on the condition of always respecting the unstable equilibrium between these two great political forces, even when others appeared (Communists, Baathists, Islamists).

Less immediately apparent was the fact that such a system allowed for the "traditionalist" management of the rural areas

MULTIPLE USES OF NEOLIBERALISM: SUDAN   179

where the majority of the population lived at the time. The two Sayyeds benefited from such a sphere of influence that it was often left to their representatives to smooth provincial tensions. These representatives were also expected to deal with customary authorities. Therefore, in some way, the co-opting of these large organizations made it possible to keep political activities at the level of the urban political elite. It is at Khartoum that the relationships of power were tested, and alliances were formed and broken because the rural areas remained the property of the religious elite who led the two main parties. Such a system could not last forever because it was being challenged internally by the growth of the monetary economy and the presence of the government in rural areas. It was from the outside via regressive environmental transformations and voluntary or forced migrations that they arose. This is the gap that the Islamists took advantage of when they took power in June 1989.

One last point deserves to be highlighted. The colonial government did not implement this policy simply to stabilize the country in terms of security. It also established itself as the largest agricultural contractor. In 1925, the British organized the largest irrigation project in the world, the Gezira project: close to 880,000 hectares located between the White Nile and the Blue Nile, where more than 100,000 tenant farmers lived with their families. While this program was the largest project established by the colonial government, it was not the only one. It emphasized that the government would remain the only real, important economic operator for decades to come.

The economic policies implemented by the colonial government continued smoothly until the October 1969 coup d'état. This coup was led by soldiers in alliance with the Sudanese Communist Party (SCP), which, at the time, was the largest Communist party in the Arab world behind the Iraqi Communist Party. For two years, the new government led by Ja'afar Nimayri embarked on a nationalization of companies and the economy that was characteristic of Communism; at the beginning of the 1970s, the public sector represented more than 50 percent of the country's GDP. An aborted coup attempted by an SCP faction led to a bloody purge of Communist activists and sympathizers in the army, government, and unions: the SCP never recovered and Ja'afar Nimayri completely transformed the government into a Western model. In 1972, 30 nationalized companies were returned to the private sector and a new, more liberal investment code was adopted. The liberal (i.e. pro-Western) inclination was also seen on the political level: Nimayri was the only Arab leader to support the Camp David Accords in 1979 and benefited during that period from the largest influx of US aid in sub-Saharan Africa.

And yet, this economic reorientation would continue and would affect Sudanese economic life in the long term for better and for worse. Even though this government acted violently starting on day one against its northern opponents, it was nevertheless capable of making peace with one revolt in Southern Sudan by the Anya-Nya people, thus bringing to a close in 1972 the initial episode of the war that had started with a rebellion in December 1955, a few days before the independence. This agreement, which granted regional autonomy to this part of Sudan, was also a strong signal with regard to Western and regional interests.

The 1973 oil crisis, as well as the emergence of petro-monarchies in the Gulf as employment pools and investors, considerably transformed the Sudanese economic landscape. The four-fold increase in the price of oil provided these monarchies with more capital than they knew what to do with; a pro-Western government on the other side of the Red Sea endowed with enormous potential in terms of both human and natural resources represented an appreciable source of profit. The Nimayri government, rid of its burdensome Communist allies, couldn't have asked for more. In just a few months, its priorities were refocused on agriculture (only 12 percent of arable land was at that time being cultivated) and transportation infrastructures, the latter made up a veritable bottleneck for any development strategy. A plan financed by the Arab Fund for Economic and Social Development aimed to spend 6 billion dollars over 25 years, and from 1975 to 1985 financed a hundred projects in the agricultural, farming, and other related industries for an estimated cost of close to 3 billion dollars. This first boost generated other projects that were less ambitious but just as important in the long run. Even so, all these development plans, without even factoring in their methodology, focused on mechanized and irrigated agriculture and large-scale industry to the detriment of the traditional sector. This led to the dispersal of rural populations, because life became more difficult, and to exodus towards urban centers. The performance of the modern agricultural sector was deceiving and was unable to compensate for the declining production of rural economies.

For the first time, Sudan was enjoying a real possibility of getting out of its underdevelopment rut. It was failing dramatically for reasons that are largely foreign to our topic.[11] What we are interested in is that Sudan, far from being the all-too-famous granary of the Arab world, rose in 1985 against Ja'afar Nimayri because the country was in extreme debt (7 billion dollars at the time, or just over 35 billion dollars at the end of 2009 (EIU, 2010), a debt that was largely due to arrears). The year 1985 marked the end of the first phase of an ambitious development plan. And yet, at that time, Sudan imported more food products than ever before.

This period is therefore very important for our study on several levels. First, it involves a development project that was based almost exclusively on foreign investments that placed Sudan at the center of the Arab world, while its elite, all political opinions taken into account, suffered from a second-class status that was most often assigned to them in neighboring countries; an enduring colonial legacy and weak Sudanese urbanization undoubtedly explain this marginalized status in the representations of modern Arab elite from Sudan. This economic project was born at a time when the economy inherited from colonization—notably growing cotton—was running out of steam. Its implementation, even if partial, also crystallized new economic players who made a dent in and transgressed the de facto monopoly that the traditional bourgeoisie had gained in the largest sectors of the Sudanese economy that marked the 1990s: high-level government officials redirected either directly or indirectly into the business world; the "corporatization" of soldiers put in charge of semi-public companies in order to buy their political loyalty; the exoneration through an alliance between the government and political party henchmen by "economically" attacking certain sectors of the traditional bourgeoisie who, as witnesses of unfailing political repression, had already largely decided to export their assets to Egypt and other countries in the greater region.

A special asterisk should be placed next to one new player in particular: Islamic banks. The first bank in this group, the Faisal Islamic Bank of Sudan, was established in 1977 in Khartoum, followed by the Bank al Baraka al Sudani. Through their connections with Islamic circles brought to the government's side in 1977, these banks benefited from tax exemptions and ease of access to hard currency, thus allowing them to display results that were unparalleled compared to more conventional banks. Their growing role and the protection that they benefited from despite numerous allegations of corruption and bypassing financial regulations set by the Central Bank of Sudan demonstrated the growing strength of the Islamic environment within Sudanese political society, their international connections, and the confrontation yet to come with the traditional business communities that had forged symbiotic relationships with the financial system largely controlled by the government, despite permanent political rivalries. Although these rivalries were systematic, they were also part of a certain division of tasks that allowed everyone to benefit from the market with periods of greater or lesser success.

It was during the Nimayri government, whose main events we briefly described, that the colonial government's regulations fell into crisis. In February 1986, the IMF announced that Sudan was no longer eligible for the organization's loans. At the end of 1987, the World Bank estimated that Sudanese debt was greater than its GDP and that exports only represented 30 percent of its economy. The government resulting from "nearly" democratic elections in April 1986 was hardly in a position—and hardly impartial—to make drastic decisions: it decided to limit debt service payments to 25 percent of export revenues. Too little, too late, and all the more so because the war resumed in Southern Sudan in 1983, and its cost (which, while admittedly exaggerated, was estimated at 2 million US dollars per day at the time) also put a strain on the already scarce resources.

The democratic government's failure to act especially highlighted the inability of its leaders to find their bearings both domestically and internationally. They proved to be prisoners to Islamic rhetoric regarding the necessity of adopting the Sharia (Islamic law) for the Sudanese state and thus cut themselves off from the road to peace that was imperative to obtaining a more conciliatory attitude from the international community. The coup d'état by the National Islamic Front just as they finally accepted to take political initiative to resume negotiations with the revolt in Southern Sudan was the perfect example of this.

REFORMS AND RECOMPOSITION UNDER ISLAMIC NEOLIBERALISM

The new government was faced with a number of challenges, the first of which was to survive despite being in the extreme minority lacking support among the vast majority of the urban population. The Islamists had led this coup mainly out of fear of being completely marginalized if an agreement between the central government and the rebels in Southern Sudan were to be reached. The task promised to be difficult: it involved increasing their strength in Khartoum; gaining control of the army, who had only followed them because of misunderstandings created by NIF officials; and breaking any attempt of resistance by an opposition made leaderless through the arrest of its leaders, which was not without social connections in the urban world and the government apparatus.

Beyond that, the NIF had reflected on its own understanding of an Islamic state and the interpretation it proposed was in fact congruent with neoliberalism: the state forfeited its economic role, and was limited to its regulatory functions; and the private sector became the medium of development and wealth because the Sudanese Islamists liked money and were not content with populist asceticism.

The Islamization of the Sudanese economy, as in Pakistan and Iran, was far from a simple affair. Even a very extensive reading of Muslim tradition and Islamic thinkers regarding this question left a number of unanswered questions. Above all, this Islamization was supposed to take into account such inescapable economic realities as the dramatic lack of hard currency, the increasing isolation of Sudan on the international scene and, as a result, the difficulty of finding investors likely to stand up to Western, or at least American, pressure.

Finally, the new government had to face up to its own internal failings. Indeed, in order to lend credibility to the non-partisan nature of the coup d'état (Is the army not, in Sudan like elsewhere, a national institution?), the Islamists' organization, the National Islamic Front, was dissolved just like the other political parties and its charismatic leader was himself imprisoned for months.[12] The dissolving of the party created a radically new situation because the decisions were most often made without any real group debate, unlike in previous years. Moreover, the positions at the heart of the government tended to create new hierarchies that were not always in line with those within the party. For example, president Omar al-Bashir was a NIF member with no real responsibility, whereas General Zubeyr Mohamed Saleh who became his vice-president in 1993 was an important leader, undoubtedly the head of the military wing. The party's ambition within the government apparatus should be properly analyzed elsewhere, the results of which should not be underestimated.

In the first two years, the economic policies were completely opposed to the liberalism extolled by Islamic theory: statism, subsidies (for critical commodities such as bread and gas) were doubled by organized rationing through local political structures based on a Libyan model, People's Committees, absolute control of hard currency and interest rates, etc. These measures were implemented with a determination that surprised all those observing

Sudan: three people were executed for having participated on the black currency market for small sums; the strict control of licenses and, even more, the legality of certain business practices caused shortages against which the regime seemed to make out better than the people.

Nevertheless, this period was not an attempt to wager on another policy, this time more state-run and isolationist, which would be corrected starting in 1992. It was not completely plausible, given the state of public finances at the time of the coup d'état. It had two major goals, which were conditions that were essential to the implementation of the Islamic economic liberalization project.

On the one hand, it involved dismantling the traditional bourgeoisie. Together, this group had a quasi-monopoly on most government contracts, with each party favoring its members for whatever opportunities were created by the nominations of its ministers. In exchanged for this, these economic players were generous when solicited by the leaders of their party of allegiance. In such a situation, factionalism and ministerial instability may have participated in the building of a more competitive market by in the long run authorizing the gaining of a savoir-faire by elements of each part of this traditional bourgeoisie and by avoiding the complete consolidation of the control of one market sector by any one group. Political factionalism achieved what competition could not. After 1989, by limiting or revoking import–export licenses, controlling access to hard currency, and prohibiting economic operators suspected of being too sympathetic to the opposition from doing any business, the Sudanese government created a void. During 1989–92, many business people abandoned the Sudanese market for this simple reason and often moved their business first to Egypt, then Europe, and then also increasingly to Asia, well before it became popular to do so at the end of the 1990s.

Because markets detest voids, the Islamic government was keen on promoting "its" economic operators and appointing them to dominant positions in the main growth sectors, especially of course those created by and for the government. This "new" bourgeoisie was different in a number of ways (social origin, education, socialization, use of the formal financial system) from most of the members of the traditional bourgeoisie, as we will see below.

Such a strict and uniquely controlled policy was also aimed at another goal that transcends more than the economic scope: the disciplinarization of Sudanese society. For the Islamic leaders—and not just the soldiers that were on their side—these controls and the brutal repression of any dissidence signaled the restoration of authority and the government (even if the government and the regime were one and the same in many peoples' eyes). This explains why many apolitical senior government officials swung to the new regime after June 1989. Indeed, we could call this opportunism or a will to survive during extensive purges throughout the government apparatus, but it goes beyond that. Tired and humiliated for several years by the preferential treatment used by key businessmen and politicians to help themselves to government resources, some thought that such repression would make it possible to restore the idea of a regulating government that defends the country's greater interests against the individual interests of the various parties. And of course they became disillusioned: yesterday's victim of exclusion proved to be a good student and quickly surpassed the traditional parties in know-how.

However, collapse couldn't be avoided. As with any coup d'état, the inaugural speech of June 30, 1989 made reference without fail to the corruption undermining the state and announced the indictment of high-level political and administrative officials. As elsewhere, once the situation was stabilized, these proceedings suddenly ended, or more accurately were directed arbitrarily at minor figures, leaving the major corrupters of the 1980s unpunished. The Sudanese people, extremely sarcastic with regard to the new government, asserted that those currently in power could not be arrested, citing the example of how Hassan al-Turabi had halted the investigations into the embezzlement and misappropriations committed by Islamic banks during the worst of the drought in the 1980s.

The topic of corruption has never stopped feeding the rumor mill or being a source of public debate since 1989. In the last section of this chapter, we will discuss the various forms of corruption because they explain both the social continuity of the Nimayri period and a never-ending quest to de-legitimize an unpopular government.

In February 1992, Sudanese economic policies changed drastically and marked a true neoliberal turning point. This had to do with a radical application of IMF formulas without the corrective measures usually set up to temper social cost. Such bandwagon behavior was all the more paradoxical because relations with the Bretton Woods organizations were deteriorating. Domestically, such a position change was made possible by previous policies: the political opposition was eradicated; its alleged partisans in the government, army, and unions were suspended and often imprisoned; and its economic supporters were ruined or ordered to leave the country.

When it was called to help Sudan in 1978, the IMF set up support measures (at that time, Sudan was a crucial ally to the United States in a region where East–West competition was as lively as the repercussions of the Israeli–Palestinian conflict). Starting in 1980, it implemented structural adjustment measures that prevented debt from racing upward. In 1986, Sudan was declared ineligible.[13] Soon after the United States listed Sudan on its list of State Sponsors of Terrorism in 1993, the IMF decided to suspend Sudan's voting rights (undoubtedly a pure coincidence). This decision was largely symbolic because Sudan's votes represented less than 1 percent of total IMF votes; however, this action provoked an escalation in the debate on the expulsion that would be fodder for discussion for years to come in Washington. This eviction did not occur because of the opposition by several countries, such as France, which maintained less conflictual relations with Khartoum than the United States, and which wanted to avoid institutions leaving Bretton Woods for reasons of global governance: if Sudan had to be excluded, ten other countries would follow and the IMF would be rendered obsolete. It was not until March 1997, thanks to a large amount of Malaysian financial support a few months before the Asian crisis, that an agreement was concluded with the IMF that required Sudan to repay 4.5 million dollars per month in debt service, drastically lower inflation (from three to two figures), unify interest rates, and reduce government loans with the Central Bank of Sudan. In August 1999, while exporting oil was still a fledgling enterprise, the IMF lifted its Declaration of Noncooperation, and in 2000 the country's voting rights were restored. At that time, the debt was estimated to be 20 billion dollars, of which 1.6 billion dollars were owed only to the IMF. It is also during this period that the normalization of relations between American and Sudanese security agencies took place.[14]

The implementation of liberalization policies took place on several levels. On the one hand, thanks to a constitutional reform adopted in 1994, the Sudanese state had become a federation.[15] This measure made it possible to get new administrations, which in general did not have sufficient resources, to cover the costs of essential public services (health, education, local infrastructure). The result was that, between 1992 and 1998, government expenditures were reduced by half as a percentage of GDP. The key effect was felt elsewhere: in the short term, provinces that had largely been ignored by previous governments were solicited and granted, at least nominally, with prestigious institutions (parliament, universities, etc.). At the end of the 1990s, before oil rent made more equal distribution possible, this experience was bittersweet: students had no professors because they were often busy with a more lucrative second job given that local government employees were still very poorly paid when they were paid at all. The increase in the number of local government employees was also accompanied by a drastic decrease in the number of federal employees; lay-offs were facilitated by ruthless political repression and a government fiscal crisis that pushed some people to return to the deregulated private sector in search of small niches and others, in greater number, to choose the path of economic exile.

Economic liberalization was also evidenced by the progressive decrease in subsidies for critical commodities, especially for bread. On this topic, the government acted in different ways: bread subsidies were reduced in stages, while market price leveling was more abrupt for other products. However, the humanity of this gesture is less apparent than the memory of the urban revolts that marked the fall of Ja'afar Nimayri in 1985. The social costs of these and other urban liberalization measures must not be underestimated and can still be observed today, despite the actual prosperity that was brought about by the peace agreements signed in January 2005, and especially the (very uneven) distribution of oil rent in the capital. For example, the most humble employees often only ate one real meal per day.

The last part of these liberalization policies attacked the Sudanese parapublic sector, a sector that had been created by the colonial government and which, in its heyday, had represented close to 70 percent of Sudan's GDP. In fact, because of the catastrophic management of the 1970s and the short supply of hard currency in the following decade, the 190 public companies were all facing similar problems: they often operated at less than 30 percent capacity (notably because of the lack of replacement parts) and lacked new investments and qualified employees, the latter had often chosen to leave the country because of the low salaries and the political climate.

Between 1992 and 1995, 17 companies were sold and 22 were restructured. Between 1996 and 1998, this number reached 50 but privatization conditions gave rise to bitter debates, not only in the opinion of a public already willing to use any pretext against the government but also within the regime itself. Indeed, Islamist or otherwise, the government repeatedly made "mistakes" that benefited its henchmen: confidential invitations to tender were hardly transparent; acquisitions were partially paid for or practically not paid at all; etc. Similar to other situations in Africa (not to mention on other continents), some say it was a veritable stripping down of the country in favor of the regime's clients much more than a process that complied with Bretton Woods standards. In fact, subject to a case-by-case analysis, it may be said that, thanks to these privatizations, Sudan at that time benefited less from an influx of fresh capital than from the disappearance of structural deficits.

We might have expected that this dismantling of the parapublic sector would have paved the way to a more liberal economy in which the government would no longer play a central role. The development of the oil industry challenged this fragile "asset": the government once again found its economic centrality and the virtuous hypothesis of the construction of a free market was ousted. Except for public contracts, there was very little room for independent and meaningful accumulation.

In the introduction, we noted that in the 1990s, Sudan was in an untenable position vis-à-vis the international community. Heavily in debt, it was not held in IMF's favor. It was truly ostracized because of its Islamic nature and its reprehensible relationships with people and organizations that were hardly in favor in Washington (e.g., Osama bin Laden and the Palestinian Hamas). It was leading a domestic war that provoked outrage among various sectors of international civil society because of recurrent massacres, allegations of slave practices, and massive, repeated human rights violations. Finally, it was the subject of sanctions voted by the United Nations Security Council following the assassination attempt against President Hosni Mubarak in which certain Sudanese officials helped a commando of an Egyptian terrorist organization. In August 1998, following the bombings of two American embassies in East Africa, a drug manufacturing plant was bombed in an industrial suburb of the Sudanese capital, which was less proof of Khartoum's involvement in criminal actions than of Washington's exasperation with the country.

All the same, despite the severe reduction of international aide—Sudan received 17 million dollars in aid in 1997, whereas it had received close to 1.9 billion in 1977—the Sudanese government proved itself able to survive and face up to the financing of its dirty war in Southern Sudan as well as the payment of its soldiers' salaries and that of government employees well before oil rent rebalanced the situation. How was this government able to do what its predecessors had failed to do in more favorable international conditions?

The answer is not simple because the analysis cannot be based simply on the accounting documents provided by the major international institutions. Moreover, these institutions have to date been extremely prudent in this regard, notably because they witnessed the acquisition of costly military equipment whose financing is nowhere to be found in government records. Various answers have been proposed. One involves the mobilization of international admirers of the former Islamic leader, Hassan al-Turabi. Often born into the royal families of Persian Gulf monarchies or as arrogant businessmen, they are suspected, at least for the first two or three years in the early 1990s, of having chipped in to help the Khartoum government to survive. This financing probably decreased greatly when purely rhetorical attacks against Persian Gulf monarchies multiplied after the Iraqi crisis. Other more realistic answers refer to some interstate agreements concluded at the beginning of the 1990s (with Libya, Iran, Malaysia, and later China) and to the promise of oil long before the building of the 1,600km pipeline brought it from the well to the port. Some cite the massive trafficking of counterfeit currency, an argument used since 2006 against the Lebanese Hezbollah.

Without deciding on the total or relative validity of these various explanations, an analysis of statistics provided by the Sudanese government offers a wholly other conclusion. During the 1990s, the agricultural areas in northern and central Sudan benefited from favorable weather, contrary to the previous decade. In addition, government policies had a ripple effect on the agricultural sector: control over prices and marketing was eliminated, exports were stimulated, and taxation was drastically reduced. The rain-fed farming sector, which had been neglected under previous governments who gave the most aid to large irrigated projects, reacted positively to these new macroeconomic policies as did the livestock sector. In the 1990s, rain-fed farming sector growth was on average 24 percent per year and livestock sector growth was 10.4 percent.

This data may seem technical but it is not so. It underlines just how much the government's agrarian colonization policy, often implemented by the regime by fire and by sword, did not only have the possible goal of eradicating populations judged "not Arab" or Muslim enough. It also provided, in a context of international isolation and weaning from bi- and multi-lateral aid, a real sustainable economic option that would make it possible to acquire hard currency, consolidate influence in the rural areas, and wear down hostile populations by using agrarian colonization as a counterinsurgency strategy. These were just a few of the myriad uses of neoliberalism.

LAND COLONIZATION AND BORDER CHANGES: THE CASE OF KORDOFAN

As soon as they arrived in power in 1989, the slogan of the Islamic leaders was *syassat al-tamkin*: exclusive control of government and society. Domination of the economic sphere was in the foreground, as previously mentioned. Since the 1970s, economic power had been at the center of the strategy to dominate political power. Today, the Islamic group, renamed the National Congress Party (NCP), has mostly carried out this hegemonic project on both the economic and political levels.

The government's agricultural policies, especially during the first years following 1989, were centered on a rhetoric of popular mobilization and insisted on economic independence and self-sufficiency. The slogans were "we will eat what we grow" and "al-nafra al-khadra," which meant the mobilization of all resources and means (human, financial, and technological) to promote the agricultural sector. However, this policy boiled down to the government's withdrawal from large agricultural projects by ending subsidies to tenant farmers and adopting Islamic systems of buying products from producers in order to export them.

The domination of the economic sphere as well as social and regional exclusion (concentration of economic and distribution activities in urban settings—especially in the capital—and the increased marginalization of the rural world) resulted in significant transformations, of which the most notable politically was the re-emergence of political ethnicity.[16] The traditional structures of political mediation and social regulation (native administration, customary law) which, historically, had been a bridge between the traditional political elite and their rural roots, and the ethnic groups and political parties, were weakened or destroyed by Islamists whose goal was to marginalize their competition once and for all. One of the effects of this today is that the revolt of the suburbs against political and economic marginalization tends to be seen in ethnic armed conflicts for lack of other channels, as in Darfur or the province of Kordofan, to say nothing of the east or north.

Analysis of the land policy shows the connection between this hegemonic economic project and the logic of war. The issue of land is also an excellent angle for understanding the current acute sharpening of political ethnicity that characterizes the political and social realities of Sudan today. Indeed, it remains at the heart of the Islamic regime's policy in terms of the rebuilding of economic links with the rural world that is still the dominant reality in Sudan. It became a sizeable political stake in the present-day context of economic openness, influx of foreign investment, increased tensions between ethnic communities in outlying regions, and at the critical moment of the implementation of peace agreements between the Sudanese government and the Sudan People's Liberation Movement (SPLM) signed in January 2005.

Indeed, in the outlying agricultural regions along the whole of the southern region, such as Southern Kordofan and the Blue Nile, land is of sizeable political interest and is a major factor in the instability between the northern and southern regions. That is because, in addition to the fact that these two regions provide great opportunities for commercial agriculture, land regains a significant immaterial dimension. It is a factor in how native peoples define their identity. Land ownership is based on ethnic group and social hierarchy: local populations, while "historical" land owners (according to customary law), make up the bulk of those working the land, while the profits of their work benefits mostly "foreign" owners, i.e. non-natives to the region.

We will focus on the practices of the Sudanese government regarding land, notably in connection to its liberal economic policy (questioning of the traditional land ownership system, selective redistribution of resources, marginalization, and exclusion) while analyzing its role in the appearance and spreading of local civil conflicts. Our field of study is the area of Southern Kordofan. Indeed, it is in this outlying region that can best be seen the connection between the government's logic for war and its liberal policies, as well as the effects that land policy has on the social fabric. We will also discuss the oil-producing areas where there is a specific connection between land, government violence, and political ethnicity.

The legal framework of land ownership, namely the hybrid systems in Sudan, is already a source of contradiction. Modern land laws and the traditional property system institutionalized by customary law are not in sync. According to the latter, rural property is communal, meaning that the land belongs to the community or ethnic group. Starting in 1970, a new law established that the government was the only owner of land that was not officially registered. The community therefore only had the usufruct and access to the land was possible only through rental or long-term lease. This was a problem insofar as, for the most part, rural land had been inherited for generations and was not registered. The enactment of this law hardly took into account the persistence of the social institutions that nevertheless made up the social order in large parts of the country.

This new situation became a problem as soon as, in the 1970s, the government got involved in the expansion of mechanized agriculture in order to promote export crops. At that time, investors could acquire land (through long-term leases), including community properties where most of the arable land was located. Most of these investors were not native to the area (the vast majority of them were from the center of the country) and had the means necessary (including access to facilities offered by the government) to farm the land and take part in these large projects.

The persistence even today of this legal anomaly, the resulting social hierarchical organization, and the juxtaposition with economic, social and political marginalization as well as government violence against certain communities during the civil war made the situation in these regions very unstable and caused very deep ethnic resentment, which today is evidenced by intercommunity confrontations.[17] This is true for our case study of the region of Southern Kordofan.

Southern Kordofan offered opportunities for large-scale agricultural investments (especially for export crops). This expansion was not without consequences on the local social order that was based on the cohabitation of various ethnic communities made possible by the respect of traditional institutions (native administration and customary law) to manage intercommunity relations. Land in this local society played an important role in the definition of identity, as well as in the social hierarchy and traditional political power structure.

The government's policy consisted of a selective and exclusive redistribution of expropriated arable land to the benefit mostly of natives of the north and Arab communities that had been residing in the region for several generations. In a society so hierarchically organized by ethnic community as Southern Kordofan, this land practice contributed first to the ethnic and economic polarization of local society. More importantly, this exclusivity and the initial expropriation created among the local people a feeling of non-ownership and even of colonization, because the introduction of commercial agriculture (or what are called mechanized agriculture projects) in this region was done most often to the detriment of the traditional agricultural system (small family-operated farms) used by the majority of the local non-Arab people, the Nubas. The 1970 law contributed largely to the expropriation of small pieces of property owned by the Nuba people, most of which were not registered.

This new social reality was reinforced by the impoverishment of small land owners who soon became workers on their own land, not for their own gain but for that of wealthy non-native land owners. Indeed, these small land owners had neither the financial means nor the know-how to compete with the new buyers and be part of these new projects. What is more, this neither benefited the region of Southern Kordofan nor its people. Profit went straight to the largely absentee land owners.

The expansion of commercial agriculture came at the expense of pastoralism, which was an important activity in the region. The historically defined pasture spaces and routes were seriously affected by this expansion. However, the government was completely unaware of this reality and no steps were taken to control these new transformations. The droughts that hit the region hard at the beginning of the 1980s excited tensions and even caused armed confrontations between farmers and shepherds. In the local societies of Southern Kordofan, the Blue Nile and Darfur, where socioeconomic division corresponded roughly to ethnic division (the Arab communities practicing pastoralism and the others practicing agriculture), the tensions deteriorated quickly into acute armed ethnic confrontations.

The government had a direct role in these rivalries for increasingly scarce resources. There have always been disputes between the shepherds and the farmers. Nevertheless, respect for the effective traditional arbitration mechanisms of the native administration and customary law made it possible to control the tension. However, the weakening of these mechanisms by the government created a conflict resolution void.

The agricultural expansion policy dated from well before the current government. And yet, it was under this government that the policy was becoming a true war strategy against a local population that was considered both hostile and a possible ally of the SPLM. The current government was different from its predecessors in three ways.

First, it involved not only promoting certain communities to the detriment of others, but the land policy operated also like true political clientelism: investors who were close to the party were favored because they were likely to fill the party's coffers and represent a political ally in local management because the NCP did not have its own social base in the region. But the fact remained that its clients belonged to specific ethnic groups. In the previous years, there had been no real distribution of major leases because the government refused to promote the agricultural sector in that region. However, the administration only renewed leases (because of state ownership) to its allies. Today, land is becoming an element of exchange between the NCP and local populations so that the former can build a social base for itself.

Second, given that the issue of profit was always factored into the choices made by decision-makers, the use of land in Southern Kordofan perhaps was due more to the war strategy against the SPLM which, since the 1990s, had militarily occupied certain parts of the region and benefited from a true popular foothold. This war was mostly led by allied local communities that were mobilized and armed by government forces. Admittedly, this community war mobilization strategy had started under the previous government (1986–89). Nevertheless, under the current government, this practice was increasing in scope and became official under the name Popular Defense Forces (PDF), a paramilitary group discussed in the next section.

Despite the signing of the peace agreement in January 2005 and the SPLM's participation in political institutions, the war continued by proxy between these two former enemies. But it switched from an open conflict to a localized and encrypted war in ethnic terms for both land and oil. On the side of the SPLM, political (and war) mobilization regarding land and against expropriation and the government's liberal capitalist policies is today at is zenith, notably with the return of displaced Nuba communities in other areas of the country because of the war.[18]

Land ownership may be the source of armed ethnic conflicts today in Sudan, notably in the regions bordering the north and the south. The signatories of the peace agreements recognize this, and a National Land Commission (NLC) as well as commissions in each state are provided for in the peace agreement as bodies to resolve land disputes and regulate land use or even request government compensation. However, at the end of 2007, this point of the agreement had not yet been implemented. In the absence of arbitration mechanisms and the clear intention of the government to make laws to regulate problematic situations, the topic of land runs the risk of fueling more and more conflicts which will grow in scope when displaced persons and refugees return home.

Finally, at the heart of the current government's land policy and its willingness to contain the Nuba people was the redefinition of the administrative boundaries of the state of Southern Kordofan. The main goal of the decision a few weeks before the signing of the 2005 peace agreement to merge the government of Western Kordofan with that of Southern Kordofan was to restructure the ethnic demography of the new administrative entity, once again to the advantage of Arab communities and to the detriment of the Nuba people, who are not Arab. The former, after the intensification of confrontations in this region and the spreading of the war close to their territory, joined the government that was arming them, even if their political allegiance remained undoubtedly with a traditional party. However, the unification of these two regions can also be explained in terms of an economic interest: oil. This brings us back to the issue of petroleum development in the region, which is also the origin of the emergence of political ethnicity and community violence.

The oil fields of Heglig are geographically located in the southern part of Southern Kordofan and, according to the SPLM, belong to Southern Sudan. The SPLM considers this region to be part of territories that were arbitrarily attached to the north by colonial authorities in 1905. This is the unresolved issue of the border between the north and the south, one of the points disputed by the NCP and the SPLM: it represents an important stake of the 2011 referendum on self-determination for people in the south provided for in the peace agreement.

The definition of borders is also essential in the allocation of oil revenues. The peace agreement provided for three distribution levels for oil revenues: the national level (which includes the northern and southern states), the Southern Sudan government (which includes the southern states) and the producing states. Each government of a producing state receives 2 percent of net revenues. The recent fusion of the two Kordofan regions created major confusion with regard to revenue allocation. In addition to the 2 percent of revenues that go to the producing state, a special provision in the agreement allocated 2 percent to Western Kordofan, which is inhabited mostly by an Arab group, the Misseriya. This created yet another point of inequality between this group and the Nuba, thus increasing the rivalries that already existed between them.

We have tried to show the relationship between the practices of the Sudanese government, its economic liberalization policy, and the re-emergence of ethnic resentment. Indeed, the ethnic elements as well as hegemonic practices (economic and social) have been characteristic of the Sudanese government ever since the country's independence. However, the difference is due to the intensity of this phenomenon and its social and political consequences. The Sudanese Islamists were successful in dominating the economic sphere and changing the economic structure to their benefit. This led them however to basically unravel the social fabric and even to question the structure of the Sudanese state. Economic liberalization and the size of oil revenues increased the stake represented by the control of the economic sphere (and of the state) and radicalized the exclusion of historically marginalized communities as well as other dominant political and social groups. They provided reasons for rebellions in outlying areas, including serious armed ethnic confrontations that today are ringing in a new political order in Sudan.

COERCION VERSUS INDIVIDUATION UNDER THE NEOLIBERAL GUISE

The new government was, by both philosophy and necessity, encouraged not to build its political project simply by using state control as other Arab authoritarian regimes had done before but had to nevertheless satisfy its supporters and ensure its survival. In what follows, we would like to emphasize three elements which, articulated or led within the frame of a neoliberal policy, had significant structural effects on the social control and individuation process in Sudanese society. These elements are, the Islamists' idea of the individual, the establishment and development of Islamic humanitarian organizations, and the growing militia-ization of the rural order.

The Islamists' political theory not only developed a neoliberal model but also a theory of the individual built on its affinities. Money and its uses had no negative connotations, even if some populist trends gave voice to them on occasion; but it was also accepted that some had a gift for business as others had a gift for politics. Hassan al-Turabi did not hesitate to entrust some of the funds to certain people so that they would make them yield a profit and pay back a significant part of the profits to his organization. This way of operating had a number of advantages: it made it possible to quickly co-opt within the economic elite younger individuals who had different training from those of older generations and who were already acquainted with the leader and his organization; it also made it possible to use people with rare talents without requiring, as in other political movements, a social capital similar to that of the elite; it also encouraged innovation because the new members attempted to show just how much their ideas were different from the old methods. Incidentally, this attitude also nourished a very globalized definition of success and individuation.

That which was possible as an organization when such opportunities existed but were not very common was no longer possible when government control was complete and dozens and even hundreds of people had to be rewarded, all the while keeping the public budget from financial asphyxiation. The creation and development of Islamic humanitarian organizations made it possible to combine two important goals. First, regarding the accumulation issue, these NGOs turned out to be perfect small businesses that employed somewhat qualified people with access to the international humanitarian market in Sudan (the law required having a local partner), while being able to import and export without having to pay the usual taxes. Second, these organizations—whether the organization itself or people within it—played a significant role in both supporting sympathizers without resources and connecting dangerous populations (typically the 4 million displaced individuals) in security networks while keeping an eye on international NGOs suspected of harboring spies.

Wanting security services to be financed through private business had several advantages. On the one hand, such a policy only had marginal costs for the state, which did not have to fake its books in order to decrease the importance of this sector in the eyes of the IMF. On the other hand, it ensured the Islamists would survive both by making an uprising (*intifada*) against the government virtually impossible and by ensuring, in the unlikely event of a changeover of political power, the financial resources necessary to regain power.

This policy, which was manifest in the 1990s, intensified with the exporting of oil. First, the normalization with Washington since spring 2000 seemed to augur a renewal of peace negotiations with the SPLM and the possible participation of non-Islamic groups in the government, starting with the former enemy, the SPLM. In a context such as this, this policy had to be consolidated in order to avoid all risk of losing power. Next, the reaffirmation of the government's economic centrality in the allocation of oil rent generated sizeable appetites, notably among the security services that considered themselves to be both the guardians of the government and those who did the dirty work. Certain deposed Islamic leaders will say that this expansion also showed that a specific partisan euergetism was running out of steam. While in its initial years the government could count on the militant generosity of Islamic economic operators, partisan fervor was fading and the simple lure of profits prevailed before the first ten years had passed. Indeed, these resources no longer had the same strategic nature: individualism was undermining the partisan logic inasmuch as these operators were taking more and more advantage of their privileged connections with specific members of the government leadership: the political dimension had lost a considerable amount of steam because of the personal enrichment not only of economic operators but also the government and political leaders, a movement not dissimilar to the second part of the Nimayri government.

Thus, at the end of the 1990s, many service companies were developing. Some attempted to conceal (often with very little success) their employees' real activities. Others increasingly entered the market and sought to earn money by taking advantage of privileged government connections in order to win public contracts. These companies were notably in the sector of activities derived from oil extraction, the financial sector, and the IT sector, without forgetting import–export. This does not mean that they completely controlled these various strategic sectors: there were, for example, niche sectors that required skills that these companies did not have. However, their presence was obvious to the point of short-circuiting official or internationally certified procedures.[19]

To the "defense" of Sudanese leaders, this economic model is almost the norm for many of its neighbors and allies. To a greater or lesser degree, despite the government's very secular nature, this is what is seen in Eritrea and Ethiopia. It is obviously similar to what is seen in Libya, Iraq under Saddam Hussein, and also in Algeria under the NLF and during the civil war. Inasmuch as they would have liked to, the Sudanese Islamists had not created anything new.

If the details of this "security accumulation" remain misunderstood, the militia-ization of the rural order gave rise to more inquiries and just as many concerns. Indeed, the premises of such a policy existed well before the June 1989 coup. The colonial government had turned to it shamelessly both in Darfur and in Southern Sudan repeatedly as long as it allowed it to spare its meager budget. The first war in Southern Sudan had provoked a re-creation of ethnic militias in order to oppose uprisings in areas where the army preferred not to go. However, this policy had been led very selectively and had no major macropolitical effects.

The renewal of war in Southern Sudan in 1983, insurgent incursions in areas of northern Sudan that were the Prime Minister's stronghold, the bankruptcy of the government, the unsuccessful reinsertion of armed opponents of Nimayri during the 1970s, the inability of the army to lead even the smallest battle: all of this converged starting in 1986 for the preparation of new militias in rural areas, at least in the war zones. And yet, this privatization of violence was partial and provoked significant domestic and international controversies, which limited its intensity and geographic scope. On several occasions, the army protested the loss of its monopoly (for reasons that undoubtedly were not only fed by constitutional worries, seeing as how the war was also a way for some officers to fill their pockets). One part of the political class denounced the return of the Mahdist war project (because, at the time, the head of the government was Sadeq al-Mahdi, the great-great grandson of Mahdi) and the coup attempt that would have transformed the Prime Minister into the first leader of a religious monarchy. As for the human rights defenders, they saw more the losses of control brought about by this forced communalization of government taxation and called to mind the massacres and impunity that it authorized, especially after the El Daim massacre in 1987.

The new government had a completely different determination. The state's fiscal situation made rearming the army and an immediate offensive against the insurgents impossible. This did not take place until spring 1992, even if in the meantime the SPLM havens on Ethiopian soil had been eliminated. Moreover, the army was demoralized and its loyalty to the new government uncertain: the war in the south was therefore used to keep unsure troops and officers a safe distance from the capital while purges were decided on and power was consolidated. Finally, the advantage of formalizing ethnic militias was to reinsert the war at the local level, depoliticize it, and ensure that battalions of combatants were available at a low cost because pillaging was designed straightaway as the necessary conclusion to a battle.

The creation of the Popular Defense Forces (PDF) in November 1989 was a true turning point in the war in the south but also in the state's management of outlying areas. In the space of a few years, the conflict in Southern Sudan was fed by a proliferation of local civil conflicts provoked by militias incited by the central government in order to contain insurgent progression or the consolidation of their positions. The war was thus becoming south versus south, even more so than it was north versus south. Moreover, the Islamic regime was sensitive to the threat that could be born out of the emergence of a strong militia alliance that could have challenged its rule. With determination, it made every effort to not only create strong militia groups but also to cultivate ambitions and rivalries among their leaders so as to be able, if need be, to divide them and provoke a confrontation between suddenly rival Sudanese branches.

This policy of war clientelization first was applied in Southern Sudan, and caused several thousand casualties and the displacement of hundreds of thousands of people. As we saw in the previous section, it was also led with determination in the border zones between the north and south where it typically appeared like a release of the state's sovereign functions appearing as an agrarian colonization that favored certain communities at the expense of others, in agreement or sympathizing with the rebellion. It was also led determinedly in Darfur even before the current conflict which started in February 2003. Starting in 1991, the repression of an attempted uprising led by former Islamist, Daoud Bowlad, who had switched to the SPLM, was led using techniques that would later be implemented regionally starting in April 2003 and would lead to the sad situation we know today.

If this analysis of the Popular Defense Forces emphasizes the privatization of public order by the state, this action is not without ambiguity or limits. Indeed, undoubtedly proof of tacit acceptance by the military institution, these militias were not completely independent from the government beyond the weapons and munitions that were given to them before the fighting. They were most often trained and supervised by Islamists who were themselves soldiers. Devolution was therefore not complete, even if there was proof of strong tension between the official armed forces and these duly controlled militias.

The Popular Defense Forces, however, were not limited to this unique phenomenon of communitarian or tribal militias. The Islamic regime intended to succeed in implementing a real process of disciplinarization and subjection of urban society. In the cities in the north, the PDF tended to regroup two very different types of recruits. On the one hand, answering a call to Holy War (*jihad*), many officers and Islamist students signed up to go fight in the south against the so-called infidels. Whether or not the cynics agree, this call was truly felt among the youth polarized by Islamism, to such an extent that enrollments were numerous and the NCP lost important officers, officers who could have been used to teach at universities and run the government apparatus. On the other hand, students and those aspiring to certain public service positions were required, at one time or another, to spend long months within the PDF either to validate their training or to have access to training. During this period, which could last up to two years, the young recruits were subject to ideological indoctrination and a fairly complete military training.

In fact, these units met several government needs. First, they made it possible to identify the most religious elements and those who supported the government's political discourse. They benefited from special treatment and could in time receive military training to become an officer or to work in one of the many security services. The most rebellious were also identified and, in addition to the punishment that was inflicted on them, were placed on a blacklist, which challenged whether or not they would have a future working within the government. Next, these units were the ones that actually went to fight in Southern Sudan while government soldiers were those who dropped bombs and attempted to avoid as much action as possible. But, there too, a certain heterogeneousness prevailed because some units were quasi-professional whereas others were generally more seen as *bassidji* (as used in the Iran–Iraq war), i.e. young people sent to the frontline to set off the mines before close combat is waged.

Thus, this was advantageous for the government in two respects. First, it had a striking power that was independent of the military institution, without being an alternative praetorian force, thus guaranteeing it independent military support. In addition, it could credit these forces rather than the official army with victories in the south, thus reinforcing their prestige among both its domestic and international partisans. The government also created a cult of martyrs extremely similar to the one that prevailed in Iran. The walls of University of Khartoum were covered with pictures of young students who had died in combat, the streets bore the names of the most heroic, and television programs praised their sacrifice.

And yet, this policy had very ambivalent consequences beyond the loss of numerous human lives. First and most paradoxically, the Islamists would have been the first to return the war to its national context, in spite of their attempt to tribalize it. Indeed, the Sudanese army was fundamentally made up of country people from Sudan's outlying regions (especially the previously mentioned Nuba Mountains), Southern Sudan, and Darfur. The officers were in most cases Arab in origin. By modifying recruitment for war, the government involuntarily encouraged the urban world to recognize that the war in the south was not a far-off reality that, for many, could be reduced to nothing more than an important part of the government budget. The children of the urban elite were suddenly risking their lives; some died and others returned permanently disabled. This cruel reality had significant effects. On the one hand, it provoked growing civil resistance during PDF recruitment campaigns. On the other hand, it gave credibility to the need for a political solution among the normal population, even if this involved no sympathy or social reconciliation with the Southern Sudanese.

The cult of martyrs also had very ambivalent effects. Of course, it provided the symbolic dimension of supporting the war but also marked individual itineraries in a country where Islamists did not by a long shot represent a significant portion of the youth. This heroism also resonated therefore as the growing social isolation of the government from the youth uninterested by the war and in search of other ways of identifying itself. After the division of the Islamists in December 1999, Hassan al-Turabi had some very harsh words, perhaps born out of absolute cynicism, about the quest for paradise through this type of holy war: "Paradise is built on earth, not elsewhere, he said, and it is here that you should look for your wives." By only proposing martyrology as the individual ideal, the government strangely strengthened other tendencies in its neoliberal policies: individualism and consumerism.

Serious anthropological studies would need to be conducted in order to possibly figure out what in the current social processes comes from individuation produced by globalization, and the withdrawal of the social and political because of the trauma from the political repression supported by the new social criteria of success. At the same time, as in other parts of the Muslim world, Islamists tend to redefine themselves a religious people who think for themselves and not simply like someone following in the paths of others. If there was an alternative between martyrdom and consumerism, Sudanese Islamists have not found it and oil rent has not made that job any easier.

CONCLUSION

The deliberate implementation of a neoliberal policy in Sudan had radical effects on the regulation of the post-colonial state. Even if this policy was congruent with the Islamic plans, we can see that the result has very little to do with the ideals developed by its theorists and bears little witness to any sort of Islamic ideology.

In a little more than a decade, using all the instruments of the state, from coercion to indoctrination to liberal macroeconomic policies, the Sudanese government reproduced itself and reconfigured its functions while acting more partisan and monopolistic than ever before. While the colonial government had given rise to a bourgeoisie highly stratified by the political history of the nineteenth century and the rural/urban divide, almost two decades of Islamic rule and neoliberal policies profoundly reorganized the market, the economic elite and its relationship with the government, political society, and the outside world.

If this government was capable of getting rid for the most part of the old elite, the new elite that it gave rise to seemed uninterested by competition and economic autonomy. While being opportunists, they demonstrated mostly the success of a hegemonic reconstruction project of the market in which the Islamization of practices serves to hide the controlling of the most dynamic or important economic operators, not only linked to the current leaders but also to their security services, to the exclusion of all others. The stake is less the expanded reproduction of a competitive market than the strategic preservation of a government undermined by factionalism like its predecessors, but also capable of—thanks to the unifying role of its security services—resisting domestic and international pressures for true democratization. We could certainly argue that this evolution is for the most part connected to the transformation of Sudan into a rentier state, given that it now produces close to 500,000 barrels of oil per day. However, this valid argument cannot overshadow the dynamics that were already at work well before oil extraction started.

This is undoubtedly an abrupt conclusion that is very far from a specific ideological vision that would have us believe that market liberalization results in the eventual liberalization of the political sphere. Not only does the case in Sudan not allow us to validate such an argument but it shows that the paradoxical result of liberalization could be the spreading of war to areas where it did not previously exist by underlining the peripheral status of large areas of the country and numerous communities.

NOTES

1. Roland Marchal is a researcher at the CNRS, based out of the CERI-Sciences Po, Paris. He is the lead author of the text. Einas Ahmed is an associate member of CEAN/IEP in Bordeaux and a researcher at the CEDEJ in Khartoum. She is the author of the third section in this chapter and participated in the development of the other sections.
2. Dissolved in 1989 like all the other political parties, the Sudanese Islamists united under the National Congress Party (NCP) in 1998. This organization, however, included non-Islamic members whose professional and/or private activities required strict alliance to the government.
3. Johnson (2003).
4. Roy (2004).
5. Without wanting to delve any deeper into this subject, the first years of the government were in many respects pre-totalitarian and underlined the extent to which the new government knew how to mobilize the repressive techniques acquired during previous periods of authoritarianism in Sudan, notably between 1969 and 1985, and the expertise of governments in the region (Baathist, Libyan, Iranian) for a national security network, notoriously in urban centers.
6. Contrary to common understanding, the North–South war hardly corresponded to a geographic, religious, or ethnic divide. Zones located in northern Sudan revolted against the central government in coordination with an insurrection led mostly in the country's south; the Nuba Mountains or the southern Blue Nile region, without even mentioning the border zone with Eritrea, rebelled for many years, but accepted ideas die hard.
7. It would be interesting to compare the NIF—which was created in the fall of 1985 and is a true, fully engaged political player endowed with significant financial means thanks to the rise in power of the Islamic economy (particularly banking) since 1977—with its predecessor, the Islamic Charter Front (ICF), which was created in 1964 and was never more than a second-tier player.
8. Pitcher (2002).
9. See, Nicole Grandin (1982), Holt and Daly (1988).
10. The first military government was as it were co-opted by the political parties who at the time were incapable of ruling the country. The second attempted with some success after 1977 to join forces with the great traditional political trends, even if it was the Islamists who finally came out on top.
11. In addition to the problems linked to cooperation between Arab countries, we must analyze the costs brought about by a blocking of Port Sudan (the only Sudanese port), numerous delays due to inefficiency and corruption of middlemen and state employees, the scale of a luxury consumerism now accessible to immigrant families, the rapid flight of capital while the domestic political situation weakened after 1976, etc. All these reasons were at one time or another essential to explaining the involution of the Sudanese economy after the 1973/74 euphoria.
12. Nevertheless, contrary to other parties whose leaders were pursued, the leaders of the NIF with the exception of Tourabi were immediately integrated

into government operations, at first discreetly and then, after the power was consolidated, more and more openly. The first internal snag was caused by the length of the Islamic leader's detention: he was expected to be released after one month, but was only finally let go after six.
13. The irony of the story is that in 1984 Washington granted a business loan to Khartoum in order to allow it to pay off its debt service. Once the US Congress got wind of this, they immediately blocked it. In 1997, at a time when relations between the IMF and Sudan were at their worst, Malaysia, under the control of Dr. Mahathir Mohamad, was doing the same thing.
14. Benjamin and Simon (2003).
15. Lavergne (1997).
16. Lonsdale (1996).
17. For the history of land ownership laws, see Awad (1971).
18. Among the main recommendations from the All Nuba Conference, which took place in Southern Kordofan in April 2005, a few months after the peace agreement was signed and which brought together the Nuba diaspora as well as all the main Nuba political factions: "... the review of all [land] leases that were granted by the state in the previous periods, and abolishing them if needs be" (par. 23); "... the listing of all lands that were confiscated from the natives in order to redistribute them as public or private schemes, and restoring them to their rightful owners or compensating them" (par. 24); "Drafting new land laws in accordance with the wishes of the citizens to own these lands" (par. 25); and "Reviewing all the legislations and the bases under which the lands were distributed for agricultural schemes in order to give the utmost priority to the local population ..." (par. 28). "The Final Communique of the All Nuba Conference," April 2–6, 2007, p. 38.
19. It is not uncommon for a foreign company wanting to set up shop in Sudan to seek the help of a local partner to facilitate procedures. When granting contracts for the construction of the Merowe Dam, the international companies were invited to choose the local companies that they wanted to subcontract to from a kindly provided list. Competition and invitations to tender open to all could wait.

REFERENCES

Awad, M. H. (1971) "The evolution of land ownership in the Sudan." *Middle East Journal*, Vol. 25, No. 2.
Benjamin, D. and Simon, S. (2003) *The Age of Sacred Terror: Radical Islam's War Against America*. New York: Random House.
Economist Intelligence Unit (EUI) (2010) *Country Report Sudan*. London: EUI (April).
Grandin, N. (1982) "Al-Sayyid Abd al-Rahmân al-Mahdi (1885–1959) et l'héritage mahdiste au Soudan oriental." In *Le Cuisinier et le Philosophe. Hommage à Maxime Rodinson*, ed. Jean-Pierre Digard. Paris: Maisonneuve et Larose, pp. 217–226.
Holt, P. and Daly, M. (1988) *A History of Sudan from the Coming of Islam to the Present Day*. London: Longman.
Johnson, D. (2003) *The Root Causes of Sudan's Civil* Wars. Oxford: James Currey.

Lavergne, M. (1997) "Le nouveau système politique soudanais ou la démocratie en trompe-l'œil" (The new sudanese political system, or image of democracy). *Politique africaine*, No. 66 (June).

Lonsdale, J. (1996) "Ethnicité, morale et tribalisme politique" (Moral ethnicity and political tribalism). *Politique africaine*, No. 61, pp. 98–116.

Pitcher, M. A. (2002) *Transforming Mozambique: The Politics of Privatization, 1975–2000*. New York and Cambridge: Cambridge University Press.

Roy, O. (1992) *L'échec de l'Islam politique* (The failure of political Islam). Paris: Le Seuil.

"The Final Communique of the All Nuba Conference." April 2–6, 2007, p. 38.

Part Three

6
Colombia: The Re-structuring of Violence

Francisco Gutiérrez Sanín[1]

COLOMBIAN VIOLENCE AND NEOLIBERALISM. IS THERE A CASE?

Neoliberalism has been a major target of the mobilization of social forces in Latin America since the late 1980s. Practically none of the major political changes and turbulences that have taken place in the subcontinent in the last 25–30 years have avoided including neoliberalism as one of their main themes (and sometimes it was really the only one). Hugo Chávez can be seen as a lagged product of the *Caracazo*, the rebellion of hundreds of shantytown neighbors who stood up against the plans of economic adjustment pushed forward by Carlos Andrés Pérez in 1989. Once in power, Chávez' opposition against neoliberalism became one of his core ideological tenets. In Ecuador, practically all the social movements that have given the streets a de facto veto power since the early 1990s have fought against the "paquetazos" (adjustment proposals of successive governments). In Bolivia, Evo Morales arrived in power from a tide of forces that furiously rejected the neoliberal proposals of Gonzalo Sanchez de Losada. More generally, today's Latin American left is an anti-neoliberal left—it developed against neoliberalism, and owes it its strength and a substantial part of its popular appeal. This is no coincidence. According to certain key indicators, the region of the world that showed the most abrupt economic opening in the period of the neoliberal great transformation—which started approximately in the late 1970s and early 1980s, see other comparative chapters in this volume—was Latin America. While the developed capitalist world had relatively open economies that further opened gently, and Africa had closed economies that opened unevenly, Latin America had closed economies that opened abruptly. And neoliberalism has substantially increased the already enormous (the highest in the world) Latin American levels of inequality. No wonder the process has been so traumatic and has created such a drastic political change.

None of this, though, seems to apply too clearly to Colombia. It is true that several social movements have launched anti-neoliberal proposals, and that several intellectual circles have actively opposed the full-fledged implementation of neoliberalism. The problematic, however, is far from the center of the political agenda. The left has grown, but it is supported much more by anti-corruption slogans than by the opposition to neoliberalism. Though it has vigorously attacked the free trade treaty that the government wants to conclude with the United States, it has done so for ideological and programmatic concerns, not for the (quite dubious) political gains. The Liberal Party, which had earlier been a staunch opponent of the treaty, glided towards a more flexible position and ended as a (tepid) treaty supporter—a change in which probably pragmatic calculation had a role: citizens were not commending an adversarial position towards the treaty, perhaps because they saw it as a form of attacking the president.[2] Opinion polls show systematically that the population is either indifferent to or divided on the issue, and this includes the most vulnerable social strata. Neoliberalism has produced in Colombia no popular explosion (as the Caracazo), no social movement (as in Bolivia), no permanent street opposition (as in Ecuador), no general mobilization against the political system (as in the Argentinean "que se vayan todos").[3] On the contrary, a highly pro-neoliberal and right-wing president has maintained high levels of popularity that have no equal in Colombian history, and that must be rather rare in any country (seven years and counting with 70 percent-plus support). The political preferences have moved to the right as well, especially among the young (*Revista Semana*, 2002). All this, of course, has to be nuanced. Specific neoliberal measures have activated popular opposition. For example, the privatization of the public utilities on the Atlantic Coast was followed by a stream of protests, and several forms of individual opposition (harassment of the collectors that the private firms send to the popular neighborhoods, burning of meters, etc.). In 2007, the intent of changing the regional financial structure of the country, which especially affected education policies, was also greeted with a tide of protest. In the aggregated landscape, though, these protests have been rather isolated, non-sustained events, overshadowed by other concerns that have regularly fed "big politics" in Colombia.

In the other direction, in Latin America the 1970s and 1980s were the decades of agrarian wars, especially in Nicaragua, El Salvador,

Guatemala, Peru, and Colombia. The advent of neoliberalism *coincided* with the cooling down of this agrarian fire. In some cases, this might have been only a coincidence. In others, however, it is more than that. Wood (2000) has made a persuasive case that peace was attained in El Salvador due to the fact that, with economic globalization, the costs of non-negotiation for economic (especially agrarian) elites surpassed those of bargaining. Intuitively, and sometimes explicitly inspired by the Central American experience, several researchers believed that this was also the case in Colombia and, unsuccessfully, tried to convince key internal audiences that striking a peace accord was indispensable for both globalization and for good business (two remarkable examples are "La paz es rentable," 1997, and Gómez, 2003). This is not difficult to explain. Rational actors may find that the duet of peace plus neoliberalism is a second best, and that the option of triumph over the guerrilla plus neoliberalism is preferable *and* available. The feeling that this optimal option is possible can also be fed by international experience. Certainly, cases like Fujimori in Peru are remarkable precedents, and there is proof that at least part of the Colombian political elites were conversant with it: they expected to achieve what Fujimori had (*El Espectador*, 1999).

It is typical of the neoliberal cycle in Latin America that it has triggered mass opposition, sometimes with violent outcomes (like in Bolivia, or in the Venezuelan Caracazo of 1989), but rarely organized violent contestation in the form of guerrillas.[4] The new Latin America has veered towards the left, but away from organized insurgent action. Obviously, none of this applies to Colombia. Contrary to Central America, the adaptation to the global economy did not imply a change in the evaluation of costs and benefits of making war by the economic elites, at least not so large and generalized so as to prompt a collective action in favor of negotiation. Or if it did then the guerrilla remained unimpressed.[5] Be that as it may, the protagonists of the Colombian confrontation seem to contradict the notion that "peace is profitable" or, in the other direction, "nobody wins with war." But perhaps not? It may be the case that rational actors engage in severely suboptimal dynamics and destructive actions, and know it, but cannot prevent it. Be that as it may, if war is ostensibly suboptimal, its continuation has to be explained. What kind of interactive structure produces such an outcome? More obliquely, the Colombian version of neoliberalism has been incapable of producing the cessation of violence. While, as argued above, the end of the peasant wars in Latin America coincided with the implementation of the neoliberal program, in Colombia war and opening not only overlapped, but sometimes even seemed to reinforce each other.

In other words, Colombia appears to have behaved in a typically bizarre fashion. Unlike in other Latin American countries, the Colombian neoliberalism has not been translated easily into political terms. The phrase should not be misunderstood. Certainly, the main armed actors—especially but not only the guerrillas—refer on an everyday basis to themes intimately and directly related to neoliberal transformations. However, the main effects—mass mobilizations, protests, the creation of an oppositional public opinion; or, in the other direction, peace agreements based on the simultaneous implementation of neoliberalism and democracy like in El Salvador—are simply not there. There does not seem to be a direct line of causality between neoliberalism and an increase or decrease in violence. The standard argument, according to which neoliberalism has caused misery and social disintegration and thus more violence, simply does not work (or has not worked until now). But, on the other hand, the sum of political and economic openings did not, despite the hopes of the architects of the 1991 Constitution and the experience of other countries, bring peace. Neither the "anti-liberal dystopia" nor the "liberal promise" have been borne out in Colombia. The sum of a clearly more democratic and transparent constitution and neoliberalism did not bring peace, contrary to the explicit hopes of the architects of this process of change. So should we simply leave the discussion at this point: the relation between neoliberalism and violence is simply non-existent? There is no story whatsoever.

In this chapter I will argue that this would be quite wrong. There is a larger story here, and it is both extremely important and interesting—a story of a continued interaction between liberalization and modes of war-waging. Its general contours are easy to draw. In the process of implementation of neoliberalism, the Colombian state suffered large-scale changes. Indeed, these changes were not necessarily an exogenous imposition or an anti-democratic conspiracy. Some of these changes responded to very long-standing traditions and demands, the obvious case being decentralization. Openers—or at least their intellectual and political vanguard—believed that the incorporation of the country into the new global world entailed the transformation of the state under the principles of decentralization, transparency, and accountability. But the implementation of these institutional reforms was determined by the fact that they were being enacted in the context of a country at war. In other words, war and the Colombian neoliberal experience shaped each other. I will show that neoliberalism also transformed the Colombian war, and quite deeply. Institutional change can influence war in two ways: quantitatively—increase or decrease in the intensity of war; and qualitatively—opening the door to new ways of combating, establishing links with the population, etc. In the quantitative dimension, it may be the case that in effect neoliberalism, in the long run, is associated both with the initiation and with the cooling down of the Colombian conflict. This in reality is open to debate, where the analyst has to juggle with mixed evidence. In the qualitative dimension, though, it is clear that *all* armed actors have suffered a process of adaptation to and learning about the new socio-economic and institutional conditions prompted by the neoliberal globalization. This is the central claim of this chapter. To make my point, I will analyze three types of situation:

- An old problem that could not be solved by the previous model of development, but that was deepened (land property rights).
- A new problem directly created by neoliberalism (resulting from the reforms in the health sector).
- A new problem related only obliquely to economic liberalism, but which has typically been pushed forward by liberal politicians and multilateral agencies (decentralization).

In all three cases, I will describe the problem, the proposed solutions and the expectations behind them, and the outcome. These outcomes will show that neoliberalism completely changed the dynamics of war, though the quantitative impact—homicide rates, for example—may go in either direction.

The chapter is structured as follows. I start with a discussion of the specificities of the Colombian neoliberalism. Though neoliberalism *is* a viable concept (see the comparative chapters in this volume), one must be aware that: (i) each country has its own neoliberalism, and (ii) neoliberalism evolves over time. To understand how neoliberalism has interacted with the Colombian armed conflict, it is necessary then to understand the trajectory of the country's specific brand of neoliberalism as it developed in the last 30 years. The second section establishes a periodization of the Colombian conflict. Contrary to the standard version of a country in perennial war, I suggest that only in the late 1970s or early 1980s do we have a genuine civilian confrontation, and I suggest some ways in which conflict and neoliberalism interacted. The final three sections constitute the main part of the chapter, and focus on the qualitative analysis of the interrelation between institutional changes prompted by neoliberalism and war. Based on the three examples (land, health, and decentralization), I explain the concrete mechanisms that show how the changes in the institutional set of restraints and opportunities, and in the modalities that link the country with global markets, have transformed the Colombian war.

THE NEOLIBERAL TRANSFORMATIONS IN COLOMBIA

The Nature of Colombian Neoliberalism

Neoliberalism came to Colombia in a non-standard fashion. The assertion has to be qualified, as in a sense each country's experience of neoliberalism is unique. Even after this caveat, Colombia seems anomalous enough. Unlike the richer countries of the Latin American Southern Cone, and also its Andean neighbors, it never had a governmental populist experience, or the clear predominance of a statist program (or party). The country never witnessed a hypertrophy of the public sector, nor was it ever governed by political elites willing to "see as a state" (Scott, 1999). The Colombian state has always been small, at least in comparison with many of its Latin American counterparts. Economic orthodoxy was never really out of fashion, as a careful survey of even the sharpest reformist politicians shows (see for example Gutiérrez, Acevedo, and Viatela, 2007). Furthermore, the Colombian adjustment to the new realities of economic globalization was typically gradual, and it is difficult to establish a clearly delimited departing point, which does exist quite ostensibly in, say, the Bolivian and Venezuelan cases. It avoided the debt crisis that so badly hit the majority of Latin American countries; the 1980s were not a "lost decade" for Colombia. Certainly, the second finance minister under Belisario Betancur (1982–86), Roberto Junguito, carried out a severe adjustment program, but probably fell short of a full-fledged implementation of neoliberalism.[6] A second key moment arrived in 1990, with the administration that issued the new Constitution. Here, both the effort and the ideology that supported it were much more sustained and articulated, and were related explicitly to a large-scale program of state modernization. The year 1990 symbolizes a key movement that in a time band—more or less between 1986 and 1994—deeply changed the state, completing a wide array of institutional reforms and introducing new bureaucratic routines. Álvaro Uribe's two administrations (starting in 2002) gave renewed impulse to the neoliberal program.

Many circles in Colombia had expected that neoliberal transformations would come, if ever, hand in hand with the closure of the political system. This fear stemmed from the experience of Latin America in the 1960s and 1970s, when the set of policies that anticipated neoliberalism—called "monetarismo" by the contemporaries—was almost invariably implemented by dictatorships. It was considered that only authoritarian governments could put in practice very severe pro-market policies, which would severely hit, and politically alienate, the majority of the population. Against these predictions, in Colombia at least, the two first economically liberal moments not only coincided but were deeply articulated with democratization processes, which cannot be ignored as mere window dressing even by the most severe of evaluations. Belisario Betancur pushed forward a broad peace process accompanied by an equally energetic political reform proposal, though it is probably true that his worldview was more developmentalist than liberal, and that for him the structural adjustment program was not a programmatic guide but rather a bitter pill to swallow. César Gaviria, on the other hand, was a convinced neoliberal, and believed in what can be called the isomorphism principle: free and open societies and economies reinforce (and resemble) each other. He managed to foster a constitutional process that included both deeply neoliberal clauses, and a genuine and ample proposal of democratization.

In Colombia, thus, the application of neoliberalism had not had—at least until very late—authoritarian overtones. This is not a local phenomenon. Globally, with some important exceptions, neoliberalism and the so-called third wave of democratization not only coincided but further buttressed each other. In part, this was the result of conscious activity, in part a result of indirect mechanisms, and in part a result of the interaction between both. Additionally, Colombia has had a strong republican tradition, associated with macro-institutional political stability, which closely matched the spirit of the "third wave." Summing up:

- In Colombia, neoliberalism was not as traumatic as elsewhere because of two factors. First, the country never had a populist-statist experience, so many of the neoliberal operations that seemed so ominous in the rest of Latin America, had in Colombia both precedents and bounded effects. For example, the number of privatizations between 1990 and 2000 was relatively modest (nearly 40 firms, see Pombo and Ramírez, 2001; CONFIS, 2001).

- There have been three key neoliberal moments: the second half of the Betancur administration (1982–86), the Gaviria administration (1990–94), and the two Uribe administrations (2002–10). There have also been frequent changes and reversals in between, which respond to another Colombian governance tradition (gradualism).
- Neoliberalism has not been a central issue for public opinion. From time to time it has been a political highlight, and certainly it has played objectively an extremely important role. But this has not been easily translated into the political realm. The opposition has combated the most audacious neoliberal actions of successive governments, especially the free trade treaty with the United States.[7] But the payoffs it has got from this activity are small.
- Neoliberalism—given both international constraints and endogenous traditions—was long associated with political liberalism. Both the Betancur and Gaviria administrations headed experiences of opening and democratization, and several times expressed their intention of reforming the "closed" Colombian traditional-bipartisan political system. The Uribe government behaved differently, and during certain periods proposed explicitly a tradeoff between security and liberty. However—be it because of international constraints or because of the weight of pre-existing traditions and world views, or a combination of both—until now it has not embarked on a clearly authoritarian path.[8]
- The guerrilla has consistently denounced the neoliberal course of the country as an anti-national cabal. Despite the fact that during the guerrilla's negotiations with different governments this issue did not crop up as regularly as in its standard propaganda, it must not be ignored that neoliberal policies shrank the feasible bargaining set between the guerrilla and the government. On the other hand, there is no evidence that the economic elites have come to the conclusion that the costs of being in war and making no concessions are higher than those of achieving peace and conceding something.

The Policies

In sum, despite the gradualist style of its application, and the fact that it was being introduced in a country without previous statist experiences or parties, neoliberalism has had significant effects, which have deeply changed both Colombia's economy and polity.

It terms of specific policies, Colombia's neoliberalism exhibits practically all the basic traits of the canonical neoliberalism, but has at the same time several specificities and rather surprising outcomes. The main one is the fact that the implementation of neoliberalism in the decisive, second moment—the Gaviria administration—entailed the growth of the state, due to increases of investment in security and justice, but also of the health and education sectors. Between 1990 and 1996, social investment by the central government grew from 3.9 to 6.9 percent of GNP; resources for health and education grew from 2.5 to 3.4 percent and from 0.7 to 1.2 percent of GNP, respectively. Investment in justice and security also grew (1.9 to 2.4 percent, and 0.6 to 1.1 percent, respectively).[9] Naturally, the scheme of fiscal decentralization, deepened and developed by the 1991 Constitution, also played a role. In other words, in Colombia neoliberalism was introduced through the establishment of a new social pact, so the subjective belief of many of its architects—that the state should be reduced—was neutralized by the immediate costs involved in the creation and sustaining of the pact.

Neoliberalism in Colombia introduced key innovations in at least seven economic realms. First, monetary policy. Colombia is one of the few countries in the world that has constitutionalized the fight against inflation (articles 371, 372, 373 of the Constitution, which were developed by Laws 31 and 35 of 1992, and 549 of 1999). The 1991 Constitution also gave the monetary policy to the central bank, restraining the latitude of the government to make investment decisions. However, this did not imply a reduction in the budget for defense and security, as some had feared.[10] Second, fiscal policy. Following a very long trend, the Colombian tax system moved towards a "flattening out," moving away from proportionality. For example, of the total taxes collected by the state, 20.5 percent corresponded to VAT-type taxes in 1975, 32.4 percent in 1990, and 35 percent in 2006. The weight of tax on income descended correlatively from 78 percent in 1970, to 64.8 percent in 1970, and 55.2 percent in 2006.[11] Third, privatizations. Fourth, stimuli to foreign investment. The country changed its rules of the game to favor the entry of international capital, once again gradually but with a successful result.[12] Fifth, the flexibilization of labor. The theme was discussed several times, and was finally implemented during the first Uribe government. The expectation was that flexibilization would reduce unemployment, but independent studies suggest that this has not been the case: it worsened the conditions of workers, without affecting the rates of unemployment.[13] Sixth, the freezing of the land problem. Seventh and last, social policy, especially health and education (see for example González, 2000[14]). The basic orientation here was to broaden the coverage of the respective system, articulate national and subnational agencies, and promote demand-driven services. The main inspiration for this set of reforms was the Chilean experience—but also the renewed emphasis of multilateral institutions in the fight against poverty. If the objectives were fulfilled, a more flexible and efficient state would provide universal services. In other words, unlike in the previous statist and developmentalist model, in the new scheme of things a small but working state, more open to the citizen and to local dynamics, would incorporate huge and excluded sectors of the population.

Neoliberalism also had some very clear and obvious *political* consequences. At least four of these deserve to be highlighted. First, the weakening of the national framework, especially due to the need to adapt to the world economy. Some of the fundamental policy levers—especially in the economic realm—have passed to transnational actors. The discussion of the free trade treaty with the United States is a notable example of this; the bargaining process has included the US executive, its congress, and specific actors. In this case, policy-making has involved a mixed set of national and foreign actors. Probably even before the neoliberal reforms, international actors participated in Colombian decision-making, but not so openly and deeply. The war against drugs represents a somewhat different, but striking, case. It has a strongly *prohibitionist* content, emanating from a very stable US policy (crafted in the second half of the 1960s). However, since neoliberal leanings in Colombia go along with certain political alignments—partisans of the continuation of the war on drugs are known to be staunch allies of the US—support for neoliberalism and for the war on drugs are strongly associated.[15] Second, the modernization of the state. Third, in the new environment political practices have also suffered a change. For example, the composition of the cabinets in Colombia was the result of a careful negotiation between political parties and regions. Attaining a party–region equilibrium was one

COLUMBIA: THE RESTRUCTURING OF VIOLENCE 219

of the main concerns of each president. The two Uribe administrations have implied a departure from this practice. Uribe's cabinets showed two characteristics: a strong regional concentration, and the predominance of figures coming from the private sector. This is a case of "requited love," as opinion polls have shown that the levels of support for Uribe—already extremely high on average—reached 90 percent levels among entrepreneurs.[16] Fourth, the intent of modernizing the security sector. This is an obvious link between the Gaviria and Uribe administrations. But at the same time the investment in security (and justice) was increased gradually, and the armed forces were modernized, new forms of private security were allowed to develop. On the one hand, the Convivir associations—private security cooperatives, many of which were instrumentalized by the paramilitary—were created and pushed forward until their complicity with criminal elements became too conspicuous. And on the other hand, as in many countries of Latin America, private security firms proliferated, becoming a silent but rather strong new type of policing force.

In sum, Colombian neoliberalism has been characterized by:

- A relatively small number of privatizations—or, by the same token, a gradual process of privatization. The biggest number in Latin America took place in Mexico, Brazil, and Argentina (and probably Peru). Between 1990 and 2000, Mexico witnessed 186 privatizations, Argentina 171, and Brazil 185; Colombia only 33.[17] This is rather modest, but the country never had a welfare state or a populist experience. The emphasis has been more on the flexibilization of labor, commercial opening, and the re-structuring of the state apparatus to make it more efficient (Echavvaría, 2000). The creation of new social policies emphasized universal coverage and economic efficiency, which in turn implied coordinating the collaboration of private–regional agencies with national funders.
- All this resulted in increased inequality. Colombia had never been able to solve the issue of its extremely high levels of inequality. However, in the 1960s and 1970s, the inequality indexes evolved slowly in the right direction. In the 1980s they stagnated, but in the 1990s there was a severe deterioration.
- Imperfect economic liberalism, due to the international prohibitionist regime over coca production. In Colombia, neoliberalism is politically marked, and increasingly so: it is

related to a geopolitical alliance with the United States. This implies adopting a staunch anti-drugs orientation. However, coca is the main agricultural staple of the country. To establish some kind of comparison, the total production of the country's primary historical export, coffee, represents 1.5 percent of GNP, while the best guesstimates of coca production fluctuate at around 5–7 percent of GNP.[18] This means that Colombia's economic liberalism has a very strong limit, and that it has to coexist with a de facto blend of economic opening and closure.
- The land problem has been particularly acute, and has interacted with other problems. Narcotraffickers were compulsive land buyers, and by the early 1990s they probably constituted the main rural sector in Colombia (Reyes, 1997). This might have opened policy windows of opportunity. Being illegal agents, narcos could be easily expropriated, and the freed lands utilized to generate a new distribution. This was the theory. In reality, the expropriation of narcos has been extraordinarily sluggish. And all the attempts of redistribution of legal lands have been shelved. Since the paramilitary consistently stole the land of petty owners, one of the most outstanding consequences of the armed conflict was to further increase the concentration of land ownership in rural areas.
- An increased concern for justice and security. There is an obvious, and public, link between such concern and neoliberal policies. For example, foreign investors regularly demand minimal conditions in terms of social order.
- The privatization of security (Convivir, growing numbers of private security agencies, and the paramilitary, are instances of the phenomenon).[19]

THE COLOMBIAN CONFLICT AND NEOLIBERALISM

Colombia, as is known, has suffered persistent violence independently of the model of development, at least since the late 1940s, and possibly even before. The first great wave of internal conflict in the twentieth century (called La Violencia) originated from insuperable differences between the two main political parties, and evolved towards a much more complex and difficult to interpret generalized peasant collision. For several scholars, what we are witnessing today is only the continuation of La Violencia. Indeed, the embryo of what would become Colombia's main guerrilla organization (the FARC) appeared in those years, and many of the original motives (especially the agrarian ones) that were associated with La Violencia appear in pristine form still today.

There are two reasons, though, that undermine the notion of Colombia as a country impaired by 50 years of "continuous political violence." The first one is that in effect there is good evidence, both qualitative and quantitative, that suggests that there was a decline in homicides, both common and political, between 1964 and 1975 (Gutiérrez, Acevedo, and Viatela, 2007). By any standard, it is difficult to characterize that period as one of conflict. True, there were guerrillas of different stripes like in the rest of Latin America, but they were quite marginal, and suffered heavy blows from the security forces. The ELN was practically dismantled by the Anorí operation in 1973; the Maoist groups vegetated on the margins; even the FARC, which from the beginning had the advantage of being much more skilled militarily, was a small and vulnerable force (that in 1967 also took a good thrashing), with no political clout. Additionally, the old bipartisan motives that had animated even the most criminalized expressions of La Violencia simply faded out.

By the mid 1970s, however, Colombia was once again heating up. Two simultaneous events played a key role in this. First, a new guerrilla group, the M-19, using new forms of "armed propaganda," was able to take the problem of war and peace to the level of national politics. Second, the country saw the culmination of a process that would change its social texture. On the one hand, Colombia urbanized at quite a rapid pace. In 1970, 57 percent of the population dwelled in cities; rising to 63 percent in 1970, 69 percent in 1980, and 71 percent in 2000.[20] On the other hand, from being basically a coffee exporter until the late 1960s, Colombia gradually became a minerals and coca producer. Naturally, this took time, but at the end of the 1980s this process had come to full fruition. Presently, the country is basically an exporter of mining products, of coca, and of people (Gutiérrez, Acevedo, and Viatela, 2007).

In sum, the initiation of the Colombian conflict cannot be separated from a very deep transformation in the country's productive structure and in the modality of its links with world markets. Colombia's bond with a global, illegal market, has determined its trajectory. The existence of this market provided illegal groups with:

- The capacity to escalate their activity through a tax on the coca production. In 1978, the FARC decided that it would allow peasants to cultivate coca in the territories where it had influence. At the time, it had no more than 800 soldiers (Ferro

and Uribe, 2002). By the end of the decade, it had more than 15,000 soldiers, all well fed and armed.
- The capacity to appear in front of peasant communities as social regulators. Since by definition the state cannot regulate an illegal market, both guerrillas and paramilitaries can aspire to fulfill this role. By not carrying out an agrarian reform in the 1960s, the state resorted to the policy of colonization instead, trying to populate huge expanses of land with peasants that had neither "social capital" (they were migrants, with scant traditions, links, networks, etc.) nor institutions to produce a cohesive social life. The entry of the coca money triggered delinquent violence and social anomie. Groups that were able to control and police the population, order social life, solve collective action problems, and unify taxation, received a certain amount of social support, independently of their authoritarian and, eventually, homicidal behavior.
- The entry to other illegal markets. The key to entering the coca market is to solve the problem of transportation. Coca entrepreneurs are overall focused on routes. These routes can be used to introduce weapons, hard currency, and so on. Big armed organizations have strategic advantages (economies of scale, fire power, discipline) over small, criminalized groups.[21]
- More generally, know-how. Especially in the case of the paramilitary, there was a rapid process of learning by the rural elites. The narcos were the vanguard of the landlords, and they taught them how to use and organize private security apparatuses.[22]
- Conflicts between the governing coalition. For both economic and political reasons, the narco market generated disarray within the governing coalition.

Less spectacular but probably equally important was the articulation of the armed non-state groups with the mining economy. At first, it was mainly the ELN who acted in this terrain, though with time it lost this monopoly to both the FARC and the paramilitaries. The ELN vindicated, defended, and promoted a nationalist policy, which justified the sabotaging of oil pipelines throughout the country. In the 1980s, through to the beginning of the new century, this activity was very intense. It also attacked the machinery of gold mining firms, who had a high percentage of foreign investment. The evolution of foreign investment gave this guerrilla group a political rationale that interacted well with extortive action (foreign investment in the oil sector nearly doubled between 1996 and 2001; in the mining sector overall, including coal, it grew from 51.1 million dollars in 1996, to 523.7 million in 2001, and 2.010 million in 2006[23]). While underscoring the political nature of these actions, the ELN collected a contribution to stop doing it, or to not start. This, of course, resembles a form of provision of security as those analyzed by Gambetta (1993) and others.

In the 1980s, the war became ever more intense and widespread. The growth of guerrilla organizations was only matched by that of paramilitaries. We know that the latter got early support by state officials, especially from security agencies, but at the same time from the narcotraffickers and the traditional rural elites. While in practice the state officials accepted the collaboration of the narcos and other criminals to combat subversion, the embattled Colombian state was, on the other hand, launching under US patronage—and imperative—a war on drugs.

In the meantime, Colombia had undergone a large-scale institutional transformation represented, but not limited to, the 1991 Constitution (the other main piece of reform was decentralization). It was supposed that the Constitution would be, among other things, a peace pact. However, after the enactment of the Constitution the conflict intensified. The M-19 and other minor guerrilla groups demobilized, but the major denominations, the FARC and the ELN, persisted. Among the factors that may have been associated with such recrudescence of the conflict in the presence of democratization, the following appear particularly relevant:

- Democratization itself. It is well known that democratizing in the aftermath of a peace process can be quite traumatic (Snyder, 2000). It was already seen that decentralization not only changed the nature of the conflict, but also increased the access of armed non-state groups to rents. On the other hand, contrary to the typical cases of "democratization and de-stabilization," in Colombia the increased competitiveness of the political system has not entailed particularly high costs.[24] It is a fact that the constitutional process, conceived by its architects as a peace pact, allowed the reinsertion of several guerrilla groups and that this actually had a de-polarizing effect.[25] There are several other ways, though, in which more political liberalism can temporarily increase the levels of violence of a country at war. It can be difficult for the executive to invest in security. Certainly, until very recently the

Colombian state's investment in security was surprisingly low, but this does not appear to have any clear relation with the new institutional constraints created in 1991: it predates that year. The more recent sharp increase in security investment could be easily negotiated within the institutional conditions crafted in 1991 (Gutiérrez, Acevedo, and Viatela, 2007). The logic of "small is beautiful" might have further fragmented the political parties, facilitating the penetration of illegal agents into the system. This is true, but once again the phenomenon predates 1991, and even after the 2003 political reform that conferred more cohesion to the system such penetration remained.
- Territorial disputes between non-state armed groups. The growth of both the FARC and the paramilitaries made them collide, as each one tried to snatch away territories from the other.
- The gradual privatization of security. Once again, this is not exclusive to the neoliberal period in Colombia. However, it did take its definite form through a decree that gave origin to the security cooperatives, Convivir, which in practice opened the door to a modality of paramilitary activities endorsed and supported by the state. There was a second form of implementation of the privatization of security: national and foreign firms that paid the paramilitaries to watch over their properties. Frequently, both modalities mingled (see for example the recent confession of the paramilitary leader Mancuso[26]). Palm oil and other staple sectors may owe part of their capacity of expansion to the combination of state support and private provision of security. When Harvey (2003) speaks of the Colombian "armed neoliberalism," this is not only a literary trope[27] (see below). It refers to a form of link between export agricultural economies and global markets that create profitable conditions by overcoming any type of resistance by armed coercion.

LAND

Knowing that violence long preceded neoliberalism, one may wonder if there is a story that links agrarian property rights, neoliberalism, and war. In effect, there is a long history of agrarian tensions that predates the inception of neoliberalism in Colombia. The instrumental use of violence to expropriate peasant property in the midst of a civil conflict was probably already widespread during the late stages of La Violencia (Posada, 1969). Similarly, the manifestations of peasant unrest in the Atlantic Coast in the mid 1960s were repressed by different forms, which did not shy away from the systematic use of vigilantism (Escobar, 1998). Furthermore, it can be comfortably conjectured that agrarian conflicts were poisoned by the entry of narcotraffickers as big landowners, which took place in the early 1980s, a phenomenon that has deepened without pause in recent decades (see for example Reyes, 1997).

Narcotraffickers were strategically interested in rural property for at least four reasons:

- Property rights and the rule of law are weaker in the countryside than in the cities. For example, cadastral records are patchy and unreliable, at best. Thus, it is easier to link rural properties to criminal activities, starting with money laundering.
- From the beginning of the second wave of the Colombian conflict, there was a strategic articulation—through paramilitarism—between the old rural elites and the narcos.
- Unlike other assets, land is a key resource for both war and the exportation of illegal products. Land can be used for the processing of coca into cocaine,[28] for installing communication networks, and for installing troops.
- Taxation. After decentralization, the main tax on land (*impuesto predial*) fell on the shoulders of municipalities. It is probably the case that small and weak municipalities, with only a handful of policemen, have not had the clout, or the will, to tax the land of the narcotraffickers and other big landowners.[29]

It has also been argued that narcotraffickers have a ruralist culture. Be that as it may, it is claimed that presently narcotraffickers hold some 48 percent of the arable land (*El Tiempo*, 2003), which represents at least one-third of the country's utilizable land (Reyes, 1997). This may seem more than sufficient to explain parsimoniously the hike in rural violence that the country has experienced in the last decades. The narcotraffickers have the know-how, the penchant, and the capacity to use extreme violence against their opponents. As has happened with many other cases—the classic case being Sicily—when organized crime regulates rural relations one immediate political consequence is the use of murderous tactics against social leaders, and the population at large. This is precisely what has happened in Colombia, transforming it into the country with the world's highest homicide rates of trade unionists and social leaders.

So where is the story? Where does neoliberalism play a role? Does it? Were all the necessary ingredients for the explosion of violence already there, without the existence of neoliberal reforms? Note that one could argue that the problem of Colombia is much more linked to the confluence of two non-liberal economic regimes: (i) The inward-looking development model predominant during the National Front ran out of gas—and with its exhaustion the most inefficient agents that thrived within it started to defend their position not (only) through cajoling and lobbying, but also through massive violence. The most obvious example is cattle ranching, an extremely inefficient and backward economy, whose leaders have not been particularly enthusiastic about economic opening. (ii) The international prohibitionist regime that regulates the cocaine market, with the effects described above. In this sense, it can be claimed that the political economy of the Colombian rural violence is intimately linked to economic closure.

This is difficult to refute. What is really interesting is that the economic opening has not mitigated the intensity of rural contradictions; it has deepened them instead. So there is actually a story out there, which is in fact quite conspicuous and can be developed in at least three dimensions. First, the neoliberal reforms of the 1990s involved changing the emphasis from asset distribution to strengthening land markets which, it was supposed, would increase productivity through the stabilization of property rights and allow for an eventual democratization of land (market asset allocation would eventually expel the most inefficient agents). Democratize rural property it did not; instead it opened windows of opportunity to illegal actors. Narcotraffickers and warlords can be analyzed from many points of view, among them as illegal entrepreneurs (Catanzaro, 1988). In both capacities—as businessmen and as illegal actors—they are interested in converting their illegally acquired capital into legal businesses. So they probably transferred enormous amounts of capital to legal activities. Once again, it is practically impossible here to gather macro, aggregated evidence to confirm this assertion. On the other hand, judicial proceedings offer plenty of support for this conjecture. Narcotraffickers invested heavily in some key sectors, such as cattle ranching and horse breeding.[30] They migrated to these legal activities with their know-how and their private armies, utilizing them generously as a competitive advantage (Duncan, 2006). This large-scale asset movement entailed choosing the winners, and a massive operation of the Weberian "political capitalism." The tinkering with property rights by the state had the consequence—intended or not—of permitting the creation, and/or consolidation, of a new class of land proprietors that play a key role in the maintenance of rural order through the systematic threat of violence. Please note that this class was created by "closed" dynamics, but consolidated by "open" ones.

Second, the political decision on property rights—in particular, the focus on guaranteeing them to foster productivity (Saffon and Uprimny, 2009)—has also frozen the extant situation of extreme inequality. This issue has had an extremely involved and traumatic story in Colombia. There were several land reform proposals (1936, 1961, and 1968), that in the end were incomplete or frustrated (for details see Hirschman, 1962; Gutiérrez, Acevedo, and Viatela, 2007). One of the main consequences of the internal conflict has been increasingly uneven land distribution in the country; some authors calculate that presently the rural Gini is as high as 0.8 (which is really unsustainable). The land problem in Colombia disappeared from the policy world, save in the form of expropriation of narco-landowners to eventually promote some kind of reform. However, this initiative has not produced any tangible result (*El Tiempo*, 2005b). The lands of the criminals have not been transferred to the rural poor in part because of the technical difficulties involved. But there has also been a set of political decisions and attempts[31] that reveal the intent of avoiding any type of redistributive use of the expropriated lands of the criminals, on the grounds that redistribution and productivity are at odds.

All this has had an institutional and organizational expression. In 2003, the institute for agrarian reform (INCORA) was changed into an agency for agrarian development (INCODER),[32] which has excluded distribution of land from its priorities and has actually been charged for aiding and abetting paramilitaries and politicians to take over thousands of hectares (*El Tiempo*, 2004a,b, 2005a). The period of opening that started in 1991 not only froze the distribution of land in Colombia, but tended to legalize the expropriation of peasants by armed actors. At least the following facts can be presented to support this proposition:

- The miserable failure of the proposal to transfer assets from narcotraffickers to peasants (*El Tiempo*, 2003, 2004a,b, 2005a,b), despite its potential high national and international legitimacy.

- The government's failure to oppose several bills that legalized the accumulation of land by networks of armed actors and politicians supporting them.
- The full incorporation of these armed actors and politicians to the power bloc that governs in Colombia. Presently, they are a substantial part of the governing coalition. When a paramilitary leader claimed that 35 percent of the congress was in his hands, many thought it was an exaggeration. Judicial processes presently suggest that it was rather an understatement.

At a somewhat more abstract level, the problem can be considered from the following point of view. The "closed" economy created dynamics of inequality that have been relatively well studied (Bonet and Meisel, 1999). One of the central tenets of the neoliberal reforms—both at the theoretical and practical levels—is to guarantee the stability of property rights. Thus, in the transition to an "open" regime, the old structures were frozen and insulated from politics. They could only be "touched" by market dynamics. In the case of Colombia this was reinforced by the transfer of assets to private agents (many of them embedded in criminal networks). At the same time, globalization of neoliberalism has been associated with the growth of huge illegal global markets. The fact that these markets coexisted with a prohibitionist regime—whose staunchest defender is at the same time, by far and large, the strongest and most enthusiastic defender of neoliberal measures in Latin America, namely, the US—has guaranteed the persistence of high levels of criminalization of the Colombian economy. Both factors together have resulted in an extremely unequal, criminalized, and because of this, violence-prone[33] rural life.

The third dimension of the violence–land–neoliberalism story is, quite obviously, displacement—a phenomenon that has taken on huge dimensions (see for example Saffon and Uprimny, 2009). Once again, nobody can claim that displacement is a "neoliberal phenomenon." Actually, a previous wave of violence in the twentieth century—La Violencia—produced a huge, and as yet un-quantified, number of IDPs. Several authors have alleged that back then the key motivation for violence was the prospect of fetching the land of the victims (Posada, 1969), which makes both waves of Colombian violence quite similar in this regard. What differentiates this second wave, and especially the dynamics unleashed by the paramilitaries from 1990 on, are the following factors:

COLUMBIA: THE RESTRUCTURING OF VIOLENCE 229

- The link of the displacement process with the promotion of macro agro-industrial projects. Actually, this is a core component of the paramilitary project, since one of the main branches of the paramilitary (in Urabá) was born as an armed wing of agro-industrialists, to combat the trade unions, the legal left, and the guerrillas. What started as an experiment intimately linked to banana production, proliferated in the 1990s, and extended to other crops. For example, it has been alleged that the expansion of oil palm in the last ten years has depended on the paramilitaries, who first evict the population and establish a vertical social order, and then "invite" the agro-industrialists to settle.[34] In some cases, this has taken place in territories that the 1991 Constitution reserved for protected communities, be it Native Colombians or Afro-Colombians. The facts surrounding this problem have been ferociously contested, but the association of palm oil producers has admitted explicitly that at least some of them—not affiliated with the association—have engaged in such practices.[35]
- The explicit acknowledgment by the paramilitaries that theirs is a two stage activity, with the first one being "cleaning," and the second "luring." They start by establishing their social order through indiscriminate violence, then keep social protest at bay by selective violence (Gutiérrez and Barón, 2005; Gutiérrez et al., 2007), and when they have consolidated their modality of governance they focus on stimulating investment, both national and foreign. For example, Vicente Castaño—one of the most murderous paramilitary leaders, who did not join the peace process with the government—made the following declaration in 2005: "In Urabá we have palm crops. I myself got the entrepreneurs to invest in those long-lasting and productive projects. The idea is that the rich invest in those projects in different zones of the country. When the rich go there, the institutions of the state also go. Unfortunately, the institutions of the state only participate in these things when the rich are there. We have to take the rich to all the corners of the country, and that is one of the missions of all our commanders."[36]
- Judicial evidence already shows amply that foreign investment played a key role in the aforementioned dynamics. In the case of oil companies, they seem to have offered a security premium to armed groups—the dominant ones, be it the guerrillas or the paramilitaries—so that they abstained from

attacking them. This allowed for a lax coexistence (Pearce, 2005) with armed groups. The agro-industrial firms are probably at the extreme end of the scale, with some of them not only funneling substantial resources to the paramilitaries but also participating in the organization of their activities (Gutiérrez and Barón, 2005). It is interesting to describe the mechanisms through which they did it. In Urabá, for example, they transferred the monies to a Convivir that had been taken by paramilitaries and narcos (*Papagayo*). In other parts of the country they actually participated in the paramilitaries' regional general staff. Be it in this capacity, or as sponsors of the paramilitary activity—frequently with the intermediation of politicians—they also provided rewards to local actors, bolstering the paramilitaries' regional legitimacy. Naturally, there is here a less spectacular but much more potent link: to the extent that the paramilitary fiefdoms do increase, or at least maintain, private investment—against the guerrilla-influenced areas—all social agents can expect gains (in the form of employment, etc.), a point that is evident in the Vicente Castaño quote above. It may be conjectured, thus, that both actors involved in this alliance are conscious of its effects.

- It must be noted, though, that the paramilitary acted both as *the* (self-represented) armed group of the private sector, and as a praetorian guard, that systematically extorts private investors.

Once again, this can be seen in a somewhat more abstract way. A Polanyi-type argument can be built. The first step is to consider what the paramilitaries have been doing in the last decades. One of their main activities has been evicting people from their lands, and establishing a new social order in which social protest is murderously repressed. This on the one hand triggers a large wave of rural–urban migration, and on the other operates in favor of a capitalist-type form of agriculture. What we are witnessing now is a huge—terribly brutal and highly criminalized, but nonetheless easily recognizable—process of encirclement,[37] the necessary condition for Polanyi's "great transformation."

While from 1980 to 1995 the official land reform institution INCORA processed a million hectares for distribution to the peasantry, the expansion of drug lands reversed this. Narcotraffickers bought up between 3 and 4 million hectares, some 12 per cent of land suitable for agriculture. The cumulative effect from 1980 to 1995 was an agrarian counter-reform. But an even bigger change was to come in the next five years, by 2001 the top 3 per cent owned nearly 76 per cent of the land. The degree of concentration is even more accentuated if the very biggest property holdings, those over 500 hectares, are considered: in 1984 this 0.4 per cent of landowners held 32.5 per cent; in 2001 the top 0.4 per cent held 61.2 per cent of all registered land. (Higginbottom, 2005, p. 123)

There is a clear correlation between land concentration and the displacement of farmers. Harvey (2003) found "method in [this] madness": evict farmers and impose an authoritarian social order concentrated on production. Harvey coined the expression "armed neoliberalism," and speaks about "accumulation by dispossession."

The encirclement empowers both capitalist producers and criminal networks that can act as praetorian guards. Enclave economies linked to global markets develop over a type of social order characterized by the permanent threat or use of overt coercion against the population.

HEALTH

The Objectives and the Tradeoffs

Contrary to standard accusations, neoliberal transformations—especially in neoliberalism's second stage—have frequently taken account of social problems. In particular, in the realm of social policies neoliberal thinkers and decision makers hoped to produce a breakthrough that would allow the country to get around the shortcomings of the "closed" period. The main argument was the following: A purely statist perspective towards social policy had stalled the initiative of both the entrepreneurs and civil society. The results were high transaction costs (bureaucracy, corruption), informational problems (expressed by the failure to provide the services to who really needed them), and poor coverage. A more agile and transparent system would help increase the investment in social policies, improve its efficiency by concentrating on the poor, and accomplish universal coverage. Fortunately, such a model was already in existence: the Chilean experience, which was being promoted in Latin America by multilateral institutions. What Colombian policy-makers had to do was to understand it and adapt it. This is precisely what was done, promoting one of the most radical and clear-cut processes of neoliberal reform in the country. It must be emphasized that these reforms cannot be conceptualized as an anti-popular cabal. Indeed, the promised hike in investment in both health and education took place (but it involved an increased social security contribution by the workers). On the other hand, the neoliberal reforms—captured in the health sector by the Law 100 of 1990[38]—implied precisely the process on which Polanyi insists so much: the reification of the market as the only regulator of social relations, and thus the full commodification of health and life.[39] This has implied a large-scale institutional transformation, with consequences well beyond, and below, the expectations of the neoliberal architects. The brunt of the reform was felt by diverse sectors. For example, the Taylorization of medical services entertained by the Law 100 hit especially hard the salaries of health professionals (doctors, nurses, etc.), but over this base essentially universal coverage was reached.[40]

The Institutional Machinery

The objective of this subsection is not to provide a full description of the Law 100 and its impact on the health of Colombian citizens (there are already good evaluations of this, see Abel and Lloyd-Sherlock, 2001[41]), but to describe the mechanisms through which the implementation of the neoliberal reforms opened windows of opportunity for the paramilitary to capture the health sector in several regions of the country.

Which are the relevant changes implemented by the Law 100 and subsequent reforms? Mainly the following:

- The privatization of the system, or in the policy-makers' slang, the transition from "subsystems" to "regimes." Before, there existed a public subsystem and a special subsystem. Now there are two regimes, the Taxed Regime ("Régimen contributivo") and the Subsidized Regime. Before, the public subsystem took care of 70 percent of the patients (while 30 percent of the service was funded by contributions from the workers). Now the taxed regime takes care of 70 percent of the patients, and the subsidized one of the poorest 30 percent (Morales, 1997).
- The transition from a state monopoly to a competitive offer of the service. Barriers to entry of private agents were radically lowered. The previous system had had very low rates of coverage (Morales, 1997; Jaramillo, 1994, p. 81).

The structure of provision of the service depended strictly on the public hospitals. Now, private entrepreneurs can initiate their own undertakings, in alliance or not with public agencies. The new private or private–public firms—in the Colombian parlance, the EPS[42]—have their own networks of provision of the service, or can subcontract with other agencies. In particular, the provision of health services to the poorest sectors of the population is funneled through the so-called ARS,[43] which can be of various types. An ARS can be: an EPS, an equalization fund (Caja de Compensación), a health cooperative, a neighborhood or community association (these last two modalities are especially important in poor regions, where both states and markets are weak). All these organizational entities provide their services through a compulsory plan of subsidized health.[44] The identification of the beneficiaries of the subsidized system is in theory made by the state.[45] On the other hand, the beneficiaries had the right to choose the ARS with which they wanted to associate with.
- The creation of a flexible system of intermediation. The ARS are intermediaries between the state and the direct, specialized, providers of the service, as hospitals, health centers, etc. These—the so-called IPS[46]—"do not have their own previously allocated budget, but are paid by the ARSs when they provide services to their beneficiaries."[47] It must be noted that this gives an incentive to IPS to *not* help poor people that are not members of an ARS.
- The new system subsidizes demand, not supply. This is a key policy principle in the implementation of neoliberal social policies. The previous system subsidized supply (hospitals, for example). Now, demand is subsidized. To avoid regulatory problems, the providers of the service are supervised by a control agency, the Superintendencia Nacional de Salud. Different forms of regulation were subcontracted, decentralized, and/or privatized.[48]

In recent years, a reform of Law 100 has been discussed, which would entail, among other things, the elimination of the intermediary role of the ARSs returning some of their functions to subnational governments (Vélez and Alba, 2002).

The Paramilitary Takeover

The study of the new institutional landscape makes it very easy to understand why and how the paramilitaries could take over the health system in several regions. The basic mechanism through which they did it was:

- Create health cooperatives or put sufficient pressure (through violence and graft) on already existing ones, so that they yielded to their plans.
- Already having an ARS, they would inflate its list of beneficiaries, capturing huge state subsidies.
- Sometimes they also collected rent from the existing beneficiaries. They could do so because through coercion they could impede the presence of any other ARS, and as seen above the system gave incentives to hospitals to *not* help a poor person not affiliated to an ARS.

This penetration of the health system allowed paramilitary leaders to kill several birds with a single stone. First, they had access to handsome economic resources. It may be claimed that these were negligible in relation to those offered by narcotrafficiking, but to maintain such a point of view would be a loss of perspective. In relation to rents, illegal armed actors are insatiable.[49] Second, these resources were provided by the state, not by a stigmatized criminal activity. Third, since many of these operations were performed through politicians and subnational bureaucrats, they allowed to cement precisely the type of alliance with extant regional powers that explains the importance of the paramilitary clout. Fourth, paradoxically enough, it became a source of (regional and local) legitimacy. Certainly, the fact that the monies of the poor were being utilized by brutal warlords produced a huge scandal. However, locally and regionally it allowed the paramilitary to insert thousands of poor citizens in patronage networks, where, the paramilitary claimed, they were being favored with access to the service. In some cases, it also allowed the paramilitary to establish working relations with social organizations and community leaders.

A key assumption of the best of neoliberal reformers was that, to put it in the classical Weberian categories, the opening of the economy would eliminate "political capitalism," a mode of production characterized by the fact that agents do not accumulate capital through competitive risk taking, innovation, and the creation of new wealth, but through political influence, patronage, and clientelism. The dynamics described above show that such an assumption is unwarranted. The typical counter-argument, repeated thousands of times in official and officious documents—"the model is correct, but the institutions are wrong", "there is a need to adapt the political institutions to the new realities"—is not satisfactory for several reasons. First, it presupposes the point that is in question. In this case we are seeing precisely the intent of adaptation of an institutional setting to the rules of openness and transparency, explicitly inspired in international examples and principles, favoring an armed non-state actor. Second, no model is applied in a social vacuum or in near ideal conditions. Models are always applied to mixed realities, and part of their validation depends on their capacity to guide reformers in a better understanding of their own reality. Third, the Law 100 was unequivocally neoliberal. The question that has to be explained, then, is how and why can violence and diverse forms of political capitalism thrive in the context of an open market economy.

Part of the answer is provided by governmental reports. According to them, in 1999 there were 242 ARSs, of which 178 were cooperative or "solidarity oriented" associations (ESSs),[50] 47 were Equalization Funds, and 17 were EPSs (ten private, seven public). The ESSs "exhibited enormous disparities in regard to their organizational development and inefficiencies in their accountancy and management" (Corcho et al., 2000). Alter evaluating 165 ESSs—using criteria such as social participation, management, and financial parameters—"43 percent of them were classified as having a low or very low level of development, 46 percent had an intermediate, and 11 percent a high level." In 40 percent of the cases, the EPS did not have accounting (Corcho et al., 2000, p. 16). There were also monopolistic trends. "Many of them [the ESSs] have accumulated resources indiscriminately ... and the community ARSs instead are heading towards extinction, so the tendency is toward the creation of monopolies" (Corcho et al., 2000). In sum, the architects of Law 100 overestimated both civil society and market dynamics. Society can be quite uncivil, and the market can favor actors that through expeditious methods—including violence and political capitalism—obtain initial advantages that eventually consolidate in the form of monopolies (monopolies that in turn can support non-state armies and illegal networks).

DECENTRALIZATION

Decentralization has been a large-scale state reform, which has taken nearly two decades to unfold, and is still taking place. Its relation vis-à-vis neoliberalism is different from land issues or social policies. First of all, decentralization has a long and rich history in Colombia,[51] which is inseparable from its institutionalization in the 1980s. Second, decentralization is not neoliberalism in itself. Indeed, there is a case for seeing decentralization as a process of deepening of political liberalism, a case that enjoys near universal support (at least verbally) in Colombia. But it does not necessarily correspond to economic opening. Last but not least, there are many decentralizations and much intense debate about key issues among those in charge of implementing decentralization. For example, the transference of funds from the center to the subnational entities has been a permanently contested issue, and is still debated today.

In sum, it cannot be reasonably claimed that decentralization depended on neoliberalism. The relation between both is more oblique, but not less clear. Neoliberal intellectuals considered decentralization, citizen participation, and so on, to be necessary conditions for the construction of a modern state. They would allow governments to introduce basic principles of transparency, accountability, and civil society participation, which can eventually generate an efficient state. Municipal administrations would be supplier and more efficient than centralized management. Regions and municipalities would have a (positive) interest in fostering private investment. Decentralization would legitimize institutions, taking them nearer to the citizens, eliminating the corrupt clientelist political intermediation. It would permit the competition of subnational entities in the global markets, and create the conditions to moderate, and ultimately eliminate, the pro-Andean (and anti-Coast) biases that had characterized the inward-looking model of development (Barón and Meisel, 2004). In other terms, it was hoped that in Colombia decentralization would be the point at which economic and political liberalism would converge. Decentralization was the epitome of the isomorphism principle:[52] modernization entailed opening society and markets, and these two openings reinforced each other.

The Colombian model of decentralization was highly concentrated on the municipalities, which were given long-repressed rights— like electing a mayor; before the introduction of the new model they were appointed—and funds in a scheme of gradual growth of transferences from the nation. The first election of mayors took place in 1988. The 1991 Constitution institutionalized the ear-marked transference of funds to the municipalities, which would respond with their own budgets and formulate/implement their own development plans. The sketch of the main lines of operation of this institutional machinery is approximately the following: Mayors were given the levers of local power, and the capacity to administer resources. Since these resources were ear-marked, and there were relatively tight financial restrictions, this would *simultaneously* give each municipality an increased decision-making capacity, and would prevent the typical gambits of clientelist intermediation (for example, channeling resources to sectors in which the clients of politicians could be favored; or patronage through the discretional right to appoint officeholders).

As the reformers had expected, the new institutional setting upset the old practices of clientelism, but the outcome was different from what they had predicted. First of all, clientelist practices found another, very substantial, field to play: contracting.[53] Since municipal and departmental investment was ear-marked, the politicians could not spend the money in other sectors, but they could indeed favor a private contractor, who in compensation had to pay the politician a percentage (generally 10 percent) for choosing him. Clientelism changed, thus, but was not weakened.[54] Institutional controls and checks and balances were much weaker at the subnational level,[55] so the margin of maneuver of the politicians to allocate funds remained big, despite the establishment of several provisions to limit it.

In the meantime, both guerrillas and paramilitaries discovered that the increased power of the mayors in weak municipalities was a godsend for them. It was guerrillas who first understood the advantages of the "socialism in one municipality." By kidnapping mayors and staging "popular tribunals" against them, they were able to force them to make key decisions (for example, building a police station or not), favoring certain populations (those where the guerrilla group had more support), and transferring funds to the insurgents through various modalities (a percentage over the contracts, placing people chosen by the guerrillas in public works, and even the relocation of assets). With a time lag, the paramilitaries understood the advantages of municipalization, and perfected the guerrillas' strategy. They were able to do so for many reasons.[56] First, contrary to the guerrillas, they were a pro-systemic force, so they could aspire to build some kind of joint governance accord with the state, which in effect they did. And this gave much more stability to their territorial control. Second, and in consequence, they could deal with state resources much more comfortably and with much less risk (for the politicians and the armed group itself). Third, they could interact with private investors from a much better position. Fourth, the new clientelism based on state contracts was more palatable to control from above, so the paramilitaries found through this mechanism a lever to administrate extant political networks and put them at their service. Fifth, the municipalities—especially the weakest ones, of course—could be forced to act in certain ways. The guerrillas had used this generously, but mainly in the military sense. The paramilitaries introduced a new, economic, dimension: protecting private agents.[57]

The Colombian conflict, thus, was municipalized, and this had several consequences. The main ones are:

- Municipal budgets became an important issue in the economy of war. As seen above, both the guerrillas and the paramilitaries collect a percentage (generally 10 percent) of the contracts of the municipality to provide services (for example, for public works).
- At the same time, neoliberal reforms implied a change in the form of provision of some services by the state. Particularly, many of them that before were directly offered to the popular neighborhoods by state agencies—and that had become a hotbed of clientelism—were now outsourced. For example, an important portion of municipalities had their own public works enterprises and which offered assistance to the neighborhood organizations (Juntas de Acción Comunal)—an assistance that arrived almost always through the intermediation of a politician. It was supposed that contracting out these activities would not only increase efficiency, but weaken clientelism. As seen above, weaken the old bipartisan clientelism it did, but it also increased the capacity of armed groups to have an influence on the municipal life and, additionally, capture rents in the process. Instead of the traditional patronage structures, the Colombian non-state armed groups put pressure—combining violent threats and monetary carrots—on mayors to take decisions regarding what to contract out to whom, and the percentage that should be given to the group.
- Municipal policy also gained in relevance. Putting pressure on the mayors, armed groups could influence decisions that could change locally the course of the war.
- Popular trials of mayors who acted wrongly according to the purported norms or objectives of the illegal group. This allowed the latter to obtain social support (for example, by appearing as an anti-corruption bastion).

As said above, many of these innovations were discovered by the guerrillas. These methods had the defect of being purely "exterior." By the mid 1990s, however, the paramilitaries—which at first had appeared in several regions as a purely punitive, or vigilante, force—understood the advantages of going into regional politics. They built fiefdoms that provided both economic and political gains not only for the paramilitary, but also for the politicians themselves (which explains their high levels of stability). The centerpiece of the new design is that in some regions the paramilitaries became the overseers and coordinators of clientelism. They did not try to take over all the clientelist networks, nor certainly to capture all the rents these produced. Instead, they decided which clientelist patron could do what, and collected sizable rents for its brokerage. The necessary condition for all this to work was the control over the contracts and payroll of the municipality, which was obtained by a combination of coercion and corruption.

CONCLUSIONS

Through a set of specific examples, this chapter has shown how neoliberal reforms in Colombia changed the institutional settings, and by doing so deeply perturbed the logic of war (and peace). Naturally, neoliberalism did not create (or solve) problems ex novo; no reform, however revolutionary, can do that. Here I have shown that—despite the permanent interplay between the new and the old—the dynamics through which neoliberalism and the Colombian conflict interacted can be specified.

There are many more examples. A crucial one that probably deserves separate attention is the privatization of security. In all these cases, the standard counter-argument—according to which neoliberalism is a correct formula, wrongly implemented due to weak institutions or lack of social capital—does not seem very effective. In every macro social reform there will be a certain distance between the prescriptions and the realities that the reformers have to deal with. If it did not exist, no reform would be necessary. The distance is not an anomaly, thus, but a sociological datum in itself: how were the initial conditions transformed? Why weren't adequate conditions created by the process of reform? Why do unintended and unexpected equilibria appear? Whatever answers are provided to these questions, it appears clear that the Colombian case invites a reconsideration of the typical evaluations of neoliberalism—on both sides of the political and academic spectrum.

NOTES

1. Francisco Gutiérrez Sanín is a researcher at the Instituto de Estudios Políticos y Relaciones Internacionales, Universidad Nacional de Colombia. This chapter could not have been written without the input of William Mancera, Jairo Baquero, and Diana Milena Mendoza.
2. Whose enormous popularity affects any adversarial move by the opposition. The president himself has warned that anti-treaty politicians are attacking dear national interests. At the same time, the Liberal Party director, ex-president César Gaviria, was for a long time an icon of neoliberal reforms.
3. It might be counter-argued that this is a consequence of the systematic assassination of the leaderships of social organizations and the legal left that has taken place in Colombia in the last decades. This may be part of the explanation. Despite that bloodletting, however, the left and other expressions of protest have developed well and actually had spectacular successes in the last years.
4. Mexico may be an exception, but the Zapatistas are much more interested in propaganda (sometimes, very rarely, armed), national and global, than in strategic violence. The other guerrilla, the PDPR-EPR, is more threatening, but politically and militarily marginal.
5. Despite suffering substantial military pressure in recent years.
6. The discussion about the intensity and modality of the neoliberal transformations is far from Byzantine. See for example Rodrik (2007).
7. That was initially proposed during the Gaviria government, and negotiated years later by Uribe.
8. Though there have been quite dramatic institutional de-stabilizations.
9. Comisión de Racionalización del Gasto y las Finanzas Públicas, Ministerio de Hacienda y Crédito Público, http://www.minhacienda.gov.co/MinHacienda.
10. Investment in defense reached a historical high of 4.3 percent by 2003.
11. www.dian.gov.co.
12. www.dnp.gov.co.
13. See also Evaluación de la reforma laboral (ley 789 de 2002). Universidad Nacional de Colombia, Facultad de Ciencias Económicas. Centro de Investigaciones para el Desarrollo–CID, March 2007, p. 75.
14. Also Departamento Nacional de Planeación: "Avances y retos de la política social en Colombia," http://www.dnp.gov.co/Archivos/PaginaPrincipal/Politica_social_2_(Oct2007).pdf.
15. This is especially clear in the two Uribe administrations.
16. It also reached similar levels in some regions.
17. Calculations based on: Privatization Data. World Bank, http://rru.worldbank.org/Privatization/.
18. See for example Steiner and Corchuelo (2000).
19. The Convivir were created by Decree 356 of February 11, 1994. They were part of a trend—not only in Colombia—consisting in the increasing strength of the market for security, and were thought to facilitate the cooperation of agrarian proprietors with the armed forces. They fell prey to the paramilitary in several regions.
20. Calculations based on DANE figures, http://www.dane.gov.co/.
21. For the case of the paramilitary, see Duncan (2006).
22. This process of learning took place in addition to the experience of La Violencia.

23. Calculations from Proexport, Reporte de Inversión Extranjera Directa. http://www.proexport.com.co/VbeContent/NewsDetail.asp?ID=8820&IDCompany=16.
24. And in recent years we have witnessed a closure of the system.
25. The political coalition headed by the M-19 declared explicitly that it did not belong to the left.
26. www.salvatoremancuso.com; Revista Semana, No. 1307, May 19, 2007.
27. This is why I asserted above that neoliberalism did not explain well aggregated outcomes, but it could work well "locally" (i.e., be indispensable to understand specific dynamics of violence in concrete contexts).
28. There is scant evidence that big narcos utilize land to raise illegal crops; probably they prefer to buy the product from peasants.
29. There are no systematic studies about the problem, though. According to the National Department of Planning, the taxation on land has grown, but this evaluation includes only legal actors.
30. Also in real estate in the cities.
31. The most famous of which was the Carimagua conflict. Carimagua was a property in the south of the country, expropriated from the paramilitary, which in principle had been allocated to IDPs and relatives of the victims of that group. The Ministry of Agriculture, however, decided to offer it to a set of entrepreneurs, some of whom were well connected in parliamentary and governmental circles. Finally, due to a huge public debate, the operation was aborted.
32. "Decreto número 1300 de 2003. Por el cual se crea el Instituto Colombiano de Desarrollo Rural, Incoder y se determina su estructura," http://www.acnur.org/biblioteca/pdf/4710.pdf.
33. There is a huge debate about the relation between rural inequality and violence. These debates, though, seldom include the analysis of threshold effects. In view of the existing literature, it is reasonable to conjecture that Ginis of 0.8 or beyond are difficult to sustain without some manifestation of malaise or unrest. The neoliberal Colombia froze the distribution of land at those levels, and actually has tended to go in the direction of worsening them.
34. Information about concrete cases can be found in: Corte Interamericana de Derechos Humanos (CIDH) Resolución del 6 de marzo de 2003. Human Rights Everywhere, Diócesis de Quibdó. Septiembre 2004. Informe del INCODER, marzo 2005. Resolución Defensorial No. 39, junio 2005. Comisión intereclesial Justicia y Paz, octubre de 2005. Procuraduría General de la Nación, agosto 2006.
35. Declaration of the representative of FEDEPALMA, the association of oil palm entrepreneurs, regarding the denunciations forwarded by the communities of Jiguamiandó y Curbaradó. Taken from: Audiencia Defensorial, "Cultivos de palma africana en territorios colectivos Jiguamiandó y Curbaradó—Chocó," Bogotá, 3 de junio de 2005. Recording of the event, given by the PIUCP Programa de Iniciativas Universitarias para la Paz y la Convivencia.
36. http://doblecero.blogspirit.com/archive/2008/06/05/palma-desarrollo-malefico-de-vicente-casta%C3%B1o.html, quoting an interview given by Castaño to Revista Semana.
37. Luz Teresa Gómez, personal communication.
38. The case of education is somewhat different because, among other things, of the presence of a strong teachers union, which has no counterpart in the health sector.

39. Sometimes, patients have not been treated by hospitals and other agencies because they are below the minimal threshold of contributions that they would need to be treatable. Some of these cases have resulted in the death of the patients, some of them children.
40. On the other hand, medical doctors argue that that very Taylorization abated the quality of the service. A very strong evidence in favor of this is the high number of special citizen actions (*acciones de tutela*) against health agencies in previous years. Even then, it may be argued that for a very poor citizen the utility curve is monotonous: getting something is always better than getting nothing. In the long run, though, a cleavage between a "good-private" and a "bad-poor" health system can appear (or may have appeared already).
41. Where the Colombian reforms fare surprisingly well. For other evaluations of the Colombian health sector see: Bustamante Ledesma (1994), Jaramillo (1994).
42. Empresas Públicas de Salud.
43. Administradoras de Régimen Subsidiado.
44. Plan Obligatorio de Salud Subsidiada (POSS).
45. Through a system called SISBEN.
46. Instituciones Proveedoras de Salud.
47. S. Quintana, "El acceso a los servicios de salud en Colombia. Médicos sin fronteras," http://www.disaster-info.net/desplazados/informes/msf/accesosaludcol.htm.
48. Ibid. Also Jaramillo (1994), p. 69.
49. More so the paramilitary, who have to support the structure of the group and at the same time provide for the enrichment of its leaders.
50. Empresas Solidarias de Salud, ESS.
51. Coincidentally, associated with the closure–opening of the economy debate.
52. Open societies, polities, and markets resemble, and support, each other.
53. This, of course, applies also to health, as there is a large intersection between the two themes (health reforms and decentralization).
54. In a sense, politicians increased their power in relation to their social base, because they did not depend on their capacity to provide favors to many people, but on their capacity to make a small number of (not necessarily publicly known) decisions.
55. Among other things, because of technical limitations. A substantial portion of mayors and municipal councils accused of corruption in recent years incurred offenses due to a lack of knowledge of the workings of the state. www.procuraduria.gov.co.
56. It is not rare that good imitators surpass innovators.
57. For example, municipalities are in charge of taxation of the land, and both paramilitary and the core social alliance that they represent have a generous representation of cattle ranchers and big landowners. Indeed, there is evidence that the FARC has protected landowners against peasants in some departments. But there is a huge difference of scale.

REFERENCES

Abel, C. and Lloyd-Sherlock, P. (2001) "Health in Latin America: themes, trends and challenges." In *Healthcare Reform and Poverty in Latin America*, ed. P. Lloyd-Sherlock. London: Institute of Latin American Studies, pp. 1–20.

Barón, J. D. and Meisel, A. (2004) *La descentralización y las disparidades económicas regionales en los noventa: Macroeconomía y regiones en Colombia.* Bogotá DC: Banco de la República.

Bustamante Ledesma, A. (1994) *Sistema de seguridad social en Colombia: ley 100 de 1993, comentarios y suplemento legislativo.* Santa Fe de Bogotá: Editora Jurídica de Colombia.

Catanzaro, R. (1988) *El delito como empresa. Historia social de la mafia.* Madrid: Taurus.

Colombia: Unidad que multiplica (1988) *Entrevista a dirigentes máximos de la Unión Camilista Ejército de Liberación Nacional sobre la historia del ELN, y una reflexión sobre la situación de las guerrillas en ese momento 1988.* Publicado en: Nicaragua, México y Perú Centro de Documentación y Ediciones Latinoamericanas.

Consejo Superior de Política Fiscal (CONFIS) (2001) *Privatizaciones y Concesiones de La Nación 1990–2001.* Colombia, Documento Asesores, 07/2001.

Corcho, A. E., Castilla Luna, M., and Acosta Ramirez, N. (2000) *Narrativa sobre la Reforma del Sistema de Salud en Colombia.* Núcleo De Acopio, Apoyo Y Difusión De Las Iniciativas De Reforma Instituto Nacional De Salud Pública. Marzo del 2000, p. 24.

Duncan, G. (2006) *Los señores de la guerra. De paramilitares, mafiosos y autodefensas en Colombia.* Bogotá: Planeta.

Echavarría, J. (2000) "Colombia en la década de los noventa: neoliberalismo y reformas estructurales en el trópico." *Coyuntura Económica*, Vol. 30, No. 3 (September), pp. 121–148.

El Espectador (1999) "Yo haría lo mismo que Fujimori," entrevista con el Ministro de Defensa Rodrigo Lloreda por Ingrid Reyes y Éver Palomo. February 14, p. 5 A.

El Tiempo (2003) "Narcos, los dueños del 48% de las tierras productivas." September 2, pp. 1–2.

El Tiempo (2004a) "Urgen suspender la vigencia de la ley de tierras." September 28, pp. 1–3.

El Tiempo (2004b) "Polemica por proyecto que legaliza tierras." September 18, pp. 5 A.

El Tiempo (2005a) "Reversazo de Incoder les quito 10 mil hectareas a campesinos." October 23, pp. 1–2.

El Tiempo (2005b) "Extincion de dominio no ha tocado latifundios ilegales." June 11, pp. 1–6.

Escobar, C. (1998) "Clientelism, Mobilization and Citizenship: Peasant Politics in Sucre, Colombia." PhD dissertation, University of California, San Diego.

Ferro, J. and Uribe, G. (2002) *El Orden de la Guerra Las FARC-EP: Entre la Organización y la Política.* Bogotá: CEJA.

Gambetta, D. (1993) *The Sicilian Mafia: The Business of Private Protection.* Cambridge, MA: Harvard University Press.

Gómez, B. H. (2003) *Conflicto, callejón con salida.* PNUD, http://www.planeacion.cundinamarca.gov.co/BancoMedios/Documentos%20PDF/creditos.pdf.

González, J. I. (2000) "Política social e indicadores sociales en Colombia: una evaluación." *Investigación y Desarrollo*, Vol. 8, No. 3, pp. 244–257.

Gutiérrez, F. and Barón, M. (2005) "Re-stating the State: paramilitary territorial control and political order in Colombia." Working Paper no. 66, Crisis States Programme DESTIN–London School of Economics.

Gutiérrez, F., Acevedo, T., and Viatela, J. M. (2007) "Violent liberalism? State, conflict and political regime in Colombia, 1930–2006, Crisis States." Working Paper Series, No. 2. London School of Economics (LSE) / Development Studies Institute (DESTIN).

Harvey, D. (2003) *The New Imperialism*. Oxford: Oxford University Press.

Higginbottom, A. (2005) "Globalization, violence and the return of the enclave to Colombia." *Development*, Vol. 48, No. 3, pp. 121–125.

Hirschman, A. O. (1962) *The Problem of Land Tenure and Land Reform in Colombia*. New York.

Jaramillo Pérez, I. (1994) *El futuro de la salud en Colombia Ley 100 de 1993: política social, mercado y descentralización / Iván Jaramillo Pérez*. Santafé de Bogotá: FESCOL, FRB, FES, Fundación Corona.

Morales, L. G. (1997) "El Financiamiento del sistema de seguridad social en salud en Colombia." CEPAL, Serie Financiamiento del Desarrollo, No. 55. Santiago de Chile.

Pearce, J. (2005) "Policy failure and petroleum predation: the economics of civil war debate viewed from the warzone." *Government and Opposition*, Vol. 40, No. 2, pp. 152–180.

Pombo, C. and Ramírez, M. (2001) *Privatization in Colombia: A Plant Performance Analysis*. Bogotá: Universidad del Rosario.

Posada, F. (1969) *Colombia: Violencia y Subdesarrollo*. Bogotá: Universidad Nacional de Colombia.

Revista Semana (2002) "Giro a la derecha." September 2, pp. 32–34.

Reyes, A. (1997) "Compra de tierras por narcotraficantes." *Varios: "Drogas ilícitas en Colombia. Su impacto económico, político y social,"* Ariel-PNUD-Dirección Nacional de Estupefacientes, pp. 279–346.

Rodrik, D. (2007) *One Economics, Many Recipes: Globalization, Institutions, and Economic Growth*. Princeton, NJ: Princeton University Press.

Saffon, M. P. and Uprimny, R. (2009) "El potencial transformador de las reparaciones. Propuesta de una perspectiva alternativa de reparaciones para la población desplazada en Colombia," in CODHES (ed.), *Desplazamiento Forzado. ¿Hasta cuándo un Estado de Cosas Inconstitucional?*, Antropos-CODHES, Volume I.

Scott, J. (1999) *Seeing as a State: How Certain Schemes to Improve the Human Condition Have Failed*. New Haven, CT: Yale University Press.

Snyder, J. (2000) *From Voting to Violence: Democratization and National Conflict*. New York: W. W. Norton and Company.

Steiner, R. and Corchuelo, A. (2000) "Repercusión económica e institucional del tráfico de droga en Colombia." Documento CEDE 3830, Universidad de los Andes.

Varios: "La paz es rentable". Facultad de Ciencias Sociales–Universidad de los Andes, Universidad Nacional–IEPRI. Financiado por el Departamento Nacional de Planeación. Mayo 1997–Diciembre 1997.

Velez, A. and Alba, L. (2002) "Nuevas bases jurídicas de la reforma a la seguridad social en Colombia." Revista de Enfermería. IMSS, p. 52.

Wood, E. (2000) *Forging Democracy from Below: Insurgent Transitions in South Africa and El Salvador*. Cambridge University Press.

7
War and Neoliberal Transformation: The Peruvian Experience

Ramón Pajuelo Teves[1]

INTRODUCTION

During the last two decades of the twentieth century, some 70,000 people were killed in Peru's fratricidal war. The conflict started on May 18, 1980, with the burning, by the PCP-SL,[2] of ballot boxes in the town of Chuschi, a peasant community in the province of Ayacucho, one of the poorest regions of the country. Following a carefully scripted political and military strategy, the guerrilla movement Sendero Luminoso launched a "people's war" against the Peruvian state on the day of presidential elections, which were supposed to reinstate democratic rule in the country after twelve years of unorthodox military dictatorship.[3]

The war between Sendero Luminoso and the Peruvian government escalated relentlessly through the 1980s, expanding across the territory and becoming the biggest violent confrontation ever in the history of the republic of Peru. The Túpac Amaru Revolutionary Movement (MRTA),[4] another Peruvian radical and armed left-wing organization, had also taken up arms in 1984, thus exacerbating the maelstrom of violence. The confrontation between the state and the insurgent movements coincided with a severe economic and political crisis, the most significant features of which were hyperinflation and a loss of credibility in political parties. In the late 1980s, the war was at its height, the national economy was on the brink of collapse, and the shaky democratic system that replaced the military dictatorship was beginning to crumble.

What happened over the next decade was therefore surprising. The winner of the presidential elections held in 1990 was Alberto Fujimori, a political outsider who, against all odds, succeeded in defeating the well-known writer Mario Vargas Llosa, who was the favorite. Although Fujimori won the elections thanks to a speech in which he openly opposed the neoliberal program of his opponent, two weeks after the beginning of his government he implemented a set of neoliberal reforms that led to a severe economic shock. The harsh neoliberal recipe Fujimori had chosen to help stabilize the economy was soon afterwards supplemented with an authoritarian political regime, through the coup d'état on April 5, 1992, with the help of which he succeeded in taking over all public powers. These changes in the Peruvian economy and politics also coincided with the defeat of the Sendero Luminoso movement and the capture of Abimael Guzmán, its top leader. The capture of Guzmán marks a turning point in the war—in the years that followed Sendero Luminoso, now without its leader, started to crumble and was eventually defeated by the state. In this same period, the MRTA, whose warring activities never reached the dimension of Sendero Luminoso's, was also defeated by the state and its leaders captured.

A cursory look at the Peruvian case could lead to the impression that it was mainly the neoliberal reforms brought in by Alberto Fujimori that led to the end of the civil war. This, in fact, was the view that the Fujimori government propagated during its years in power, from the top echelons of the state down. This chapter disagrees, arguing that the chain of causality went in the opposite direction: the success of the neoliberal stabilization program was, in fact, greatly facilitated by the end of the civil war. The way the war ended permitted the effective imposition of neoliberal policies, together with the establishment of an authoritarian political regime.

The neoliberal economic stabilization program, the de-escalation of war, and the political onslaught against the so-called "traditional parties," assured Fujimori wide popular support, which made the strengthening of his authoritarian regime easier. His government implemented an effective social-aid strategy aimed at the poorest regions of the country, and created social programs administered by a wide-reaching network of executives appointed on the basis of patronage and political privilege. This government system, set up by Fujimori and his allies, was based on an iron-tight power alliance between the state, neoliberal techno-bureaucracy, the armed forces, and the business sectors.[5]

Fujimori managed to stay in power throughout the 1990s, through successive presidential re-elections. Fujimori won his first re-election in 1995, defeating Peruvian diplomat Javier Pérez de Cuéllar by a large margin. He was again re-elected in the 2000 elections, which were widely thought of as fraudulent and led to the political isolation of Fujimori by the international community. Despite this and despite the growing social opposition to the regime, he was sworn into office for a third time in July 2000, amid strong protests. However, two months later the Fujimori regime surprisingly collapsed, when it was revealed that the government had secured control of Parliament by bribing congressmen from other political groups.

Although allegations about the existence of a huge corruption network set up by Fujimori and his allies to ensure political control had been commonplace in Peru since the early 1990s, they could not compete with the popularity of the regime. Finally, in September 2000, the disclosure of a video showing Vladimiro Montesinos, the regime's close advisor, buying the support of a congressman with wads of banknotes, revealed the mafia-like nature of the regime and sparked a political crisis that forced Fujimori to announce a new election in which he would not participate. Shortly afterwards, and taking advantage of a trip abroad, Fujimori fled the country, surrendering all presidential powers through a fax sent from Japan.

While the democratic transition that followed the downfall of Fujimori brought about major reforms aimed at restoring the democratic governance of the state, it also ensured that the economic system Fujimori's regime left behind remained untouched. The three democratic governments that followed—the short transitional government of Valentín Paniagua, the government of Alejandro Toledo, and the current government of Alan García—were all committed to sustaining the neoliberal stabilization. After nearly two decades of the orthodox adoption of neoliberal reforms in Peru, it is surprising that the neoliberal model is still being implemented without major adjustments. After the 1990s, when neoliberalism was introduced as the only way out of the severe economic crisis and internal war, it is now being promoted as a development strategy, considered the only option for ensuring peace and economic growth. This hegemonic ideological paradigm in Peru is a sort of "neoliberal consensus" heartedly advocated by the country's economic and political elites.

Nevertheless, this neoliberal consensus, which during the Fujimori time had elicited wide popular support, has been steadily losing ground since the start of the democratic transition in the early 2000s. In recent years, the validity of neoliberalism has been questioned by a growing climate of discontent, as witnessed by a large number of protests and social unrest. Although the neoliberal model has generated strong economic dynamism, most of the population still lives in poverty and some in extreme poverty. Poverty feeds discontent, while the contrast between high macroeconomic growth rates and social instability in the country grows more visible. Besides protests and social conflicts, there have been local instances of political violence reminiscent of past decades, together with increased drug trafficking.

In short, what happened in Peru was a successful neoliberal stabilization experience that, political ups-and-downs notwithstanding, managed to remain in place for almost two decades. The effectiveness of a political patronage-based distribution of state resources should be highlighted as among the mechanisms that allowed for the consolidation of the neoliberal stabilization during the Fujimori administration. Using huge amounts of money from privatization schemes and increased tax revenue, the government set up a wide distribution network, through highly customized social programs dependent on the regime's political needs. At the same time, the state was co-opted by a political mafia, which successfully managed to centralize their criminal activities within the public apparatus, under the iron-tight control of Fujimori himself, as well as his closest associates and partners. Among the factors contributing to the neoliberal stabilization, which brought broad popular support to the regime, controlling inflation and the state's victory in its war against the armed insurgent groups should be stressed. Economic growth figures and the population's repudiation of the so-called "traditional politicians," who became the target of the regime's anti-political rhetoric, also widened the regime's social support.

With the democratic transition of the early 2000s, and following an authoritarian neoliberal stabilization scheme, a new political and social scenario opened up in Peru. The neoliberal economic model was kept by the democratically elected governments that followed the Fujimori regime, although severe social fragmentation and contradictions have remained, which have been largely fueled by the insufficiencies of the neoliberal stabilization program.

Peru has been unable to overcome problems that gave rise to the war-marked 1980s, the economic crisis, and the crumbling of the system of political representation. Despite the economic growth resulting from the neoliberal stabilization program, long-standing social, territorial, and ethno-cultural inequalities still remain in Peruvian society. The neoliberal order has failed to transform the structural exclusion and poverty that have impacted on popular sectors. This situation has been reflected in growing protests and social conflicts, which could give rise to new critical situations in the future.

WAR AND NEOLIBERAL TRANSFORMATION: PERU   249

The first section of this chapter is a summary of the war experience in Peru. The second section describes the links between war termination and neoliberal transformation, examining the characteristics of the neoliberal "revolution" since the early 1990s. In the third and final section, the situation after the neoliberal reforms is addressed, and an analysis is made of the evolution of both social unrest, and of the reasons for a focused resurgence of subversive activities.

THE WAR

According to calculations made by the Truth and Reconciliation Commission (CVR)[6] set up in Peru to examine human rights violations during the internal war, the total number of casualties was some 70,000 people. This figure exceeds both the number of victims in the previous civil wars, and in the wars fought by Peruvian soldiers in international conflicts.

Regarding the social background of dead and missing people, they were mostly poor people, belonging to the most marginal social sectors in the country. Most of them were indigenous peasants who, caught up in the maelstrom of war, became its main victims (see Figure 7.1). Quechua was the mother tongue of 75 percent of people

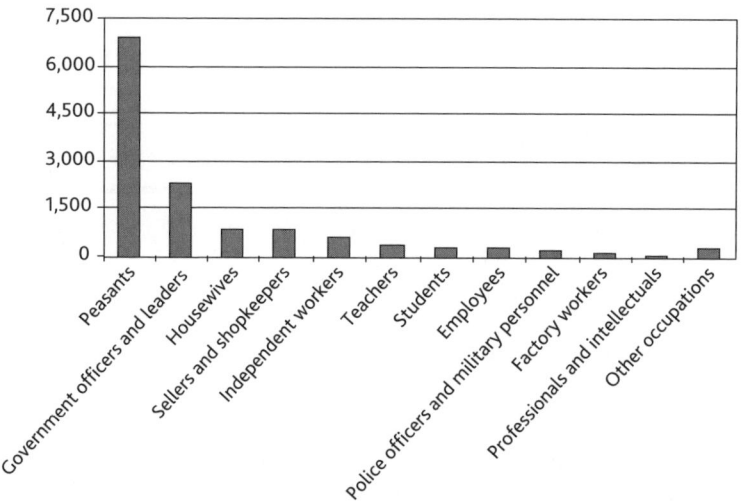

Figure 7.1 Casualties according to occupation

Source: CVR (2003).

killed (see Figure 7.2) and, because of their place of origin—the poorest, most excluded, and remotest regions of the country—the fact is that the most vulnerable sectors of Peruvian society were most affected by the violence (see Figure 7.3).

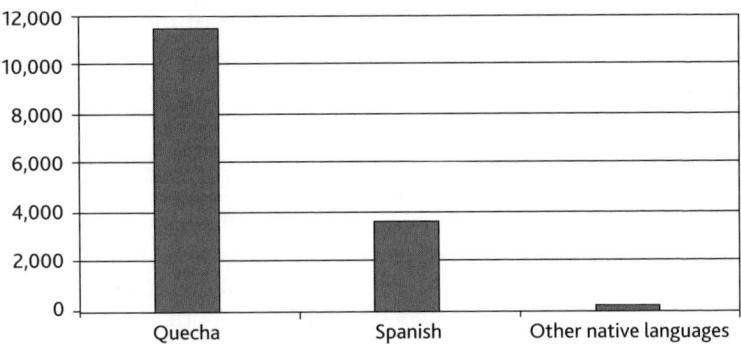

Figure 7.2 Casualties according to mother tongue

Source: CVR (2003).

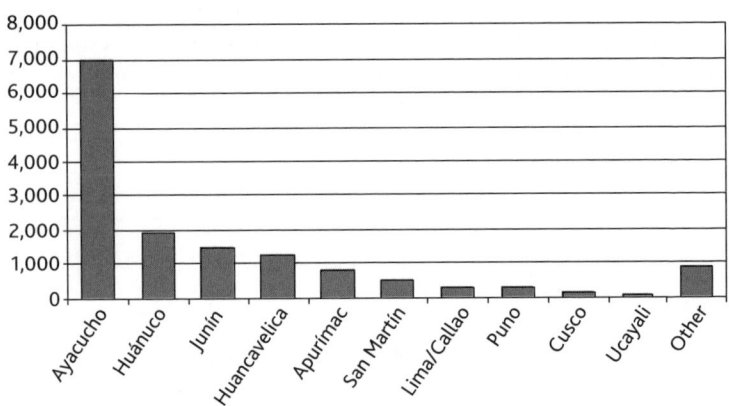

Figure 7.3 Casualties according to place of birth

Source: CVR (2003).

Looking at the evolution of the war in terms of the number of victims, the conflict shows two high-intensity periods. The first period corresponds with the early 1980s, when the militarization of the country was ordered by the state. The second period corresponds with the end of the decade when Sendero Luminoso unleashed a severe confrontation with the state, aiming to create a so-called "strategic equilibrium" with state forces (see Figure 7.4).

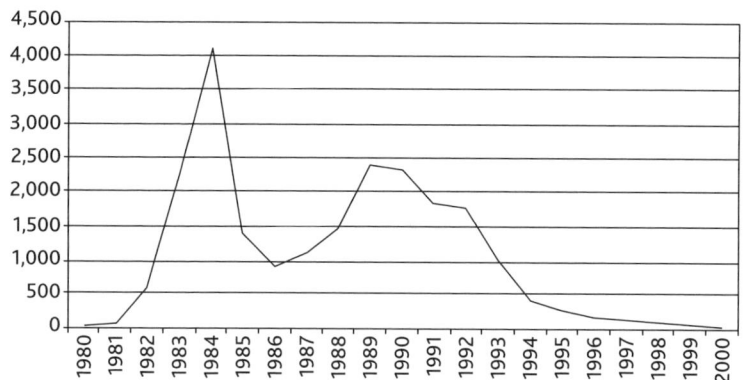

Figure 7.4 Number of casualties according to year of death/disappearance, 1980–2000

Source: CVR (2003).

When the Truth and Reconciliation Commission made inquiries into the reasons why this war had become the deadliest conflict in Peruvian history, it found that the violence unleashed by the PCP-SL had opened a Pandora's box that proved to be difficult to deal with by any of the various armed actors. During the 1980s, violence increased exponentially, feeding on simmering conflicts that had built during previous decades. Extreme poverty and marginalization experienced by many people, as well as the many conflicts unleashed by the swift modernization of previous decades, provided fertile ground for Sendero Luminoso's activities. At the same time, many of these conflicts had been suppressed by the persistence of an extremely restrictive and exclusionary political regime.[7]

The Historical Background

Peruvian society has undergone profound modernization since the mid twentieth century, during which the traditional features of the country became swiftly transformed. The following changes are examples of how deeply modernization changed the country: (i) the traditional rural settlement patterns were transformed in a few decades into a new urban settlement pattern; (ii) deep socio-cultural and habitat changes were brought about by speedy urbanization and the expansion of the cities, reaching back to the rural areas from where the newly-urbanized population had come; (iii) an industrialization process never seen before in national history started to take shape, and new salaried employees began to emerge; (iv) the state expanded and experienced significant institutional growth, increasing its presence in the national territory; (v) the media (radio, TV, and print media) began to flourish; (vi) market activities greatly expanded, reaching areas previously characterized by geographical inaccessibility and territorial remoteness from economic and social power centers; (vii) education expanded at an unprecedented rate, not only at basic but also at higher levels (universities and colleges).

The Peruvian society that gave rise to the PCP-SL, resulting in the biggest conflict in the recent history of the country, had thus evolved from a thwarted modernization process. While completely changing the country's face, this process had also sown the seeds of conflicts and contradictions, which broke into the open due to Sendero Luminoso's activities. Progress in the late 1970s towards a more open political system, in the form of democratic transition from a protracted military regime, arrived too late to change the course of events already set in motion.

The Trajectory of the War

The PCP-SL, the political group that launched the war, was born out of a split within the Peruvian communist left in 1970.[8] At the time it emerged, it was a fairly small group led by Abimael Guzmán, an Arequipa-born teacher of philosophy, who had come to Ayacucho to work at the Universidad Nacional San Cristobal de Huamanga (UNSCH). This university of colonial origin, renowned for being the place where the PCP-SL emerged, had been reopened in 1959, after having been closed for a long time. UNSCH's importance can be understood as an outcome of the fact that Ayacucho is one of the poorest regions of the Peruvian highlands. In this rural region—characterized in the 1960s and 1970s by extreme poverty and economic stagnation, and the population predominantly made up by indigenous peasants who were attached to large estates or belonged to indigenous communities—the reopening of the university came with an expectation for change.

During the 1970s, the PCP-SL—a small group made up by hardly two or three dozen militants loyal to Abimael Guzmán, who was already seen as an ideologue—managed to gain control of the university and firmly expand their activities across the Ayacucho rural regions. This happened thanks to the recruitment of university teachers and students as militants. Sendero Luminoso was thus able to link the university to other social sectors strategically important to its growth plans: the rural communities and popular urban neighborhoods. Towards the end of the decade, a broad, national-level popular movement was created, which succeeded in holding out against the military dictatorship still in power at the time, forcing the Francisco Morales Bermúdez government to convene a Constituent Assembly and to call general elections in May 1980. The withdrawal of the military from power and the return to democratic rule was a real challenge for the left, which was forced to re-define their participation in (and opposition to) the democratic electoral system. Unlike most left-wing groups who made a decision to participate in the elections, the PCP-SL opted to keep out, stating their opposition to joining the democratic system. Not only that, this tiny party also decided to put their rhetoric on the need for an armed struggle into practice.

On May 17, 1980, supported by a scant—if growing—social base both in the city and in the countryside, the Senderistas launched their war by burning ballot boxes in the small town of Chuschi. The initial stage of the war, lasting about three years, was the biggest moment of success for Sendero Luminoso, not only because it significantly expanded the number of party militants—a party that was also getting internally consolidated—but also because the Senderistas were able to take root in many Ayacucho communities, which were becoming "support bases" for the PCP-SL. Sendero Luminoso thus succeeded in making an important impact on national politics by conducting multiple armed actions that took government forces by surprise.

In late 1982, faced with the growing Sendero Luminoso armed struggle in Ayacucho, which had rapidly spread out towards the neighboring regions of Apurimac and Huancavelica, the government made a decision to take drastic measures: It declared a state of emergency in territories directly affected by violence, and instructed the armed forces to fight the PCP-SL army. Because of this, conflict conditions were completely changed, and the second stage of the war began, defined by the militarization of the confrontation between the state and the Senderistas. Under the new counter-insurgency policy, Political Military Command was set up in Ayacucho, which, from 1983 onwards, was in full control of regional political affairs. The state was thus leaving political and institutional control in the hands of the military, leaving civil roles in emergency-declared areas under military control.

The decision to militarize the conflict led to its escalation to levels that not even the Senderistas themselves would have predicted at the time they were designing their political-military plans. This was reflected in an increase in violent actions, the impact of which was particularly harsh on the civilian population. Both the members of the armed forces and the Senderistas violated villagers' and peasants' human rights as a result of this escalation.

Between 1983 and 1985, Ayacucho was in the midst of a civil war. It was not only the confrontation between the PCP-SL and the armed forces that were a part of the war, but also the tensions between these armed groups and the communities, which were viewed as allegedly subversive by the military and as state collaborators by the Senderistas. This ended up in many brutal collective massacres and murders committed by both warring parties. At the same time, the conflict between the communities themselves was aggravated.

With the rise to power of president-elect Alan García Pérez in 1985, the situation was expected to improve. Indeed, during its first months in office, the government seemed to regain control of the civil war, asking the warring parties to respect human rights. However, on June 18 and 19, 1986, following a Senderista strategy to exacerbate violence, state prisoners revolted in jails, and the government responded by indiscriminate use of force, slaughtering hundreds of prisoners, and starting a new period of the war. This also forced the Túpac Amaru Revolutionary Movement (MRTA), a second armed organization born in 1984, to declare the end of the one-year truce the MRTA had given the Aprista government, and resume armed actions against the state. The MRTA, a Guevarista-inspired organization, thus contributed to the national escalation of the war, though it had always been a rather different group from the PCP-SL. (Ideology was a major difference between the MRTA and the Senderistas, as the MRTA was not a Maoist group but, rather, had taken on a leftist ideology inspired from Latin American guerrillas. Also, the members of the MRTA wore war uniforms and followed the Geneva Conventions, stating their respect for human rights, which enabled them to establish a better relationship with the civilian population.)

The slaughter of prisoners signaled the third period of war, which lasted until March 1989. This period was mainly characterized by the territorial spread of violence over most of the national territory. While the war continued to spread in the areas originally made up by the departments of Ayacucho, Apurimac, and Huancavelica, other regional battlefronts of a similar, and even larger size, emerged in Lima, Puno, the central jungle, the coastal region, and the Northern highlands.

From 1989 until Abimael Guzmán was captured in September 1992, a new and critical period of the war emerged. This is the time in which the biggest state crisis and the largest territorial expansion of the conflict coincided. According to the political plans of the PCP-SL Central Committee, it was the moment at which what they called the "strategic equilibrium" was going to be achieved, i.e., a parity of forces with the state. According to Abimael Guzmán, an increase in violence was to break the backbone of the government's resistance, allowing the PCP-SL to gain power in the country. With this aim in mind, the PCP-SL increased its destruction spree, blasting electrical pylons to cause widespread power failures, staging raids and stepping up calls for so-called "armed strikes." This situation coincided with a severe economic and political crisis which, in addition to the Senderistas trying to reach the "strategic equilibrium," helped to generate a situation of chaos. However, after almost a decade of war, the counter-insurgency policy was beginning to bear fruit. Superseding the "scorched earth" policy of earlier years that was responsible for so much havoc, the military since 1989 had become more selective in its anti-subversion fight, attempting to win the civilian population's support. Also, infiltration and other intelligence activities were beginning to help military and police actions. An event that decisively changed the balance of forces in favor of the state was the peasant mobilization, which was achieved through the establishment and expansion of local "rounds" or "self-defense committees" that were allied with state law enforcement agencies. The peasants' rejection of the PCP-SL and their siding with the state was a strategic shift during the war, the real dimension of which the Senderista leadership failed to apprehend at the time.

This critical situation, the Senderista offensive and the state counter-offensive taking place between 1989 and 1992, would come to an end in September 1992, when Abimael Guzmán was captured. What followed was the political collapse of the PCP-SL—the more so, because its leadership in prisons was facing severe internal differences, which ended up creating a split. Abimael Guzmán's call to negotiate a "peace agreement" with the Alberto Fujimori regime was rejected by the PCP-SL party members, who also accused the government of media manipulation. Thus, the PCP-SL members were split between the so-called "agreement-seekers" (followers of a tactic to seek a peace accord) and those calling for armed struggle to be sustained (the group called "to go on," mainly combatants still fighting in the central jungle region). After 1992, the defeat of Sendero Luminoso was skillfully used by the Fujimori regime to increase its political authority and to implement an aggressive neoliberal transformation plan from the state. The perseverance of a corrupt and authoritarian regime in the next decade thus coincided with the end of war and the introduction of a new hegemonic neoliberal order.

THE NEOLIBERAL "REVOLUTION"

Starting in the early 1990s, neoliberal reforms were introduced in Peru by a political coalition made up of newly-elected president Alberto Fujimori, the armed forces and the country's business elite. The neoliberal techno-bureaucracy, responsible for the state's management of reforms, and the National Intelligence Service, controlled by the presidential advisor Vladimiro Montesinos, joined this coalition. It is important to understand the background to this power coalition shepherding the neoliberal opening and stabilization of the Peruvian economy during the 1990s. Since the 1970s, several governments had made stabilization attempts in an effort to overcome the economic crisis the country was involved in since the outbreak of the international oil crisis. None of them, however, came close to having the same impact as the coalition led by Alberto Fujimori.

The Political Background of Neoliberal Stabilization

In 1968, General Juan Velasco Alvarado led a coup d'état installing a progressive military regime self-styled as a "Revolutionary Armed Forces Government." During those years in-depth changes in the Peruvian society were taking place, major reforms were being implemented, including land reform, one of the most radical land-tenure schemes being applied in Latin America. Land reform completely transformed land tenure in the country, removing the traditional landowner sector from the scene. In replacement of the manor-like landowner structure, based on estate dominance and control of serf peasant workforce, a cooperative production system was introduced in the countryside through the creation of social-property enterprises, known as the Agricultural Social-Interest Societies (SAIS). Land reform came together with other measures seeking the structural transformation of the national economy, under the aegis of the state, aiming at promoting industrialization and internal dynamism. The most important productive sectors were placed under state management, through a far-reaching nationalization policy, which went hand in hand with similar reforms in education and employment.

Nevertheless, in 1975, the Velasco experiment came abruptly to an end prompted by a military coup d'état headed by Francisco Morales Bermúdez. Although Morales announced a second phase of the so-called "Revolutionary Armed Forces Government," in practice he began dismantling the statist developmental model of his predecessor. The political cornering of the military regime became acute over those years, reaching a critical point when mass mobilizations and national strikes, such as the July 1977 stoppage, began to take place, forcing the military to negotiate the restoration of democracy. Elections were thus convened to install a Constituent Assembly, which would be responsible for drafting a new Constitution. Presidential elections in which the winning candidate was Fernando Belaúnde (who had been overthrown by Velasco Alvarado in 1968) were held in 1980. Within this transition-to-democracy framework, left-wing parties attempted to shape up an electoral coalition through the formation of the UI.[9] However, not all left-wing groups, which had multiplied in the 1960s and 1970s, agreed to join in the democratic game. As mentioned above, the PCP-SL decided to launch its armed struggle against the state the same day presidential elections were being held, thwarting the polls by burning polling boxes in the peasant community of Chuschi, Ayacucho. The return of democracy thus coincided with the outbreak of war.

During the first half of the 1980s, the Fernando Belaúnde regime used the 1979 Constitution—which stipulated that the Peruvian State was based on a "social market economy"—to advance the dismantling of the vestiges of the Velasco regime. This involved a push towards trade liberalization, especially to encourage the growth of non-traditional exports. However, state economic management constraints, linked with the lack of a clear monetary policy, management difficulties within state-owned enterprises, and the inability to handle the increasing external debt (especially in an international setting in which the so-called debt crisis had broken out) weighed more. The social market model, failing to emerge as a consistent development strategy, was reduced to a political rhetoric detached from state control in real terms (Wise, 2003, p. 199). Other critical factors were added, including the expansion of Sendero Luminoso's actions, and the occurrence of natural disasters, such as El Niño-associated floods and droughts, on account of which large areas in the country were devastated. Thus, the Belaúnde regime helped to give rise to the crisis that was to erupt during the second half of the decade.

Alan García, candidate of the Peruvian APRA party, was the winner of the 1985 elections. His government had generated great expectations, not only because it was the first time Aprismo came to power after 60 years of playing a leading role in Peruvian politics, but also because the young president was bringing with him promises of change and renewal. The formula the Aprista government applied was to expand fiscal spending and to use the huge state apparatus to boost the economic take-off and increase the performance of private actors. Thus, during the first two years of the new government, high growth levels and a strong economic dynamism were achieved, together with increasing domestic consumption. However, things abruptly changed in 1987, because fiscal spending by far exceeded revenues. The government's economic heterodoxy, as reflected in decisions such as restricting the payment of foreign debt, state control of the financial sector, and boosting economic welfare through a wide-ranging subsidies policy, crashed with the worsening fiscal deficit. In 1988, inflation soared to seven times the previous year's level, unleashing an economic imbalance the government was unable to control. At the same time, increasing political violence fed the feeling of chaos and lack of governance.

At the end of the 1980s, the state of affairs could not have been worse. A feeling of national failure pervaded, not only because of the acute economic crisis but also because of the threat Sendero Luminoso was posing through its actions, which had managed to put the state in check. Inflation reached amazing figures: nearly 3,000 percent in 1989, and 7,000 percent in 1990, while in the last three years of the Aprista government, the GDP fell by 24 percent, the fiscal deficit increased and real wages fell over 150 percent. Neoliberalism, and the need for a "heavy hand" in politics, appeared in this chaotic setting as the only option for a way out of the crisis, even more so because of the failure of previously implemented economic models (see Table 7.1).

The Introduction of Neoliberalism: 1990–92

Three factors paved the way for the introduction in 1990 of neoliberalism in Peru: (i) the national crisis resulting in the election of political newcomer Alberto Fujimori; (ii) the debacle of the political parties and the loss of credibility of democracy; (iii) the existence of a military plan whose purpose was to stabilize the political situation in Peru by imposing an authoritarian government.

Table 7.1 Developmental models before the implementation of neoliberalism

Presidential administration	Economic policy	Developmental model
1968–80 Revolutionary Armed Forces Government	State capitalism	• Import substitution • Investment in infrastructure • Wide nationalization • Land tenure reform
Phase I: 1968–75 Juan Velasco Alvarado	Expansionist phase	• Redistribution policy • Tied exchange rate • Erratic monetary policy • Growth of public indebtedness
Phase II: 1975–80 Francisco Morales Bermúdez	Adjustment phase	• Promotion of non-traditional exports • Trade liberalization • Competitive exchange rate • Monetary adjustment • External debt negotiation and growth
1980–85 Fernando Belaúnde Terry	Orthodox stabilization with populist policies	• Promotion of primary exports • Investment in public infrastructure • Fiscal expansion • Floating exchange rate • Erratic monetary management • Debt renegotiation and growth • Decelerated trickling down of social policy
1985–90 Alan García Pérez	Neo-structuralism	• Price and wage controls • Consumer-led reactivation • Trade protection • Redistributive rhetoric • Layered exchange rate • Expansive fiscal and monetary policy • Infrastructure neglect • Unilateral debt moratorium

Source: Wise (2003), pp. 32–33.

The favorite candidate in the 1990 elections was the writer Mario Vargas Llosa who, in 1987, had become the leader of the Freedom Movement, formed to oppose an attempt by the Aprista government to nationalize private banks. Vargas Llosa jumped into the political arena by disseminating a neoliberal economic discourse, proposed as the only solution for a country in the midst of chaos, reflected in hyperinflation and the worsening war. Economist Hernando De

Soto, who in 1986 had published his book *The other Path*, a clear allusion to Sendero Luminoso, also played a meaningful role in the positioning of neoliberal thinking in the country. Vargas Llosa and Hernando De Soto suggested that the major problem in Peru was the continuity of mercantilism and statism, and that drastic liberalization, capable of sweeping away the bureaucratic hurdles that prevented the drive towards the free market, was therefore required. The purpose of De Soto's book (Vargas Llosa wrote the prologue to it) was to demonstrate the latter's political thesis in a specific field: the management of real estate and its conversion into an economic asset for development and overcoming poverty (De Soto, 1986). Around this time, in association with the Freedom Movement, a group of young neoliberal politicians emerged, mainly economists and lawyers, who were later to become the technicians who, from their positions within the state, led the government's economic stabilization program.

The 1990 elections buried the presidential aspirations of Vargas Llosa, who was to be defeated by the previously unknown university teacher Alberto Fujimori. Weeks before the elections, Fujimori attracted popular sympathy against the candidacy of Vargas Llosa, who was being deemed as the candidate of the rich. Thus, Fujimori became the second most-voted candidate in the first ballot and the unquestioned winner in the second voting round. During his campaign, Fujimori used a direct anti-neoliberal discourse, openly opposing the economic shock program that Vargas Llosa was proposing. Fujimori's campaign slogan, simply offering "honesty, technology, and work," was seen as an alternative to the onslaught of the rich, embodied in the candidacy of the famous writer, who ended up being defeated. Thus, at the head of an independent movement called Cambio 90, Fujimori came to power by profiting from the crisis engulfing the political parties.

Just one day after the electoral victory of Alberto Fujimori, the introduction of neoliberal reforms in the country got under way. The key event was the meeting between the elected candidate and economist Hernando De Soto, who persuaded Fujimori of the need to implement an extreme agenda of neoliberal reforms as the only possible way out of the serious crisis Peru was immersed in. What followed was a succession of key events: before taking office, Fujimori got rid of his first economic team, embarking on a tour abroad in which he contacted neoliberal businessmen and bureaucrats, several of whom were to become Peruvian state officers. Nearly two weeks after he was inaugurated, the so-called

August 1990 "Fujishock" was implemented, followed by hundreds of decrees imposing neoliberal reforms. Also, on April 5, 1992, Fujimori forced a coup d'état, signaling his government's slide into a long authoritarian period.

All these events went hand in hand with a political plan designed in 1989 by the armed forces, to implement a package of reforms aimed at liberalizing the economy and defeating Sendero Luminoso, through the imposition of an armed forces-led dictatorial government over a 25-year period. This plan, known as "The Green Plan," was unveiled a few years later and disclosed by *Oiga* (Listen) magazine (1993). Later on, it was revealed that, in order to become president, Fujimori had to assure the armed forces that he would at least partially implement their plan. This was beneficial for both sides: Fujimori obtained some crucial components for his own governmental plan that he had been missing, while the military had found the person that could implement their plan, without having to resort to a typical coup d'état to directly control the reins of power.

Between the arrival of Fujimori to power in 1990 and the April 1992 coup d'état, two finance ministers were called upon to give impetus to economic reforms. The first, Juan Carlos Hurtado Miller, announced a drastic economic shock, deemed as one of the more stringent and orthodox reforms applied world-wide (Chossudovsky, 1992). This happened just eleven days after Fujimori had taken office (see Table 7.2).

Table 7.2 Main economic measures after the August 8, 1990 economic shock

- Removal of exchange controls.
- A 3,000 percent petrol price increase.
- Removal of subsidies of all sorts.
- Overall liberalization of goods and services prices, to be further regulated by the market.
- Implementation of a tariff regime with a 10 percent minimum and a 50 percent maximum.
- A 300 percent minimum wage increase.
- Delivery of a 100 percent extraordinary compensation to July wages.
- Removal of all tax exemptions.
- Increase to 14 percent on the general sales tax (IGV).

Source: Lajo (1991).

But Carlos Boloña Behr, the second finance minister of the Fujimori regime, was the real neoliberal transformation architect. He had replaced Hurtado Miller in February 1991, and remained in his position even after the 1992 coup. In his book *Cambio de rumbo* (Changing Course), Boloña (1993) made a thorough description of the implementation of the structural adjustment program (SAP) by the government. The main objectives of this program were: (i) unlimited economic liberalization; (ii) the country's reintegration into the international financial system; and (iii) the institutional transformation of the state.

During Boloña's term in office, structural reforms were implemented in three waves.[10] The first one took place between March and April 1991, through 61 supreme decrees aimed at liberalizing the economy. Among other measures, tariffs were reduced, the foreign exchange market was liberalized, the initial impetus to enterprise privatization was given, and the labor regime was liberalized. The second wave of reforms took place between May and November 1991, a period in which 171 legislative decrees were approved. The executive was able to enact them through an act of delegation of authority granted by Congress to legislate on three issues: the promotion of investment, the promotion of employment, and pacification. The third and final wave of structural reforms during Boloña's term in office took place between April and December 1992, i.e., after the coup d'état. The government issued 745 supreme decrees, through which neoliberal reforms were deepened in the trade, financial, public, and productive sectors.

If the economic adjustment changed the course of national economy, the political turn consolidating neoliberal reforms was the April 1992 coup, through which Fujimori assured himself control over all state powers. Thus, neoliberalism was being associated with the imposition of a dictatorial regime lasting until 2000.

1992–2000: Neoliberalism and Authoritarianism

During the years following the authoritarian imposition of the neoliberal model between 1990 and 1992, Peruvian neoliberalism went through two well-defined moments. The first one, from 1993 to 1997, can be viewed as a booming period for the economic model in place. The country's economic stabilization began to bear fruit, through the improvement of macroeconomic indicators. The economy's dynamism was substantially increased, a fact clearly reflected in GDP growth, fiscal deficit control, the stabilization of inflation, increasing foreign investment, increased trade by lowering tariffs, and so on. (see Figures 7.5, 7.6, 7.7, 7.8, and 7.9).

State revenue was also increased over this period, not only because of improvements in tax collection, but also through capital inflows

WAR AND NEOLIBERAL TRANSFORMATION: PERU 263

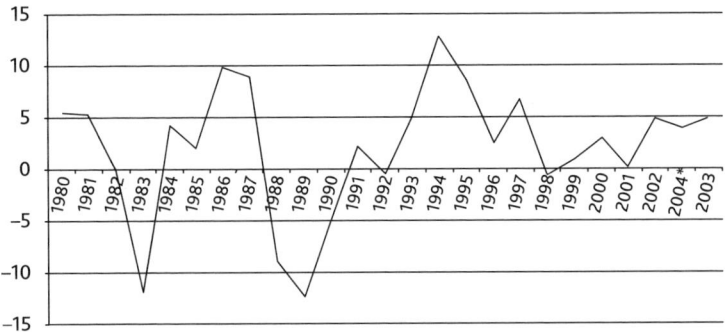

Figure 7.5 Evolution of the gross domestic product (GDP), 1980–2003
Source: INEI.

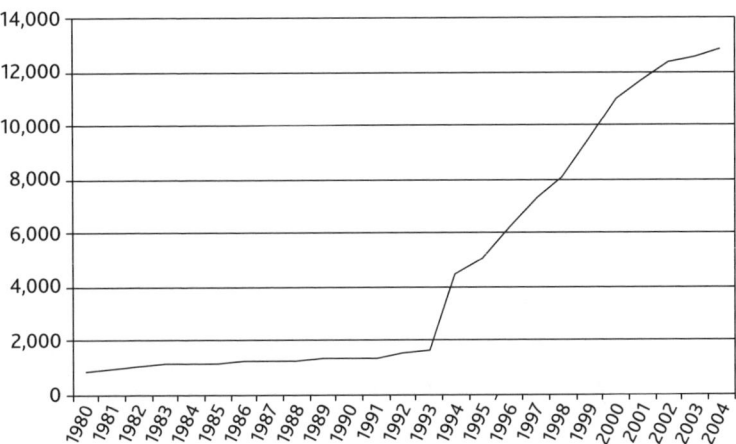

Figure 7.6 Foreign Direct Investment (in millions of US dollars), 1980–2004
Source: INEI.

from the privatization of state enterprises. With these resources at its disposal, the government was able to implement an aggressive social aid program, and execute works in sectors such as education, transportation, and health (see Figure 7.10). The confluence of the defeat of the insurgency, economic stabilization, and the implementation of social aid policies, resulted in strong approval for the regime. This allowed Fujimori to be re-elected in the 1995 elections, defeating Javier Pérez de Cuéllar, the former Secretary General of the United Nations.

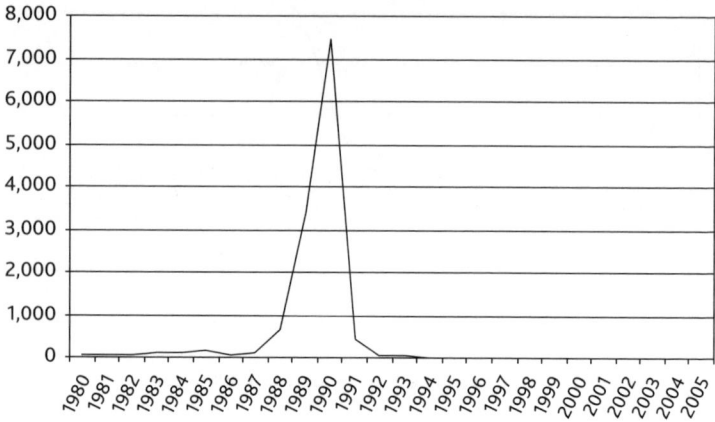

Figure 7.7 The evolution of inflation, 1980–2005

Source: INEI.

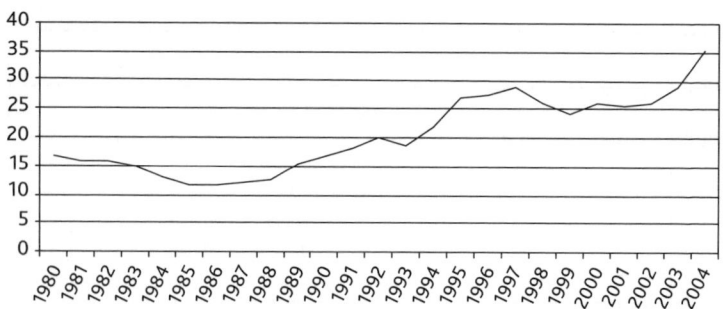

Figure 7.8 Foreign trade as a percentage of the 1980–2004 GDP (External Opening Ratio)

Source: INEI.

Over those same years, under the neoliberal cloak of success, an apparently democratic government was institutionalized which, in practice, was a fairly unique authoritarian regime. Hence the confusion surrounding its description: since it wasn't an overt dictatorship, some analysts used other terms, such as *dictablanda* and *democradura* (Lopez, 1993).[11] There was talk of a triumvirate, consisting of President Fujimori, General Nicolas de Bari Hermoza, the top head of the armed forces, and advisor Vladimiro Montesinos, head of the National Intelligence Service.

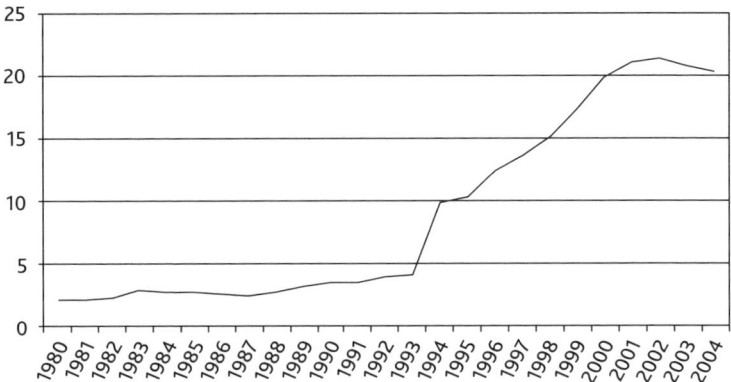

Figure 7.9 Foreign Direct Investment as a percentage of the 1980–2004 GDP

Source: INEI.

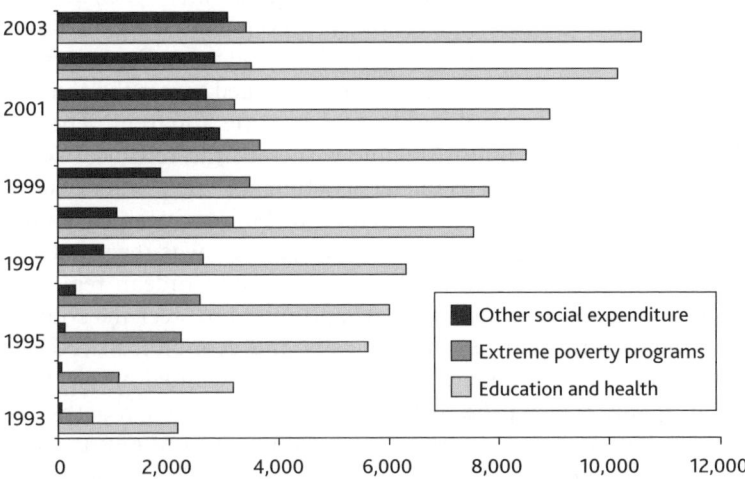

Figure 7.10 State social expenditure budget (in millions of New Soles), 1993–2003

Source: INEI.

During the Fujimori regime, this entity became a real surveillance team, monitoring institutions, and—through the use of the media, several of which were in the service of the government through juicy bribes—managing public opinion.

From 1998, a second period in which the economic situation began to show traits of a crisis began to surface. The deterioration of the global economy as a result of a series of crises, like the Mexican and Asian ones, meant the transformation of external conditions on which, to a large extent, the model relied. For the first time since neoliberalism had been implemented, macroeconomic indicators showed a worrying situation, with a reduction of GDP, while it was becoming increasingly clear that the economy was entering into a recession. Although this situation was to last during 1989 and 1990, it did not reach the destabilization and hyperinflation stages; public opinion thus continued to perceive a stable situation. Discontent and a loss of credibility in the regime did not come out of public awareness about the economic slowdown, but above all out of the feeling that only a few had benefited from the sacrifice that came with the 1990 economic adjustment, and poverty and inequality had not been reduced.

The slowdown in the economy coincided with an attempt by Fujimori to get re-elected once again. He forced the congress to enact the so-called "Act of authentic interpretation," which allowed him to apply for a new re-election. The political setting, however, was different from the one during the 1995 elections. Organizations opposed to prolonging the dictatorship emerged across the country, and criticism of the neoliberal order became apparent. The last three years of the Fujimori regime witnessed the return of social protests by sectors such as university students and workers. In the 2000 elections, the leading contender to Fujimori was Alejandro Toledo, an economist of provincial origin who was regarded as a successful "cholo" (term used throughout the Andean region to refer to a person of mixed race). He promised to steer the country on a democratic path, both politically and economically. To get re-elected, the government had to resort to a scandalous electoral fraud, against which protests spread over the following months. On the day Fujimori was sworn in for his third term of government, the opposition led by Toledo convened a mass mobilization for the recovery of democracy, called the Marcha de los 4 suyos ("The March of the Four"). While the swearing-in by Fujimori was taking place in Congress, the streets of Lima filled with thousands of people who were attempting to stop Fujimori from being sworn in again, and who were ruthlessly suppressed by law-enforcement police officers.

The fall of the regime, however, did not come about because of popular mobilization; rather, it was due to the disclosure, in September 2000, of a video in which advisor Vladimiro Montesinos could be seen buying the political support of an opposition congressman with wads of cash. The uncovering of the Fujimori's regime corruption was, thus, a completely destabilizing factor for the regime. While Montesinos was fleeing the country, Fujimori announced that new elections, in which he would not participate, would be held. In November that year, and taking advantage of an invitation to an international forum, Fujimori fled to Japan, sending his letter of resignation to the presidency via fax.

The Neoliberal Transformation of the State

According to economist Efrain Gonzáles de Olarte (1993, 1998), the transformation of the state within the framework of neoliberal reforms had three essential parts: (i) tax reform; (ii) the dismantling of the state's economic role through the privatization of public enterprises; and (iii) the reform of decentralized institutions within the state apparatus.

Economic liberalization coincided with a far-reaching institutional state readjustment process. This plan was supported by international agencies, like the International Monetary Fund and the World Bank, mainly, and included the introduction of reforms in areas such as state employment, tax collection, management of the financial system, design and implementation of social-sector policies, and streamlining of the administration of justice, among other sectors. The goal was to redefine the role of the state, ensuring the effectiveness of governance for the expansion of free markets.

According to Durand and Thorp (2000), a drastic reform of the state was introduced as the only way out of the excessive bureaucracy and lack of control vis-à-vis the economic crisis. Theoretically, this reform should have been gradually implemented in order to move from a large and unmanageable developmentalist state to a smaller but active state, that was more functional in terms of the free market development (Wise, 2003). Employment is one area in which this goal was clearly reflected. Thousands of workers were dismissed, as a way to get public companies ready for privatization and shrinking the institutional dimension of the state (see Figure 7.11).

Institutional changes were introduced along three successive periods (Gonzáles de Olarte, 1993), together with the implementation of the structural adjustment program (SAP). The first one included the "Fujishock" in August 1990, and lasted until January 1991. The second one began with the enactment of neoliberal decrees in February 1991, and lasted until the April 5, 1992 coup. The third one was the consolidation of reforms, including the adoption of a new political constitution in late 1992.

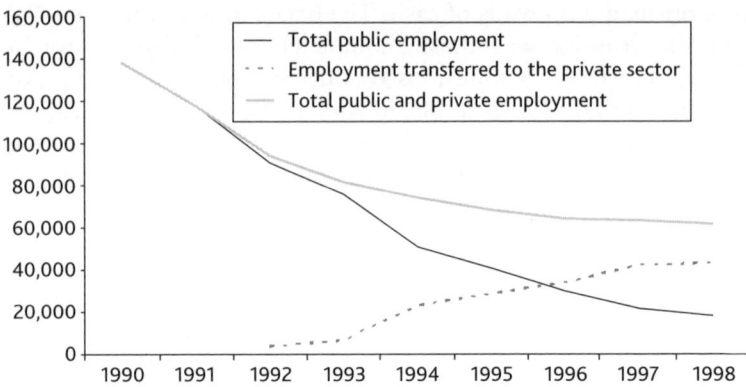

Figure 7.11 Evolution of public and private employment, 1990–98

Source: INEI, Ministerio de Trabajo, Ministry of Finance.

The neoliberal transformation of the state's institutional apparatus was carried out according to the structural adjustment program's timing priorities, including economic acceleration and backward trends during the successive Fujimori governments.[12] Key reforms include, among others, the readjustment of state agencies critical to the economic management, including the Central Reserve Bank (BCR) and the Ministry of Economy and Finances (MEF). Subsequently, with a view to speeding up the privatization process, a Commission for the Promotion of Private Investment (COPRI) and several Special Privatization Committees (CEPRIS) were set up. The next step was the creation of state entities aimed at achieving economic policy goals. The tax collection system was thus revamped through the reform of entities such as the National Tax Administration Superintendence (SUNAT), which allowed for an increase of state revenues to provide for social aid programs.

The tax reform was begun with the restructuring of SUNAT. In 1991, this institution had about 3,000 workers, who earned US$50 monthly on average. After the reform process, the number of workers was much lower and an elite sector was generated, earning wages averaging US$800 a month.[13] The next step was to increase revenue by leveling taxes to international scales, and creating a thorough taxpayers registry. SUNAT was endowed with powers to enforce tax laws, thus becoming one of the most influential institutions during the stabilization process.

Foreign trade was another area that was the subject of a deep institutional restructuring, designed to increase private participation and endowing the state with strict regulatory powers. From 1990 to 1994, the customs system was reconverted to the neoliberal system, through a series of rules including a new customs law focused on the promotion of the primacy of import/export free markets. Regarding social policy management, in August 1991 a new institution was created: the National Fund for Compensation and Social Development (FONCODES). The goal of this agency was to concentrate social spending and target the poorest sectors, in order to offset the structural adjustment impacts and win the political support of the population in areas directly affected by the civil war. Rural and urban areas where extreme poverty was rampant were privileged through the build-up of infrastructure for education and health, together with the provision of aid in the form of food, donation of clothing, etc. FONCODES became a major source of governmental legitimacy, because it was able to carry out a lot of work, thanks to resources from privatizations and the budgetary support received from agencies like the World Bank, the Inter-American Development Bank, and some international cooperation agencies.[14]

The flow of resources to the government for investment in social programs, leading to broad social support particularly in the poorest sectors, came mainly from the privatization of state enterprises. To date, 235 state-owned enterprises have been privatized in Peru, completely dismantling the productive and entrepreneurial capacity of the state, largely inherited from the Velasco military regime. The privatization scheme achieved its highest success during the first half of the 1990s. Over 65 companies had been sold until 1996, generating an income of more than US$3 billion to the state. Among the most significant and financially substantial privatizations, one could mention the state telephone, electricity generation and transmission, mining, oil, manufacturing, and agriculture enterprises, among other sectors.

During the second government of Fujimori, the pace of privatization slowed, and the focus shifted to infrastructure works concessions to private companies linked to the Fujimori political power network. Likewise, lucrative import and export businesses were promoted, through which the government's close allies managed to amass huge wealth. The creation of an extensive political patronage network, personally led by President Fujimori and his advisor, Vladimiro Montesinos, was sustained with money originating from privatization. This corruption network spread to within the state apparatus, generating several Mafia rings which controlled major economic sectors, through the provision of facilities for conducting business and investment. Thus, privatization ensured the upholding of the neoliberal economic stabilization, through the indiscriminate use of the huge resources from the sale of state-owned enterprises (see Figures 7.12 and 7.13).

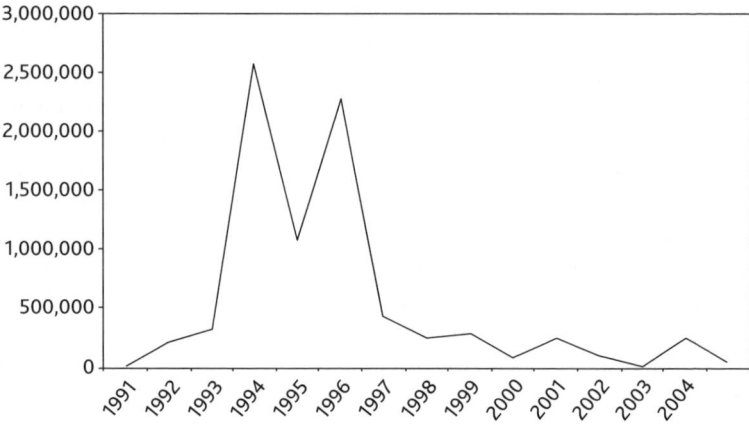

Figure 7.12 Amount raised from privatizations (in thousands of US dollars), 1991–2004

Source: INEI, Ministry of Finance.

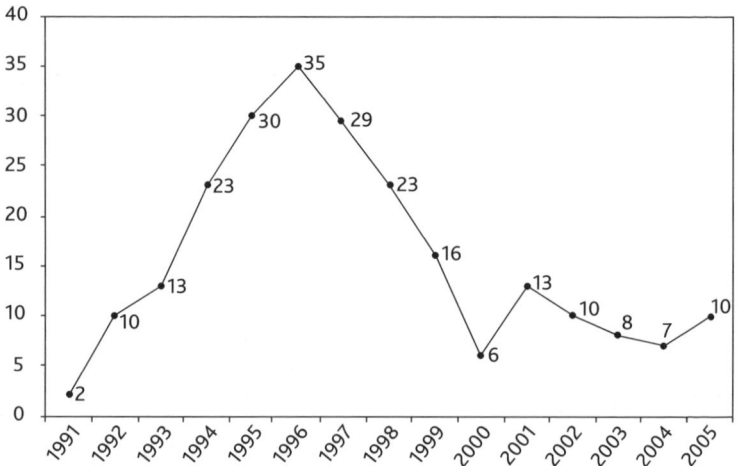

Figure 7.13 Number of firms privatized, 1991–2005

Source: INEI, Ministry of Finance.

The privatization of public enterprises went hand in hand with the setting up of several agencies responsible for regulating and supervising the operation of the new privatized enterprises, as well as with the granting of concession contracts and pricing estimation for basic services, such as telephone and electricity (see Table 7.3). However, these entities have been opened to questioning so far, due to conflicts of interest with transnational corporations benefiting from privatizations, thus giving rise to a great deal of consumer protests.

Table 7.3 Major regulatory agencies set up as a result of neoliberal reforms

Comisión de Tarifas Eléctricas (CTE)	Committee on Electricity Rates
Comisión Nacional de Medio Ambiente (CONAM)	National Commission on the Environment
Instituto Nacional de Defensa de la Competencia y de la Protección de la Propiedad Intelectual (INDECOPI)	National Institute for the Defense of Competition and the Protection of Intellectual Property
Organismo Supervisor de la Inversión Privada en Energía (OSINERG)	Supervisory Body of Private Investment in Energy
Organismo Supervisor de la Inversión Privada en Transporte (OSITRAN)	Supervisory Body of Private Investment in Transportation
Organismo Supervisor de la Inversión Privada de las Telecomunicaciones (OSIPTEL)	Supervisory Body of Private Investment in Telecommunications
Superintendencia de Banca y Seguros (SBS)	Superintendence of Banking and Insurance
Superintendencia nacional Aseguradoras de Fondos de Pensiones (SAFP)	National Insurance Superintendence of Pension Funds
Superintendencia Nacional de Servicios de Saneamiento (SUNASS)	National Superintendence of Sanitation Service

THE POST-NEOLIBERAL STABILIZATION SCENARIO

The post-Fujimori scenario in the 1990s shows that while a successful neoliberal stabilization was in place, severe economic, social, and regional fractures were still persistent in the country. A significant change in state–society relations in the country has been apparent as an outcome of the introduction of neoliberalism, which replaced the state-centrist model in force since the mid twentieth century. However, social inequalities and regional fractures have not vanished. A sharp contrast between high economic growth rates and extreme poverty is still prevailing. New conflicts and violence are often a result of this situation, as can be demonstrated by recurrent social protests and the resurgence of Sendero Luminoso.

Since the end of the authoritarian Fujimori regime and the return to democracy, the inconsistencies of neoliberalism seem to be breeding the conditions for the outbreak of a large number of social conflicts, accountable for serious governance problems in the country. The expectations associated with the democratic transition have been thwarted by the continuity of the neoliberal model, whose growth figures mean little to the popular sectors, due to the persistence of high poverty rates and exclusion. Moreover, recent years have seen strong growth in the cocaine economy. Increasing drug trafficking has meant an opportunity for the remnants of Sendero Luminoso, which have released a brand-new political discourse. This shows that Sendero Luminoso has entered a new phase in its history: it has regrouped politically and its increased armed actions confirm that Peru could be facing a focused resurgence, linked to the economic expansion of drug trafficking. However, this should not be seen as a threat to state hegemony, as was the case in the 1980s.

2000–07: Democratic Reconstruction and Neoliberal Continuity

In November 2000, when the Fujimori regime came to an end, a promising democratic transition period started in Peruvian politics. Overseeing this change was entrusted to Valentín Paniagua, who for eight months (until July 2001) presided over a transitional government. The heights of corruption reached during the Fujimori government were disclosed by this government, when the so-called "vladivideos" or corruption videos, showing the corruption of the state, were made public.

A new electoral process was convened during Paniagua's government, and Alejandro Toledo, who in 2000 had led a broad social mobilization against Fujimori and became the victim of electoral fraud, was elected president. Meanwhile, the neoliberal right-wing candidate, Lourdes Flores Nano, was eclipsed by the re-emergence of Alan García Pérez. In order to maintain macroeconomic stability, an exemplary political agenda for democratic recovery was drawn up by the transitional government in its few months in office, albeit leaving economic aspects untouched.

Alejandro Toledo's government needed to provide clear signals about its economic policies and it announced that the economic model would remain unchanged. This was to help in the economic re-stabilization effort, after the 1998 slowdown, and to increase the appeal for foreign investment. At the same time, a statement was made that a second round of reforms, designed to strengthen the macroeconomic success of the model on the basis of institutional consolidation, were to be launched. To that effect, a process of regionalization and decentralization of the state was announced to begin in 2003.

The new launching of the neoliberal model was made in a favorable international climate, greatly boosting growth sectors such as mining. Insofar as the economic model implemented since the 1990s had been targeted on primary product exports, it is strongly dependent on increasing raw materials exports. The high price of minerals over the past few years has, in this way, brought about a new economic expansion cycle, which has continuously shown upward trends linked to high yearly GDP growth levels since 2000. Peru is, therefore, being considered as a country showing one of the strongest growth figures in Latin America.

However, the economic re-stabilization, achieved from 2000 to 2005 failed to become associated with a higher level of redistribution, and with an appropriate institutional reform of the state. Rampant poverty and increasing inequality attest to the current model's inconsistencies—based on a primary-product economy and the boom of the economy's tertiary sector—and its difficulty in generating effective linkages with other economic sectors generating employment and a higher growth redistribution. On the other hand, the regionalization process has resoundingly failed, not only because of design flaws in the institutional reform, but also because of fears it would conflict with local identities, long settled in Peru since the nineteenth century. But political parties are also a part of the institutional fragility because efforts made so far to rebuild a political representation system based on the existence of soundly formed parties have failed. The distrust in politics in general and in the so-called "traditional parties" remains, which helps independent groups gain popular support—these groups, regardless of political ideologies, have instilled an extremely pragmatic perspective on political participation, which is seen as a business.

The difference between economic growth and redistribution has in recent years been reflected in increasing social protests. Several places in the country have witnessed outbursts of strong social conflict, generated by local or regional grievances. Likewise, new organizations capable of social mobilization have been set up, among which is the National Confederation of Communities Affected by Mining (CONACAMI), bringing together communities impacted by the recent mining expansion.

In addition to the return of social protest, a resurgence of subversive activities linked to increased drug trafficking has been another unexpected reality, as shown by recent data on Sendero Luminoso.

The current government of Alan García, who was elected president in the 2006 elections, made a decision again to go on with the neoliberal program. This is a new democratic government choosing the path of continuing neoliberal economic policies. The growth trend continues, but so do the model's inconsistencies generating real problems with the redistribution of wealth.

Conflicts and Social Protests

Neoliberalism has brought about a new wave of social unrest in the country. The classical trade union or political social protests, which had virtually disappeared from the political scenario over the last decade, have been replaced in the last few years by the constant outbreak of fairly focused, often violent, protests and social conflicts, usually responding to local demands. Unlike the situation prior to the neoliberal stabilization, the current social conflict cycle is not associated with leftist political parties' activities, nor does it show clear political representation in the form of clearly identifiable organizations and leaderships.

In the late 1970s and into the 1980s, social protest in Peru was marked by numerous strikes and work stoppages organized by politically-linked trades unions, such as the General Confederation of Workers of Peru (CGTP), the Unitary Union of Educational Workers in Peru (SUTEP), the National Federation of Mining Workers (FNTMMSP), among others. While strikes continued throughout the 1980s as a privileged form of social protest, they took a downturn during the next decade to the point where they nearly vanished. The implementation of neoliberal reforms, as well as the political parties' crisis, have led to a serious erosion of organizational arrangements of unions. Labor restructuring linked to the neoliberal economic stabilization also meant the disappearance of many trade unions, and the loss of union influence upon workers.

In the context of neoliberal reforms and the establishment of an authoritarian regime, other forms of social protest, such as marches, demonstrations, local and regional strikes, and so on, vanished during the 1990s (see Figures 7.14 and 7.15). In the second half of the decade, only a scant number of protests and demonstrations, mostly by young university students, took place in protest against the Fujimori regime. Several regional mobilizations were convened later on, organized by new organizations, such as the Regional Fronts and Defense Fronts, which had emerged in several parts of the country. Mobilizations, such as those undertaken by the Regional Front of Loreto during the late 1990s, helped voice the demands for political and economic decentralization, and the opposition to the regime.

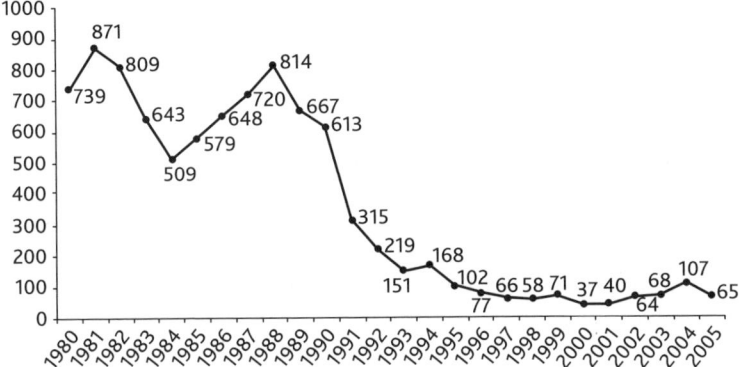

Figure 7.14 Number of strikes, 1980–2005

Source: INEI, Ministry of Labor.

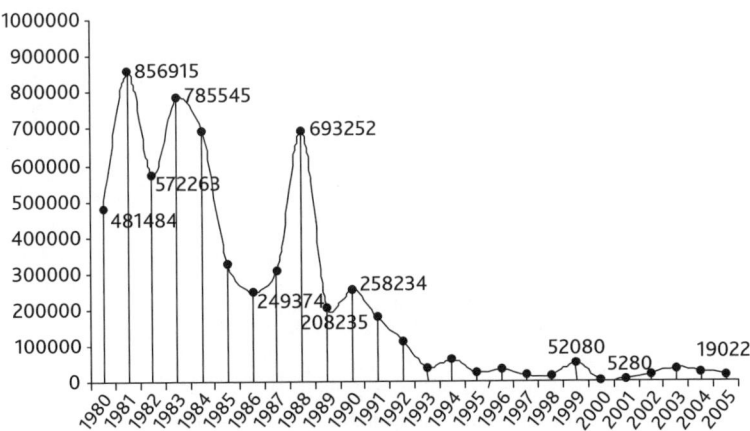

Figure 7.15 Number of workers participating in strikes, 1980–2005

Source: INEI, Ministerio de Trabajo.

Strikes also recorded a slight resurgence towards the end of the 1990s, and, in particular, since the democratic transition. While these are not like the strikes of the 1970s and 1980s, in terms of the number of participants and the type of political discourse associated with the protest, it is important to note that growing labor sectors have opted to again take up this form of protest to defend their interests against the entrepreneurs and the state.

This return of union protests and the calls to strike should be understood as part of a new social conflictivity cycle, emerging after the fall of the Fujimori regime. Since 2000, a remarkable resurgence of social mobilizations and protests by a variety of social actors has been noticed. To date, more local and regional protests have been taking place, showing no effective national articulation but occasionally shaking people's local realities (Pajuelo Teves, 2004).

Grievances underlying conflicts fall into at least five categories: (i) local and regional conflicts between people and their authorities; (ii) conflicts between local populations and extractive companies (mining, oil, timber, etc.); (iii) conflicts based on unions and labor situations; (iv) protests by peasants and farmers (coca growers, communal workers), demanding better prices and protesting against state policies; and (v) disputes between different social sectors. (See Table 7.4.)

Table 7.4 Social conflicts, 2004–07

Scenario/type	Description	2004	2005	2006	2007 (April)
Municipal	Questioning of local authorities	64	35	39	22
The environment	Clashes between populations and firms involved in exploitation of natural resources	6	14	20	27
Community	Conflicts between communities on account of boundaries, propriety titling, access to resources	–	12	17	9
Union–sector	Labor and/or union claims	18	7	11	7
Regional	Conflicts between departments for territorial boundaries or access to resources	5	2	7	7
Coca growing	Questioning by coca leaf growers of government crop eradication policies	–	2	3	4
Higher education centre	Questioning of university authorities or administrative staff	3	1	–	–
	TOTAL	96	73	97	76

Source: People's Ombudsman, press, author's collection.

Under the Alejandro Toledo government, the emergence of these protests and conflicts highlighted the contrast between institutional precariousness and political instability vis-à-vis the economic boom, reflected in high growth rates. The proliferation of protests has also highlighted the difference between peoples' increase in expectation that they should be better off and the persistence of high poverty levels, something not consistent with economic growth trends. This situation has remained unchanged during the current Alan García regime. The neoliberal model restricts the spread of economic benefits to all social sectors, and has given rise to sensitive situations of social discontent, as the wave of protests and conflicts currently shaking up the country shows. Social conflictivity is linked to the disparities and inequalities that neoliberal transformations have generated: economic stabilization has not counterbalanced unfulfilled demands by the population. Rather, it has generated higher inequality and discontent. The current government's response has left the management of the economy untouched.[15] To handle the situation, a social conflict unit has been set up by the government within its Council of Ministers, which barely manages to monitor the evolution of conflicts, and has only been able to settle a few negotiations to defuse protests. This is clearly inadequate in the current situation, which could lead to further violence and increased political instability.

The Focused Resurgence of Sendero Luminoso

Three major political-military plans were carried out by Sendero Luminoso in the 1980s, each more intense than the previous one. This organization significantly increased their subversive actions between 1980 and 1990, reporting a total number of 20,139 military actions, such as the blasting of electrical pylons, takeovers of civilian populations for agitation and propaganda purposes, downing of bridges, attacks on police posts, and attacks on local municipalities.

In the late 1980s, Sendero Luminoso entered a second phase of its "protracted war," which in supporting documents was referred to as the beginning of a "strategic equilibrium." This meant implementing new political and military strategies to expand the armed struggle, even to other countries. In Peru, this situation was expressed in the resurgence of actions, involving the use of car bombs, a call to the so-called "armed strikes," and an intensification of targeted assassinations.

Nevertheless, the purported "strategic equilibrium" coincided with a significant shift in the state's counter-subversive strategy:

replacing indiscriminate military actions by a patient process of intelligence and infiltration of subversive organizations. This change in government strategy began to bear fruit in the early 1990s, under the Fujimori regime, when the key Sendero Luminoso and MRTA leaders were captured. With the capture of Abimael Guzmán, the top Sendero Luminoso leader, in September 1992, the war entered into a new phase defined by the strategic victory of the state.

One year after being imprisoned, in letters sent to then president Fujimori, Abimael Guzmán requested that talks get under way to enter into a peace agreement. Fujimori made the Guzmán letters public and the outcome was a split within Sendero Luminoso, between a faction that ignored Abimael Guzmán and announced the continuation of the so-called "people's war," and a faction that decided to support its leader in his search for a peace agreement. Throughout the 1990s, the government used the divisions within Sendero Luminoso to achieve political returns, both in the domestic and the international arena. Meanwhile, Sendero Luminoso was being greatly reduced in its operational capability. Many of its militants decided to lay down their arms, while others opted for repentance. However, some contingents remained, seeking refuge in the most remote areas of the jungle and the mountains. There was talk about one or two contingents carrying out sporadic propaganda actions.

However, since the early 2000s, military actions carried out by the Senderistas have been on the increase, in particular in a fairly localized area of the jungle and the central highlands (see Figure 7.16). The setting for this Senderista resurgence has been the growth of drug trafficking activities. Coca-growing areas are spreading to other neighboring places. The economic growth of drug trafficking has given the Senderista remnants—who have weapons, military experience, and the need to control economic resources—a favorable opportunity for regrouping. According to journalistic sources, Sendero Luminoso groups now control cocaine production and marketing, support coca growers, and provide protection to some drug traffickers. Many Senderista members who had lost contact with their units, are said to have enlisted in the coca economy, changing their discourse to one of defending the coca growers. This fact has made it possible for the Sendero remnants to persist until today in two areas at least: the upper Huallaga and the Ayacucho jungles, from which propaganda actions, ambushes, takeover of populations, and armed incursions are carried out.

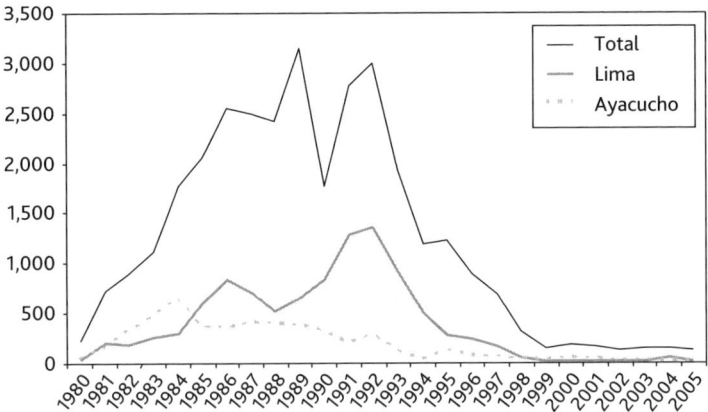

Figure 7.16 PCP-SL subversive actions, 1980–2005

Source: CVR, Home Secretary.

Over 800 subversive actions have been reported since 2000, in particular in areas such as Ayacucho, Huancavelica, Junin, Huanuco, San Martin and, to a lesser extent, in Lima, and La Libertad (see Figure 7.17). Thus, the type and number of actions, and their implementation in places where Sendero Luminoso had previously been present, suggest that we are witnessing a true, if localized, resurgence of this organization, linked to the economic expansion of drug trafficking. Sendero Luminoso members have begun to reunite after years of divisions, assuming a new political discourse to go along with their actions. Although this is not a threat to the strategic victory the state achieved in the 1990s, a new moment in the historical development of this organization, a new attempt at political regrouping, could be forthcoming.

CONCLUSIONS

The Peruvian case shows a positive correlation between the termination of war and the introduction of neoliberalism. However, war in Peru did not end as a direct result of the neoliberal stabilization; indeed, it would be more appropriate to say that neoliberal stabilization was largely facilitated by the military victory of the state.

Even after the defeat of rebel groups, war became a highly influential factor in Peruvian politics. Throughout the 1990s,

280 ECONOMIC LIBERALIZATION AND POLITICAL VIOLENCE

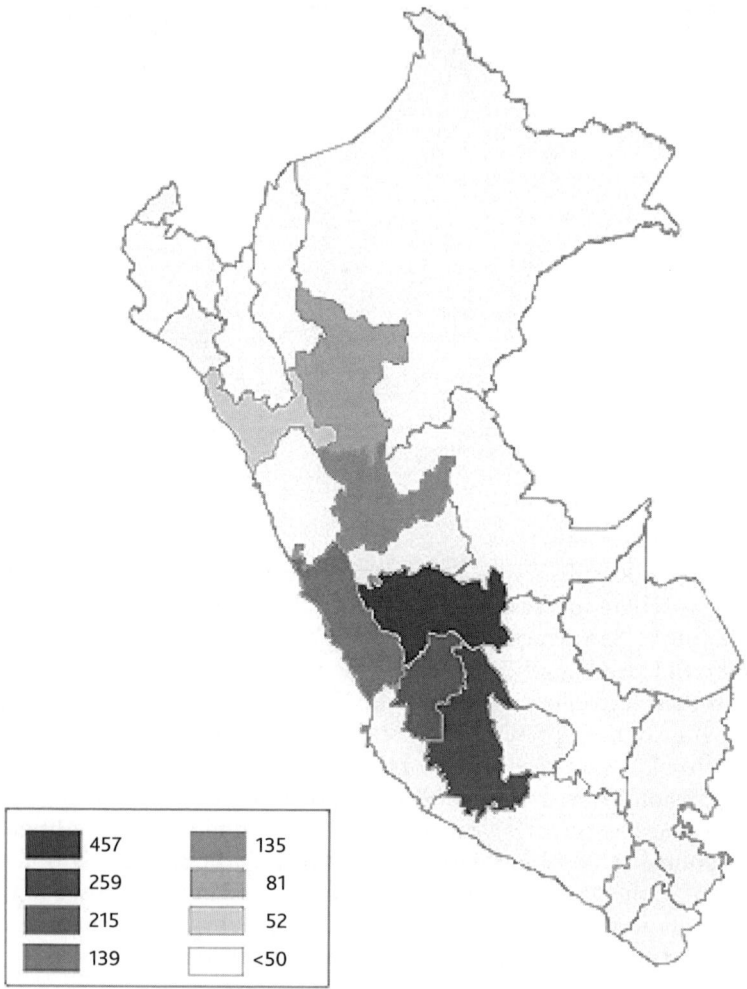

Figure 7.17 Total number of subversive actions by department, 2000–05

Source: INEI, Home Secretary.

the Alberto Fujimori government took advantage of the Sendero Luminoso defeat to make progress in implementing the neoliberal reforms, with the political aim of showing that these reforms bring order, stability, and growth. This rhetoric proved to be rather effective because large population sectors associated peace with the deepening of reforms.

Stabilization was also maintained through the establishment of an authoritarian political regime that lasted over a decade. The privatization policy allowed the government to have access to a large amount of money, which supported the implementation of several social welfare programs aimed at the poorest sectors of the population. At the same time, a vast patronage network was built up within the state, apparent in the customized management of public affairs, and social aid programs in particular. The mafia-style control of the state, and corrupt management of public resources through the state apparatus itself, allowed for the regime to maintain centralized corruption networks, closely linked to political participation in organizations loyal to Fujimori.

After the downfall of the authoritarian regime, the neoliberal economic model remained popular. However, new social and political problems sprouted up. Undeniably, the Peruvian economy has become diversified and more dynamic, reaching high growth levels in what could be described as a new neoliberal economic cycle that has no place for the centrist-state in force for the previous few decades.[16] But the success of neoliberal stabilization has also concealed many things. Not only did extreme poverty levels among many sectors of society remain unchanged, but protests and social conflicts erupted, signaling problems with neoliberal growth and persistent inequalities.

In addition, a focused resurgence of Sendero Luminoso has been recorded over the last few years. This is an attempt by this organization, now closely linked to the expansion of drug trafficking, to return. In this new configuration, the Senderistas are seeking to change their political discourse and their action in an effort to become embedded in grass-roots organizations, and from there, build up a new social base and trigger radical protest actions.

These new conflicts and protests, as well as the increasing presence of Sendero Luminoso, show a paradoxical scenario. As much as the successful neoliberal stabilization in Peru is strengthened, new social actors come into being and renewed social protest forms emerge, increasing social conflicts across the country. Neoliberalism seems to be breeding social expectations which it is unable to meet because of its incapability to generate growth with equity. These difficulties could give rise to new situations of instability and violence in the future.

NOTES

1. Ramón Pajuelo Teves, a researcher at the Instituto de Estudios Peruanos (IEP), is an anthropologist from the Universidad Nacional Mayor de San Marcos in Lima, Peru. He holds a Master's degree in Latin American history from the Universidad Internacional de Andalucía, as well as a Master's degree in Andean history from the Universidad Andina Simón Bolívar in Quito, Ecuador. His research revolves around indigenous and peasant communities, social movements, as well as ethnicity and politics. He wrote this chapter with the help of Dynnik Asencios.
2. Partido Comunista Peruano Sendero Luminoso (Peruvian Communist Party–Sendero Luminoso, hereafter referred to as PCP-SL, or Sendero Luminoso).
3. General Juan Velasco Alvarado had taken power in 1968 thanks to a coup d'état, inaugurating a rather peculiar military regime responsible for a number of fairly forward-looking reforms, among which the agrarian reform, one of the most sweeping changes ever to take place in Latin America, stands out. In 1975, General Francisco Morales Bermúdez had ousted Velasco from power, through a coup d'état, thus starting the so-called "second phase" of the military regime. Severe popular protests prompted the government to convene a Constituent Assembly in 1978, and organize general elections in 1980.
4. Movimiento Revolucionario Túpac Amaru.
5. For an overview of this regime, known as "fujimorism," see Murakami (2007), Cotler and Grompone (2000), Degregori (2000), Crabtree and Thomas (2000), and Quijano (2005).
6. Comisión de la Verdad y Reconciliación.
7. In this regard, some figures could be useful as an explanation. While in the 1940s, 35 percent of the population were city dwellers, and 65 percent were living in rural areas, in 1980, only 40 years later, this pattern was reversed: only 35 percent of the population were living in rural areas, while 65 percent were living in urban areas. Only in 1979 were illiterate people conferred a right to vote (most of the indigenous and rural population were illiterate).
8. The origins of the Peruvian left go back to the foundation of the Socialist Party by José Carlos Mariátegui in 1928. Upon his death, in 1930, the party came to be known as the Peruvian Communist Party (PCP). A split took place within the PCP in 1964 into a "pro-Russian" side and a "pro-China" side, one represented by the PCP-Unity, of Leninist leaning, and the other by the PCP-Red Flag of Maoist leaning. The PCP-SL is a split from the PCP-Red Flag, taking place in 1970.
9. The Left Unity, a political front that was to be known as the United Left (Izquierda Unida, or IU), winning the Lima Town Hall office in the 1983 elections under the leadership of Alfonso Barrantes Lingán. In 1989, due to inner struggles, this leftist front was to break up for good.
10. Following is Boloña's own description (1993, p. 55) of the structural reforms architecture.
11. The Spanish term for dictatorship is *dictadura*: "dura" means harsh; "blanda" means soft.
12. To this date, there has been talk in Peru about the still pending reform of sectors such as the judiciary, notwithstanding that, for some years, attempts have been made for these changes to be introduced counting on huge monetary resources.

13. However, under a regime known as "golden payroll," a tiny number of officers were earning salaries much higher than the average.
14. The work of FENCODES was reflected in the construction of many school buildings, thousands of kilometers of roads and health centers in the poorest areas of the country. Many a time these works were inaugurated by Fujimori himself, who used to travel to barren places. Thus, the feeling that, with the "chino" (Spanish for Chinese, despite Fujimori's Japanese ethnic roots) government, the state was reaching out to the poorest, at last, who welcomed the aid they were receiving with their wide support to the government. As years went by, however, the rampant corruption in social program management, and in the administration of international cooperation and privatization-originating funds, was to be unveiled.
15. Management of mining companies' earnings is a fair example. Since a taxation framework for fiscal requirements these firms must abide by is non-existent, the Alan García government made a decision to require them to make a voluntary contribution to state social programs.
16. This trend is currently underway throughout Latin America. See Garretón (2002).

REFERENCES

Boloña, C. (1993) *Cambio de rumbo. El programa económico para los '90*. Lima: Instituto de Economía de Libre Mercado–Universidad San Ignacio de Loyola.
Comisión de la Verdad Reconciliación (CVR) (2003) "Informe final." Lima: CVR.
Cotler, J. and Grompone, R. (2000) *El fujimorismo: ascenso y caída de un régimen autoritario*. Lima: Instituto de Estudios Peruanos.
Chossudovsky, M. (1992) *Ajuste económico: el Perú bajo el dominio del FMI*. Lima: Mosca Azul Editores.
Crabtree, J. and Thomas, J. (eds.) (2000) *El Perú de Fujimori*. Lima: Instituto de Estudios Peruanos–Universidad del Pacífico.
Degregori, C. I. (2000) *La década de la antipolítica. Auge y huída de Alberto Fujimori y Vladimiro Montesinos*. Lima: Instituto de Estudios Peruanos.
De Soto, H. (1986) *El otro sendero: la revolución informal*. Lima: ILD.
Durand, F. and Thorp, R. (2000) "La reforma tributaria: análisis del experimento SUNAT." In *El Perú de Fujimori: 1990–1998*. Lima: Instituto de Estudios Peruanos–Universidad del Pacífico.
Garretón, M. A. (2004) *América Latina en el siglo XXI: hacia una nueva matriz sociopolítica*. Santiago: Ediciones LOM.
Gonzáles de Olarte, E. (1993) *Privatización y nuevo rol del Estado en el Perú*. Lima: Instituto de Estudios Peruanos.
Gonzáles de Olarte, E. (1998) *El neoliberalismo a la peruana*. Lima: CIES–Instituto de Estudios Peruanos.
Lajo, M. (1991) "Perú: efectos sociales y agroalimentarios de las políticas de estabilización y ajuste." *Comercio Exterior*, Vol. 41, No. 6, pp. 547–557.
Lopez, S. (1993) "Perú: golpe, democradura y democracia." *Cuestión de Estado*, No. 4–5. Lima: IDS.
Murakami, Y. (2007) *Perú en la era del chino. La política no institucionalizada y el pueblo en busca de un salvador*. Lima: Instituto de Estudios Peruanos.
Oiga (1993) "Historia de una traición. Muchos misterios quedarán revelados al conocerse el plan militar que se consolidó el 5-IV-92." Lima, 12 de julio.

Pajuelo-Teves, R. (2004) "Perú: crisis política permanente y nuevas protestas sociales', en Observatorio Social de América Latina." *OSAL*, No. 14. Buenos Aires: CLACSO.

Quijano, A. (2005) "El fujimorismo y el Perú. Lima." Seminario de Estudios y Debates Socialistas.

Wise, C. (2003) *Reinventando el Estado: estrategia económica y cambio institucional en el Perú*. Lima: Universidad del Pacifico.

8
Economic Liberalization and War: The Central American Scenario

Ricardo Peñaranda and Mauricio Barón[1]

INTRODUCTION

The revolutionary period set in motion in the 1960s in Central America came to a close 30 years later. With the end of this period came an uncertain balance of power, especially for insurgent movements, which in three out of the five countries in the region—Nicaragua, Salvador, and Guatemala—had opted for armed struggle in the early 1980s.

The misery of the poor and their social exclusion—most of them live in the rural areas—does not by itself account for the emergence of revolutionary movements. Neither does the influence of the Cuban revolution, regardless of its symbolic value and the assistance it provided to insurgent organizations. It is rather the confluence of two contradictory processes that accounts for the revolutionary wave: a swift economic growth deeply disturbing existing social relations, and the closure of venues for participation, resulting in a political deadlock unlikely to be institutionally overcome. Indeed, the revolutionary processes taking place in Central America were the expression of the population's discontent with the inequalities inherent in capitalist development, against the backdrop of a political system that between 1950 and 1980 was defined by authoritarianism.

The economic boom of the post-conflict period allowed for the sustained growth of GDP in the region, ranging between 4.8 percent and 6 percent on average (Vilas, 1992). The Central American "golden decades" came hand in hand with a diversification of the agricultural-export supply: other than coffee and bananas, the sugarcane, cardamom, and cotton industries were developed. Increasing pressure on peasant farming, growing pauperization of the rural workforce, and heightened income and rural property concentration all came together during this boom. In all these cases, the monopoly of other sectors, such as transport, services, and the food industry, was also included in the capital expansion process.

The revolutionary wave emerging in Nicaragua in the mid 1970s, and its spread throughout the region over the next decade, had a common origin in the impact of capital expansion on a deeply globalized world, making the transformation of political regimes, worn out by decades of authoritarian domination, mandatory. A space for political transition was then opened up and seized by popular sectors advocating radical, even revolutionary democratization, which in the end was unsuccessful in all instances. However, this does not mean that old authoritarian regimes,[2] which eventually also had to give in, prevailed. On the contrary, what can be discerned is the triumph of a "new elite" with strong links to international capital, deeply committed both to the liberal reform agenda in the economic arena, and to the strengthening of democratic regimes in the political one.

Two distinct cases will be examined in this chapter: El Salvador and Guatemala. Both countries are illustrations of different strategies for overcoming conflict and different ways of opening up political transition.

In the first case of El Salvador, our claim is to show that the costs of war were increased, traditional economic elites were weakened, and the continuation of the conflict was made untenable by the sheer size of the insurgent threat, backed by a broad popular movement (Wood, 2000), a fact which opened up the way to a large-scale implementation of public policies designed to undermine the foundation of the insurgency, forcing the insurgents to agree to a political negotiation.

In the case of Guatemala our claim is different. In this case, armed insurgent organizations did not, in any way, succeed in jeopardizing the social order or amount to a real threat to the government buttressed by the military apparatus (Rouquié, 1992). In fact, the climate of insecurity the guerrillas had generated was used by the state to unleash repression against the insurgency's social bases, repression applied not just as a solution to the insurgent threat, but also as a means to restructure society. Economic reforms implemented since the late 1980s were a reflection of the expectations of a new modernizing elite, which succeeded in linking their aspirations with the desire for peace of society as a whole.

MODERNIZATION AND ARMED CONFLICTS

El Salvador

Inequality in land property distribution is one of the many factors triggering revolutions in the twentieth century (Skocpol, 1994), and the Salvadoran experience is a case in point. Although land reform does not necessarily entail the transformation of society, in primarily agrarian societies, such as El Salvador, a reform of this kind may end up significantly upsetting the economic and political power structure (Paige, 1993).

One of the main sources of conflict in El Salvador has been the land tenure system because the country's land use model is marked by the dominance of large landholdings and the limited availability of arable land. Additionally, the large number of workers available and the expectations a large percentage of the population has for access to landed property add to this equation. The 1971 agricultural census data showed that 1.5 percent of rural properties, measuring 290 hectares on average, were taking up 40 percent of cultivated land, including the best-quality lands, endowed with better topographical and irrigation conditions. By contrast, 73 percent of rural properties were smallholdings of marginal quality land that constituted only 10 percent of arable land.

The land oligarchy in El Salvador was supported by coffee production, standing out from other regional hegemonies because of its homogeneity, its ability to control other social sectors, and the dominance it exerted on the state until the 1970s. The concentration of economic power and wealth reached such a degree that the bulk of the coffee business was in the hands of 40 families, which were the basis of a small group of 26 companies ruling the agricultural coffee, cotton, and sugar export activities, getting the most out of the economic diversification process (Colindres, 1976). This concentration of power was to become a hindrance to the development of democracy, and blocked any modernization attempt likely to hurt the owners' interests (Paige, 1993). This situation also involved the owners' control over a plentiful and cheap workforce that had no other employment options, the control of which became critical to ensuring the development of the agricultural export projects, and entailed the strengthening of coercive economic measures, ensuring a hold on labor relations, and preventing the peasant population from entering into any organizational form whatsoever.

The frustrations of modernization

The Salvadoran economy was streamlined on the basis of an "authoritarian-capitalist" model corresponding to what Barrington Moore described as "conservative modernization" (Wood, 2000). It therefore ended up strengthening traditional sectors which expanded into other activities, such as banking and exports, and were thus able to consolidate their control over the state.

In fact, this process getting under way in the mid 1950s accelerated the diversification of the economy. However, it did not involve either substantial structural changes, or a more equitable distribution of resources. On the contrary, it became an opportunity for the economic elite to spread its control to new production fields (sugar, cotton) and other activities (banking, industry), ending up with a virtual monopoly on the economy. Although some differences eventually emerged among the two elite sectors—agro-finance and agro-industrial—in the end, the first of them, an advocate of an economic-plantation outlook in favor of land concentration and wage restrictions, ended up the winner. This is why El Salvador came to be regarded in the 1970s as the most "efficient" world coffee grower and the third-largest coffee exporter after Brazil and Colombia (Paige, 1993).[3]

Under these circumstances, both the expansion of the job market, and economic and social democratization were left on hold. Eduardo Colindres' work shows that, in 1976, 92.49 percent of landed properties (250,539) were holding 27.12 percent of the country's arable land, and that only 0.7 percent of farms (1,941 measuring more than 100 hectares each) amounted to 38.67 percent of the agricultural area (Colindres, 1976). Land concentration also included processing activities: only 15 firms—family businesses directly involved in production—were holding 80 percent of coffee processing facilities. A similar situation could be found in terms of the market: in 1974, the ten largest companies were in control of 62 percent of exports (Paige, 1993). With regards to the outcomes of scant efforts made to expand access to land, the figures speak for themselves: in 47 years of re-distributional policies, from 1932 to 1979, the state managed only to achieve the acquisition of 82,000 hectares, benefiting 14,500 families (Flores, 1998).

The unfulfilled expectations for democracy that the modernizing process had generated paved the way for the emergence of non-conformists who, since the 1970s, had heartedly started to make their demands known. There is a clear link between this process and the growth of left-wing and centrist sectors, as well as the proliferation of urban and rural popular organizations, the mobilization of which was to become acute with the onset of the coffee price crisis and the failure of the democratizing attempts of 1976–77, bringing about a narrow political opening and a thwarted "agrarian transformation" process (Guido, 1979). By 1977, the occasional popular mobilizations had been transformed into mass movements supported by the newly formed guerrillas, while the threatened elites created a paramilitary force, ORDEN, the original purpose of which was to safeguard the status quo in rural areas. ORDEN quickly turned into a repressive apparatus, parallel or supplementary to the military and police agencies.

Political crisis, war, and agrarian reform

The prevailing economic model in El Salvador ended up making social asymmetry worse, and was responsible for the social and political crisis of the late 1970s. By becoming intertwined with other factors, this economic model made the country swing from social crisis to war. The following are some of the factors that contributed to this: (i) the conflict with Honduras in 1969, driven by mass migrations of Salvadorans compelled to leave their country by the failure of economic modernization; (ii) the growth of trade union and peasant protests; (iii) the steady rise, at local level and in congress, of the "opposition" represented by the reformist Christian Democratic Party; (iv) the political crisis, leading to government intervention in the 1972 electoral process to prevent an eventual triumph of the Opposition Union, headed by the Christian Democrats; (v) the beginning of a decline in coffee production, as a result of the drop in international coffee prices from 1978 onwards; and (vi), finally, the Sandinista victory in Nicaragua in 1979 which energized the most radical sectors who thought that the revolution was now imminent.

The Salvadoran economy plunged into a deep crisis in 1979, after 30 years of sustained growth. The cost of war was estimated at nearly US$3 trillion, but the fall of GDP by more than 23 percent and the massive flight of capital, should be added to that estimate. As Elizabeth Wood stresses, the most obvious aspect of the crisis was the collapse of agricultural exports, which in 1977 accounted for 25 percent of GDP but in 1985 fell to 10 percent, and in 1993 represented only 3 percent of GDP (Figure 8.1).

Correspondingly, the unstable political system collapsed. The 1979 military coup tried to launch a reformist model headed by a civilian-military junta, which called for a stop to violence,

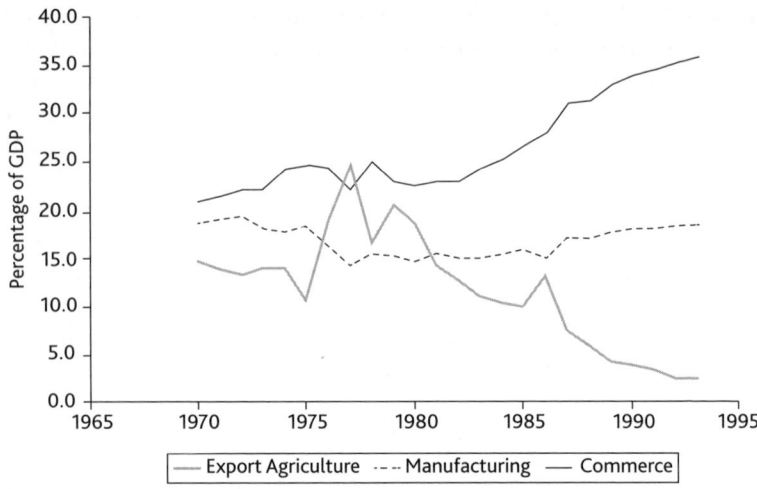

Figure 8.1 El Salvador: productive sectors' share of GDP, 1970–93

Source: Wood (2000).

committed itself to disarming paramilitary groups, promised to ensure free political expression and association, and guaranteed the equitable distribution of wealth and, especially, a wide-ranging agrarian reform. Amid a deepening political crisis, seeking to remove the causes of social violence and snatch from the left their main sources of grievance, the most conservative reformist sector of the government managed to get hold of power, launching three forward-looking projects in early 1980: (i) agrarian reform; (ii) nationalization of the banking industry; and (iii) nationalization of foreign trade. Although the armed conflict continued unabated, the reformist project, despite all its constraints, partly achieved its goals and, by the end of the decade, would help avert a social crisis and keep the rebel advance in check.[4]

In March 1980, the Basic Agrarian Reform Law was enacted. The Law provided for the encumbrance of all properties of over 100 hectares, in the case of high-quality lands, and properties of more than 150 hectares of medium-quality land. Moreover, regardless of their size, all properties failing to fulfill a social function, as defined in terms of employment, productivity, management of resources, and enforcement of labor laws, could be seized. In practice, the reform did away with the economic power of the coffee elite. The land was to be handed over to cooperatives and worker organizations, registered before the Ministry of Agriculture, and made up by landless farmers, tenants, laborers, or settlers. The estimated value of the reform as a whole was estimated at US$500 million, and should have involved 50 percent of the land devoted to agriculture (Flores, 1998).[5]

In 1992, twelve years later, when the peace agreements were signed, 295,000 hectares had been redistributed among 85,000 peasant families as a result of the Agrarian Reform. Seventy percent of the land encumbered had been distributed as a cooperative. The area of land actually encumbered exceeded by 50 percent the area scheduled to be encumbered at the time the process had started. The number of families that benefited from the reform represented one-fifth of the rural population, while the area involved was equivalent to 20 percent of the arable lands in the country. The political consequences were striking: on the one hand, the most traditional coffee elite sectors, those directly involved in production, were the most affected by the measures and by the accompanying instability. Conflict costs were thus increased for them, implying that the continuation of war was no longer deemed as beneficial (Wood, 2000); the way to a peace agreement was thus paved.

Insurgent forces were also affected by the reforms, although they retained their military capabilities and popular support until the end of the conflict. Undoubtedly, the reform process managed to wear out, or at least neutralize, some of their social bases, preventing the rebel forces from advancing beyond the stalemate they had reached with the government forces. In the end, the Farabundo Martí Front for National Liberation (FMLN) was compelled to put the idea of a revolutionary victory aside, moderating their expectations and adopting a more pragmatic attitude. This meant, in the words of Joaquín Villalobos, "accepting reality and turning it into an agreement" (Villalobos, 1989).[6]

The peace process in El Salvador

The 1989 FMLN offensive was a turning point in the conflict. From that time onwards, all actors involved in the conflict agreed that armed struggle was at a dead end. Having failed in its attempt to get hold of power, the insurgency was forced to seek an alternative to a military victory. For its part, the government managed to overcome the insurgent's offensive, although it acknowledged that its opponent was able to withstand the huge military pressure exerted by government forces. The insurgent offensive generated political problems for the United States government, which did not want to support an army that did not appear to be on the brink of achieving victory, and was still involved in acts of violence against civilians, including the murder of the members of the Jesuit community (Byrne, 1996).

The decline of the traditional elites and the emergence of new entrepreneurial elite are key elements in explaining the willingness of El Salvador's dominant groups to seek a peace agreement. While the traditional agro-export elites and the army had for decades shared the concern about preserving their ability to capture state resources (protection racketeering), in the late 1980s this model had become outdated. On the one hand, the army had failed to become an effective fighting force able to conclusively defeat the guerrillas; all it was able to do was to unleash indiscriminate repression, which, instead of weakening popular support for the FMLN, strengthened it. In addition, the results of the civil war, land reform, and political transformations coincided and thus modified the composition of the civilian elite and of the Salvadoran economic structure, so that, instead of preserving a regime that had undoubtedly become obsolete, peace negotiations became something more desirable than the continuation of war.

As an outcome of the agreements entered into in January 1992, the FMLN was to become a political party. In return for the demobilization of the FMLN, the state security forces were replaced by a National Police Force. The peace agreements also involved major reforms to the army;[7] further reforms to the judicial and electoral systems, and a land transfer program benefiting both guerrilla fighters and the military, were also implemented as a result of the peace agreements. Peace negotiations were agreed upon in six covenants, and a provision was made for a human rights monitoring program to be implemented by the United Nations observers in El Salvador (ONUSAL).

The termination of war meant that neoliberalism was to emerge as the hegemonic ideology of the new commercial and financial elite. This sector strongly believed that a new democratic order, arranged around neoliberal premises, would leave behind the authoritarian past and would return to the path of economic development. Although peace negotiations had been conducted and ended up with the signing of agreements on January 16, 1992, they did not involve society as a whole—they were developed, behind closed doors, by high-ranking army officers, the Salvadoran elite, and the top FMLN leadership. Negotiations included issues such as the electoral reform, a land distribution agreement (to benefit former

FMLN combatants and civilians living in their areas of influence), and new tools to renegotiate economic and social reforms. However, the core of the Salvadoran institutions remained untouched, thus opening an avenue for the new elite to make ARENA (Nationalist Republican Alliance) a viable electoral alternative to an electorate that was feeling tired of war and disillusioned with the Christian Democrat Party's inefficiency and corruption.

Guatemala

During the protracted period from independence until the mid twentieth century, Guatemala's economy and society experienced a retreat to traditional forms of concentrated land ownership and control of the workforce. This process, reinforced by the country's isolation from the world market, had not been substantially changed by the consolidation of the coffee economy in the late nineteenth century, nor by the presence of United States investments as enclave economies during the first half of the twentieth century.

In 1950, 72 percent of the total agricultural area was concentrated in 2 percent of farms, while 88 percent of up to seven-hectare farms were taking up just 15 percent of the land. Land concentration was a reflection of an exclusive social structure, unable to provide for mobility channels. Ownership structure and traditional-oligarchy control were only threatened from 1944 to 1954, during the short-lived democratic experiment known as "Guatemalan Revolution." It was at this time that nationalist middle-class sectors, with the Agrarian Reform as one of its main banners, tried to consolidate themselves by promoting a political and economic modernization process (Rouquié, 1992). The Arena project, benefiting a quarter of the peasantry, provided for the expropriation and distribution of landowners' idle lands, amounting to about one-fifth of arable land. This proposal, seeking to make peasants into agricultural entrepreneurs, also included access to credit and improved crop techniques.[8] The 1954 coup d'état by colonel Castillo Armas meant the immediate suspension of the reform and the repeal of measures taken. Expropriations were reversed and Agricultural Committees disjointed. All reformist measures were quickly reversed: Congress was dissolved and trade unions outlawed, along with left-wing parties. The Labor Code was suspended and universal suffrage revoked (the illiterate were again excluded from political rights), thus marginalizing the indigenous population, which made up 55 percent of the national population (Torres, 1981).

The unexpected end of the democratic experience of the 1950s also paved the way for a new developmental strategy, aimed at preserving highly concentrated land ownership patterns and at easing pressures from the agrarian elites through a policy of expansion into forested areas. This project was consistent with the development of a new agro-export model giving renewed impetus to the coffee economy, and introducing new export products such as cotton, sugar, and cardamom. The crisis of the traditional farm system, with its traditional pre-capitalist arrangements to fix wages, was quickened by these developments, and ultimately replaced by a new agro-industrial model that resulted in the development of a rural migrant proletariat (Paige, 1983).

A decision was made in the 1960s to establish settlements in potentially arable but uninhabited lands, and land was given to settlers in plots with individual legal titles. This model was established in 1962 by the Agrarian Reform Law (Decree 1151), which, with some amendments, remained in force for more than 20 years. The National Institute of Agrarian Reform (INTA) was created by this law to design and implement the land tenure and use policy, and the colonization of new areas. The law ratified private land ownership and made the expansion of agricultural areas the privileged tool for awarding new land titles. While the provisions for the expropriation of idle lands were kept, they were never implemented. Beginning in the 1960s, the drive for colonization was the most outstanding feature of the agrarian reform. By diminishing the social urgency of the land question, colonization became a solution for large landowners.[9]

Paige's (1993) assumption about the formation of a migrant proletariat is in agreement with the findings of Le Bot (1995) and Rouquié (1992) that the accelerated development of agricultural exports, in the Pacific region in particular, involved the disintegration of the nineteenth-century "traditional farm" and its replacement by smaller, export-oriented farms following a capitalist logic. This led to the dissolution of pre-capitalist labor relations, and the eviction of sharecroppers and their replacement by migrant labor from the highlands. In this sense, colonization was a safety valve for social tensions, keeping temporary access to a cheap and stationary workforce. During the 1960s and 1970s, the new production lines, such as sugar, cotton and cardamom, coupled with renewed coffee exports, employed between 400,000 and 500,000 laborers a year. In the late 1960s, sugarcane plantations alone employed 277,000 laborers for a four-month period, 85 percent of them from three highland regions: Huehuetenango, 51 percent; Quiché, 22 percent; and Guatemala, 12 percent.

With the growth of land property in the late 1970s, as compared with the 1950s, came a large decrease in large land holdings, along with increased medium-size holdings. Added together, these two categories constituted 64 percent of all land property, suggesting that what happened was not so much a distribution of land as a subdivision of large property holdings into more efficient farms, which had to absorb much of the nearly 400,000 hectares being incorporated into arable land (figures do not include the more than 1 million hectares awarded in settlement areas). As far as small properties are concerned, micro-plots (less than 0.7 hectares) doubled in number during the 1950–79 period, but nevertheless continued to account for just 1 percent of the total area (Table 8.1).

Table 8.1   Guatemala: land distribution according to farm size, 1979

	No. of farms	% of all farms	Total area (ha)	% of total farmland in Guatemala	Average area of each farm (ha)
Less than 0.7 ha	166,724	31.0	55,331	1.0	0.3
Family (0.7–7 ha)	301,736	57.0	622,038	15.0	2.0
Family (7–44.8 ha)	49,509	9.0	779,610	19.0	15.7
Multi-family Medium size (44.8–900 ha)	13,176	2.0	1,814,311	44.0	137.7
Multi-family Large (more than 900 ha)	478	0.1	834,022	20.0	1,744.8
Total	531,623	100.0	4,105,318	100.0	

Source: ECLAC (2001).

The two phases of war

A deep impression was made on Guatemalan society by the failure of the democratic experience of the 1950s, highlighting the main authoritarian features of its political system: increasing military power, weakness of the party system, and control over opposition of any kind. In the early 1960s, a moderate conservative transition attempt towards democracy, under the rule of General Ydígoras Fuentes, was thwarted by the 1963 military coup, introducing more than 15 years of "façade democracy" (Torres, 2006).

This was a pact between the elite and the army, ensuring control of the executive and the legislative branches of the government and employing pseudo-democratic means to hide the lack of any real competition, while ensuring the demobilization of popular organizations through the implementation of selective violence targeted at both radicals and democratic political forces. According to Torres Rivas, this stage shaped the future course of the country and combined: (i) the worst period of selective repression against democratic forces; (ii) the most important period of economic modernization until then; (iii) the pre-insurrectional moment in which whatever remained of the social movement would lean towards armed struggle (Torres, 2006).

The first phase of the Guatemalan armed conflict started with the military uprising of November 13, 1960, led by nationalist officers revolting against corruption within the army and against the government's decision to allow that some of the forces involved in the attempted "Bay of Pigs" invasion in Cuba were deployed from Guatemalan territory. Although the uprising was quickly put down, it laid the groundwork for a group of army officers who, upon their return from exile in 1962, created the Revolutionary Movement 13th November (MR-13), the predecessor of the Revolutionary Armed Forces (FAR) (the Guatemalan Labor Party, TMP, also participated in its creation). The insurrectional climate in which these armed organizations emerged reached its highest point during the "March and April 1962" demonstrations, which were characterized by a large student participation and the support of unions and popular organizations. For six weeks, three major cities came to a standstill in a mass protest action voicing the political and social discontent that had been accruing since 1954 (CEH, 1999).

The second phase of the Guatemalan war had something in common with the first, and the personal histories of the new leaders also allowed for these two moments to be connected. However, both because of their characteristics, their venues, and their intensity, we can talk about two different stages in the conflict, as opposed to the traditional narrative that talks about a single 36-year period of war (1960–96). Several new features were introduced in the 1970s: (i) Since the 1972 oil crisis, serious cracks started to show up in the economic development model which, despite retaining its dynamism a few more years, showed serious changes, such as an unusual inflation growth, which acted as a pivot to renewed forms of social protest; (ii) Since 1975, social movements recorded a new intensity that largely responded to economic tensions, and included the emergence of trade unions in response to the demands of a growing working population; also, the formation of peasant leagues and organizations supported by the

Catholic Church and the Christian Democrats, grouped around the Peasant Unity Committee (CUC); (iii) The triggering of indigenous movements around the Mayan identity reconstruction efforts, the internal fighting against "custom," from which a new leadership emerges, and the neo-community dynamics in the highlands and the Petén region, supported by the Catholic Action (Le Bot, 1992; García-Ruiz, 1997).[10]

In January 1972, the first column of the second guerrilla wave crossed the border with Mexico, entering the country through Ixcán, and headed south past Quiché and Huehuetenango: the setting for a slow deployment during the following years. This guerrilla nucleus, led by Rolando Moran, would give birth to the Guerrilla Army of the Poor, which made its first public appearance in 1975. Likewise, a second guerrilla column, in which former guerrillas from the old insurgent stage were involved, crossed the border with Mexico in 1972, and formed the Organization of People in Arms (ORPA), which sought to establish itself in the regions of San Marcos, Quetzaltenango, and Chimaltenango, in an attempt to control a corridor between the border with Mexico and the country's central region. Later on, after too long an incubation period, ORPA would launch public actions in 1979. Finally, the Revolutionary Armed Forces (FAR) made an attempt to establish itself in the region of Petén at about the same time, approaching and sometimes being in conflict with the Guatemalan Workers' Party (TMP) already operating in the capital and in the Pacific coastal cities.

In the Guatemalan armed conflict there are therefore two clearly identifiable phases. The difference between them lies in the fact that during the second phase the indigenous population acted as the social support base for the guerrillas. This development was not forced or inevitable, and it requires explanation. First, an explanation can be found in the modernization process which the indigenous populations were undergoing at the time, and their social exclusion. And, second, in the tools the guerrillas used to strengthen their relationship with the communities living in those territories. These mechanisms were explained in terms of "benefits" that the guerrillas offered the indigenous people, including "class benefits," such as the popular rallies intended to strengthen the political power of local communities, the execution of medium and large landowners to strengthen territorial control, and "security benefits," such as the execution of collaborators with the authorities, attacks on army patrols, and attempts to create "liberated zones," the security of which was in theory guaranteed by the guerrillas.

At an early stage (1977–80), army actions seemed to confirm the guerrillas' mobilization capacity on the basis of these mechanisms (REMHI, 1998).[11]

Yet, the mobilization of the rural population did not succeed in the expected popular uprising that would have allowed for the emergence of a popular army. Still, it was strong enough to warrant a large-scale intervention by the Guatemalan armed forces, an intervention that subjected this population to many abuses of power and violence. The answer to the insurgent challenge was operation "Ash," in 1981 and 1982, which resulted in the army taking control of the Pan-American highway, and deploying more than 15,000 troops in the regions of Quiché and Huehuetenango (CEH, 1999; Ball et al., 1999), and was followed by operation "Victoria" in 1982, and operation "Strength" in 1983. The militarization of Guatemalan society and the rhetoric of a "terrorist state" were developed in tandem with the exponential growth of violence. Out of a total of 55,021 victims of political violence REMHI recorded between 1969 and 1996, 80 percent were concentrated in the 1980–83 period (REMHI, 1998). Most of these victims were rural people and indigenous people in particular, as shown by the following indigenous population density figures: Quiché, 31,400; Alta Verapaz, 6,485; Huehuetenango, 4,776. During the most intense period of the war (1980–83), the army adopted a strategy to fight the guerrillas by repressing the civilian population, deliberately acting against communities living close to guerrilla operation regions.

The primary tool used by the insurgency policy was the Civil Defense Patrols. This military intervention mode was initially set in motion under the government of General Lucas García, in the late 1970s, and stepped up under the government of General Ríos Montt, who arrived in power after a coup in March 1982, and who intensified the struggle against insurgent movements after the annulment of the constitution and the establishment of a state of siege. The Civil Defense Patrols (PAC), the para-state nature of which allowed them to enjoy wide impunity, included more than 900,000 members who deliberately encouraged interethnic rivalries.[12] The PAC were a low-cost mechanism to ensure control in areas the guerrillas had been expelled from, and eventually joined the army in the deployment of offensive activities.

The end of conflict and political realignment

The Guatemalan peace process began in the mid 1980s, when Vinicio Cerezo, the Christian Democratic candidate, was elected

President in November 1985, and went hand in hand with the implementation of democratic reforms giving civilians access to power. It should be highlighted that this process coincided with the end of the military campaign and the defeat of insurgent organizations, paving the way to negotiations with armed groups within the framework of a regional peace agreement, outlined in the Esquipulas I (1986) and Esquipulas II (1987) covenants. From the time the first talks between the insurgents and the government took place in the late 1980s to the signing of the Agreements for a Lasting Peace in December 1996, careful negotiations were under way to ensure the alignment between the democratization process and the peace agreements.

Among the documents allowing the final peace agreements to be signed in May 1996, special mention should be made of the Indigenous Peoples' Identity and Rights Agreements, signed in Mexico in March 1995 (Azpuru, 1999). The text depicts the indigenous community's grievances so as to ensure their democratic integration into Guatemalan society; their demands amount to the minimum to be negotiated between the state and indigenous peoples. The main components of this document were the recognition of the indigenous peoples' identity, the recognition of the validity of international instruments against discrimination, and the commitment of the Guatemalan government to include a series of guarantees in the constitutional reform that would translate these principles into specific provisions. These provisions included respect for local indigenous authorities, expansion of political participation of indigenous communities, respect of customary law, the regularization of land tenure by indigenous communities, and ensuring their ability to exercise their cultural rights.

The implementation of the agreements was tied to the approval of a constitutional reform, which was to be done through a referendum. The drawbacks of the entire process were brought to light by the failure of the Popular Consultation (Arnson, 1999) in May 1999. Besides the obvious flaws in the referendum mechanics and huge abstention rates (reaching 81 percent of the ballot), what was made clear through this process was the polarization of Guatemalan society around the issue of what political space it was prepared to grant to indigenous people who, because they constituted more than half of the country's population, were seen as a threat.

A strong link is apparent between the negotiations leading to the peace agreements, democratic transition, and the economic modernization process. This link is apparent in the rise to power of a "new elite," which had close links with international banks and cooperation agencies. The emergence of this new actor signaled the demise of the "old oligarchy" and the breakdown of its pact with the army.

MODERNIZATION, TRANSITION, LIBERALIZATION

In the midst of armed conflict in the first half of the 1980s, Central American countries underwent a crisis: it was an outcome of a weakening import substitution-based economic model, which relied on excessive tariff protection and inefficient industrial production processes. This widespread crisis prompted the redirection of these countries' economies towards the implementation of neoliberal policies. It is clear that this reorientation was largely a response to pressures from international organizations, like the World Bank and the International Monetary Fund. In the 1980s, Costa Rica and Honduras recorded a real 3 percent GDP growth, while for other countries in the region, real growth rates were less than 1 percent (El Salvador and Guatemala) and for Nicaragua the GDP growth rate was negative (–2 percent). The countries with economies that sustained the hardest recession impact were those affected by armed conflicts, while Costa Rica and Honduras, free of armed conflicts, managed to achieve very moderate economic growth rates (Aguilar and Elizondo, 2005). The 1990s showed a regional economy working and growing under the influence of structural reform policies. Real GDP growth rates were positive in all countries: Costa Rica, 4.9 percent; El Salvador, 4.3 percent; Guatemala, 4.1 percent; Honduras, 3.5 percent; and Nicaragua, 3.2 percent. GDP per capita grew in all countries except for Nicaragua, where it was negative (–0.1 percent), although in the second half of the decade it showed a slight recovery (1.1 percent).

The disparity among countries without internal conflict and countries with internal war helps us understand how convenient peace was to the neoliberal program. The Central American countries not involved in internal conflict (Costa Rica, Honduras, and Panama) began to implement their structural reforms in 1985, complementing in this period their World Bank structural adjustment programs with economic stabilization programs funded by the International Monetary Fund to address their balance of payments-related problems. The remaining countries, El Salvador and Nicaragua, engrossed in their internal military conflicts, had no choice but to wait until the early 1990s to implement the new development strategy suggested by international financial institutions.

Changes in El Salvador and the New Economic Scenario

El Salvador underwent one of the most drastic economic changes on the continent during the first half of the 1990s. The traditional economic profile based on the concentration of production and financial activities, the heavy burden of agricultural exports and the stakes for an import substitution model, had collapsed under the weight of the economic crisis and armed conflict. The nature of the Salvadoran economy was to be completely changed by structural reform programs undertaken by successive National Republican Alliance (ARENA) governments, including trade liberalization, privatization of the banking industry and public services, the reform to the pension system, and the adoption of a private investment-focused incentive system. The World Bank's 2003 Country Economic Memorandum (World Bank, 2003) shows that El Salvador stands out among Latin American countries in terms of market liberalization reforms, and considers its economy as one of the world's most liberalized in 2000.

El Salvador's political and economic achievements during the first half of the 1990s were indeed remarkable: the termination of war, democratic transition, economic stabilization, implementation of a new world market-oriented strategy, and renewed growth. GDP per capita, which had dropped by an average of 3 percent per year during the previous decade, recovered at an average rate of 6 percent per year between 1990 and 1995, while poverty levels were reduced by 12 percentage points.

A four-goal structural adjustment program (SAP) was launched by the new ARENA government, led by Alfredo Cristiani, in July 1989: (i) reaching sustained growth; (ii) reducing the economic participation of the state; (iii) making more efficient use of resources available to the country; and (iv) eradicating poverty. The program was to be implemented in two phases: an initial stabilization phase, designed to last for an 18-month period, and a second restructuring phase to be developed in the medium-term (Segovia, 1997). Although the implementation of this program was delayed in comparison to other Central American countries, it was nevertheless quickly deployed thanks to the swift progress of negotiations leading to the signing of a peace agreement in 1992. Immediately after the signing of the agreement, the government of El Salvador entered into negotiations with the International Monetary Fund, UNDP, World

Bank, and the United States Agency for International Development about implementing the Salvadoran economy restructuring policies. The National Reconstruction Program (NRP), an upshot of peace agreements already underway, did not condition the implementation of the structural adjustment program. Both the government and international organizations considered them as complementary, insofar as the NRP helped reduce the social impact of the SAP and to the extent that the inflow of international financial resources, together with local investment, improved the real outlook for economic change (Segovia, 1997).

Although working along different paths, both the economy liberalization process of the 1990s and the state intervention program carried out during the previous decade, convey a paradigmatic example of the power public policies have to change economic structures and to reorient conditions under which political life evolves, which are the core "lessons" of Salvadoran experience (Boyce, 1996).

Although undoubtedly relying on the political will of the Salvadoran state, the implementation of the structural adjustment program could only become viable in a new context defined by five key elements:

- First, deep economic structural changes accounting for decreasing agricultural exports, whose GDP share dropped from 25 percent in 1977 to only 3 percent in 1993. This decrease required the agro-export model to be reoriented towards a commercial-and-service sector-led economy, while signaling the decline of the traditional land elites and the relinquishing of the rural setting as the main social conflict axis (Wood, 2000).
- Second, the recovery of political stability following the end of armed conflict and the signing of the peace agreements in early 1992. The peace agreements were to become a turning point making economic activities flourish as a result of the new transition to democracy and the return of confidence in institutions (Azpuru et al., 2007).
- Third, re-established confidence between private entrepreneurs and the new government after 1989, allowing for the adjustment program implementation phase to count on the support of the business sector (Segovia, 1997).
- Fourth, the growth of remittances flows allowing for the expansion of trade and consumption, despite the steep decline

in donations and international aid that had buttressed the economy deficit during the 1980s (Rivera, 1996).
• Fifth, the expansion of Central American economies which, except for Nicaragua, recorded, during the first half of the 1990s, a two-fold growth on average, rising from 2 percent to 4 percent. Trade increased, strengthening regional growth, improving economies such as the Salvadoran one, which recorded a two-fold increase in exports to Central America.

The structural adjustment program

The liberalization of market forces was the key axis of economic adjustment, the market being, according to well-established economic thinking, the most efficient resource allocation and price fixing mechanism. In the particular case of El Salvador, the promotion of free markets meant that the state was relieved of its role as the main economic actor, the result of the interventionist policies of the 1980s, and was subsequently replaced by the market. According to the model, the liberalization of private economic forces would lead to an efficient allocation of resources and would allow for sustained economic growth, the benefits of which would, in the medium-term, spread to society as a whole, resulting in the eradication of poverty. The structural adjustment program was launched in 1989, two years before the peace agreements. Its three key axes were the privatization of banking, trade reform, and fiscal reform.

Probably, the privatization of the banking system was the most urgent step of economic adjustment. The banking industry had been nationalized in March 1980, and its management was appointed using political criteria, leading to a crisis that was to become manifest ten years later. Bank deposits, as well as total loans, had recorded a 30 percent drop, arrears levels had tripled, and liquidity levels were so low that only recurrent state intervention had prevented widespread bankruptcy (SAPRIN, 2000). As a result of this situation, distrust in the banking system was widespread further spurring capital flight.

The privatization process began with the enactment of the Commercial Banks Restructuring and Strengthening Law, in November 1989, seeking to make the increase in capital reserves mandatory. A year later, in November 1990, the Financial Restructuring and Strengthening Fund was established, to recover financial institutions' overdue loans, replacing the latter by bonds issued by the Central Reserve Bank, which made successive issues totaling 2,450 million colones (US$250 million). Finally on November 29, 1990, the Commercial Banks and Savings and Loans Association Privatization Law was enacted, the aim of which was the sale of all financial institutions, ownership democratization, efficient administration, and the de-politicization of the credit system (Rivera, 2000).

Eight banks and four financial institutions had already been privatized in 1992. This process was sharply criticized for its lack of transparency, its inability to ensure democratization of the system, and for having set up a new capital concentration framework allowing prevailing economic groups to reconfigure themselves. On the other hand, considering the size of the refinancing the Central Bank had implemented, the amount of money from privatization was virtually negligible. Nevertheless, the most important achievements were the restoration of confidence in the financial sector, the application of real interest rates, and the emergence of a new competition framework within the system, allowing for new financial instruments to be generated. All this contributed to a huge credit development helping the expansion of domestic consumption.

A speedy economic opening was facilitated by the trade reform. The reduction of import tariffs was carried out quickly: tariff rates that in some cases reached up to 290 percent, were reduced to 50 percent in 1989. This percentage was to be further reduced in the following years to reach 20 percent in 1992, with some exceptions such as textiles and footwear. Additional measures included the reduction of import procedures, facilities and subsidies granted to exporters, and the opening of lines of credit designed to encourage international trade.

The tax reform sought to simplify the tax structure, streamlining the tax system and making state operations more efficient. The reform was launched in 1990, with measures to make income tax procedures easier and remove some exemptions. In May of that year, both the Stamp and Stamped Paper Law and the Property Tax Law were amended. In 1992, new income tax changes were introduced, the different income types were grouped together, the number of taxpayers was reduced to exempt employees with a lower income, albeit, control over companies was made tighter, and a single 25 percent rate was set on income. Regarding indirect taxes, the main novelty was the introduction in 1992 of the VAT (Value Added Tax) at a rate of 10 percent, exempting some goods and services at the start. Three years later, this tax would be increased, reaching a 13 percent rate.

Along with these reforms, additional measures were applied, such as the early liberalization of the exchange rate, subsequently suspended to adopt a fixed rate, leading in practice to the dollarization of the economy. On the other hand, interest rates were gradually liberalized, including foreign currency deposits, which were regularized. The Stock Exchange was established in 1992. Many benefits were offered to encourage foreign investment, and traditional institutions regulating main agricultural exports (INCAFE and INAZUCAR) were dissolved. The privatization of several public services, such as pensions, energy, and telecommunications, which had been scheduled to take place in 1993, was finally launched in 1996.

All these measures, in particular those pertaining to banking and foreign trade, brought about conditions conducive to a domestic consumption boom, which was spurred by the unexpected growth of international remittance flows.

Flow of external resources

At the time the armed conflict came to an end, concerns were growing over the impact on the Salvadoran economy of the unavoidable reduction of transfers from international organizations, which in practice had supported it during the decade of the 1980s. This coincided with the implementation of the adjustment plan. Surprisingly, the decreasing international donations, slowly shrinking during the first half of the 1990s and then more quickly in the second half, were more than offset by the growth of family remittances from Salvadoran people living abroad, mainly in the United States[13] (Table 8.2).

Table 8.2 El Salvador: growth of external resource flows (in millions of colones), 1989–98

	Official donations	Private remittances	Total transfers
1989	282.4	236.8	519.2
1990	223.3	345.4	568.7
1991	178.5	542.8	721.3
1992	226.5	707.9	934.4
1993	220.3	823.2	1,043.5
1994	284.9	939.3	1,224.2
1995	197.2	1,196.8	1,394.0
1996	64.4	1,194.9	1,259.3
1997	55.4	1,308.2	1,363.6
1998	31.1	1,486.0	1,517.1

Source: Central Reserve Bank, El Salvador (Rivera, 2000).

Returning to the figures compiled by Roberto Rivera, these show how private remittances, already high at the beginning of the 1990s, began to gradually increase, recording a five-fold rise in the first half of the decade, at which time they showed a trend to becoming stabilized. In terms of international donations, these progressively decreased during the first half of the decade, recording a sharp drop later on. What is surprising is that the overall result was not affected at any time; on the contrary, the amount of resources from abroad recorded a three-fold increase in this ten-year period.

As a result of banking privatization, and coincident with trade reform, the growth of remittances was the basis for the consumption boom, also facilitated by exports liberalization and the expansion of credit. Some specific niches, such as vehicles and household appliances for example (the replacement of which had been put on hold by the armed conflict), emerged as a result of this consumption boom, which also resulted in the expansion of housing construction, brought to a standstill for a decade for the same reason. Speculative bubbles emerged as a result of this focus on consumption, the decline of which in the mid 1980s is reflected in the loss of momentum in economic growth. The other major distortion was a huge imports growth vis-à-vis the slow exports increase. In 1989, exports accounted for US$497 million vis-à-vis a US$1,161 million imports volume. In 1992, this ratio was 597 vis-à-vis 1,587 and, in 1995, the ratio was 1,005 vis-à-vis 2,642. The adverse trade balance rose during those same years from 13 percent of GDP to 17.2 percent, a situation that remained constant throughout the decade.

As Rivera stresses in his work on family remittances (Rivera, 1996, 1998), and as the World Bank in its Economic Memorandum (2003) corroborates, the growth of external resource flows through remittances brought with it an outcome similar to the so-called "Dutch disease," including: a worsening trade deficit; inflationary pressures; currency revaluation; an exports drop; and an increasing monetary imbalance. In the face of inflationary pressures and remittances behavior, the exchange rate that had been floating in the early years of adjustment program was finally frozen in 1992.

Overall, the unmistakable progress the Salvadoran economy had achieved during the first half of the 1990s, as a result of the Economic Stabilization Program, shows that the stabilization program was successful. However, the behavior of the external resources flow led to the relinquishing of some of the most important goals the adjustment plan was seeking to achieve (i.e., the non-traditional exports-led growth strategy). This situation, coupled with the collapse of agro-exports and the presence of family remittances, which had become the main source of foreign exchange earnings, led to the ultimate transition towards a trade and service-oriented economy (Segovia, 1997). More than exports, economic growth during the post-armed conflict years was led by consumption, which also was a key economic stabilization factor during the second half of the 1990s (Rivera, 2000).

Looked at as a long-term trend, between 1979 and 1985 the Salvadoran economy behavior showed a strong recovery (Figure 8.2): an outcome of the Adjustment Plan stabilization measures. From that period onwards, growth was rated around a 3 percent average. Under these conditions, the economic model was unable to meet the expectation to generate high growth rates, capable of providing the welfare of society as a whole. According to Segovia, the feeble growth pattern made it impossible for the state to meet the poverty reduction goals, which were the ultimate objective the economic program was intended to achieve. It was also an expectation of a country that had managed to break away from a ten-year armed conflict through a negotiated peace, which in turn was a recognition of the legitimacy of demands for enhanced social and economic equality (Segovia, 1997).

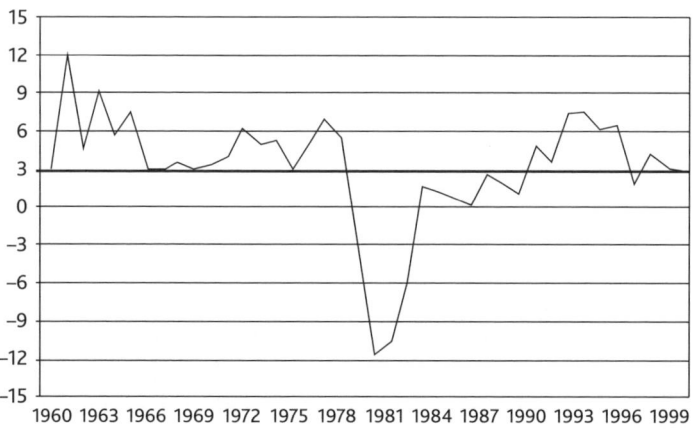

Figure 8.2 El Salvador: economic growth (%), 1960–99

Source: ECLAC, BCR (Rivera, 2000).

Crime and the privatization of security

According to the World Bank Economic Memorandum, a major factor responsible for growing social instability and for threatening the way the economy operates and grows in El Salvador are the high crime and violence rates, which account for an economic cost ranging between 13 and 25 percent of GDP (World Bank, 2003). Overall causes have been often associated with social imbalances and the consequences of war. This report also highlights the widespread use of firearms, low income, poverty, low educational levels, and lack of employment opportunities, as elements adding to criminal behavior.

The relationship between the termination of war, the launching of the economic stabilization program, and growth in crime, seem to suggest that a relationship existed between economic boom expectations at the time and the constraints of the economic model. In fact, after the signing of the peace agreements, extremely high levels of homicidal violence, attributed to common criminals, were recorded. However, as Figure 8.3 shows, homicide rates have shown a downturn trend.

The Maras, or youth gangs, first appeared in El Salvador in 1991, and have been pinpointed as the main source of violence, striking San Salvador initially. There are two types of gangs in El Salvador: student gangs and street gangs. In 1996, the National Civil Police estimated that some 20,000 young people were street gang members (Cruz, 1999).

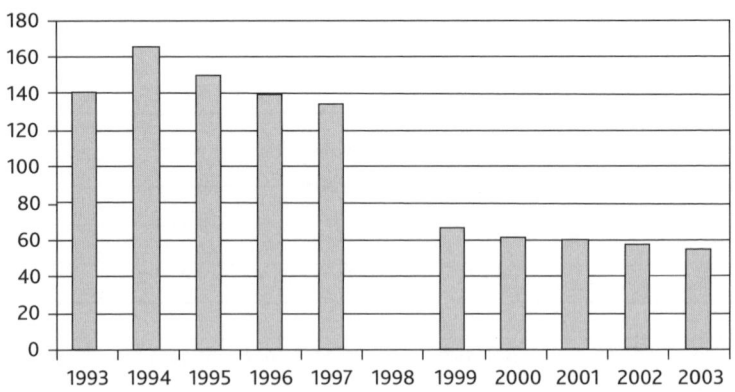

Figure 8.3 El Salvador: homicide rates (per 100,000 people), 1993–2003

Source: UNDP 2005 El Salvador Report.

In 2003 in El Salvador there were 2,388 homicides, and common criminals accounted for 57 percent of this figure, while gang members were responsible for only 8 percent. Thirty-eight percent of the total number of deaths for the same year were young people between 15 and 24 years of age, and 20 percent were young people aged between 25 and 29 years (i.e., people who tend to belong to the Maras and other youth gangs). On the other hand, homicides accounted for 7 percent of the total number of crimes committed, and the highest number, corresponding to 51 percent of crimes, referred to thefts and robberies. It is important to note the very low kidnapping (0.1 percent) and extortion rates (1 percent) in 2003. These rates could reflect a low organized crime level vis-à-vis the concentration of violence in the hands of common criminals.

An important conclusion of the 2003 report is the fact that regions recording the highest homicide rates are those less affected by the war in the 1980s, whereas those showing the lowest rates (Chalatenango and Morazán) were those in which the war was most intense. In comparison, the high rate recorded in the most urbanized areas is highlighted. This rate is probably a result of demographic changes, the increase in urbanization rates, and the concentration of large numbers of young people in cities.

The security issue has become a very important matter in El Salvador since the 1990s, especially when considered alongside the low efficiency of the National Civil Police (PNC) and the distrust this lack of efficiency arouses (UNDP, 2003). A steady increase in the number of agencies providing private security services has thus been recorded since 1994 (Table 8.3). Today, the Salvadoran law has classified security services as follows: Private Security Agencies (ASP); Associations of Security Guards and Independent Guards (AVI); Private Investigation Agencies (AIP); and Patrimonial Protection Services (SPP).

Table 8.3 El Salvador: number of Agencies providing private security services, 1994–2000

	1994	1995	1996	1997	1998	1999	2000
ASP	11	24	23	18	26	33	26
SPP	1	14	21	12	11	13	3
AIP	2	3	4	4	2	2	1
AVI		6	1	1	2	1	

Source: PCN Division for Registration and Control of Private Security Services; Melara (2001).

The expansion of the private security industry in El Salvador is linked to complex problems. First, official regulation is not very efficient. The first private security regulatory scheme was the outcome of the peace agreements, turning into the "private security services law" in 1994 (UNDP, 2003). One of the main drawbacks in this legislation is a provision that a series of bureaucratic procedures before the Prosecutor's Office, the Directorate General of the PNC, and the Ministry of the Interior have to be completed within a one-month period. It is therefore rather usual for a number of agencies to be only partially legalized. Secondly, the 1994 law provided for the PNC to enact a regulation, which never materialized. Thirdly, accurate records of personnel hired by private security companies are not kept by the PNC, the entity responsible for regulating the operation of the private security industry. Fourthly, despite the PNC's shortcomings in keeping records on the sundry aspects regarding private security agencies, these are issues the PNC is well aware of because they could potentially trigger violence. The fact is that more than 9,000 firearms are in the hands of private security companies, and over 20,000 security guards are on their payroll, each one carrying at least one weapon. Although there are no detailed records on the profile of private security guards, it is well known that, to save on training costs, private security employers would rather hire ex-military men or former guerrilla fighters (UNDP, 2000).

The UN has warned that unchecked crime in Central America can mean harmful effects to the economy (United Nations, 2007). On the one hand, the UN has warned that many foreign businessmen consider that high crime rates amount to an obstacle to investment in Central America. On the other hand, tourism—the second largest source of foreign exchange in El Salvador and Guatemala after remittances from abroad—is impaired by the warnings foreign governments issue to their citizens about the risks they may face visiting these two countries.

Guatemala: Liberalization and Economic Changes

In the triad of Central American countries beset by internal armed conflicts, Guatemala followed a path of its own towards the adoption of neoliberal policies. In 1986, the Marco Vinicio Cerezo (1986–91) government implemented a package of structural adjustment measures. His was the first democratic government after decades of military governments. This trend was to be continued by subsequent administrations, Jorge Serrano Elías (1991–93), and Ramiro de León Carpio (1993–96).

The government led by businessman Alvaro Enrique Arzú Irigoyen (1996–2000) was meant to play a key role in the adoption of neoliberal policies because this was the government giving the greatest emphasis to state modernization, through decentralization and privatization of some state assets, as well as the enactment of measures aimed at the opening of the economy. The Short-Term Program for Economic and Social Reactivation (PRES) was carried out under the Vinicio Cerezo government in clear acceptance of a mandate from the World Bank and the International Monetary Fund to reduce state intervention in the economy and to redress financial and taxation imbalances.

In 1987, two new structural adjustment programs were implemented: the National Reorganization Program and the Guatemala 2000 Plan, to promote free trade zones, booming exports and the reduction of tariffs. The plan Economic and Social Policy 1991–96: Towards an Economic and Social Democracy was approved by Serrano Elías, and targeted higher economic deregulation and decentralization of the management of the economy on the basis of market tools. Tariff reductions, reforms to the financial system, reduction of public expenditure, and reforms to the financial system were also mandated by Serrano Elías.

The impacts of neoliberal policies

The negotiation process with the guerrillas was reactivated and brought to an end with the signing of the peace agreements during the administration of Álvaro Arzú, who had defined himself as a representative of the most modern business class sector. Also, during his administration, two plans were implemented: (i) the Economic and Social Modernization Program; and (ii) the Political Agreement to Fund Peace, Development and Democracy in Guatemala, involving adjustment measures to strengthen the Guatemalan state finances. One year after the signing of the peace agreements, an arrangement was made with the World Bank to support the Program for Economic and Social Modernization over a six-year period. During 2000, the Political Agreement to Fund Peace, Development and Democracy in Guatemala was incorporated, and 46 tax reforms, with tax and public expenditure implications, aimed at reorganizing and strengthening the Guatemalan state finances, were negotiated. Secondly, this administration promoted the decentralization of public functions through the "Let us Change" plan, guided by the principle of a "regulatory centralization" and "operational decentralization" (the allocation of duties according to local skills and needs), thus encouraging local participation. Thirdly, the process of privatization of public enterprises and services was sped up under this administration: in this four-year period, the maintenance of roads, the state-owned railways, the telecommunications company, and the national telephone company were privatized; also completed was the privatization of the distribution companies. Fourthly, the removal of import and export tariffs, and the reimbursement of the Value Added Tax to all exporters was enacted. Finally, disagreements between the government and the insurgents, who had temporarily stalled the negotiations, were overcome, and the Agreement on Social and Economic Aspects and the Agrarian Situation was signed on May 6, 1996, and an agreement called the Strengthening of Civilian Power and the Army Role in a Democratic Society was signed on September 19, 1996, providing for the restructuring of state security agencies. Basically, the goal was to reduce the size of the army, and confine its role to that of safeguarding national sovereignty by protecting borders. In tandem, the restructuring of the police force took place, with a goal of changing its military nature.

The Alfonso Antonio Portillo Cabrera (2000–04) and Óscar Berger (2004–08) administrations—the latter a well-known agricultural entrepreneur—kept the policies of their predecessors in place; as regards Portillo, despite his speech favoring the implementation of social and wealth re-distributional policies. It is worthwhile pointing out that the adoption of neoliberal policies in Guatemala went hand in hand with major political changes: the return to democracy in 1986; the peace agreements in the 1990s, which, among other things, implied the incorporation of the Guatemalan National Revolutionary Unity (URNG); the formal if not actual recognition of indigenous rights, and the need for state policies to be implemented to offset widespread poverty in the country. Even President Berger, in his September 2007 speech before the United Nations, spoke about the consolidation of Guatemala as a "multicultural, multiethnic, and multilingual nation."

At the same time, during the 1990s, the United States stopped their military support for counterinsurgent campaigns deployed by Central American governments faced with internal conflicts, in favor of a strategy based on the political, economic, and social restructuring of countries in conflict. The Guatemalan business community was promoting a negotiated solution with the guerrillas. In a globalized economy, costs involved in not negotiating with the guerrillas exceeded the costs of reaching an agreement. It can be said that the end of armed confrontation and the advent of neoliberalism in Guatemala were not unrelated.

In short, the introduction and consolidation of neoliberalism in Guatemala was signaled by a transition from military regimes to democratic governments committed to: neoliberal policies; support from a business elite whose members saw themselves as forward-looking; the signing of the peace agreements with the guerrillas; and the implementation of economic adjustment measures.

For the most modern sector of the Guatemalan elite, linked to international markets, the peace agreements amounted to an opportunity to achieve the institutional stability their new economic project was calling for. Unlike what happened in El Salvador, the Guatemalan guerrillas were never close to coming to power; however, they were capable of indefinitely waging war, thereby preventing the achievement of the stability transnational employers required to carry out their business activity in the country without any constraints (Robinson, 2000). This was a double-edged issue: (i) The guerrilla made landlords and employers into a military target by considering their business representatives as allies of the military regime; as a result, not only economic but also political kidnappings became commonplace; (ii) The fight against the guerrilla became the raison d'être of the Guatemalan state, which was a heavy burden for employers and other members of the oligarchy because of the costs the protracted armed conflict imposed upon them.[14]

Since 1986, virtually all governments in Guatemala have been committed to the implementation of measures to the benefit of the liberalization of the economy. This process, which was developed in tandem with the transition to democracy and ended with the 1996 peace agreements, provided all the conditions transnational elites required to become consolidated. This sector was seeking to modernize the state and society to establish conditions that would allow them access to international markets, while avoiding to commit themselves to implementing fundamental changes to the concentration of property and wealth.[15]

Meaningful impacts on the economic arena have been generated by the implementation of neoliberal policies, mainly focused on the diversification of traditional and non-traditional product exports:

- First, the Guatemalan tax system is characterized by its limited contribution to the GDP; this contribution has ranged between 5.3 percent and 10.1 percent since 1955. Between 1985 and 2000, the Guatemalan tax burden fluctuated between

6.1 percent and 10.1 percent of GDP (World Bank, 2003). The setting in which structural adjustment and free market promotion measures have been implemented since 1987, witnessed the dismantling of export tariffs and, in the late 1990s, tariffs on raw materials, equipment, and intermediate products were virtually ruled out. Likewise, a provision was stipulated for the VAT to be reimbursed to all exporters (Ganuza et al., 2001).

- Second, while public expenditure shows an increase, Guatemala is one of the countries with the lowest share of social spending (as a percentage of GDP) in Latin America. According to the Ministry of Public Finance figures, public expenditure in Guatemala as a percentage of GDP has shown a downward trend between 1995 (10.5 percent) and 2004 (3.6 percent). This reduction in public spending would correspond to the fact that adjustment measures had an impact on the tax policy, the central government's funding instrument. Tariff contraction in Guatemala was widespread, gradual, and systematic, and had to be rectified by increases in consumption rather than income taxes, since the income tax collection was already low due to difficulties in its application. This offsetting process allowed for the tax burden of Guatemala vis-à-vis the GDP to remain relatively constant over the period structural adjustment measures were being applied; eventually, governments' spending capacity to address not only the provision of basic services, but also the transfers to solve re-distributional problems of the population, was hurt (Ganuza, 2001).
- Third, foreign investment was encouraged by the state through the enactment of the Foreign Investment Law (Decree No. 9-98), ensuring that foreign investors were accorded treatment similar to that being given to domestic investors. Additionally, a total income tax exemption was granted for a 15-year period on incomes exclusively derived from business activity.
- Fourth, Guatemala's economy has become dependent on foreign currency remittances that workers living abroad send to their families. According to Bank of Guatemala figures, since 1994 this flow has shown a steep increase, and by 2006, remittances accounted for 9 percent of GDP.

The land issue in Guatemala

The neoliberal reforms of the mid 1990s included the implementation of a land reform. The reform avoided resorting to a land distribution-based model and, instead, turned to a land market-based model, expecting property rights over land to become democratized. It is worth noting that this change in emphasis played a key role in the peace agreements the government entered into with the URNG. This agreement envisaged the creation of a fund to purchase land, as a market-based strategy to solve the distributive inequality problem.[16] In addition, an agreement was reached that the state would ensure respect for the working conditions of rural workers (Saldivar and Wittman, 2002; Garoz and Gauster, 2005). Likewise, international aid institutions, like the World Bank, advocated for a land market-based solution.[17]

The World Bank, the Inter-American Development Bank, and the United Nations Economic Commission for Latin America made two claims to intervene in the debate around land ownership concentration patterns. The first assertion is that this inequality gives rise to an inefficient use of agricultural resources. The second argument contends that land ownership concentration brings poverty. In general, these organizations believe that the growing number of growers has a positive impact on production, efficiency, and equality, while the excessive concentration of land has the opposite effect (Garoz and Gauster, 2005). The peace agreements and the World Bank proposals converged in that the land market-based agrarian reform should include the strengthening of property rights, titling, registration and cadastre, payment of taxes, improved funding mechanisms to facilitate land purchases, technical assistance and facilities to revamp farms, additional social and economic investment, as well as environmental protection. However, despite the government alignment with neoliberal policies, these measures have not been fully implemented. The Partido de Avanzada Nacional (PAN) government, which signed the peace agreements, showed reluctance to implement neoliberal measures provided by the Agreement on Social and Economic Aspects and the Agrarian Situation, signed on May 6, 1996. Subsequent governments have kept a similar political line. An additional distinctive feature of economic development in Guatemala is an economic growth strategy based on the free market and the boost to non-traditional agricultural products exports implemented in the 1980s (ECLAC, 2001; World Bank, 2005).

In short, a claim could be made that the agrarian problem in Guatemala can be linked to economic regimes combining liberal and conservative reform components, the outcome of which has benefited and consolidated rural elites involved in the export of non-traditional products. Neoliberalism has become articulated with the agrarian problem in Guatemala along two different dimensions.

First, as pointed out above, neoliberal reforms have led to a strategic change in tackling the agrarian problem by shelving the land expropriation and distribution scheme and instead fostering a peaceful land market democratization plan. Guatemalan landowners have profited from the land market characteristics, and in particular the voluntary purchase-and-sale scheme. Typically, this negotiation principle works as follows: peasant farmers' organizations seek out a plot of land they are interested in buying and negotiate its price with the owner, on the basis of the FONTIERRAS appraisal listing. On occasion, the owner is not interested in the offer to purchase and refuses to sell his property. In this case, peasants are forced to start a new process (ECLAC, 2001; Garoz and Gauster, 2002). The owners' attitude is not arbitrary; their motivation is related to their interest in keeping their social status and their privileged access to the non-traditional agricultural products market. As a series of studies about the land market dynamics in Guatemala shows, large landowners are usually reluctant to split up or sell their land to peasant groups for fear that the latter's demand for land or land invasions may be increased by transactions of this sort (Saldivar and Wittman, 2002; ECLAC, 2001). Additionally, land has become a key resource vis-à-vis the non-traditional agricultural exports boom, because firms involved in agro-export businesses, more skilled and endowed with edge-technology capabilities, would rather stock up on supplies from large-scale growers (ECLAC, 2001; Gauster, 2007).

The second dimension refers to the scant commitment shown by the Guatemalan state to the strengthening of property rights—a fact linked to the thwarted history of land reform in Guatemala, which lasted only two years (1952–54). Reform efforts were then followed by an in-depth agrarian counter-reform, supposedly coming to an end with the implementation of the peace agreements, which, among other things, advocated for the strengthening of property rights. The role the Land Fund (FONTIERRAS), established in 1999 in compliance with the peace agreements and World Bank advice, was intended to give fresh impetus to the land market; however, a lack of both political will and proper funding have rendered this initiative useless (Pillay, 2006).

The larger opening period in Guatemala has not only meant the freezing of the agrarian structure, but has also given rise to conditions conducive both to preserving the hegemony of the landowners, and to boosting land expansion and expropriation at their hands:

- The government's tendency to enact laws benefiting landowners to the detriment of peasants and indigenous population rights and interests. For instance, Article 260 of the Guatemalan Labor Code, amended in 2001, provides that once a labor contract has expired, the worker has one month to claim his employment benefits, after which this right expires. In accordance with complaints made by peasant organizations, owners of ranches and farms resort to "indirect dismissal," which is to say they orally terminate the peasant's employment, promising to soon re-hire him, but with the hidden intention to wait out the 30-day deadline the law provides for claiming employment benefits. In this way, farm owners take advantage of the importance Maya Indians usually place on verbal agreements.
- For a series of reasons, when rural workers resort to legal means to claim their labor rights, judgment is seldom passed in their favor. To begin with, agencies responsible for the protection of workers' rights, such as the Labor Inspectorate and the Labor Court, have no logistical or financial resources available to provide sufficient support to peasants. Also, there are many cases in which these agencies' officers ally themselves with landowners to intentionally delay processes hoping to wear out the plaintiff's resources and patience. Thus, labor-related lawsuits become weakened and remain unsolved. The persistent coffee crisis has made this problem more acute: since 2000, international coffee prices have shown a downturn trend, adversely affecting the number of jobs available at coffee farms, while many dismissed workers are demanding their employment benefits.[18]
- In Guatemala, land ownership rights are guaranteed by unreliable state institutions, which makes these guarantees volatile, effectively encouraging extra-legal actions to validate them. Two basic components are involved in the legal recognition of property: title registration and cadastre. Both inefficiency and illegitimacy characterize these two components. Since 1963, a public entity is in charge of title registration, annotation, and cancellation of title and other rights over identifiable movable and real property in Guatemala: the General Property Registry (RGP).[19] The

Guatemalan registration system is declaratory rather than formal; it is based on the principle that the first to declare ownership of a property by relying on documents recognized by the RGP has precedence over the rights declared by other documents to be subsequently filed. The picture is even bleaker in the cadastral field than in the registry: a land registry office was nonexistent in Guatemala until 2005; thus, a duly updated cadastral map is not available in the country.[20] The absence of a consolidated cadastral system implies that the registration of property in Guatemala is unreliable, because it is based on inaccurate measurements and files. To a large extent, this deficiency accounts for disputes over land ownership in the country[21] becoming a widespread phenomenon, in particular among rural communities that lack legal documents endorsing their claims to land ownership (lands which are being held by landowners).

Both in the case of conflicts arising out of the non-recognition of work-related benefits and in property rights disputes in some areas, the illegal takeover of lands—a violence-triggering factor—is common practice among organized peasants or peasant communities, and neoliberalism has been linked to violent conflicts over access to land. The suggestion that violence in the dispute over land in Guatemala is a neoliberal phenomenon is obviously untrue. In fact, the Commission for Historical Clarification (CEH, 2004) has fairly well documented land disputes triggering violence within the framework of the counter-guerrilla struggle. A claim could however be made that neoliberalism has a relationship with violence-generating changes linked to the struggle for land. Conflicts over land share a common pattern: the abdication of the state's responsibility when it comes to advocating the peasants' interests vis-à-vis those of landowners.

Security and private protection

In Guatemala, the privatization of security is a phenomenon that precedes neoliberalism: as an instrument consistent with agrarian counter-reform policies, the privatization of security has been key to the problematic agrarian situation in the country since the mid twentieth century. It seemed like this practice would become extinct with the termination of the armed conflict, but the result has been exactly the opposite.

One of the goals of the peace process was to consolidate democracy by reducing the scope of action of the armed forces, and to strengthen civil institutions. But the transition from a military police to a civilian police force was a massive failure, because the process was structured around a very feeble institution. The National Civil Police (PNC), besides lacking the resources to efficiently operate, counts on just 19,000 police officers to ensure the security of the 12.3 million inhabitants of the country, and is weighed down by a huge mistrust among the population, due to regular claims accusing its members of being involved in criminal activities.

An additional factor explaining the boom in private security in Guatemala is the extremely high crime levels in the country since the mid 1990s. According to a UN report (2007), the homicide rate increased by 64 percent between 2001 and 2006. In the midst of this desperate situation, the last two governments (Alfonso Portillo and Óscar Berger) resorted to getting the army out into the streets to ensure urban security: Alfonso Portillo sent army patrols to outlying areas of the capital city, while Óscar Berger, ordered that 2,400 troops were to support the PNC by conducting joint patrols to ensure citizen safety. This measure has not been successful either.

Despite the termination of the internal conflict, private security has been kept in place in rural areas of Guatemala, mainly because of resource shortages on the part of the Guatemalan police. In many cases, the police are in short supply of either vehicles or fuel to move, and they don't have the resources to buy food for officers. In the face of this shortage of resources, and in their eagerness for eviction proceedings to be carried out, landowners provide the police with transport, water, and food.[22] Also, landowners have their own private security forces, which carry out evictions on their own or in cooperation with the police. It is worth pointing out that these private security forces have been accused of the forced disappearance of peasant leaders, of issuing threats to rural communities, and of raping women. Thirdly, agro-industrial enterprises also have their own security forces which, in addition to protecting company facilities, are also involved in labor disputes, resorting to force to break up workers' protests, threatening or killing workers and union leaders.

Two types of private organizations responsible for providing security exist in urban areas of Guatemala: private security companies and neighborhood associations. Private security companies, legally or illegally operating,[23] provide service to private homes, residential complexes, factories, industries, shopping places, businesses, schools, and so on. Illegal companies, putting them within reach of poor areas, often provide a more economical service. A tight control over private security companies is not enforced by the state. To begin with, the number of private security companies in the country is unknown, as well as the exact number of personnel working for them. For example, according to a statement made by the Minister of the Interior in Guatemala in 2004, there were 110,000 guards, and only 40,000 were working legally; while the head of the National Civil Police's Private Entities Section stated there were 60,000 private guards, and only 25,560 were working for legally established companies. Staff credentials are also unknown: education, training, criminal history, and so on. As with the police, a large number of private guards have been involved in criminal activities. Finally, it is worth noting that the ex-military are more involved in private security, either as entrepreneurs or as guards. As for neighborhood associations, these are organizations formed with PNC support, with an aim to back up police work. As the CEG (2005) points out, these associations have often exceeded their role, since they engage in the prosecuting and punishing of offenders. They have even been involved in the lynching of suspected criminals.

Both the privatization of security and the insecurity issues have become a key factor in Guatemalan politics, and there is a likelihood that they will adversely affect the country's entrance into international markets. For example, in 2005, bearing in mind the upsurge in killings of union leaders, a United States congressman was critical of the approval of the Central America Free Trade Agreement (CAFTA). On the other hand, these two issues have also become problems in which international organizations like the UN and countries like the United States, have intervened. For example, in early 2007, the UN convened a meeting with representatives of political parties competing for the presidency to voice the UN concern about high levels of violence in the country, and to suggest that party representatives incorporate measures to counteract the problem into their agendas.

CONCLUSIONS

A scenario conducive to implementing deep political and economic changes is long overdue because of, first, the authoritarian nature of political regimes and the absence of a democratic space, and secondly, the destabilizing effects created by the termination of war in El Salvador and Guatemala, and in Central America in general.

The liberalization of the economy and the democratic transition went almost hand in hand with the implementation of the peace agreements. This coincidence endowed the whole process with strong internal legitimacy, bolstered by a huge international support. The transition-to-democracy phase has concluded, leading to a political-institutional regime in which the enforcement of constitutional entities and electoral competition prevail. The challenge now is the consolidation of democracy.

When will the Salvadoran and Guatemalan democracies be consolidated? This is the question academics and opinion leaders are regularly endeavoring to solve.[24] However, other questions should be posed beforehand. For example: Are the conditions necessary to ensure that this consolidation can take place at present? In both countries considered here, it is clear that the armed conflicts have left behind a number of unresolved issues that, unless overcome, may significantly delay the process: the integration of demobilized fighters into the countries' economic and political life; economic reconstruction; and the demilitarization of the state. Also, the consolidation of democracy will only be possible if strong public support is at hand, which in turn depends on democracy delivering results in areas such as social welfare, education, health, and economic opportunities—something that still needs to happen. In the years to come, in both Guatemala and El Salvador, the answer to these challenges—and indeed the future of democracy itself—will depend on the neoliberal model's ability to fulfill the "social prosperity" expectations hoped for by the population.

NOTES

1. The authors are affiliated with the Institute for Political Studies and International Relations of the Universidad Nacional de Colombia (IEPRI). The authors wish to acknowledge comments and ideas gathered at meetings with several Central American armed conflict experts, including Edelberto Torres Rivas, Elizabeth Wood, Manolo Vela, Ricardo Saenz, Alexander Segovia, and Ruben Zamora.
2. All kinds of political authoritarian systems seem to have come together in Central America: from the concentration of power in one individual in Nicaragua, to the militarization of society in Guatemala, to authoritarian reformism in El Salvador (Rouquié, 1992).
3. The Salvadoran coffee production efficiency did not have a positive impact on working conditions. In 1961, 60 percent of the economically active population was working in agriculture. This fell to 47 percent in 1971, and to 43 percent in 1980, reaching only 33 percent in 1991 (Seligson, 1995).
4. In El Salvador, war took on distinct characteristics largely due to geographical conditions. These made it unlikely that guerrilla "foci" could be developed, as had been the case in other Central American countries. Instead, insurgent groups

took advantage of social unrest, population density, and the emergence of trade unions and peasant associations. An armed action tripartite model—popular/party/guerrilla organizations—had its origin in El Salvador (Rouquié, 1992). Insurgency became articulated into "popular organizations," which, in turn, gave rise to "mass fronts." The war in El Salvador, unlike any other country in Central America, was really an armed mobilization of the people.

5. Phase I, including the expropriation of large (more than 500 hectares) estates, was immediately implemented, initially affecting 326 properties, which were handed over to peasant cooperatives jointly administered by the Salvadoran Institute for Agrarian Reform (ISTA). Phase II, which was only partially implemented, included the expropriation of lands not directly being tilled by their owners, benefiting tenants and sharecroppers, within a seven hectares limit for each plot of land being transferred. Phase III included properties exceeding the basic limit: 100 or 150 hectares, depending on their soil quality, and measuring less than 500 hectares. Precisely, the economic and political importance of the sector being affected in this phase—corresponding to the export coffee agriculture axis—allowed the government to have more room to maneuver and use balance-of-power changes to its own advantage, which is to say to achieve successive deferrals which, in practice, ended up in the non-application of Phase III (Browning, 1993).

6. Most insurgent organizations had emerged in the 1970s: Popular Liberation Forces (FPL), People's Revolutionary Army (EPR), and Central American Workers Revolutionary Party (PRTC). Together with several popular organizations, these three trends converged to give birth, in October 1980, to the FMLN. A failed attempt was made by the Front in January 1981 to topple the government in the "Final Offensive." War then became stabilized and, although the Salvadoran government, with United States financial support, successfully managed to deter the rise of the insurgency, it was nevertheless unable to prevent the emergence of a "dual power," which finally led to a balance of forces, making political negotiations mandatory.

7. The idea that the army should be under civilian control was shared by the new emerging elite and the Salvadoran left. Their criticism was mainly aimed at the army's poor military performance and high corruption levels (Gibb and Smyth, 1990).

8. A total of 600,000 hectares were seized and distributed amongst 100,000 families in eleven departments. About half of these lands were located in the fertile Southern coast area, in the department of Escuintla, and in the Eastern region in the department of Izbal, where the United Fruit Co. banana plantations were located. The United Fruit properties accounted for nearly 26 percent of the total land expropriated (Kay, 1998).

9. According to the National Environment Commission (CONAMA), 850,000 hectares had been awarded up to year 1992 in the Northern Transversal Strip (FTN) (crossing the departments of Izabal, the Northern Alta Verapaz region, Quiché and Huehuetenango), while in the Department of Petén, 210,000 hectares had been awarded. The individual awarding of lands allowed for a large share of this land to enter the land market. Many sources point to senior army officers as being the final beneficiaries of large tracts of land in the northern regions of the country.

10. These changes were already under way but were given a fresh impetus in the aftermath of the February 1976 earthquake, which in its wake left more than 27,000 people dead, 77,000 injured and more than 1 million people homeless

(approximately 10 percent of the population). A huge social and economic shock was brought about by this tragedy, making clear Guatemalan society fractures and its high inequalities. Although communication lines between social mobilization and leftist organizations were in place, the so-called "mass movement boom" of the mid 1970s started independently of the reconfiguration of guerrilla groups (CEH, 1999). The merging of these two trends, which would only take shape at the end of the decade, accounts for the sheer size of the tragedy the Guatemalan society, and the indigenous population in particular, would have to endure afterwards.

11. These circumstances came mixed together with a regional political climate undoubtedly conducive to the insurgent organizations' expectations. The arrival of the Sandinistas to power in Nicaragua in 1979, and the progress being made at the time by the Salvadoran guerrillas, seemed to indeed show that the time was ripe for the Guatemalan guerrillas to launch an offensive. Towards late 1979, the EGP considered itself to be consolidated enough to enter the next stage, that of "widespread guerrilla warfare." The deployment of the Ixcán's EGP guerrilla towards the Ixil triangle coincided with the presence of ORPA south of the region of Quiché. The transition to the "war of positions" that Guatemalan guerrillas were after called for a formation of a regular armed force, the "popular army," which guerrilla leaders believed they could achieve through the spontaneous mobilization of indigenous settlements.

12. This figure accounts for 80 percent of the indigenous male population, and it is likely to include people coming under PAC control and forced to collaborate (REMHI, 1998, chapter 2).

13. Ninety-seven percent of Salvadorans abroad live in the United States. Based on the 2000 United States Census, this population was estimated at 932,117 inhabitants, showing a big rise during the 1980s, which is a result of the United States' government granting various types of asylum and residence permits during the armed conflict (Restrepo, 2004).

14. The increase in military spending can be accounted for by the growing Army manpower: between 1980 and 1982, the number of troops rose from 14,000 to 42,000.

15. Vis-à-vis this point, two approaches may be considered. The first approach believes that, because they prevented any basic change whatsoever from being implemented in the Guatemalan social and economic structure, the 1996 peace agreements laid the foundation for the consolidation of a transnational elite (Chase-Dunn, 2000). The second one believes that a suitable framework for the necessary steps towards the solution of major social problems in Guatemala, such as poverty and social inequality, to be taken, was provided for by peace agreements (Burgerman, 2000; Edelman, 1998).

16. Within the framework of peace agreements, a commitment was made by the government to set up a Land Fund to improve land-property access capacity through a Market-based Land Reform (Palma Murga, 1997).

17. Two arguments were put forward by the World Bank, the Inter-American Development Bank and the United Nations Economic Commission for Latin America for the land property concentration pattern to be intervened. The first is that an inefficient use of agricultural resources is generated by this inequality. Second, land property concentration results in poverty. In general, these organizations believe that increasing the number of growers has a positive

effect on production, efficiency and equality, while opposite effects are the outcome of excessive land concentration (Garoz and Gauster, 2005).
18. Guatemala Economic Performance Assessment. USAID (2006).
19. The General Property Registry was set up in 1963 by Act 106, and renovated in 1985, 1987, and 1990.
20. Only until the promulgation of Decree Law on Cadastral Information Registry (Decree no. 41-2005), published on July 20, 2005, the Guatemalan Registry on Cadastral Information Guatemala, RIC, was to be established.
21. According to the Presidential Commission on Legal Assistance and Land Conflict Settlement (CONTIERRA), a total of 1,659 conflicts took place between 1997 and June 2002, while in 2005, 1,052 land disputes in Guatemala were still awaiting resolution.
22. According to Amnesty International (2006), violent incidents have been present in 51 percent of evictions since 1997, involving the police and/or private security forces.
23. Inseguridad Publica. El Negocio de la violencia, Guatemala Study Centre. September 27, 2005.
24. See, for example, Azpuru et al. (2007).

REFERENCES

Aguilar, J. and Elizondo, M. (2005) "Las políticas de reforma en Centroamérica y la nueva economía regional." Instituto de Investigaciones en Ciencias Económicas, Universidad de Costa Rica.
Amnesty International (2006) *Guatemala: Land of Injustice?* AI Index: AMR 34/003/2006. London: Amnesty International.
Arnson, C. (ed.) (1999) *La consulta popular y el futuro del proceso de paz en Guatemala*. Washington, DC: Woodrow Wilson International Center for Scholars.
Azpuru, D. (1999) "Peace and democratization in Guatemala: two parallel processes." In *Comparative Peace Processes in Latin América*, ed. Cynthia Arnson. Palo Alto: Stanford University Press.
Azpuru, D., Blanco, L., Córdova Macías, R., Loya Marín, N., Ramos, C. G., and Zapata, A. (2007) *Construyendo la democracia en sociedades posconflicto. Un enfoque comparado entre Guatemala y El Salvador*. Guatemala and Ottawa: F&G Editores/IDRC.
Ball, P., Kobrak, P., and Spirer, H. F. (1999) *Violencia Institucional en Guatemala, 1960–1966: una reflexión cuantitativa*. Washington, DC: Centro Internacional para Investigaciones en Derechos Humanos (CIIDH).
Boyce, J. (ed.) (1996) *Economic Policy for Building Peace: The Lessons of El Salvador*. Boulder and London: Lynne Rienner Publishers.
Browning, D. (1993) "Agrarian reform in El Salvador." *Journal of Latin American Studies*, Vol. 15, No. 2, pp. 399–426.
Burgerman, S. (2000) "Building the peace by mandating reform: United Nations-mediated human rights agreements in El Salvador and Guatemala." *Latin American Perspectives*, Vol. 27, No. 3, pp. 63–87.
Byrne, H. (1996) *El Salvador's Civil War: A Study of Revolution*. Boulder and London: Lynne Rienner Publishers.
Comisión de Esclarecimiento Histórico (CEH) (1999) *Guatemala: Memoria del Silencio*. Guatemala: F&G Editores.
Centro de Estudios de Guatemala (CEG) (2005) *Inseguridad Pública. El Negocio de la violencia*. Guatemala: CEG.

Chase-Dunn, C. (2000) "Guatemala in the global system." *Journal of Interamerican Studies and World Affairs*, Vol. 42, No. 4, pp. 109–126.
Colindres, E. (1976) "La tenencia de la tierra en El Salvador." *ECA (Estudios Centroamericanos)* No. 335-36.
Cruz, J. M. (1999) "Maras o pandillas juveniles. Los mitos sobre su formación e integración." In *El Salvador, Sociología General*, ed. O. Martinez. San Salvador: Editorial Nuevo Enfoque.
Economic Commission for Latin America and the Caribbean (ECLAC) (2001) *La estructura agraria y el campesinado en El Salvador, Guatemala y Honduras*. Santiago: ECLAC.
Edelman, M. (1998) "Transnational peasant politics in Central America." *Latin American Research Review*, Vol. 33, No. 3, pp. 49–86.
Flores, M. (1998) 'El Salvador: Trayectoria de la reforma agraria, 1980–1998', *Revista Mexicana de Sociología*, Vol. 60, No. 4.
Ganuza, E. (2001) "Apertura, pobreza y desigualdad: Guatemala." In *Liberalización, desigualdad y pobreza: América Latina y el Caribe en los 90*, eds. E. Ganuza, R. Paes de Barros, L. Taylor, and R. Vos. Buenos Aires: Editorial Universitaria de Buenos Aires.
García-Ruiz, J. (1997) "Modernité et sociétés paysannes: le rôle du religieux dans la recomposition des identités au Guatemala." *Archives de sciences sociales des religions*, Vol. 97, No. 1.
Garoz, B. and Gauster, S. (2002) *Fontierras: El modelo de mercado y el acceso a la tierra en Guatemala. Balance y perspectivas*. Guatemala: Coordinación de ONG y Cooperativas (CONCOOP) y Coordinadora Nacional de Organizaciones Campesinas (CNOC).
Garoz, B. and Gauster, S. (2005) "FONTIERRAS: Structural Adjustment and access to land in Guatemala." Land Research Action Network.
Gauster, S. (2007) "DR-CAFTA Year Two: Trends and Impacts Report." Stop CAFTA Coalition.
Gibb, T. and Smyth, F. (1990) *El Salvador: Is Peace Possible?* Washington, DC: Washington Office on Latin America.
Guido Véjar, R. (1979) "La crísis política en El Salvador (1976–1979)." *Estudios Centroamericanos*, Vol. 19 (July–August), pp. 507–526.
Kay, C. (1998) "El fin de la reforma agraria en América Latina? El legado de la reforma agraria y el asunto no resuelto de la tierra." *Revista Mexicana de Sociología*, Vol. 60, No. 4.
Le Bot, Y. (1995) *La guerra en tierras mayas*. Mexico: Fondo de Cultura Económica.
Melara Minero, L. M. (2001) "Los servicios de seguridad privada en El Salvador." *Estudios Centroamericanos*, Vol. 56, No. 636 (Oct.), pp. 907–932.
Paige, J. (1983) "Social theory and peasant revolution in Vietnam and Guatemala." *Theory and Society*, Vol 12, No. 6, pp. 699–737.
Paige, J. (1993) "Coffee and power in El Salvador." *Latin American Research Review*, Vol. 28, No. 3.
Palma Murga, G. (1997) *Promised the Earth: Agrarian Reform in the Socio-economic Agreement*. London: Conciliation Resources (http://www.c-r.org/our-work/accord/guatemala/promised-earth.php, accessed October 6, 2009).
Pillay, R. (2006) *Evaluation of UNDP Assistance to Conflict – Affected Countries. Case Study Guatemala*. New York City: UNDP.
Recuperación de la memoria histórica (REMHI) (1998) *Guatemala: Nunca Más*. Guatemala: REMHI.

Restrepo, C. (2004) *La población salvadoreña en los Estados Unidos*. San Salvador: FUSADES.

Rivera Campos, R. (1996) "Remesas familiares, mal holandés y política económica." *Boletín Económico y Social*, No. 124. Fundación Salvadoreña para el Desarrollo Económico y Social (FUSADES).

Rivera Campos, R. (1998) "Mal holandés, esterilización monetaria y tasa de interés real en El Salvador." *Cuadernos socioeconómicos del BCIE*, Cuaderno No. 23. Honduras: Banco Centroamericano de Integración Económica (BCIE).

Rivera Campos, R. (2000) *La economía salvadoreña al final del siglo: desafíos para el futuro*. San Salvador: FLACSO.

Robinson, W. I. (2000) "Neoliberalism, the global elite, and the Guatemalan transition: a critical macrosocial analysis." *Journal of Interamerican Studies and World Affairs*, Vol. 42, No. 4, pp. 89–107.

Rouquié, A. (1992) *Guerres et paix en Amerique centrale*. Paris: Seuil.

Saldivar Tánaka, L. and Wittman, H. (2002) "The Agrarian Question in Guatemala." Land Research Action Network.

Segovia, A. (1997) *Cambio estructural, politicas macroeconomicas y pobreza en El Salvador*. San Salvador: UNDP.

Seligson, M. (1995) "Thirty years of transformation in the Agrarian structure of El Salvador, 1961–1991." *Latin American Research Review*, Vol. 30, No. 3, pp. 3–12.

Skocpol, T. (1994) 'What makes peasants revolutionary?' In *Social Revolutions in the Modern World*, ed. T. Skocpol. Cambridge: Cambridge University Press.

Structural Adjustment Participatory Review International Network (SAPRIN) (2000) *La liberalización del sistema financiero*. Washington, DC: SAPRIN (http://www.saprin.org/elsalvador/research/els_res_financiero.pdf, accessed October 6, 2009).

Torres Rivas, E. (1981) "Guatemala medio siglo de historia política." In *América Latina Historia de medio siglo*, ed. P. González. Mexico City: Siglo XXI Editores.

Torres Rivas, E. (2006) *La piel de Centroamérica*. Guatemala: FLACSO.

United Nations (2007) "El crimen y las drogas paralizan el desarrollo en Centroamérica." UN press release, see http://www.un.org/spanish/News/fullstorynews.asp?NewsID=9532 (accessed October 6, 2009).

United Nations Development Program (UNDP) (2000) *Violencia en una sociedad en transición: Ensayos*. San Salvador: UNDP.

United Nations Development Program (UNDP) (2003) *Armas de fuego y violencia*. San Salvador: UNDP.

USAID (2006) *Guatemala: Economic Performance Assessment*. Washington, DC: USAID (http://pdf.usaid.gov/pdf_docs/PNADG260.pdf, accessed October 6, 2009).

Vilas, V. (1992) "Después de la revolución: Democratización y cambio social en Centroamérica." *Revista Mexicana de Sociología*, Vol. 54, No. 3 (July–September).

Villalobos, J. (1989) "A democratic revolution for El Salvador." *Foreign Policy*, No. 74 (Spring), pp. 103–122.

Wood, E. (2000) *Forging Democracy from Below*. Cambridge: Cambridge University Press.

World Bank (2003) *El Salvador – Creciendo en el nuevo milenio – Memorando económico sobre el país*. Washington, DC: World Bank.

World Bank (2005) *Guatemala – Country Economic Memorandum – Challenges to Higher Economic Growth*. Washington, DC: World Bank.

Conclusions

Gerd Schönwälder[1]

If there is one principal conclusion emerging from the case studies in this volume, it is that they confound both proponents and adversaries of neoliberalism and economic globalization more broadly. In simple terms,[2] advocates of neoliberalism hold that economic liberalization, through freer trade, greater foreign investment, fewer restrictions on capital transfers, and the like, stimulates economic growth, which ultimately trickles down to the larger population. At the same time, a smaller and more efficient state produces not just greater accountability and transparency, but much improved service delivery. Civil society also benefits in the process: greater political liberties and a decline of corporatism promote the flourishing of groups and associations that aggregate interests and hold governments to account. Opponents of neoliberalism, of course, counter that instead of promoting growth and equity, economic liberalization damages domestic industry, services and agriculture, further aggravating existing cleavages and leading to more, not less inequality. A "streamlined" state apparatus is synonymous not with improved public services but with their sharp deterioration, particularly in health and education, but also in public security. Civil society, finally, is both weakened by the devastating social and economic impacts of neoliberal policies, and spurred into opposition and resistance.

Not surprisingly then, the two camps also hold very different views on whether neoliberalism generates peace or violence, which is the central problematic of this book. Proponents of neoliberalism maintain that economic opportunities and political liberalization act as disincentives to armed opposition and illicit activities, while its adversaries contend that greater inequality and other socio-economic cleavages breed discontent, and that a diminished state is helpless in the face of growing crime and illegality.[3] What *is* surprising, perhaps, is that—at first glance at least—the contributions to this volume seem to back the former view. Jairo Baquero Melo's chapter provides some quantitative evidence. He finds that more "globalized" countries are less prone to be involved in armed conflict and even when they are, the conflict is likely to end sooner than in countries less integrated into the world economy.[4] Ramón Pajuelo Teves's chapter on Peru, and Ricardo Peñaranda's and Mauricio Barón's piece on Central America, respectively, come to similar conclusions: in both cases, the onset of neoliberal policies coincided with the end of vicious civil wars that had raged on for years, sometimes decades. In both Uganda and Sudan, as shown by Frederik Golooba-Mutebi and Roland Marchal and Einas Ahmed, embracing neoliberalism allowed the ruling regimes to mobilize resources to buy off their opponents—or to repress them more effectively in the case of Sudan—in both cases enhancing political stability. Only in Côte d'Ivoire, the focus of the chapter by Richard Banégas, Alain Toh, and Yao Kouman Adingra, was the onset of neoliberalism clearly associated with a rise in political instability and ultimately civil war. Colombia falls somewhere in between: Francisco Gutiérrez Sanín shows how armed groups exploited new opportunities to tap into state resources brought about by neoliberal reforms, operating behind a façade of legality and with no decisive impact on the overall political stability.

While the assertion of the relationship between neoliberalism and conflict may seem convincing at first, a closer reading reveals a much more nuanced picture. In fact, there are good reasons to question the existence of a cause–effect relationship between neoliberalism and a decrease in political violence, certainly in the terms offered by globalization advocates. For one, neoliberalism may simply be part of a larger puzzle, involving broader processes of socioeconomic transformation whose principal drivers lie elsewhere. In El Salvador and Guatemala, for example, the ongoing civil wars were a major obstacle for emerging new elites who tried not only to replace the traditional land-based oligarchies, but to implement their far-reaching economic and political projects. More outward-looking than their predecessors, these new elites needed greater world-market integration and larger inflows of foreign capital to follow their economic ambitions, and they were prepared to accept a more democratic political regime if that entailed a modernized state apparatus that also provided a more propitious environment to do business. If anything, therefore, the cause–effect relationship was inverted: a political settlement to the armed conflicts was necessary to open the way for subsequent neoliberal reforms, not the other way around.

A similar dynamic was in play in Peru. Here, too, political considerations trumped economic ones and the defeat of the Sendero

Luminoso guerrilla movement was a precondition for the later implementation of a radical neoliberal reform program. Unlike in Central America, however, this program was driven not by emerging new elites but an unlikely coalition between the security establishment and a political newcomer, President Alberto Fujimori, heading up an amorphous anti-party movement with strong roots in Peru's indigenous and "cholo" (mixed-race) majorities. While the initial success of Fujimori's stabilization program undoubtedly helped to forestall the re-emergence of the Sendero Luminoso and other armed groups—lending some credence to the claim that neoliberalism begets peace—this success was made possible in large part by the memory of the disastrous economic management of Alan García's previous government, which produced hyperinflation and generalized economic chaos, as well as a widely-held belief that Fujimori's extremely harsh neoliberal stabilization package was the only way out.

In Uganda, too, a political settlement to the previous civil war and the acceptance of a new "way of doing politics" by the major players *preceded* the introduction of neoliberal policies, in the guise of an IMF-led structural adjustment program. More importantly perhaps, here—as well as in Sudan—the ruling elites were able to shape these policies to their own benefit, using them to strengthen their own position and to hold opponents at bay. In Uganda, this took a fairly benign form, accompanied by greater social spending, particularly on health and education, as well as government handouts and patronage appointments to please political adversaries, making skillful use of an otherwise very successful decentralization program.[5] Nonetheless, the turn towards neoliberalism—together with significant donor largesse—resulted in a larger economic pie, as well as a more open political system.

In Sudan, the story is more sinister: the adoption of neoliberal policies enabled the regime not only to strengthen its control over the economy, but also to step up political repression and marginalize its opponents. Land policies in particular were employed to weaken regime opponents and to empower supporters: the introduction of capitalist ownership principles upset customary land use practices and led to significant land transfers, mostly to the detriment of non-Arab populations in the south. In addition, the centrality of the state in the Sudanese economy, strengthened by increasing oil revenues, permitted the regime to channel resources and opportunities to its supporters, to the point that existing elite arrangements were thoroughly transformed. Remarkably, the regime was able to carry out this program without seriously trying to mitigate its social consequences, aside from encouraging the activities of Islamic humanitarian organizations. Equally remarkable is the fact that the Sudan's regime was able to bridge the divide between its policies and its Islamist rhetoric, explicitly endorsing personal enrichment. New opportunities for economic advancement certainly helped to dispel political opposition, but the repressive capacities of the Sudanese state were stepped up as well, by funneling resources to Sudan's security organs and encouraging the creation of ethnic militias under the regime's tutelage. Overall, this certainly helped to keep political violence down, but at the price of deepening old fault lines and opening new ones.

The case of Côte d'Ivoire, as mentioned, is somewhat different: instead of helping to mitigate or prevent political violence, neoliberalism clearly stoked political instability, ultimately leading to civil war. Here too, though, a more complex picture emerges than what is typically offered by globalization critics. The introduction of neoliberal policies struck at the core of the pre-existing system of political and economic regulation, a form of state capitalism with deep roots in the export-oriented farm economy. Its centerpiece, the "Caistab" (Caisse de Stabilisation des Produits Agricoles), was dismantled and as a result the state's capacity to channel resources and to hand out favors and patronage also suffered. But instead of reaping the hoped-for economic efficiencies, as well as greater transparency and accountability from a streamlined state, the simultaneous introduction of greater political liberties unleashed a wave of pent-up xenophobia against Côte d'Ivoire's large immigrant population. Based mostly in the north and often long-standing inhabitants of the country, these populations saw their basic citizenship rights threatened and responded by taking up arms against the regime. Once the old political and economic order lay in ruins, the entrenchment of a "war economy" in the north and that of a "power economy" in the south ensured the continuation of patronage and cronyism, a flourishing of illicit resource extraction activities (including different forms of "taxation"), a surge in private militias, and a general militarization of social and political spaces.

Colombia, finally, is peculiar in that the gradual introduction of neoliberal policies didn't seem to have much effect on the ongoing civil conflict in the country, one way or another. At first glance, this would confirm the idea that neoliberalism is just one piece of a larger puzzle: what really needs explaining is how a decades-old guerrilla war and widespread drug trafficking can go hand in hand with economic dynamism and political stability, including the perseverance of one of the longest-standing democratic regimes on the continent. However, a second look reveals some less apparent but nonetheless profound impacts of neoliberalism. Land markets, for example, were liberalized and property rights formalized and made more secure. However, instead of the hoped-for "democratization" of land tenure and an increase in productivity, the new policies allowed drug-traffickers and paramilitary groups to buy up large tracts of land, often laundering the proceeds of their illicit activities in the process. The introduction of market principles in the health sector, another example of neoliberal reforms, allowed paramilitary groups to create or infiltrate health cooperatives, thereby capturing state resources, sometimes even acquiring some legitimacy in the eyes of beneficiaries. Extensive political decentralization, finally, put growing municipal budgets within reach of armed groups, who exacted a percentage of municipal contracts for service delivery or carrying out public works. In all these instances, the effects were not just economic: the reforms gave illicit groups a foothold in the formal system, and fostered a creeping "mafianization" of the public sphere.

The six cases examined in this volume are obviously quite different from one another and display an astonishing variety in terms of the economic, political, and social repercussions of neoliberal reforms. What is not in dispute, however, is that these reforms had profound and lasting impacts at all these levels. While obviously not recreating the world "ex novo," as pointed out by Francisco Gutiérrez Sanín in Chapter 1, they did result in profound transformations that fundamentally reordered the incentives for "war making" and for resorting to political violence more generally. Neoliberalism, in other words, is not inconsequential.

Going a step farther, and despite the variety just noted, there are some basic patterns that emerge from the six cases studied. At the most fundamental level, one can identify some common traits that distinguish the Latin American from the African cases. In Central America, Peru, as well as Colombia, notwithstanding strong pressure from international actors, neoliberalism was embraced by important domestic constituencies who then became the principal drivers of neoliberal reforms. Neoliberalism thus became a tool to pursue a number of strategic goals, such as a new and more outward-looking development strategy, a re-ordering of existing elite arrangements, and the modernization of the state apparatus to put it in line with more business-friendly principles. In Uganda,

Sudan, and Côte d'Ivoire, by contrast, pressure to reform came chiefly from the international financial institutions and especially the International Monetary Fund (IMF). Pro-reform constituencies were weak or non-existent; at the same time, the ruling regimes—except in Côte d'Ivoire—were better able to manipulate the reforms in their favor.

Perhaps because of these stronger domestic constituencies, neoliberal reforms tended to be applied more deliberately and consistently in the Latin American cases, making it easier to assess the extent to which they reached their stated objectives, as well as their inherent limitations. In both Peru and Central America, for example, neoliberal reforms went a long way in opening up domestic economies, bringing them closer to world markets, and in reducing the size and role of the state apparatus, not least through extensive privatization programs. At the same time, they were unable to reverse a history of marginalization and exclusion, or to address the key problem of widespread poverty. In the African contexts, by contrast, where the implementation of the reforms was less thorough, the emphasis shifted to the unforeseen and often unintended consequences of neoliberalism. In at least two of the three cases studied—Sudan and Côte d'Ivoire—the most profound impacts of the neoliberal reform programs enacted there—the strengthening of a repressive regime in the former and the descent into civil war in the latter—cannot have been the intent of the international policymakers driving them. In both regions, though, there were exceptions. Colombia is one of them. Here, neoliberal reforms allowed armed groups not only to devise ingenious new ways of "looting" state resources, but also to gain a foothold in the formal system, both certainly unintended effects. Uganda, too, falls outside the standard pattern: a fairly coherent reform program produced important—and by and large, expected—changes both at the level of the economy and the state, although here, too, some doubts remain as to its long-term sustainability.

What, then, *were* the effects of neoliberalism on the incentives for "war making" and for resorting to political violence more broadly speaking? Is it possible to generalize across the six cases in this volume and to draw some more widely applicable conclusions? With all the usual provisos that apply to such a limited sample,[6] it would appear that it is. In the following, I will draw three such conclusions, first on the economic and political implications of neoliberal reforms, and then on some of their unintended and unexpected impacts. It is with regard to the latter that this book makes its richest and most interesting contributions. Neoliberalism may well be all-encompassing and global, as Francisco Gutiérrez Sanín argues in Chapter 1, but its practical application is nonetheless often incomplete and messy, and it may be hijacked to serve other purposes.

The first conclusion is that neoliberalism can produce economic gains, but that these tend to be unevenly distributed and often hard to sustain.[7] One of these gains is greater macroeconomic stability, especially when implemented against a background of economic uncertainty and turmoil. In Peru, for example, Fujimori's neoliberal reform package helped to slash hyperinflation, put public finances on a more stable footing, and even to create some room for increased social spending, using proceeds from the privatization of state assets. A similar dynamic could be observed in Uganda, albeit against a somewhat less challenging economic panorama, where neoliberal reforms, together with significant financial transfers, also resulted in a larger economic pie. Furthermore, neoliberal reforms can speed up the transition to a new development model and reinvigorate lagging economies, as was the case in Central America where the previous economic model, based on large agricultural estates in the hands of land-based oligarchies, was clearly exhausted. In a context of increasing globalization and a growing appetite for raw materials on the part of rising economies such as China, closer world market integration is necessarily beneficial for producers of minerals or oil, such as Peru and Sudan in this volume. Even producers of agricultural goods sometimes benefit.

The problem is that many of these initial gains level off and that growth rates tend to shrink over time. In several of the countries examined in this book, national economies became more and more dependent not on their own vitality and resilience, but on external resource flows. In Uganda, for example, transfers from external donors became an ever-more important factor, whereas in Central America, remittances from nationals residing abroad, largely in the US, helped to pad national balance sheets. In Peru, diminishing proceeds from the privatization of state assets affected the state's capacity for implementing social and regional policies. This raises important questions about the sustainability of the underlying economic model.

But even when growth rates remain relatively high, some doubts remain. Essentially, these relate to the fact that gains from neoliberal reform programs tend to be shared unevenly. Typically, such gains accrue to a limited set of beneficiaries, often better-educated, urban-based, and relatively younger groups of the population who are well-placed to seize the economic opportunities resulting from a more dynamic and open economic system. By contrast, and notwithstanding the limited increases in social spending just mentioned, neoliberal reforms often fail to address the deep-seated, structural problems stemming from the marginalization and exclusion of large parts of the population in many countries in the developing world, including those under study in this volume. In Peru, for instance, neoliberalism—in reality, a return to a previous development model based on the export of minerals and agricultural products—did little to ease the grinding poverty of most inhabitants of the Peruvian Andes. In Central America, and especially in Guatemala, the reforms had a negligible impact on the lives of the large rural-based indigenous majorities far away from Guatemala City. And even in Uganda, neoliberalism failed to put a dent in existing poverty levels in any significant way.

It follows that even the more successful examples of neoliberal reform programs examined in this book—not to mention the others, to which I will turn below—did not produce economic policies that convincingly addressed one of the principal root causes of armed violence in preceding years. Why, then, did these struggles not reignite? Essentially, because the roots of armed violence are more complex and single-cause explanations never go very far.[8] But this doesn't mean that there are no warning signs of potential trouble ahead. In Peru, political contestation has become more intense over the years, accompanied by a corrosive sense of disillusionment with political institutions and the political system in general. In Guatemala as well as El Salvador, crime and public insecurity have reached disturbing levels, possibly an indicator for growing social anomie and a deep-seated sense of powerlessness vis-à-vis legal routes of political and social change. In Uganda, finally, political violence has been kept in check, but only at the price of an ever-expanding network of cronyism, patronage, and mutual pay-offs, with worrying implications for the legitimacy of a regime whose transition to democracy is not yet complete.

This leads me to my second conclusion, regarding the impact of neoliberalism on political stability. The examples in this book show that the record is mixed: neoliberalism can sometimes help to modernize states and to strengthen political pluralism, but more often than not, it accentuates governance deficits and sharpens political contestation. Uganda is perhaps the most positive example: increased social spending on healthcare and education, and a broadly successful decentralization program led to better public services and brought them closer to the citizens. At the same time, a cautious political opening resulted in more opportunities to express opinions and voice dissent, which had a salutary impact on the legitimacy of the regime. Importantly, this did not amount to full democratization: the activities of political parties were severely restricted and the 2006 elections were the first multi-party elections in 20 years. But even these fairly modest results were only made possible by a prior elite pact that implied serious governance deficits, as just mentioned. Without it, a surge in political opposition and even a return to violence would have been a distinct possibility. The other cases in this volume are less encouraging. For one, initial improvements in public service delivery were often not sustainable. In Peru and elsewhere, they were financed by extraordinary revenues from the privatization of state assets, which leveled off over time. More importantly, the "streamlining" of public bureaucracies that was an essential part of neoliberal policy prescriptions implied a retreat of the state in a number of key areas, often accompanied by the privatization of the relevant services. One of the most visible trends was the privatization of security in several of the countries studied, which meant that public security was transformed from a public good—at least in theory—to one that only the relatively wealthy could afford. In some of the countries studied, such as Côte d'Ivoire or Sudan, this went a step further, with private militias competing with the state for the monopoly on the exercise of violence. Privatization programs in other areas—notably the provision of clean water—produced discontent and popular protests, although not in the countries examined in this volume.[9]

Perhaps most troubling are the many instances in which the "modernization of the state" under neoliberal auspices produced the opposite of the hoped-for improvements in public accountability and transparency. One example are the just-mentioned "governance deficits" in the Ugandan case, to which the international donor community shut both eyes. Another one is the centralization of power and resources in President Alberto Fujimori's office in Peru, which did great damage to the institutional fabric and encouraged a revival of both clientelism and political co-optation. In Colombia, the absence of effective democratic controls allowed criminal elements to infiltrate public institutions in less visible but perhaps even more insidious ways than in Peru, where Fujimori's security advisor, Vladimiro Montesinos, set up an elaborate mafia-style network to shore up support for the regime. Political liberalization in these circumstances can backfire, and at best, it may lead to a "formal" democratic system without effective structures for the representation and aggregation of interests, accompanied by low levels of political participation.[10] But it can also produce heightened levels of political contestation, without at the same time opening institutional channels for addressing legitimate demands, as happened in Peru and elsewhere in the Andean region. Perhaps most damaging in the long run is the loss of legitimacy and public trust that occurs when democratic institutions and processes are undermined by illegal practices such as corruption, graft, and nepotism; or even worse, when non-democratic or criminal groups gain control over parts of the political system and use it to further their illicit activities and ends.

As mentioned, Colombia and Peru are good examples for this trend, but Côte d'Ivoire and Sudan exemplify it even better. What sets these latter cases apart is the fact that here neoliberal reforms weren't just deficient—most policy schemes are in some way—but that they either failed completely, furthering the collapse of the state and the onset of civil war, or were manipulated by an authoritarian regime interested in consolidating its hold on power. In a sense, therefore, focusing on the "results" of neoliberal reforms in these two countries misses the point, since their unexpected and often unintended consequences turned out to be much more significant.[11] This in fact is my third conclusion: neoliberalism's "blind spots" and accidental side-effects can have a more profound impact on the incentives for "war making" and resorting to political violence than the changes resulting from neoliberal policies as such. When this happens, neoliberalism acts as a catalyst for other processes of change, releasing pent-up energies and propelling dynamics that can't be explained simply by linking them back to the neoliberal reforms that set them off in the first place. Neoliberalism doesn't have to result in xenophobia; neither does it have to produce "war economies" based on extortion and the looting of resources to fuel civil conflicts. But it can do so when it undermines a system of political and economic regulation that hitherto had held these tendencies in check, as happened in Côte d'Ivoire. Likewise, neoliberalism doesn't have to further political authoritarianism. In fact, in its more recent incarnations, economic and political liberalization are meant to go hand in hand. But when repressive regimes apply neoliberal policies selectively, skillfully molding them to their own advantage as in Sudan, this may well be the net effect.

In sum, then, neoliberalism can alter the incentives for "war making" and resorting to political violence in three fundamental ways. In extreme cases, as those just mentioned, neoliberal reforms can contribute to the collapse of entire regimes, resulting in "shadow states" as described by Bill Reno[12] or fueling the kinds of "new wars" that Mary Kaldor talks about.[13] Alternatively, neoliberalism may tilt the balance firmly in favor of repressive regimes, helping them tighten their stranglehold on their opponents. Whether or not this happens depends to a large extent on the specific contexts into which neoliberal reforms are introduced.

More typically, neoliberalism's impacts will be less dramatic but still profound. The "streamlining" of the state and the resulting reduction in public services in particular can produce weak governance structures and a lack in public oversight that favor the growth of illicit and criminal activities. This may signal a transformation from political to criminal forms of violence, especially in circumstances where insurgent groups have been defeated by the state.[14] It also heralds the emergence of new opportunities for illicit economic activities, particularly around drug trafficking. Most troubling perhaps are the instances where armed or criminal groups were able to infiltrate the state apparatus itself, not only capturing resources but acquiring some form of legitimacy for their actions. In the end, this could obviate the need for open violence directed at the state, but at the price of creating a climate of generalized repression directed at citizens.

Over time, finally, neoliberalism tends to sharpen political and socio-economic cleavages, thereby increasing the potential for violent conflict further down the road.[15] For the reasons explained above, neoliberalism seems ill-suited to address fundamental problems of poverty and socio-economic equity, and it seems equally incapable of rectifying long-standing patterns of political exclusion and marginalization. This isn't inevitable, but contrary examples are rare, certainly among the cases studied in this book. Uganda is the only case in this volume where neoliberal reforms had some success in spreading economic benefits and opening up the political arena, even if large inflows of foreign aid were at least as important. Elsewhere initial progress quickly stalled, even though the greater macroeconomic stability resulting from neoliberal reforms was an important achievement.

Taken together, the studies in this book offer numerous insights, reflections, and avenues for new research, which will be valuable to researchers, policymakers, and social activists alike. Each one in their own way, the different chapters confirm that the linkages between neoliberalism and violent conflict are multifaceted and don't lend themselves to facile generalizations, especially when seen against the even broader background of globalization in its different forms. While only scratching the surface of a very complex *problématique*, the studies do point to some interesting correlations and patterns, both within the different countries studied and between them, in different regions of the world. These will provide useful guideposts for researchers, who will want to enlarge the evidentiary base by producing additional case studies, as well as better understand the underlying dynamics by refining their theoretical approaches. Further comparative work combining "large-n" quantitative research and in-depth qualitative case studies seems particularly promising. The various "blind spots" of neoliberalism and its many unintended consequences—such as transformations from political to criminal violence or the use of neoliberal policies for other ends— also deserve greater attention. Likewise, more research is needed into the positive aspects of neoliberal reforms, and especially into possible ways of shoring up and consolidating initial gains.

For policymakers, this book also has much to offer. For one, it is a forceful reminder of the limits of social engineering, highlighting the incomplete and sometimes haphazard nature of neoliberal reforms and their many unforeseen and unintended consequences. Especially with regard to violent conflict, as we saw, the impacts of neoliberalism can be as surprising as they are diverse, if still very profound. This reinforces the need for a more careful analysis of the conflict-related impacts of neoliberal reforms, before embarking on a project of economic and political change of this magnitude.[16]

In particular, policymakers at both national and international levels will need to devise ways of spreading the economic gains from neoliberal reforms more widely, and to better control for their adverse effects. Some change in this direction is already happening: structural adjustment programs (SAPs) and the "Washington Consensus" driving them are a thing of the past,[17] and the Poverty Reduction Strategy Papers (PRSPs) spearheaded by the World Bank put much greater emphasis precisely on poverty reduction. But some doubt as to whether this will be enough. Some academics are calling for the resurrection of the "developmental state" especially in conflict-ridden countries,[18] not only to put in place a more equitable and sustainable model of economic development, but also to provide greater protection from external shocks. This would imply major changes in the way international economic relations are structured today, and go far beyond current levels of protection for vulnerable economies under the World Trade Organization.

Even more importantly, policymakers will have to address the corrosive impact of neoliberal reforms on the stability of states and political systems. As we saw, these reforms weaken already feeble governance structures, even when not leading to complete collapse (unless one counts an increase in state repression and the kind of stability resulting from it as a positive development). Part of the remedy lies in stepping up governance efforts around neoliberalism's most obvious "blind spots": greater emphasis on fighting crime and improving public insecurity; more effective regulation and law enforcement to clamp down on illicit economic activities; and stepped-up institutional oversight to prevent the "capture" of public resources by non-state groups. But aside from obvious capacity shortages holding back such efforts, these sorts of "flanking mechanisms" will fall short if they aren't accompanied by fundamental improvements to the quality of democracy as such. Creating more opportunities for political participation—including for expressing dissent—will help, especially when accompanied by institutional channels and capacities to deliver on legitimate demands.

Social activists, finally, will find support for their critique of neoliberalism throughout this book, but also some contrary suggestions that should give them pause. The case studies draw attention to the many pitfalls associated with neoliberal policies, often producing more conflictive and less peaceful societies. Evidence of such shortcomings can and should be used to hold governments to account, and to demand greater responsiveness and transparency with regard to policy formulation and implementation. Some activists will want to use this research for building social alternatives. At the same time, the studies in this book should sharpen our perception of cracks and fissures in the neoliberal edifice. In at least some of the cases studied, neoliberalism helped end civil conflicts, resulting in some economic gains and more open political systems. The question, for social activists as well as policymakers and researchers, is whether these are exceptions to the rule, or potential openings for positive change.

NOTES

1. Gerd Schönwälder is Director, Policy and Planning, at the International Development Research Centre (IDRC).

2. Perhaps too simple: the debate on neoliberal adjustment policies and its epitome, the Washington Consensus, has moved on. See the latter part of this chapter.
3. See the introduction to this book.
4. Some of this may be explained by Baquero's sample, which includes highly industrialized countries that typically score high on globalization indicators but low on violent conflict. Baquero's other findings, revealing an association between armed conflict and inequality, ethnic fragmentation, residual violence, and ongoing conflicts in neighboring countries, seem more applicable to many developing countries, although his results don't allow this kind of disaggregation.
5. Frederik Golooba-Mutebi stresses that the Ugandan government was careful to also increase its repressive capacities.
6. Baquero's quantitative study of course draws on many more cases than the six that are examined in more detail in Chapters 3–8. However, "large-n" studies, such as Baquero's, generally don't lend themselves to the sort of conclusions that are implied here. What studies such as Baquero's can do is show statistical correlations and probabilities, but these always need to be confirmed by qualitative analyses.
7. The cases studied in this book don't support the argument, often made by opponents of neoliberalism and economic globalization, that neoliberal reforms result in the wholesale destruction of domestic economies. Even in Côte d'Ivoire, what was destroyed was a system of political and economic regulation, not the domestic economy as such. Elsewhere, the changes were more subtle, with neoliberal reforms leading to a variety of economic transformations and adaptations that yielded mixed results. Obviously, though, outcomes can be different in other contexts.
8. Consistently high or even rising levels of poverty and inequality are not a good predictor of political violence, at least when taken alone. Intermediate variables, which are highly context-dependent, are crucial. As mentioned, still vivid memories of preceding civil wars, together with those of economic turmoil and despair in some cases, acted as a disincentive in some of the cases studied. Furthermore, grievances need to be "framed" and spearheaded by resistance movements, whose formation takes time and has to overcome many hurdles, especially when their predecessors have been soundly defeated as in Peru or Guatemala. Greed-based theories assume of course that what really matters are opportunities for personal enrichment; even here though, the enabling conditions need to be in place.
9. See Introduction, note 6.
10. This can be very detrimental to unfolding peace processes, which are delicate by their very nature. In Guatemala, for example, a poorly attended referendum rejected the Peace Accords that had been arrived at through long and complex negotiations with extensive international participation.
11. A similar argument was used by US "neo-cons" to attack the reform agenda of their "liberal" adversaries. See, for example, Meyerson (2006). As everyone knows, the "neo-cons" got caught in the "unintended consequences" of their own radical agenda for change, most notably in Iraq.
12. See Francisco Gutiérrez Sanín's discussion of Bill Reno's work in Chapter 1.
13. Mary Kaldor (2007) argues that these "new wars," which she observed first in the Balkans and later in Iraq, involve a blurring of the distinctions between war and organized crime, increasing privatization, and a much greater emphasis on identity politics.

14. More research is needed on this issue, both to establish causal relationships and to compare experiences across countries and regions.
15. As mentioned, the actual outbreak of violent conflict is a different matter. See note 8.
16. Conflict impact analysis has acquired some importance in the area of international development (OECD-DAC, 2001), but much less so in the field of economic reform or neoliberalism more specifically.
17. Although no-one quite seems to know what will replace them. See, Rodrik (2006).
18. For example, Julien Barbara (2008). See also Starr (2006) who proposes a "social economy" based on cooperation and reciprocity, instead of the individualistic motivations underlying neoliberalism.

REFERENCES

Barbara, J. (2008) "Rethinking neo-liberal state building: building post-conflict development states." *Development in Practice*, Vol. 18, No. 3, pp. 307–318.
Kaldor, M. (2007) *New and Old Wars: Organized Violence in a Global Era.* 2nd Edition. Stanford, CA: Stanford University Press.
Meyerson, H. (2006) "For neocons, the irony of Iraq." *Washington Post*, May 24, 2006, page A23. See, http://www.washingtonpost.com/wp-dyn/content/article/2006/05/23/AR2006052301527.html, accessed January 27, 2009.
OECD-DAC (Organization for Economic Co-operation and Development—Development Assistance Committee) (2001) "Helping Prevent Violent Conflict." The DAC Guidelines. Paris: OECD-DAC. See, http://www.oecd.org/dataoecd/15/54/1886146.pdf, accessed January 28, 2009.
Reno, W. (1999) *Warlord Politics and African States.* Boulder, CO: Lynne Rienner Publishers.
Rodrik, D. (2006) "Goodbye Washington Consensus, Hello Washington Confusion?" Harvard University. See, http://ksghome.harvard.edu/~drodrik/Lessons%20of%20the%201990s%20review%20_JEL_.pdf, accessed January 28, 2009.
Starr, M. A. (2006) "Growth and conflict in the developing world: neo-liberal narratives and social-economy alternatives." *Review of Social Economy*, Vol. 64, No. 2, pp. 205–224.

Index

Compiled by Sue Carlton

Page numbers followed by n refer to chapter endnotes

Abidjan, Young Patriots 157–62
Adja, Damana ('Pickass') 158, 162
Africa 16, 33, 56, 66, 67, 74, 77
   nationalism 38
   neoliberal reforms 13, 25, 59, 331–2
   see also Côte d'Ivoire; South Africa; Sudan; Uganda
agrarian reform 37–8, 290–1, 293, 294, 322n
   see also land ownership
Agrarian Reform Law (1962) (Guatemala) 294
Agreements for a Lasting Peace (1996) (Guatemala) 299
Agricultural Social-Interest Societies (SAIS) (Peru) 256
aid *see* foreign aid
Akindès, Francis 134
Alliance of Young Patriots for National Survival (AJPSN) (Côte d'Ivoire) 157, 158
   see also Young Patriots
Allied Democratic Forces (Uganda) 119
Amin, Idi 93, 94, 101, 105, 117, 120
anti-globalization activists 2
anti-neoliberalism 39, 209, 210, 260
AP-Wê (Patriotic Wê Alliance) (Côte d'Ivoire) 154
Aprista government (Peru) 245, 258, 259
Arab Fund for Economic and Social Development 180
ARENA (Nationalist Republican Alliance) (El Salvador) 293, 301
Arena project (Guatemala) 293
ARS (Administradoras de Régimen Subsidiado) (Colombia) 233, 234, 235

Arzú Irigoyen, Alvaro Enrique 311
Audrain, Xavier 169n
Ayacucho 252, 253–4

Banao, Gabriel 155
Bank al Baraka al Sudani 181
Barrantes Lingán, Alfonso 282n
al-Bashir, Omar 183
Basic Agrarian Reform Law (1980) (El Salvador) 290–1
Bayart, J.-F. 133, 134
BDR (Central Reserve Bank) (Peru) 268
Bédié, Henri Konan 135, 139–40, 164
Belaúnde Terry, Fernando 257–8, 259
Berdal, M. 52
Berger, Óscar 312, 319
Bertin, Kadet 154
Betancur, Belisario 214, 215, 216
Birdsall, N. 82n
Blé Goudé, 'General' Charles 157, 158, 162, 163
Bobo, S. 155
Bolivia 2, 29, 32, 45n, 209
Bollen, K.A. 84n
Boloña Behr, Carlos 261–2
Bouaké 127, 143, 144, 145, 151, 168n
Bourguignon, F. 53
Bowlad, Daoud 200
Bretton Woods institutions 95, 164, 174, 185
Buganda 111, 117
Burkina Faso 143
Bussmann, M. 8n

CAFTA (Central America Free Trade Agreement) 320

343

Caistab (Caisse de Stabilisation des Produits Agricoles) (Côte d'Ivoire) 3, 35, 128, 131–2, 146, 164–5, 330
Cambio 90 (Peru) 260
Camp David Accords 180
Campbell, J. 19, 23
capitalism 19, 31, 37, 285
  and democracy 51
  and land ownership 141, 227, 230–1, 294, 329
  liberal 194
  political 227, 234–5
  and racism 30
  state 130–1, 137, 330
Caracazo (Venezuela) 209, 210, 211
Caribbean 59, 77
Carimagua conflict (Colombia) 241n
Castaño, Vicente 229, 230
Castillo, Armas 293
Centeno, M.A. 31
Central America 285–324, 328
  economic boom 285–6
  and neoliberalism 4, 333, 334
  privatization of security 41
  revolutionary period 285, 286
  and transition to democracy 321
  see also El Salvador; Guatemala; Nicaragua
Central Bank of Sudan 181, 186
La Centrale (Côte d'Ivoire), structure of 145–6
CEPRIS (Special Privatization Committees) (Peru) 268
Cerezo, Marco Vinicio 298–9, 310, 311
CGTP (General Confederation of Workers of Peru) 274
Chauveau, J.-P. 155
Chávez, Hugo 209
Christian Democrats (Guatemala) 297
Chua, Amy 2
Chuschi 245, 253, 257
civil society 21, 33, 231, 235, 236, 327
  international 188
  organizations 104, 115–16
clientelism 17, 36, 129, 133, 164, 194, 234, 236, 237–9, 335
Clinton, Bill 14

cocaine 59, 74, 225, 226, 272, 278
coca production 45n, 219–20, 221–2, 225
coffee trade *see under* Côte d'Ivoire; El Salvador; Guatemala; Sudan
COJEP (Congress of Young Patriots) (Côte d'Ivoire) 157
Cold War, end of 49, 59
Colindres, Eduardo 288
Collier, P. 2, 53
Colombia 20, 25, 45n, 209–42
  1991 Constitution 212, 217, 223, 229, 236–7
  clientelism 36, 237–9
  and coca production 45n, 219–20, 221–2, 225
  conflict periodization 213–14, 220–4
  decentralization 34–5, 213, 223, 225, 235–9, 331
  democratization 212, 215, 216, 223, 321
  displacement 228–9
  fiscal policy 217
  flexibilization of labour 218, 219
  and foreign investment 217–18, 222–3, 229
  and free trade agreement with US 210, 216, 218
  guerrillas 216, 221–3, 237–8, 239
  health sector 213, 231–5, 242n
  Law 100 34, 232–3, 235
  paramilitary takeover 233–6
  privatization 34, 232–3
  Taylorization of medical services 232, 242n
  inequality 26, 37–8, 219, 227, 228, 241n
  land property rights 213, 218, 220, 224–31, 331
  mining sector 221, 222–3
  monetary policy 217
  narcotraffickers and land ownership 225–6, 227, 230–1, 241n, 331
  and neoliberalism 4, 7, 28, 210–13, 214–20, 330–1, 336
  new political practices 218–19
  oil sector 222, 223, 229
  palm oil production 224, 229
  paramilitaries 223, 224, 227, 229–30, 237–8, 239

Colombia *continued*
  privatizations 30, 32, 210, 216, 217, 219
  health sector 34, 232–3
  security sector 40, 220, 224, 239
  security sector 40, 220, 223–4, 239
  social policy 20, 217, 218, 231–2
  see also Colombia, health sector
  state modernization 214, 218
  and structural adjustment 215
  war against drugs 218, 223
community-based organizations (CBOs) 115
CONACAMI (National Confederation of Communities Affected by Mining) (Peru) 273
Conaghan, C. 21
CONARECI (National Coalition of Resistance of Ivory Coast) 158
conflict
  conflict impact analysis 338, 341n
  and conflict in neighbouring countries 59, 66, 112, 127
  determinants 62–3
  higher-level 50, 77
  intensity 50, 55, 63–8, 72–3, 74, 76, 77, 78
  occurrence 50, 55, 63–8, 72–3, 74, 76, 77
  origin and rationale (greed v. grievance) 53–4, 147–53, 160–1
  termination 50, 55, 58, 69–72, 78, 79
  see also under individual countries
Conflict Data Project (Uppsala University) 1
Congo, Uganda incursions 114
contracting 36, 184, 198, 205n, 237–8
Convivir associations (Colombia) 219, 220, 224, 230, 240n
COPRI (Commission for the Promotion of Private Investment) (Peru) 268
Cornia, G. 82n
Costa Rica 300
Côte d'Ivoire 45n, 126–70
  citizenship 126, 128–9, 130, 137, 138, 140, 143, 150
  see also Côte d'Ivoire, Ivority/ Ivorian identity

coffee and cocoa 126, 127, 130, 132, 133–4, 164–5
  corruption 132–3, 164, 165, 167, 170n
  criminalization of economy and state 127, 128, 129, 143, 164
  decentralization 34, 147
  democratization 139
  economic predation 164–6
  explanations of violence 126–9
  foreign aid 167
  and immigrants/immigration 135–8, 141–2
    see also Côte d'Ivoire, Ivority/ Ivorian identity
  impact of liberalization 129, 133, 139, 140–3, 146, 153, 163, 164
  inequality 28
  informalization of state 143, 155, 162–7
  Ivority/Ivorian identity 139–42, 143, 150, 155, 156, 158
    see also Côte d'Ivoire, citizenship
  land ownership 38, 136, 137, 141, 154, 156
  neoliberalism 4, 35–6, 44, 166, 167, 328, 330, 336, 340n
  oil resources 126, 167, 168n, 170n
  paramilitarization 153–62, 335
    of rural areas 153–7
    see also GPP (Group of Patriots for Peace); Young Patriots
  privatization 32, 129, 139, 142, 146, 163, 164–5, 167
    of violence 129, 143, 153
  state control of agro-export sector 130–5
  structural adjustment 128, 131, 134, 139, 141, 164, 167
  taxation 127, 144–5, 146, 156, 164, 167, 168n, 170n
    road duties 147
    tax agents 146, 168n
  war economy 127, 129, 142, 143–8, 151, 153
Coulibaly, Staff Sergeant Ibrahim ('IB') 143
Credit du Nord (Côte d'Ivoire) 146
crime/criminality 50, 53, 56, 73–4, 76, 308–9, 310
  organized crime 9n, 45n, 53, 225–6

Cristiani, Alfredo 301
Cuba
  Bay of Pigs invasion 296
  revolution 285
CUC (Peasant Unity Committee) (Guatemala) 297
CURMA (Center for Unification of Mining and Agricultural Resources) (Côte d'Ivoire) 145
CVR (Truth and Reconciliation Commission) (Peru) 249, 251

Darfur 175, 200
de León Carpio, Ramiro 310
decentralization 33–7
  see also under individual countries
Dembelé, O. 136–7, 166
democracy/democratization 33, 35–7, 49, 82n
  and conflict/violence 1, 24, 51, 53, 56, 73, 74, 78
  and economic globalization 66, 68, 73
  and neoliberalism 22, 24–5
  third wave 33, 37, 215
  Vanhanen democracy index 58
developmental state 6, 21, 29–30, 31, 32, 267, 338
developmentalism 23, 30
diamonds 54, 59, 69, 74, 81n, 83n, 127, 145, 146
DIRMOB (Directorate for Resource Mobilization) (Côte d'Ivoire) 145
divestiture 100–1, 110
Djué, 'Marshall' Eugene 158, 162
Dozon, J.-P. 138
Dreher, A. 53
drugs trade 32, 218, 223, 272, 274, 337
  see also Colombia, narcotraffickers and land ownership
Duffield, M. 52
Durand, F. 267

economic globalization
  relationship with armed conflict 3, 5, 49–50, 51, 52, 55–86, 128
  control variables 76–7
  database 57, 60, 65, 80, 83n
  dependent variables 57–8, 60, 64, 67, 75
  direct effects 50, 51, 55, 63–5, 68
  explanatory variables 58–9, 60, 69, 70, 84n
  indirect/spillover effects 50, 52, 55, 56, 65–9, 78
  statistical methodologies 50, 59–61
  statistical results 62–77
  and termination of conflict 50, 55, 58, 69–72, 78
economic liberalization
  arguments for and against 327
  and opportunities for armed groups 79–80, 83n, 85n
  see also neoliberalism
Economic and Social Modernization Program (Guatemala) 311
Ecuador 45n, 209
El Daim massacre (1987) 199
El Salvador 25, 210–11, 287–93
  1979 military coup 289–90
  army 292, 322n, 323n
  coffee production 287, 288, 289, 290–1, 321n
  and crime 45n, 308–9
  democratization 321
  economic reforms (1990s) 300–10
  Economic Stabilization Program 306
  exchange rate liberalization 305
  flow of external resources 302, 305–7
  foreign aid 303
  inequality 26, 287
  insurgent organizations 285, 322n
  Jesuit community murders 292
  land property distribution 287, 288
    agrarian reform 290–1, 322n
  modernization 288–9
  National Civil Police (PNC) 309–10
  National Reconstruction Program (NRP) 302
  peace process/agreements 8, 14, 52, 82n, 212, 291–3, 301, 302
  privatization
    of banking system 303–4, 306
    of public services 305
    of security 2, 309–10
  remittances 305–6

El Salvador *continued*
  structural adjustment 301–5, 307
  tax reform 304
  trade reform 304
  and war 285, 286, 289–90, 320, 321–2n, 328
ELN (National Liberation Army) (Colombia) 221, 222–3
EPS (Empresas Públicas de Salud) (Colombia) 233, 235
ERP (economic recovery program) (Uganda) 116
Esquipulas peace agreements (Guatemala) 299
ESS (Empresas Solidarias de Salud) (Colombia) 235
ethnic fragmentation 50, 54, 58, 63, 66, 74, 77, 340n
Evans, P. 20
external resource flows 5, 8, 83n, 114, 302, 305–7, 333
  see also foreign aid; foreign investment

factor analysis 59–60
failed/failing states 13, 52, 127, 167
Faisal Islamic Bank of Sudan 181
FAR (Revolutionary Armed Forces) (Guatemala) 296, 297
FARC (Revolutionary Armed Forces of Colombia) 220, 223, 224, 242n
Fearon, J. 54, 69, 83n
Federación Colombiana de Cafeteros 35
Fesci (student union) (Côte d'Ivoire) 116, 144, 146, 159, 162
FHRI (Foundation for Human Rights Initiative) (Uganda) 116
Financial Restructuring and Strengthening Fund (El Salvador) 303–4
FLGO (Forces for the Liberation of the Great West) (Côte d'Ivoire) 154
Flores Nano, Lourdes 272
FMLN (Farabundo Martí Front for National Liberation) (El Salvador) 291, 292–3
FNTMMSP (National Federation of Mining Workers) (Peru) 274
Fofana, Moussa 148–52

FONCODES (National Fund for Compensation and Social Development) (Peru) 269, 283n
FONTIERRAS (Land Fund) (Guatemala) 315, 316, 323n
foreign aid
  Côte d'Ivoire 167
  Sudan 180, 188, 189
  Uganda 109, 112–13, 119, 121, 337
foreign investment 71–2, 85n
  Colombia 217–18, 222–3, 229
  Guatemala 314
  Peru 262, 263, 265, 272
FPI (People's Front) (Côte d'Ivoire) 138, 139, 140, 155, 157
Freedom Movement (Peru) 260
Friedman, Thomas 1
FS LIMA 155
Fu, Hung-der 54
Fujimori, Alberto 7, 211, 248, 263–7, 283n
  and authoritarianism 246, 248, 264–5, 281, 335
  clientelism 36
  and corruption scandal 247, 266–7
  defeat of PCP-SL 246, 255–6, 278, 280
  election (1990) 25, 245–6, 258
  end of regime 247, 266–7, 272
  and neoliberal reforms 246, 247, 256, 260–2, 267–70, 329, 333
  re-election (1995) 246, 263
  re-election (2000) 246–7, 266
Fujimori regime 20
  cutting inflation 28
  and neoliberal stabilization 248, 329
  protests against 274–5
  'Fujishock' 261, 267
Fukuyama, Francis 1

Galeano, Eduardo 22
Gambetta, D. 223
Gammi, 'Pastor' 154
García, General Lucas 298
García Pérez, Alan 254, 258, 259, 272, 329
  and mining companies 283n
  and neoliberalism 247, 274, 277
Gaston, N. 53

Gaviria, César 20, 215, 216, 217, 219, 240n
Gbagbo, Laurent 126–7, 131, 134, 138, 142, 143, 165
and paramilitarization 153, 157, 158
Geneva Convention 254
Gezira project (Sudan) 179
Ghersi, E. 44n
globalization 1–3, 49
and contention 1–2
and inequality 53, 68, 79, 82n
see also economic globalization
Gonzáles de Olarte, Efrain 267
Gordon, General Charles 177
GPP (Group of Patriots for Peace) (Côte d'Ivoire) 159–60, 169n
'great transformation' 5, 15, 16, 31, 49, 51, 209, 230
grins (teapot gatherings) (Côte d'Ivoire) 148, 169n
Groguhé, Charles 159
Guatemala 25, 211, 285, 293–300
agrarian reform 293, 294
and Arena project 293
armed conflict (1960-96) 295–300, 328
end of 298–300
two phases of 295–8
Catholic Church 297
Civil Defense Patrols (PAC) 298
coffee 293, 294, 317
constitutional reform 299
decentralization 311
and democracy 293, 295–6, 298–9, 310, 311–12, 321
earthquake (1976) 322–3n
foreign investment 314
guerrillas 286, 297–8, 323n
indigenous peoples 293, 297, 298, 299, 312, 317, 323n
inequality 27, 323n
land ownership 38, 293–5, 314–18, 322n, 323n, 324n
registration system 317–18, 324n
military coups
1954 293
1963 295
1982 298
military uprising (1960) 296
National Civil Police (PNC) 319

neighbourhood associations 319–20
and neoliberalism 310–20, 334
peace process/agreements 8, 14, 298–9, 311, 312, 313, 315, 316, 319
and privatization, private security organizations 2, 318–20
public expenditure 311, 314
remittances 314
rural migrant proletariat 294–5
security organizations/agencies
privatization of 2, 318–20
restructuring of 312
structural adjustment 310, 311, 314
taxation/tax system 311, 312, 313–14
Gueï, General Robert 142, 143, 158, 164
Guerrilla Army of the Poor (Guatemala) 297
Guizot, François 135
Guzmán, Abimael 246, 252, 255, 278

Hansen, H.B. 96, 108
Hanson, M. 20, 39
Harvey, D. 20–1, 224, 231
Heglig oil fields (Sudan) 195
Hentz, J.J. 20, 39
Herbst, J.W. 81n
Hermoza, General Nicolas de Bari 264
Holy Spirit Movement (Uganda) 119
homicides 50, 57, 73–6, 77, 221, 226, 308–9, 319
Honduras 300
Houphouët-Boigny, Felix 126, 127, 136, 137, 164
Houphouëtist system 130–5, 138, 139
Huehuetenango 295, 297, 298
Humphreys, M. 52, 54, 69, 71, 83n, 85n
Hurtado Miller, Juan Carlos 261
hyperinflation 28, 245, 259, 266, 329, 333

ICF (Islamic Charter Front) (Sudan) 204n
illegal trafficking 50, 53, 54, 56, 59, 74–6, 79, 80, 83n, 221–2
see also drugs trade

IMF (International Monetary Fund) 2, 267, 300, 311, 332
  Peru and 267
  Sudan and 88, 174, 182, 185, 186, 205n
  Uganda and 95, 97, 98, 99, 107, 108, 122n, 329
INCODER (agency for agrarian development) (Colombia) 227
INCORA (institute for agrarian reform) (Colombia) 227, 230
Indigenous Peoples' Identity and Rights Agreements (1995) (Guatemala) 299
inequality 43, 44n, 45n, 79, 82n, 85n
  and armed conflict 54
  and conflict/violence 24, 25, 50, 65, 68, 340n
  and crime 74
  Gini index 26–8, 53, 58, 68, 83n
  and globalization 53, 68, 79, 82n
  horizontal 83n, 84n
  measuring 25–6
Institut Marie Thérèse d'Adjamé (Côte d'Ivoire) 160
INTA (National Institute of Agrarian Reform) (Guatemala) 294
Inter-American Development Bank 269, 315, 323–4n
international institutions
  as agents of neoliberal reform 16
  creation of 15–16
  see also IMF; World Bank
IPS (Instituciones Proveedoras de Salud) (Colombia) 233
isomorphism 17, 21–2, 23, 37, 215
IU (United Left) (Peru) 257, 282n

Junguito, Roberto 214

Kaldor, Mary 9n, 337, 340n
Kant, Immanuel 2
Keynesian state 21, 23
Khalil, Fadiga 150
Khatmiyya Sufi brotherhood (Sudan) 177
Klein, Naomi 1
KOF economic globalization index 58, 82n

Laitin, D. 54, 69, 83n
land ownership see under individual countries
  see also agrarian reform
Latin America 16, 56, 59, 66, 67, 68, 74, 77
  agrarian wars 210–11
  debt crisis 214
  economic crisis (1980s) 214, 245, 248, 257–8, 267, 300
  and inequality 85n
  nationalism 38
  neoliberal reforms 25, 331
  opposition to 209, 211
  see also Central America; Colombia; El Salvador; Guatemala; Nicaragua; Peru
Law 100 (Colombia) 34, 232–3, 235
Le Bot, Y. 294
liberal dystopia 1, 3, 5, 13–14, 18, 31, 42, 43
liberal pacifism/pacification 51, 69
Liberal Party (Colombia) 210
liberal peace thesis 2, 50, 69, 79
liberal promise 14–15, 31–2, 42, 43, 212
liberal utopia 1, 3, 5, 7, 14, 18, 43
Liberia 127, 143
LISREL model 59
Logit model 50, 69–70
Lord's Resistance Army (Uganda) 111, 115, 118
Losch, Bruno 131, 133

M-19 (Colombian guerrilla group) 221
McCarthy, J. 21
al-Mahdi, Sadeq 199
al-Mahdi, Sayyed Abdel Rahman 178
Mahdist movement 178
Maho Glofiéhi, 'General' Denis 154, 155, 169n
Malaysia 2
Malloy, J. 21
Mangou, P. 160
Maras (youth gangs) (El Salvador) 308, 309
Marcoussis negotiations/agreement (2003) (Côte d'Ivoire) 144, 158
Mariátegui, José Carlos 282n
Mayall, J. 109

MEF (Ministry of Economy and Finances) (Peru) 268
Midlarsky, M. 54
militarized commerce 13, 14, 40
military expenditure 58, 66, 68, 72, 74, 78, 85n
MILOCI (Ivorian Movement for the Liberation of the West of Côte d'Ivoire) 154
al-Mirghani family 177
al-Mirghani, Sayyed Ali 21
Misseriya 195–6
MJP (Movement for Justice and Peace) (Côte d'Ivoire) 143, 168n
mobilizations 50, 56, 57, 73, 74, 76, 212, 274–6, 298
monetarism (monetarismo) 22, 215
Monpého, Julien Gnan ('Colombo') 154
Montesinos, Vladimiro 247, 256, 264, 266–7, 269, 335
Moore, Barrington 288
Morales Bermúdez, Francisco 253, 257, 259, 282n
Morales, Evo 209
Moran, Rolando 297
Morrison, C. 53
MPCI (Patriotic Movement of Côte d'Ivoire) 143, 144–5, 168n
MPIGO (Popular Ivorian Movement of the Great West) 143, 168n
MR-13 (Revolutionary Movement 13th November) (Guatemala) 296
MRTA (Túpac Amaru Revolutionary Movement) (Peru) 245, 246, 254
Mubarak, Hosni 188
Muller, E. 54
multiple equilibria 18, 42
multiple regression 59–60
multivariate analysis of variance (ANOVA) 59
Museveni, Yoweri Kaguta 4, 5, 36, 96, 109, 110, 111–12, 115, 118
Mutesa, Edward 93
Mwenda, A. 100, 114

National Intelligence Service (Peru) 256
natural resources 2, 50, 52, 54, 58, 66, 74, 114

NCP (National Congress Party) (Sudan) 175, 190, 194, 201, 204n
neoliberalism 3–5, 18–24
 and agrarian reform 37–8
 and case studies 3, 7, 25, 331–7
  see also under individual countries
 and de-concentration of power 32–7
 and democracy 44n
 and economic growth 28–9
 impact on political stability 334–6, 339
 and inequality 25–8, 30, 43, 209, 277
 and isomorphism 17, 21–2, 23, 37
 myth of 44n
 producing economic gains 332–4
 promoting contentious politics 25, 38–9
 relationship with conflict 4–5, 13–18, 24–5, 42–3, 129–30, 175, 212–13, 327–39
 and termination of conflicts 25, 30, 39–40, 43, 211, 279–81
 Thatcherite phase 19, 20, 24, 31, 33
 unintended consequences 336, 338, 340n
  see also economic globalization; economic liberalization
New Forces (FN) (Côte d'Ivoire) 127, 142, 143–7, 168n
 and combatant engagement 148–53, 169n
new wars 9n, 82n, 337, 340n
NGOs (non-governmental organizations) 33 104, 115–16
Nicaragua 210, 285, 286, 289, 300–1, 303
NIF (National Islamic Front) (Sudan) 173, 175, 182–3, 204–5n
Nimayri, Ja'afar 179–81
Nkemdirim, B.A. 16
N'Krumah, Kwame 130
NLC (National Land Commission) (Sudan) 194
NRM (National Resistance Movement) (Uganda) 96, 97, 112–14, 118, 121
 dealing with insurgency 118–19

NRM *continued*
and economic reforms 98–101, 103, 104
impact on logic of war 109–16
and political liberalization 104–8
and pressure to reintroduce multi-party politics 104, 105–9
Nuba people 193, 194, 195, 196, 205n

Obote, Milton 93, 105, 110, 114, 118, 120
second administration (Obote II) 94–7, 112
oil 54, 58, 63, 69, 72, 84n
see also under individual countries
Okello, General Tito Olara 96
ONUSAL (United Nations observers in El Salvador) 292
ORDEN (paramilitary force) (El Salvador) 289
Ordinary Least Squares (OLS) (MCO model) 50, 62–5, 68, 73–7, 84n
ORPA (Organization of People in Arms) (Guatemala) 297
Ouagadougou agreement (2007) (Côte d'Ivoire) 126, 127, 146–7, 162, 163
Ouattara, Alassane 140, 162
Oulaï, Eloi 154, 169n

PAC (Civil Defense Patrols) (Guatemala) 298
Paige, J. 294
PAN (Partido de Avanzada Nacional) government (Guatemala) 315
Paniagua, Valentín 247, 272
patronage 113, 134, 246, 281, 329, 330, 334
and divestiture and privatization 100, 110–11, 129, 165, 269
paramilitaries and 234, 238
PCP-SL (Peruvian Communist Party–Sendero Luminoso) 245, 250–1, 252–6, 258, 260, 274, 282n
burning ballot boxes 245, 253, 257
and cocaine production 278
defeat of 246, 255–6, 261, 328–9
resurgence of 272, 277–9, 281
split over peace negotiations 255, 278

PDCI (Côte d'Ivoire Democratic Party) 138, 140
PDF (Popular Defense Forces) (Sudan) 194, 199–202
Peck, J. 22
Pedersen, O. 19
Pérez, Carlos Andrés 209
Pérez de Cuéllar, Javier 263
Peru 25, 44n, 45n, 211, 245–83, 328–9
cocaine production 272, 278
and corruption 247, 256, 267, 269–70, 272, 281, 283n
counter-subversive strategy 277–8
coups d'état
1968 256, 282n
1975 257, 282n
1992 246, 261–2
decentralization 273, 275
democratic transition period 272–4
drug trafficking 272, 274
economic crisis (1980s) 245, 248, 258, 266
economic slowdown (1998) 265–6
elections
1980 257
1990 245, 260
foreign direct investment 262, 263, 265, 272
foreign trade 268–9
free-trade agreements 29, 39
'Green Plan' 261
inequality 27, 248, 266, 271, 273, 277, 281
land reform 256
nationalization 256–7, 259
natural disasters 257
neoliberal reforms 7, 28, 246–9, 256–81, 333, 334, 336
and authoritarianism 262–7, 281
introduction of 258–62
political background 256–8
and previous economic models 258, 259
regulatory agencies 271
and social protest 273, 274–7, 281
transformation of state 267–71

and transition to democracy
271–9
new Constitutions 257, 267
poverty 247, 248, 251, 252, 266,
269, 271–2, 273, 281, 334
prison riots 254
privatization 30, 262, 267, 268,
269–71
and social spending 248, 263,
269, 281, 333, 335
social conflicts 274–7
social policy 246, 248, 263, 267,
268, 269, 281
strikes 274–6
structural adjustment 262, 267, 268,
269
tax reform 267, 268
urbanization 251, 282n
war 38, 245, 249–56
casualties 249–50
historical background 251–2
strategic equilibrium 251, 255,
277
trajectory of 252–6
Polanyi, Karl 38, 81n, 175, 232
and 'great transformation' 5, 15, 16,
49, 51, 230
self-regulating market 21, 32, 45n
Political Agreement to Fund Peace,
Development and Democracy
(Guatemala) 311
Popular Resistance Army (PRA)
(Uganda) 118
population aging 59, 66, 76
Portillo Cabrera, Alfonso Antonio 312,
319
Poverty Eradication Action Plan
(PEAP) (Uganda) 103
Poverty Reduction Strategy Papers
(PRSPs) 338
PRIO (International Peace Research
Institute) (Oslo) 1
prisoner's dilemma 35–6
privatization 335
of security 41, 43, 335
see also under individual countries;
divestiture
Probit model 55
public expenditure 59, 67
reduction in 68, 72–3, 81n, 85n, 99,
311, 314

Quiché (Guatemala) 295, 298

Rachel, Sian 169n
RDR (Assembly of Republicans) (Côte
d'Ivoire) 140, 144, 162
remittances 305–6, 314, 333
Reno, William 13, 18, 32, 52, 337
Revolutionary Armed Forces
Government (Peru) 256–7, 259
RGP (General Property Registry)
(Guatemala) 317–18
Rivera, Roberto 306
robberies 50, 57, 73–6, 77, 309
Rouquié, A. 294
Roy, Olivier 174
Rural Land Code (Côte d'Ivoire)
140–1

SAA (African Farming Union) 168n
Saleh, General Zubeyr Mohamed 183
Sanchez de Losada, Gonzalo 209
Schneider, G. 8n
Schock, K. 54, 82n
Schumpeter, Joseph 51
SCP (Sudanese Communist Party) 179
Segovia, A. 307
Sekou Touré, Ahmed 130
self-regulating market 21, 32, 45n
Seligson, M. 54
Sendero Luminoso *see* PCP-SL
Serrano Elías, Jorge 310, 311
Sharia (Islamic law) 174, 182
Short-Term Program for Economic and
Social Reactivation (PRES)
(Guatemala) 311
SIAMO (inter-professional union to
channel the workforce) (Côte
d'Ivoire) 136
Sierra Leone 127, 143
socialism 108, 131, 237
collapse of 14
Soro, Guillaume 127, 143, 145, 146,
162, 165
Soto, Hernando de 259–60
South Africa 30, 39, 52, 72
peace negotiations 14, 72, 82n
privatization of security 41
SPLM (Sudan People's Liberation
Movement) 173, 191, 193, 194,
195, 197, 199, 200

state/states 32, 40–1, 51, 85n
  impact of economic globalization
    50, 72–3, 78
  and neoliberalism 17, 19–20, 21,
    24, 31, 33, 40–1, 43, 51–2, 56
  retreat of 30–1
  state intervention 17, 19, 29–30,
    104, 302, 303, 311
Stewart, F. 44n
Stiglitz, Joseph 16
Stine, R. 84n
structural adjustment 20, 23, 71, 81n,
    85n, 109–10, 338
  see also under individual countries
Structural Equation models (SEM) 50,
    57, 59–61, 84n
  results 62–77
Sudan 33, 173–205
  agricultural sector 189
  Anglo-Egyptian condominium
    period 177–9
  and attempt to assassinate Egyptian
    president 174, 188
  before 1989 coup d'état 175,
    176–82
  border changes 195–6
  coffee trade 52, 69, 86n
  corruption 185, 204n
  coups d'état
    1969 179
    1989 173, 182, 185
  and debt 181, 182, 186, 188
  decentralization 34, 186–7
  decrease in subsidies 187
  development plans 180–1
  and financing of war 188–9
  and foreign aid 180, 188, 189
  and Holy War (jihad)177 200–1,
    202
  and IMF 181, 185–6, 188, 204n,
    205n
  inequality 27, 196
  Islamic banks 181–2
  Islamic humanitarian organizations
    196, 197
  and Islamists' idea of individual
    196–8
  land ownership 176, 189, 190–5,
    205n

  militia-ization of rural order
    198–202
  and neoliberalism 44, 174–6, 203,
    328, 329–30, 332, 336
  Islamic 182–90
  Nimayri period 179–81, 182, 185
  and oil crisis (1973) 180
  oil resources 7, 174, 189, 195, 196,
    329
  Ottoman period 176–7
  peace agreements (2005) 176, 187,
    191, 194–5, 205n
  privatization 32, 187–8
  security sector 174–5, 197, 198,
    203, 335
  privatization of 176, 197
  structural adjustment 186
  UN sanctions against 174, 188
  under Mahdist government 177
  on US State Sponsors of Terrorism
    list 174, 186
Sudan People's Liberation Army
  (SPLA) 112
SUNAT (National Tax Administration
  Superintendence) (Peru) 268
Superintendencia Nacional de Salud
  (Colombia) 233
SUTEP (Unitary Union of Educational
  Workers in Peru) 274
syllogisms 24–32

Tangri, R. 100, 114
taxation 58, 66, 67, 68, 72, 74, 78,
    81n, 85n, 86n
  see also under individual countries
Terreblanche, Sampie 45n
Thorpe, R. 267
Tickel, A. 22
Tilly, C. 51
Tinyefuza, Major-General David 115
TMP (Guatemalan Workers' Party)
    297
Tocquevillian question 16, 18, 22,
    35–6
Toledo, Alejandro 247, 266, 272, 277
Torres Rivas, Edelberto 296
trade liberalization 1, 32, 71, 257, 301
al-Turabi, Hassan 173, 185, 189, 196,
    202
Twaddle, M. 96, 108

UDC (Uganda Debt Coalition) 116
UDN (Uganda Debt Network) 116
UEMO (Economic and Monetary
    Union of West Africa) 126
Uganda 32, 33, 93–123, 328, 329,
    331–2, 334
  1995 constitution 106, 108, 111
  ban on political competition 93, 94
  civil war 95, 96–7, 105, 121
  and corruption 96, 100, 102,
    114–15, 122n
  decentralization 99, 104, 107–8,
    110–11, 113, 334–5
  economic decline 93–4, 101
  economic reforms 95–104, 333
    divestiture process 100, 110
    implementation of 99–101
    outcomes 101–4
    and relationship with donor
      community 111, 335
    under NRM administration
      98–101, 103, 104
    under Obote II 94–7
  elections (1980) 94, 95, 105,
    117–18, 121
  exiles and insurgency 117, 120–1,
    122n
  expulsion of Asians 94
  and foreign aid 109, 112–13, 337
  inequality 28
  insurgencies 93, 94, 105, 107,
    116–20, 122n
  members of parliament 113–14
  military coups
    1971 93, 105
    1985 96, 97
  peace and stability 111–12, 113,
    117–18, 120, 121
  political liberalization 104–8
  reintroduction of multi-party
    politics 104, 105–9, 110, 117–18
  security 94, 112, 121
    security agencies 97, 109, 113,
      115
  social spending 99, 103–4, 334–5
  structural adjustment 95–6, 103,
    329
  taxation 103
  see also NRM (National Resistance
    Movement)

UMAS (Union of Self-defense
    Movements of the South) 159
United Nations (UN)
  and crime in Central America 310
  Development Program (UNDP) 301
  Economic Commission for Latin
    America 315, 323–4n
  sanctions against Sudan 174, 188
  and violence in Guatemala 320
United States (US)
  and Central American counterinsur-
    gency campaigns 312
  and El Salvador insurgency 291–2
  promoting democracy 14
  State Sponsors of Terrorism list 174,
    186
USAID (US Agency for International
    Development) 302
UNLF (Uganda National Liberation
    Front) 121
UNRG (Guatemalan National
    Revolutionary Unity) 312, 315
UNSCH (Universidad Nacional San
    Cristobal de Huamanga) 252
UNU-WIDER, World Income
    Inequality Database (WIID) 58
UPC (Uganda People's Congress) 93,
    94, 118
UPDF (Uganda People's Defence Force)
    114–15
UPLTCI (Union for the Total
    Liberation of Côte d'Ivoire) 158
UPM (Uganda Patriotic Movement)
    118
UPRGO (Union of Patriots for the
    Resistance of the Great West)
    154–5
Urabá 229, 230
urbanization 37, 57, 66, 76, 181, 221,
    251, 309
Uribe, Álvaro 215, 216, 218, 219

Vanhanen democracy index 58
Vargas Llosa, Mario 245, 259, 260
Velasco Alvarado, Juan 256, 259,
    282n
La Violencia (Colombia) 220–1, 225,
    228

Walter, B.F. 69

war economies 336
   Côte d'Ivoire 127, 129, 142–8
Washington Consensus 338
Wood, E. 52, 211, 289
World Bank 17, 33, 54, 58
   2003 Country Economic
     Memorandum 301, 306, 308
   and Central America 300, 301–2,
     311, 315
   and Peru 267, 269
   and Uganda 95, 99, 100

Ydígoras, General Fuentes 295
Yoko Yoko, Bouazo 159
Young Patriots (Côte d'Ivoire) 126,
   127, 137–8, 153
   Abidjan 157–62
   rural 155–6

Zambia 39, 103, 110
Zapatistas 240n
Zéguen, Touré 159